AF477572

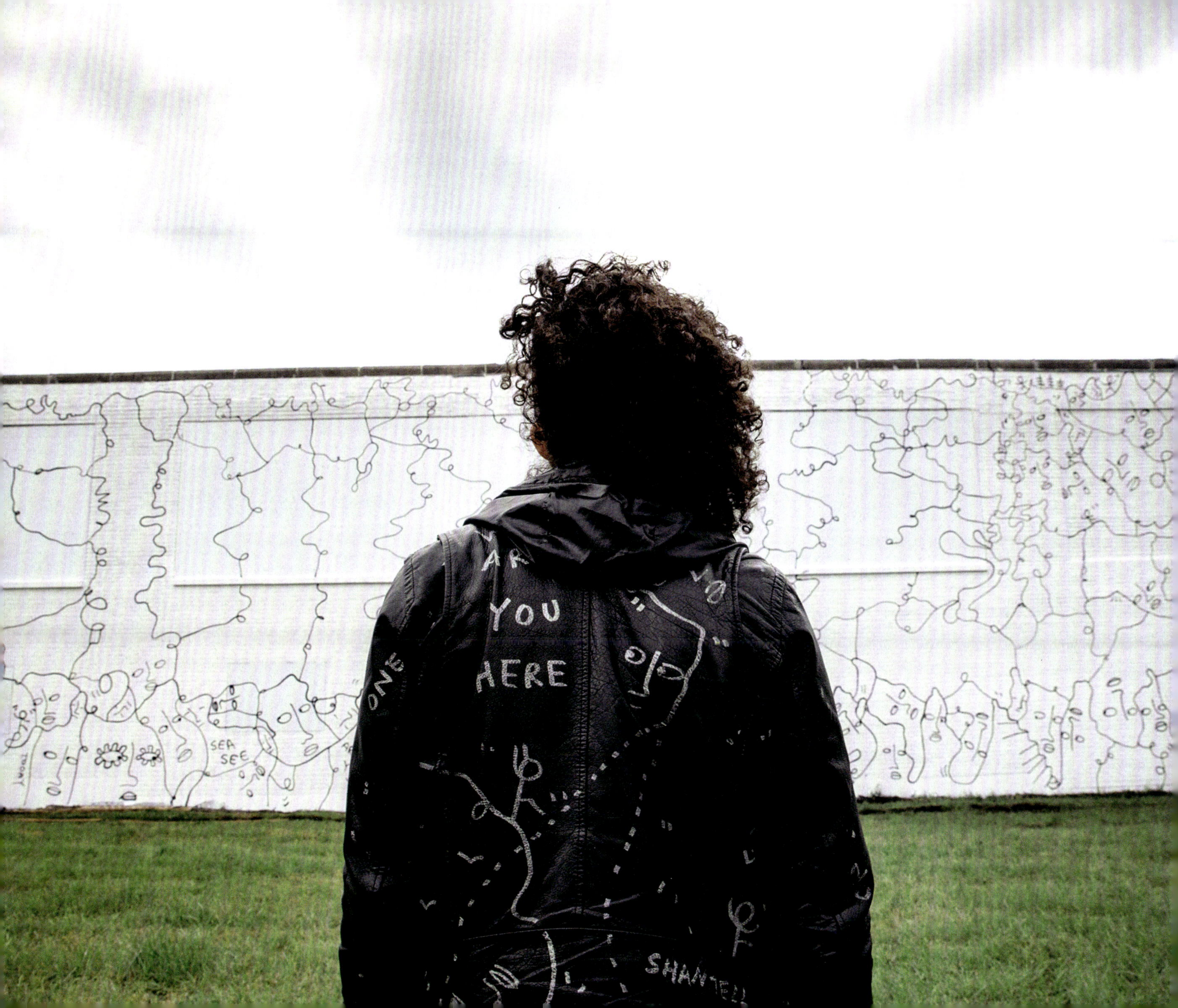

ONE
YOU
HERE
SEA
SEE
SHANTELL

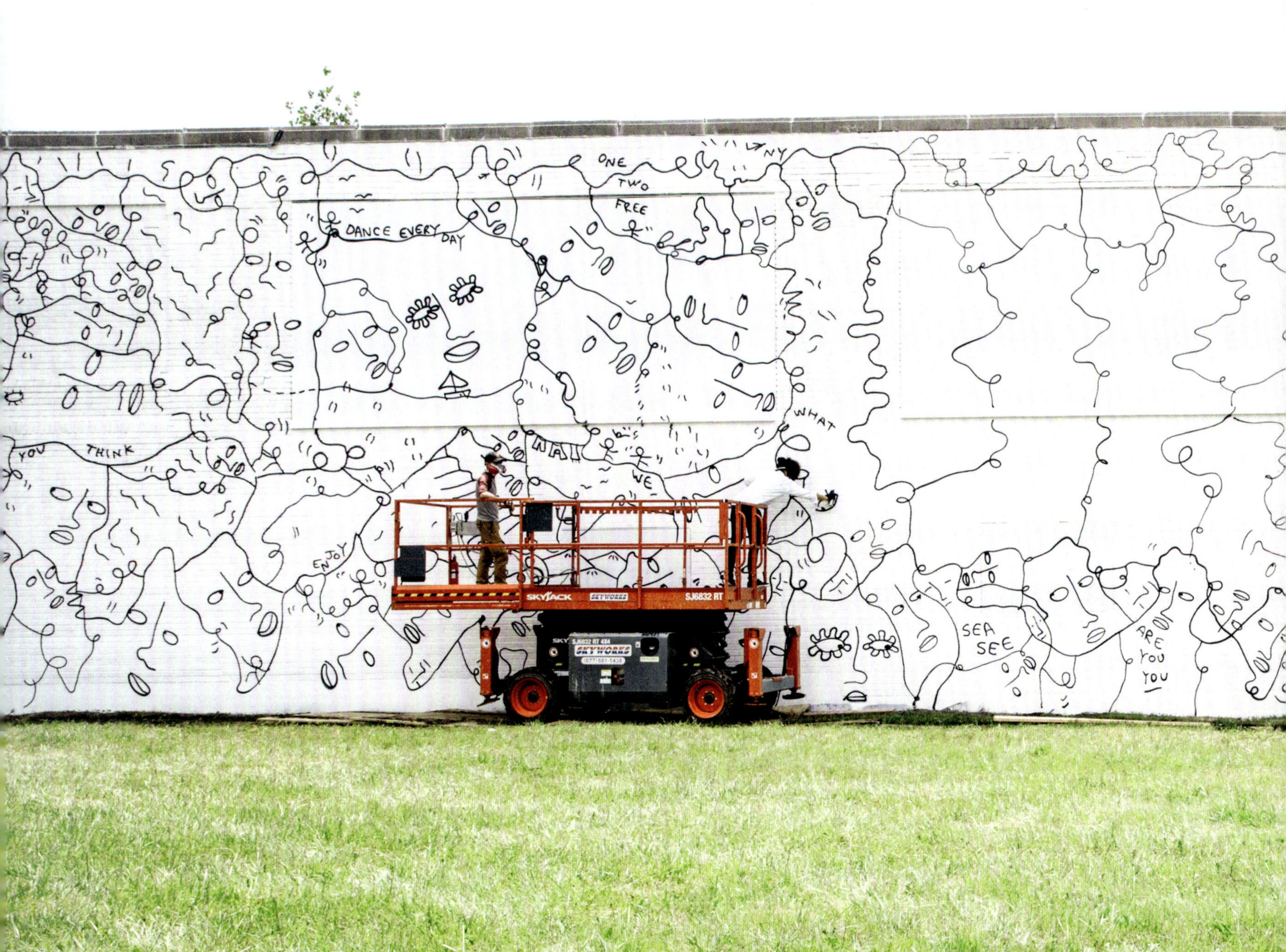

ONE
TWO
FREE
NY
DANCE EVERY DAY
WHAT
YOU THINK
WE
ENJOY
SEA
SEE
ARE
YOU
YOU

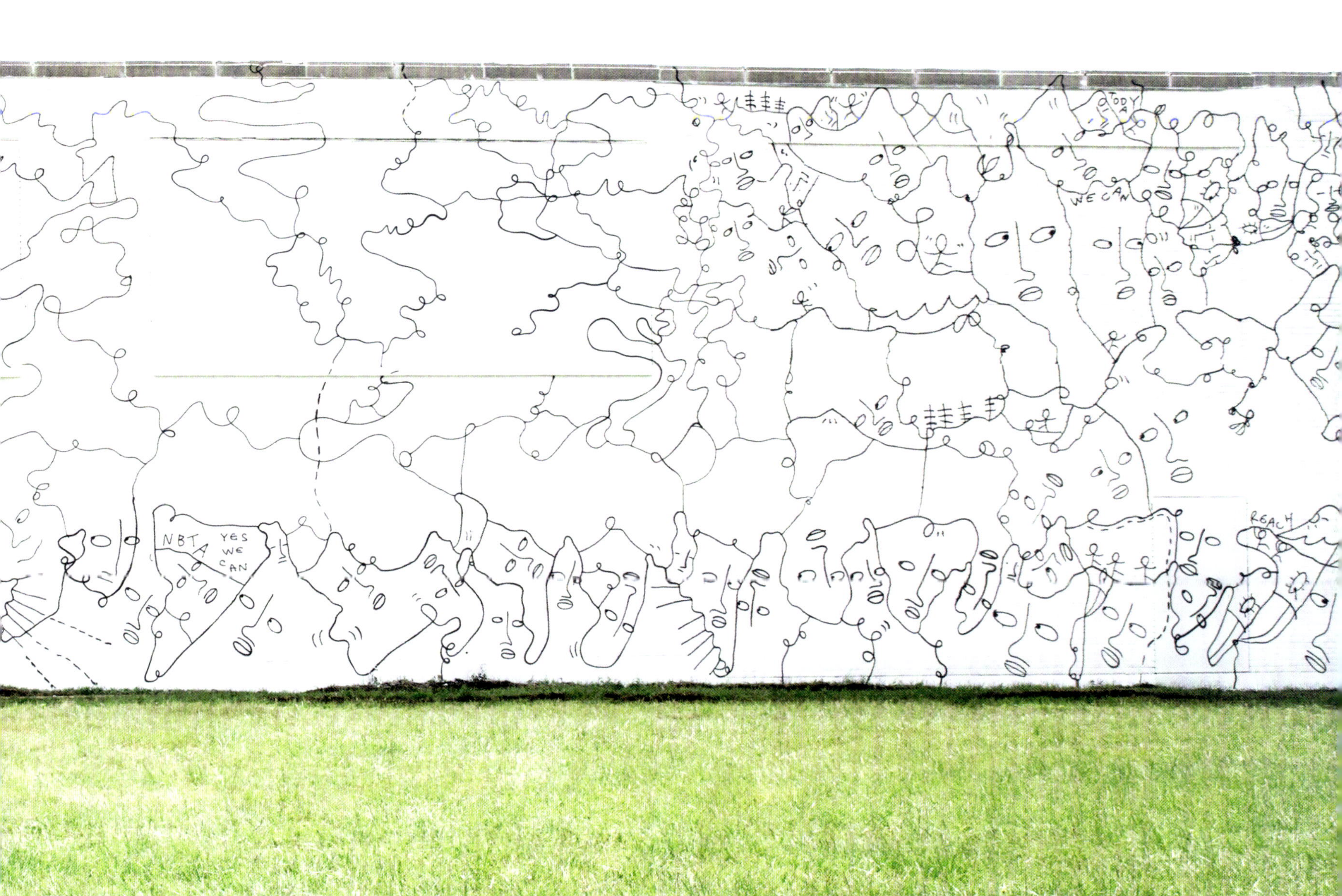TODY
WE CAN
NBT
YES WE CAN
REACH

All incidental drawings are by Shantell Martin.

p. 1 Martin in front of *Dance Everyday* (2017), Buffalo, NY, June 2017.
pp. 2–3 Martin working with mobile-lift operator Scott Bye on *Dance Everyday* (2017), Buffalo, NY, June 2017.
p. 6 Martin working on the '#ShantellOnTheRoad' series (2017) on the Derby Dam, Reno, July 2017.
pp. 8–9 Martin working on *Open Your Door* (2018) for Pow! Wow! Long Beach, California, June 2018.
p. 31 Works from the 'Dear Grandmother' series (2002–15) and other objects at Dot Martin's home in Thamesmead, London, c. 2013.
p. 51 Pens and ink in Martin's Broadway studio, 2013.
p. 91 Martin at work on *Sea You* (2013) for *Out of the Box: The Rise of Sneaker Culture*, Bata Shoe Museum, Toronto, July 2013.
p. 173 Hand-drawn toys and bottles in the Sculpture Court for *Someday We Can*, Albright-Knox Art Gallery, Buffalo, NY, 2017.
p. 197 Projection from the 'Hidden Ora' series (2006–11) at 303 Grand, Brooklyn, New York, 2010.
p. 235 Martin up a ladder for a mural at Rolf & Daughters restaurant, Nashville, May 2013.
pp. 238–9 Martin drawing *Top of the Mountain* (2017) for the '#ShantellOnTheRoad' series (2017) at Eden, Utah, July 2017.
p. 240 *Future Higher Self, Two Faces*, 2014. Ink on paper.

ISBN 978-1-912122-27-1
Limited Edition ISBN 978-1-912122-34-9

Commissioning Editor Jacky Klein
Designer Sylvia Ugga
Editor John Jervis
Editorial Assistant Kirsty Watling
Production Manager Sarah McLaughlin
Printed and bound in Italy

SHANTELL MARTIN.

LINES

HENI Publishing

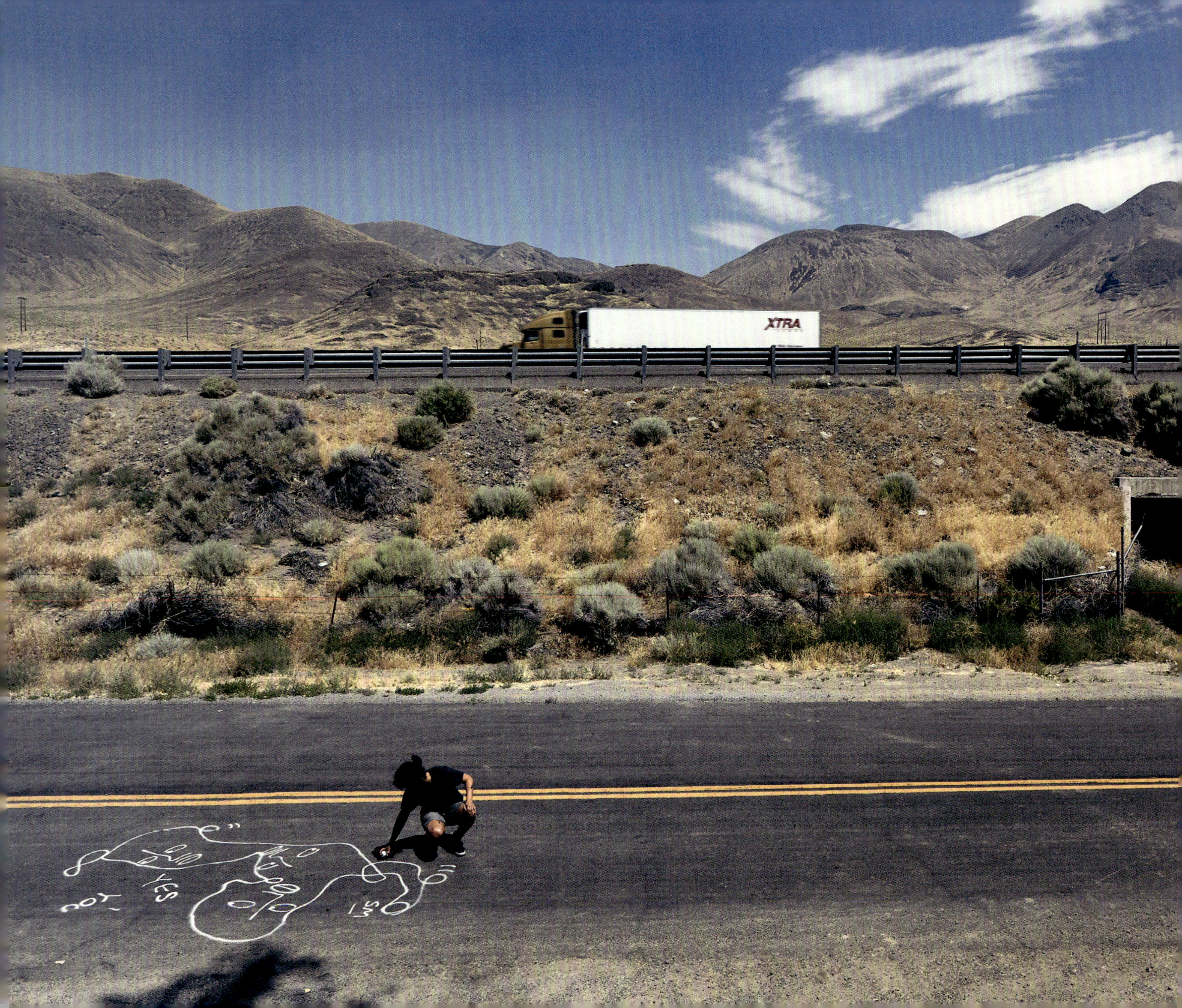
YES
YOU
YES

CONTENTS

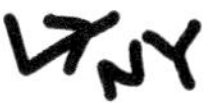

1   **2**   **3**   **4**   **5**

TEXTS

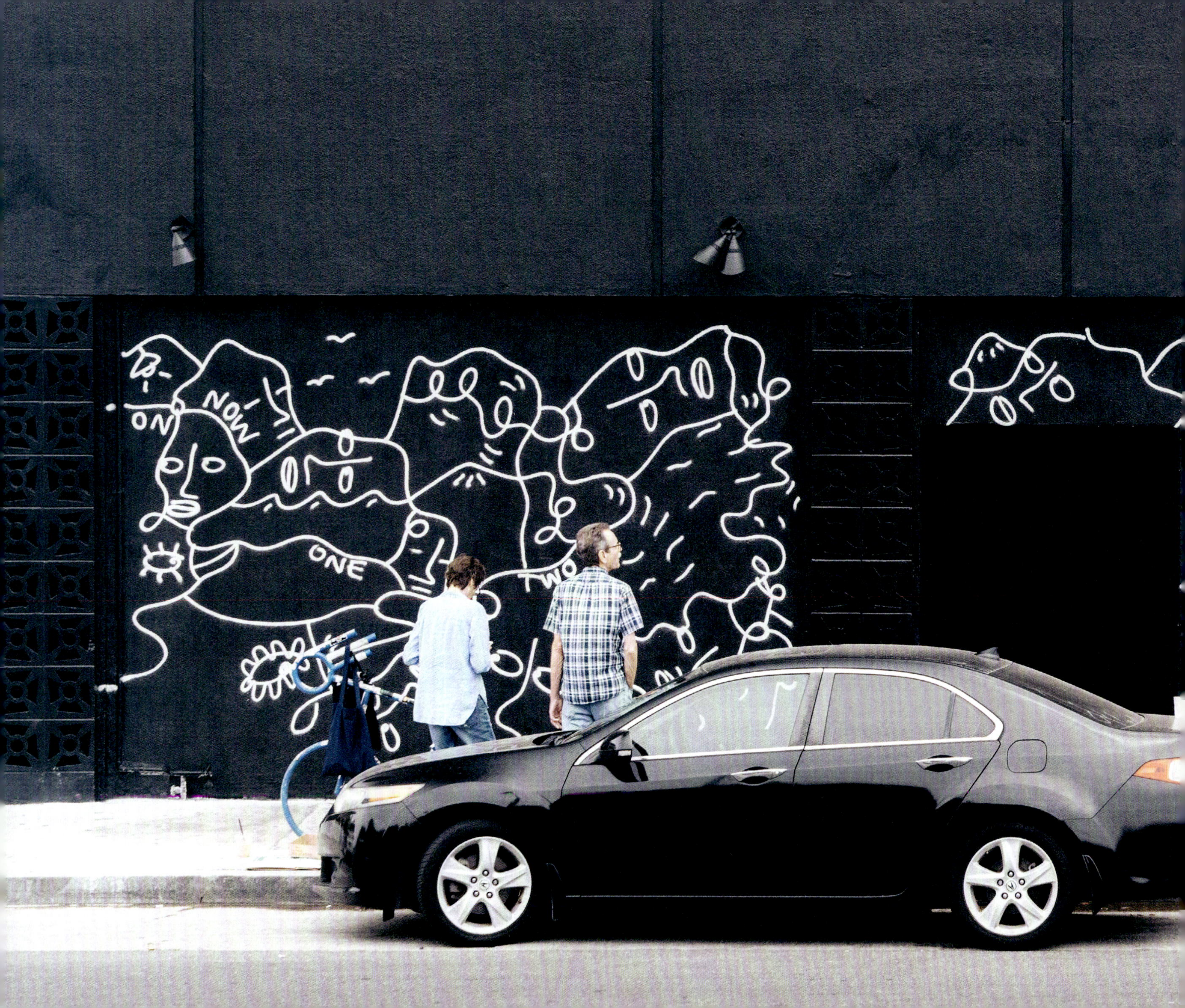

NOW
ONE
TWO

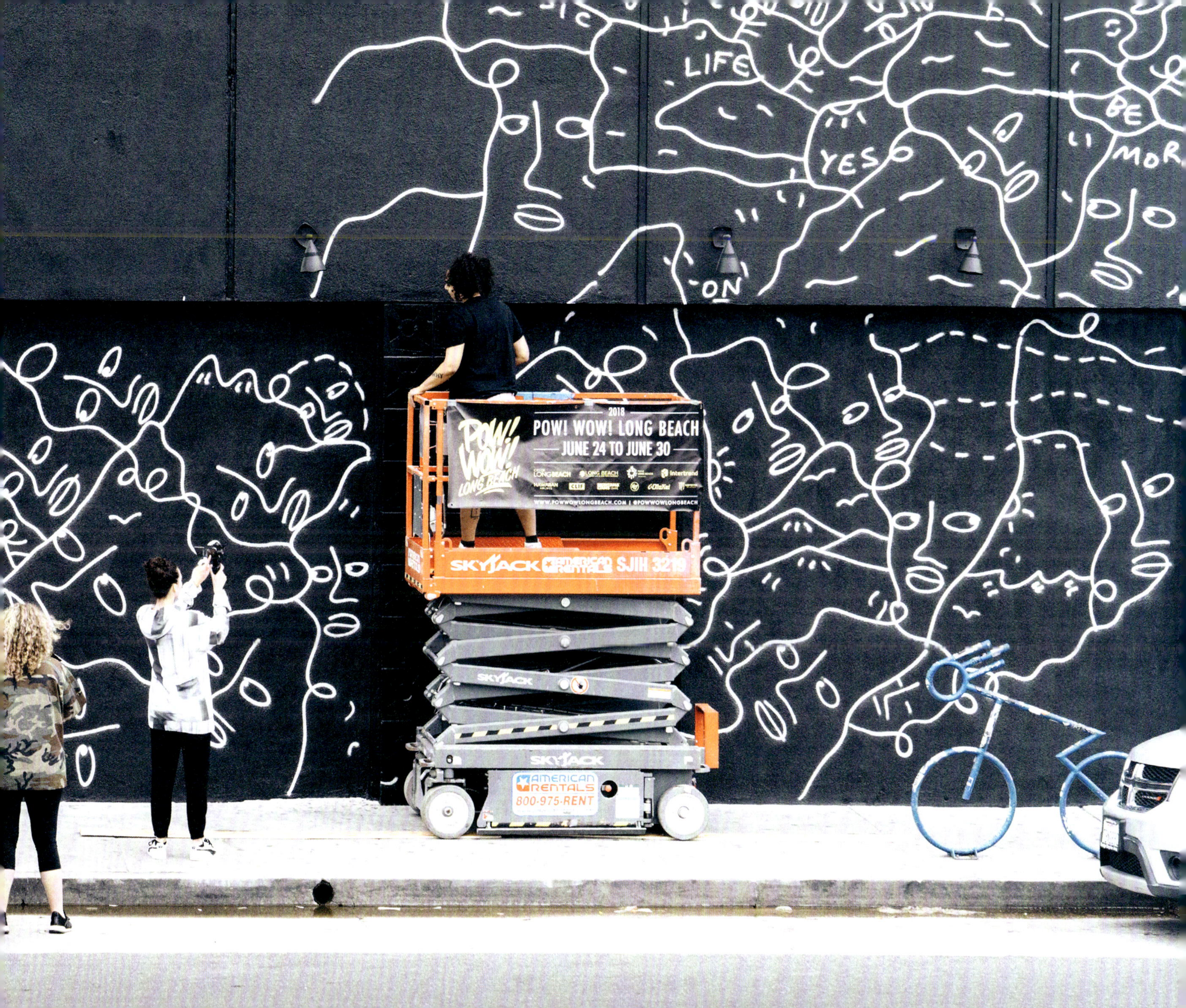
LIFE
BE
YES
MOR
ON
2018
POW! WOW! LONG BEACH
JUNE 24 TO JUNE 30
LONG BEACH
WWW.POWWOWLONGBEACH.COM
SKYJACK
SJIH 3219
AMERICAN RENTALS
800-975-RENT

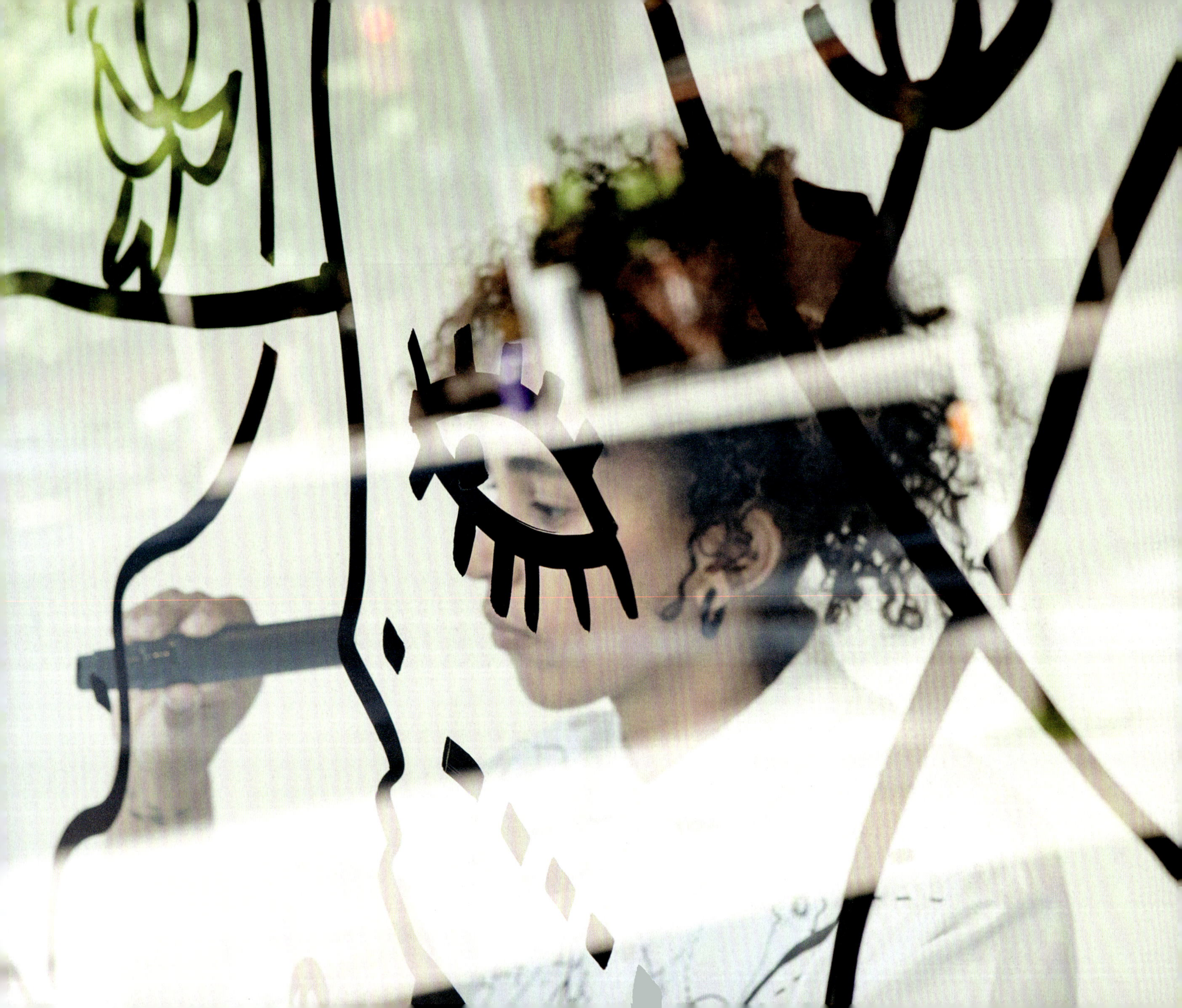

SOMEDAY WE CAN

KATHARINE STOUT

Martin working on *Sea You* (2013) for
the exhibition *Out of the Box: The Rise
of Sneaker Culture* at the Bata Shoe
Museum, Toronto, July 2013.

*'A little bit of my goal by doing what I do quite
naturally is to find the word and the vocabulary
of who we are at the core, as people.'*

The distinct character of Shantell Martin's line resonates across her work, whether this line is drawn on paper, the wall or an object, and whether it is found in the art gallery, in the classroom, on stage in a club or on the catwalk of a fashion show. Martin's line is a line of enquiry into the endless possibilities of drawing, into experimental technology for this most primordial of mediums, and into the freedom to express who we are – and through this expression, discover who we are.

Curiosity is what drives Martin's attention and energy. Through the disarmingly simple means of line drawing in black ink, she harnesses the full potential of each project to explore fundamental questions with her audience about what connects us to people and environments, while also challenging what it is we use to define ourselves.

Martin has lived and worked in New York since 2009, having moved there from London via Tokyo. Her career is multifaceted and often defies the conventions of the various worlds she inhabits. Although well known for both her commercial collaborations and her museum exhibitions, Martin is also a committed teacher and researcher. It is no coincidence that drawing is her chosen means to create this plurality of outputs, as it provides an exceptionally flexible and unique tool for artists to develop their own language and style. Indeed, drawing's heterogeneity has been cited as a reason why it is hard to classify as a medium, yet perhaps it is this single characteristic that continues to give it such currency as a useful and generative discipline for artists.

WHO ARE YOU

*'The one thing I've learned
to do is to create a line that
looks and feels like me.'*

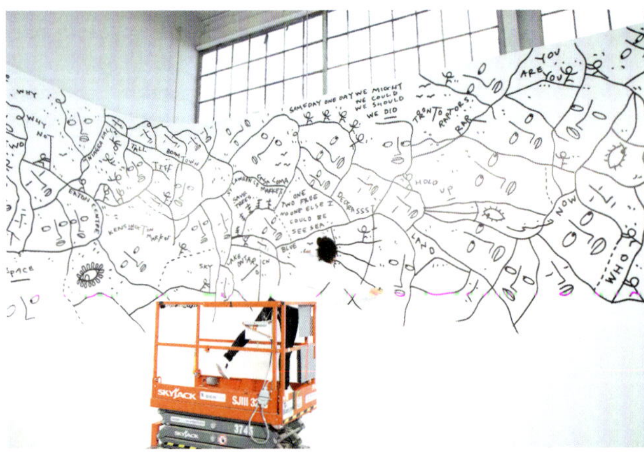

Martin working on *Niagara Falls* (2015) at
District 28, Toronto, November 2015.

Each of Martin's works starts as a continuous black line on a white background – usually from the left-hand corner. She refers to this line as the drawing's foundation: 'The initial line for me is the DNA. It's the structure. It's the foundation of the drawing. It's what holds it all together.'[1] Forming the core of the drawing, this aleatory line works its way across the white surface, filling the available volume. Once the line is completed, Martin steps back to assess the pockets of negative space that remain, using her own vocabulary of signs and symbols to respond to the character of each void. If a space appears to need support, she will draw in a stick figure. If there is a space that looks like air, then she might draw in birds. If a space lends itself to a face, she will add eyes.

One impromptu decision leads to another in an intuitive yet physical stream of consciousness, Martin's hand moving across and up and down the drawing until the mass of white space is filled and it 'feels' like it is done. Martin describes a feeling 'called stop', which starts in the toes, and is akin to reaching the bottom of a rope that is being pulled up. It's an automated instinct, formed through trial and error over countless iterations, and has created the inbuilt knowledge of when it is time to stop and walk away.

Once the work has reached its conclusion, it will inevitably resonate as a 'Shantell Martin drawing', its DNA and component parts instantly recognisable, and yet each one is unique. As she states, 'The one thing I've learned to do is to create a line that looks and feels like me.' Over the years, Martin has acquired the techniques and confidence to develop a signature style that looks so simple and yet is complex enough to offer an infinite number of variations and compositions. Instinctive yet precise, each work is created through an open response to the circumstance of its making, while founded upon a system – or algorithm – that Martin has stored in her head like a data bank.

In 1921, in a section of his lecture notes discussing 'from point to line', Paul Klee famously wrote, 'A line comes into being. The most highly charged line is the most authentic line because it is the most active. In all these examples the principal and active line develops freely. It goes out for a walk, so to speak, aimlessly for the sake of the walk.'[2] At the time, Klee was teaching at the Bauhaus in Weimar, and was engaged throughout his practice with the relationship between a line that creates a plane or form and its subject. Here he expresses the joy of allowing the line to be free of descriptive purpose. This was a methodology also advocated by his peers, including André Masson and Hans Arp, who together pioneered the Surrealist practice of automatic drawing as a means of enabling

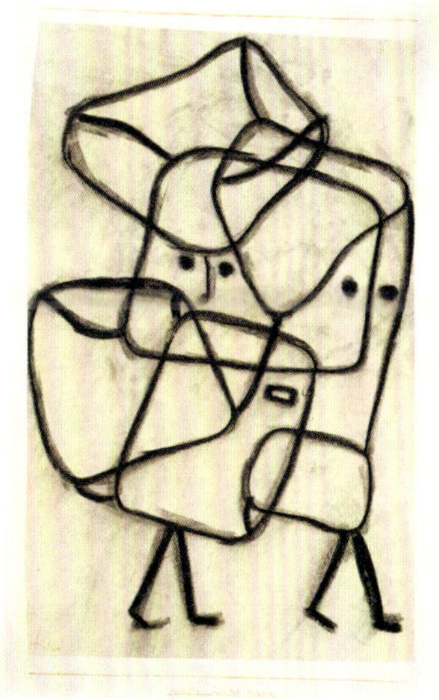

Paul Klee, *Burdened Child*, 1930.
Graphite, crayon and ink on paper
on board, 65 x 45.8 cm (25 5/8 x 18 in).
Tate, London. Bequeathed by Elly Kahnweiler
1991 to form part of the gift of Gustav and
Elly Kahnweiler, accessioned 1994.

the subconscious to be expressed. In automatic drawing, the hand is allowed to move 'randomly' or 'machine-like' across the paper as a method to remove rational control and release the psyche, which was otherwise thought to be suppressed. However, the drawings invariably resulted in forms of representation, whether because figurative forms seemed to suggest themselves from within the abstract composition, or due to the impossibility of suppressing a conscious intervention to make an image comprehensible. Klee's own non-abstract drawings display a dreamlike figuration that deliberately employs a childish or naive approach of using basic anthropomorphic forms.

In 1949, Marcel Duchamp commented on Klee's work: 'The first reaction before a painting by Paul Klee is a very pleasant realisation of what each one of us did or might have done when we tried to draw, in our childhood. Most of his compositions show at first this attractive side of unsophisticated, naive expression which is found in children's drawings... When we look closer we immediately discover how incomplete the first impression was and if Klee often uses a "childish" technique it is applied to a very mature form of thinking which the second analysis discovers rapidly.'[3] At first sight, Martin's drawings display a similar childlike simplicity, which soon reveals itself as more complicated thanks to a delicate tension between the unconscious line that has been allowed to go for a walk, and the display of skill and knowledge – derived from years of practice – in directing it. The second stage of adding the figurative elements, such as a stick figure or a face, is a more analytic process of assessing how to fill the remaining gaps in the drawing, which also shifts the work from the realms of abstraction to that of representation. Lying behind Martin's modes of representation are direct philosophical questions, revealed and made explicit in the words and concise texts that she incorporates within the work in a primarily visual way, such as her ubiquitous mantra:

WHO ARE YOU
YOU ARE YOU
ARE YOU YOU

By incorporating language within her drawings, Martin harnesses the direct power of words or phrases to cut through consciousness and trigger instant recognition in a world dominated by images. The first letters of the phrase 'Who Are You' spell out 'way', another key word for Martin, for whom each work can be described as a step on an ongoing journey exploring her own identity. Yet each of these works has also enabled a more literal journey, in which her talent for drawing has taken her away from her childhood on London's periphery to one of the best art schools at its centre, then to Japan and now on to New York. She comments:

> A little bit of my goal by doing what I do quite naturally is to find the word and the vocabulary of who we are at the core, as people. We can describe what we do, where we're from, the roles we play: teachers, mothers, fathers, cousins, sons, daughters. When answering the question 'Please tell me who you are?' without providing any of those things – it's baffling to me every time. As travelled, educated, amazing human beings, we don't really have that vocabulary to describe who we are at the core, and that baffles me a little bit. Exploring these words within my work, maybe I can start to find out what some of these words, vocabulary or phrases are.

One of her earliest works that foregrounds language is also one of her most personal, and for many years it remained a private form of connection and communication with her grandmother. The collaborative project 'Dear Grandmother' began around 2002, when Martin commissioned her grandmother Dot Martin to embroider a pair of works called *Half White 1980* as a way to allow Martin to reflect upon her own racial identity.

Growing up in Thamesmead in the 1980s meant that Martin was one of very few people of colour in her community, or indeed in her family, to the extent that she wasn't even recognised as such. She was largely treated as any other person within a population predominantly made up of low-income, working-class, white inhabitants – albeit someone who looked a little different and, because of her interest in art, also acted differently. For those unfamiliar with this area, Thamesmead is an extensive purpose-built housing estate on the outskirts of south-east London, built by the government from the late 1960s to address the lack of housing in the capital. Conceived as a modernist and progressive social project, the estate was fraught with problems from the outset when the large quantities of concrete used as the main building material turned out to be prone to damp and condensation. Schools, shops and accommodation for older people were incorporated within the estate, but this well-intended provision for self-sufficiency actually produced a

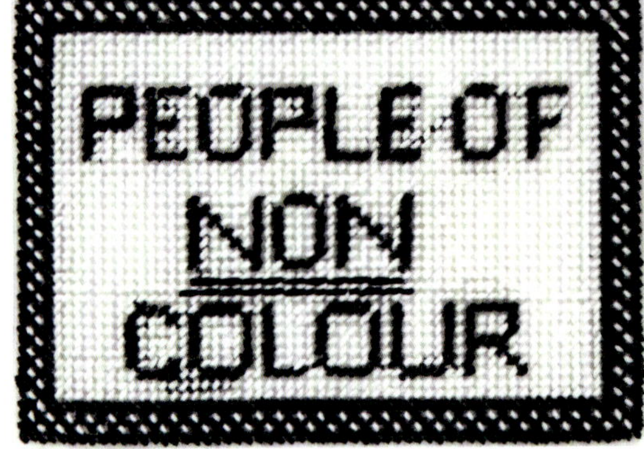

People of Non Colour, 2011.
Needlepoint, 20.3 x 30.5 cm (8 x 12 in).
Collaboration with Dot Martin.

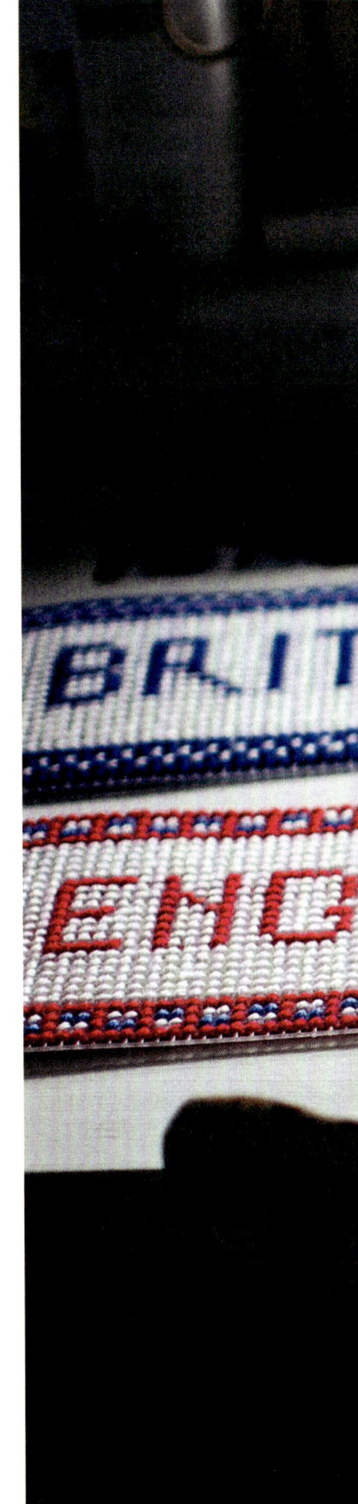

Needlepoints from the 'Dear Grandmother' series (2002–15) on the desk at Martin's studio in Bed-Stuy, Brooklyn, 2012.

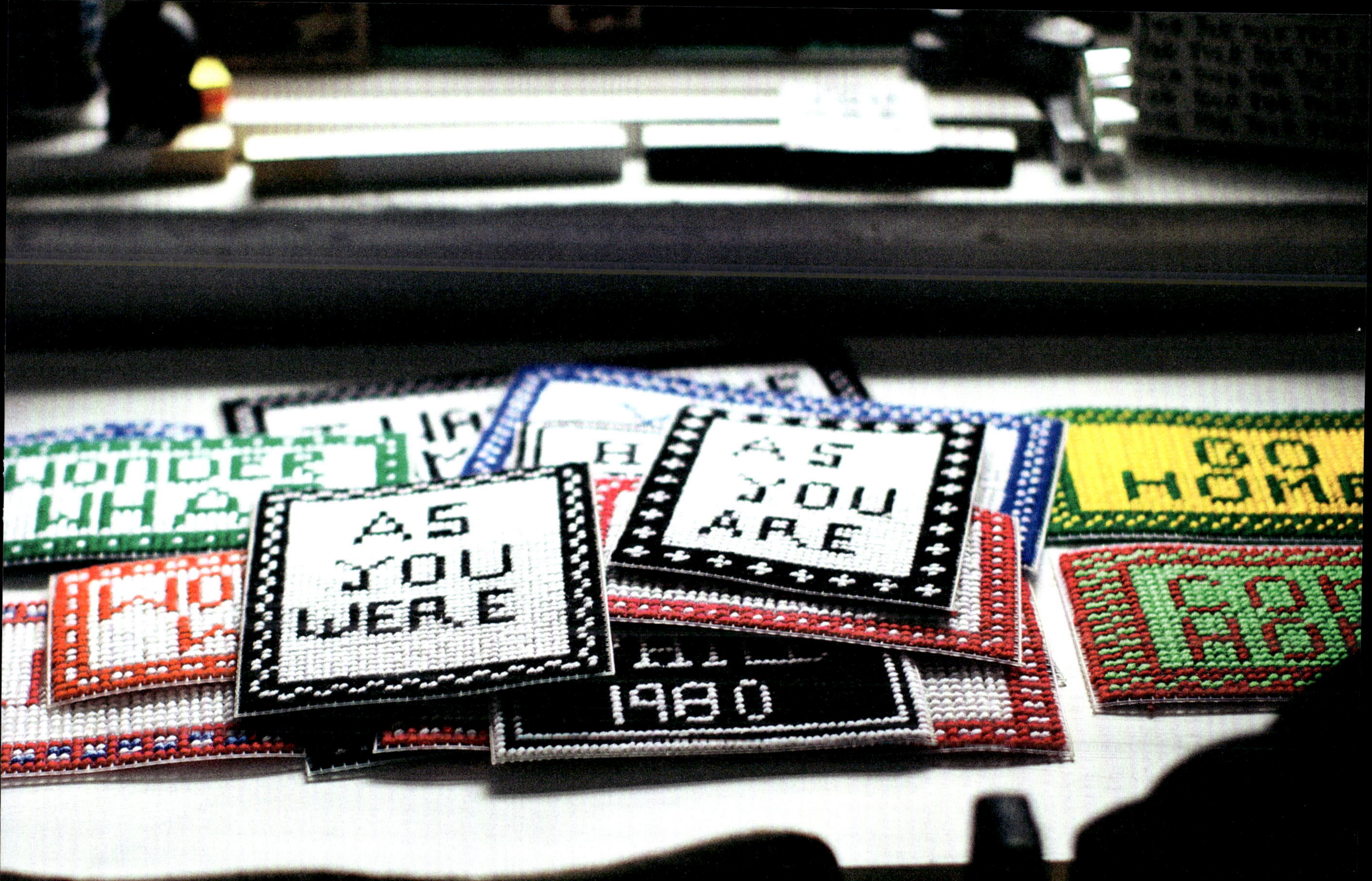

WONDEE
WHA
AS
YOU
WERE
AS
YOU
ARE
GO
HARR
1980

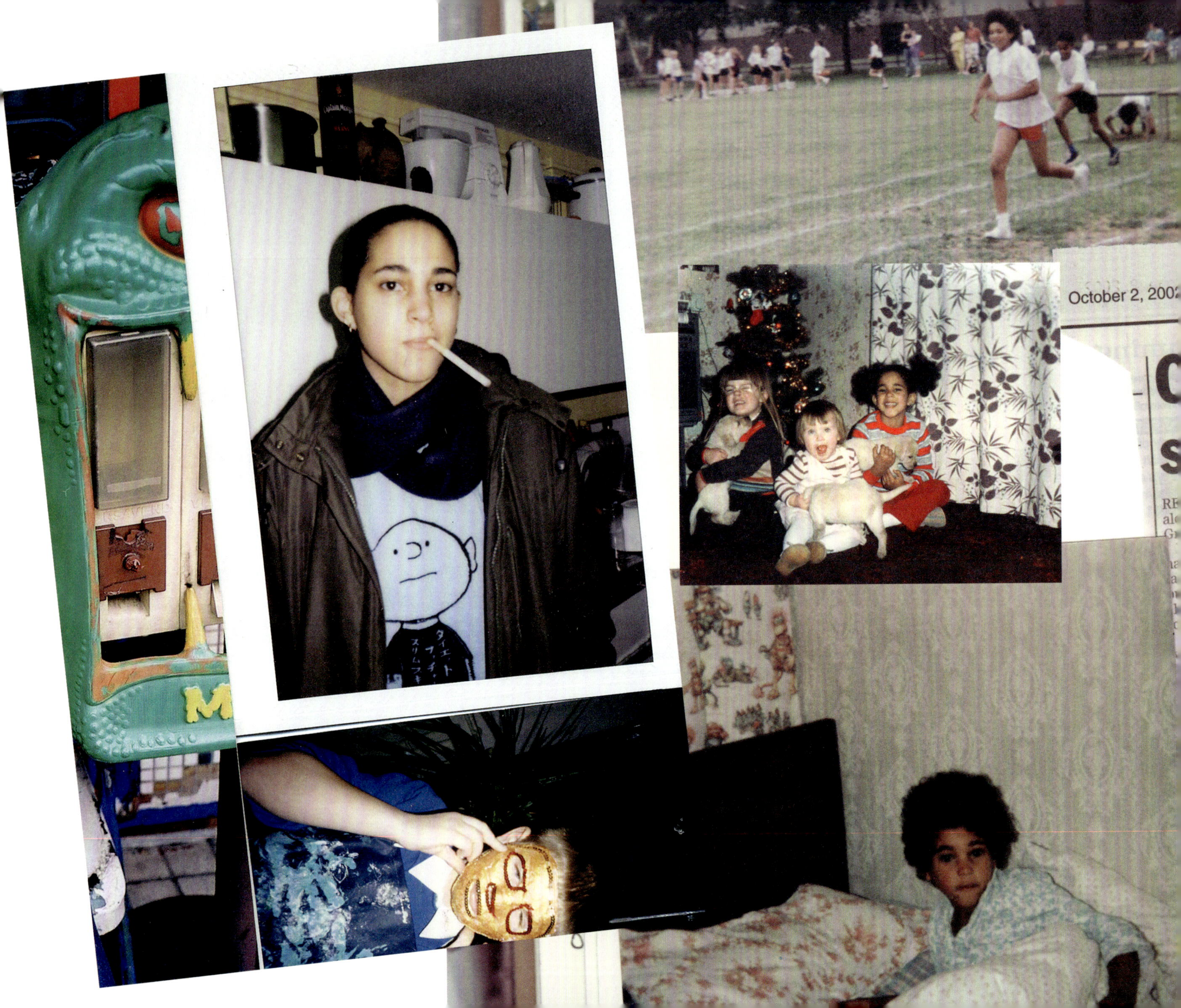
October 2, 2002

ASTEST RV

Newspaper clipping and photographs from Martin's childhood
in Thamesmead, London, taken
from the artist's scrapbooks.

LC

rity in a
ep on T

and clean-up work
of waterfront in east
been completed.
last two years, work
esurfacing, the instal-
ustrial artefacts and
oden steps to the fore-
were carved by sculp-
awrence.
tal charity Ground-
s Gateway London
celebration to mark the
rk at Endersby Wharf.
sented with a wooden
mbers of the Green-
Riverwood Project and
and live music added

JOE THE
AGE CON

NICE

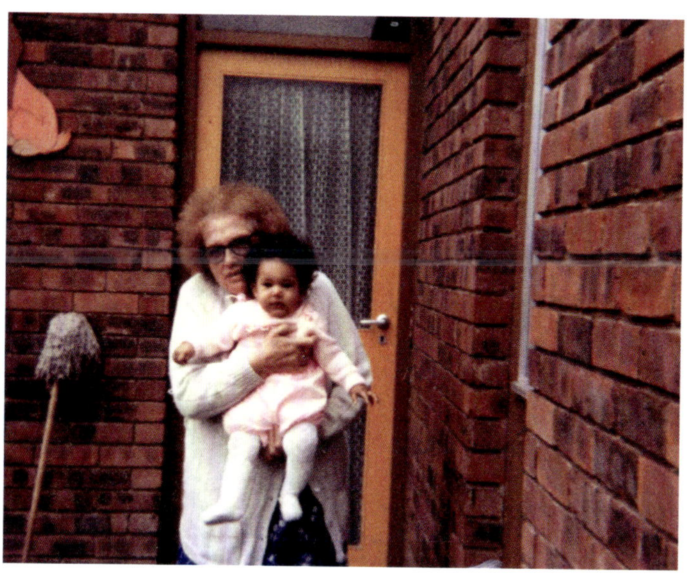

Martin with her grandmother
Dot Martin in Thamesmead, 1981.

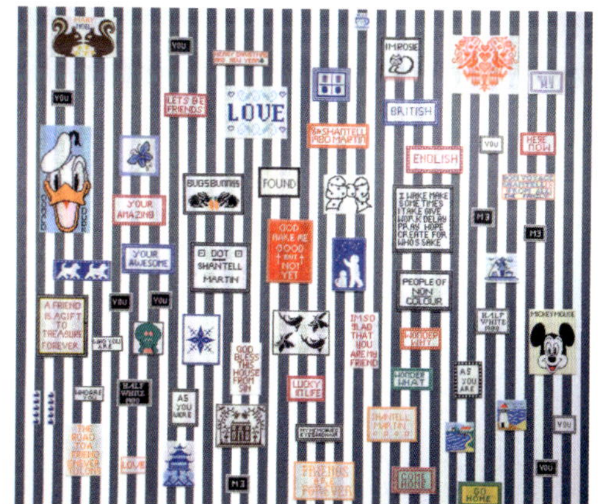

The 'Dear Grandmother' series (2002–15) on
display at the *Crossing Brooklyn* exhibition at
the Brooklyn Museum, New York, 2014.

community that became isolated and introverted. For those seeking
to break out of increasingly normalised expectations of low-income
jobs, petty crime or 'signing on' for unemployment benefits, it was
deemed necessary to leave.

With Martin working away and Dot still living in Thamesmead,
their initial embroidery series led to a collaborative process that
produced almost a hundred works. Aided by Dot's suggestions
for text and colour to complement her granddaughter's requests,
these pieces served to bridge the distance between them and to
communicate across generation, race and culture. Phrases such
as 'Come Home/Go Home' and 'British/English' revealed the latent
racism of Martin's upbringing and allowed the pair to work through
some of the challenges behind exploring such a complex topic,
and do so in a way that was playful, sincere and productive. These
works comprise a rare break from drawing within Martin's oeuvre,
providing a different form of haptic making as a means to connect
and bond with her grandmother before she passed away at the age
of 84 in 2015. Just a year prior, an exhibition at the Brooklyn Museum
in New York gave Martin the opportunity to bring the majority of the
pieces together as one installation, which enabled a more public
statement of this highly personal and emotive collaboration.

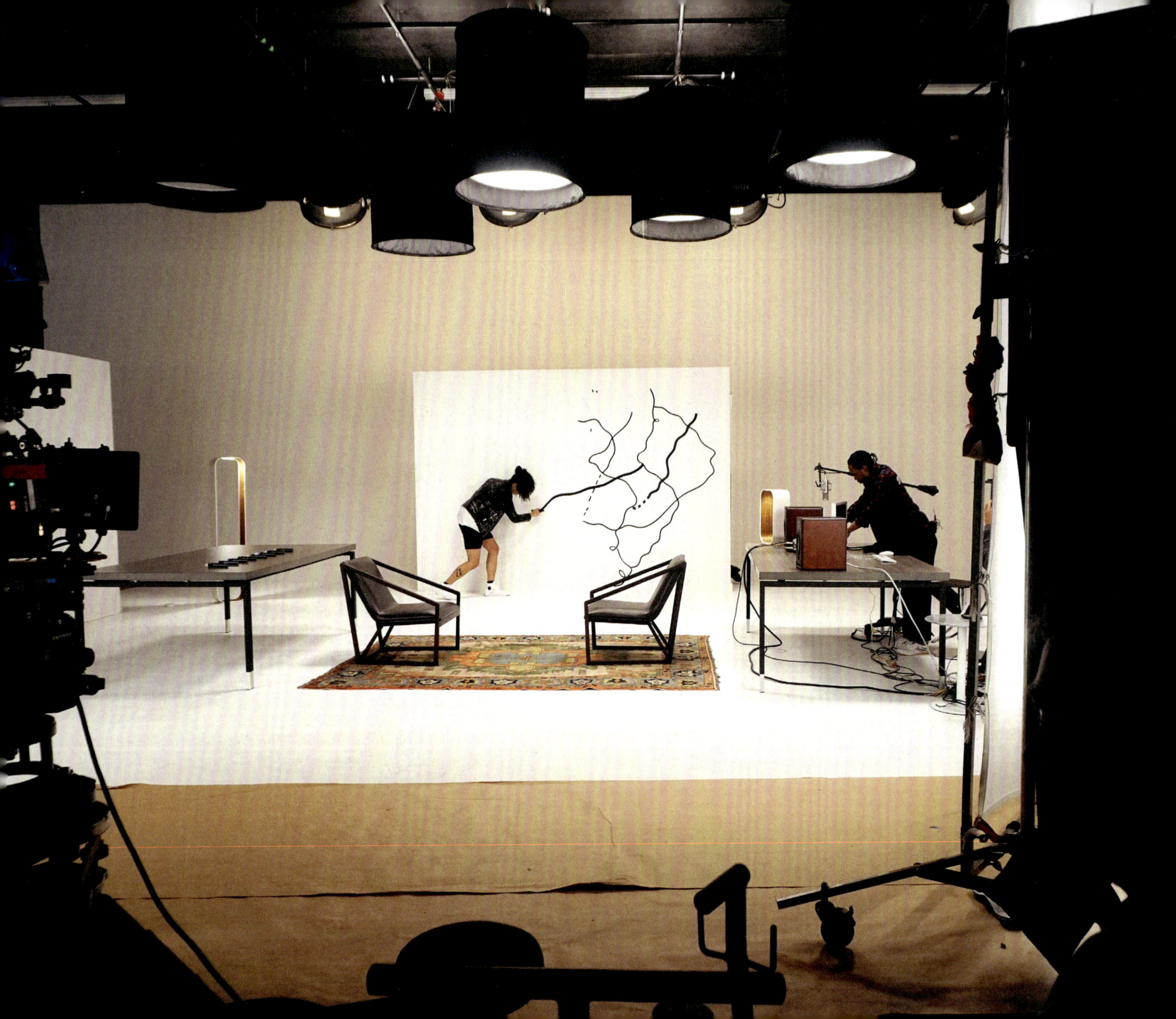

PROCESS, COMMISSIONS AND TECHNOLOGY

'You can expose the magic and it will still be magical, you can expose the process and it will still be yours.'

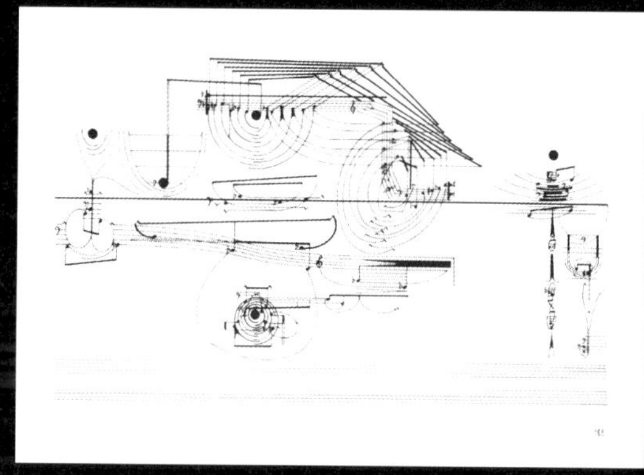

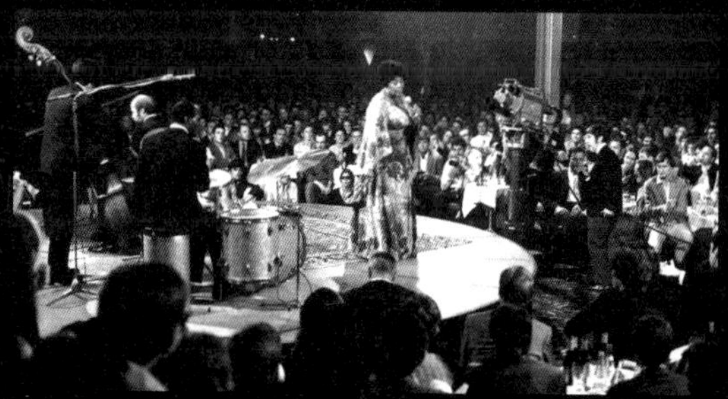

Top: Page from the score of *Treatise* (1963–7) by Cornelius Cardew.
Bottom: Ella Fitzgerald with the Tommy Flanagan Trio at the Montreux Jazz Festival, June 1969.

Collaboration often provides an experimental platform for Martin to take her practice in different directions. Indeed, many of the foundations of her practice have been borne out of a process of sharing ideas with others in different situations, particularly during her time living in Japan from 2003 to 2009. Having graduated in 2003 from Central Saint Martins' Graphic Design department in London with honours, she found her options limited given her lack of existing contacts in the relevant industries. She decided to move to Japan, initially to teach English, and continued to draw in sketchbooks, more as a hobby until some friends asked her to do some live drawing at an avant-garde music club. This environment, in which people made their own music, often using DIY instruments, prompted Martin to set up an overhead projector and make a durational drawing to music being created live. This methodology is reminiscent of the Scratch Orchestra, an experimental music ensemble founded in the UK during the spring of 1969 by Cornelius Cardew, Michael Parsons and Howard Skempton. Defined by Cardew in a draft constitution published in the *Musical Times* of June 1969 as 'a large number of enthusiasts pooling their resources (not primarily material resources) and assembling for action (music, making, performance, edification)'.[4] In accordance with this philosophy, anyone could join the orchestra, and graphic scores were used rather than traditional sheet music. There was also an emphasis on free improvisation. Although the formal ensemble was relatively short-lived before internal tensions led to its break-up, the radical principles of the Scratch Orchestra's 'do your own thing' free aesthetics continue to influence musicians and artists today.

In a similarly pragmatic way, while working as a VJ in Japan Martin established her capacity to create a drawing 'in the moment' through making the visuals as responsive as possible to the music that the band was playing. Using the increasingly addictive momentum produced by not having time to plan, hesitate or think too much, she found that she was left with a drawing that reflected who she was as an artist, in a way she describes as 'formed from the inside out'. An earlier precedent for this spontaneous improvisational approach can be found in scat singing, a form of vocal jazz developed throughout the twentieth century in which the singer improvises melodies and rhythms with nonsense syllables or no words at all, using the voice as an instrument. Regarded as one of the greatest scat singers, Ella Fitzgerald gave an extraordinary performance on 22 June 1969 at the Montreux Jazz Festival, including a rendition of 'One Note Samba' in which she and the musicians – Ed Thigpen on drums, Frank De La Rosa on bass and Tommy Flanagan on piano – intuitively follow each other's musical prompts and leads to create an astonishing six-minute display of pure, hedonistic improvisation.[5]

The adrenalin of producing drawings under extreme pressure – and, as she became better known, in increasingly large Japanese clubs – allowed Martin to both refine and become confident about her signature style, which at the time she described as 'creepy cute'. One of her Japanese sketchbooks, with its imaginative creatures and characters in this style, later informed her colouring book *Wave: A Journey Through the Sea of Imagination for the Adventurous Colorist*.[6] In its introduction Martin writes, 'Before I moved to Japan, my work was pretty dark; I was an angry teenager and young adult. But working and living in a wholly new culture helped me shed some of that anger, and as a result my drawing started to become much lighter, freer and even whimsical.'

This personal style can be set within the context of a wider movement that Japanese writer and curator Midori Matsui has described as 'Micropop', in which artists working in Japan in the late 1980s and 1990s used an assimilation of drawing styles found in popular subcultures, including comics, children's illustrated books and visual satire, to offer a hybrid mix of fantasy, social critique and personal memoir. According to Matsui, Micropop's 'efforts to mark out unique ways of perception and spaces of cohabitation, free from institutionalised pressures, or the reifying influences of global capitalism and mass media, indicate a radical assertion of individual agency.'[7] Writing about the work of Japanese artist Ryoko Aoki, Matsui proposes that the unconscious can be understood both in the Freudian sense as an archive for memory, but also 'as a vehicle for the "mobilisation" of images', a description that is arguably also applicable to Martin's work.[8] During her time in Japan, Martin created a cast of characters that offers an identifiable set of likenesses, for example the 'Eye', the 'Bird Boat' or 'Headless', to represent people, things or feelings – and as a way to exorcise memories – and these continue to populate her work. In Martin's own words:

Eye has always existed in the world but she was not always open, let alone aware and responsive. A singular string of events led Eye to the practice of meditation, which helped her become much more accepting of new experiences and more responsive towards the world at large. This new openness is visually manifest in the smooth and regularly shaped flower eyelashes that now frame Eye.

Equally at home in the air or water, Bird Boat helps you sail over all and any obstacles and gets you through those hard times when you're not sure which way to go.

Headless used to get lots of headaches and was extremely troubled by the past. In an attempt to escape all this he cut off his head but quickly realised that the shadow of his past was still firmly attached. Headless is now on a journey to find peace with his shadow.

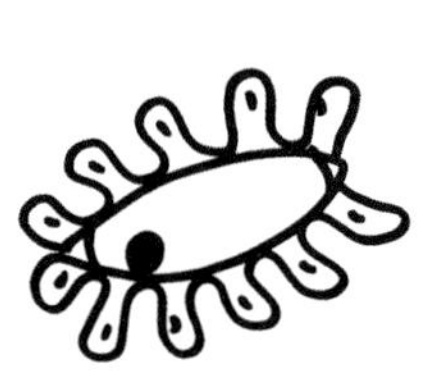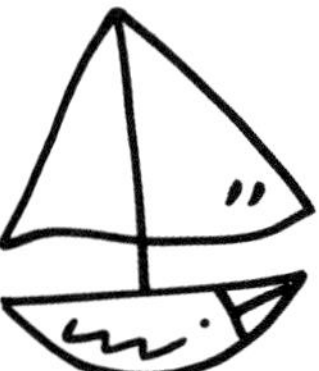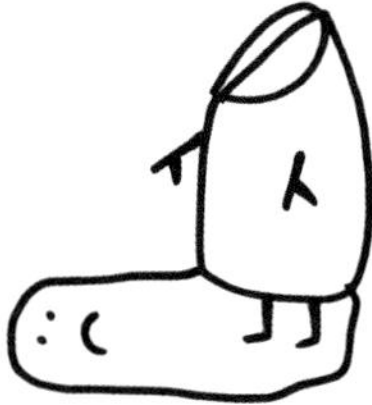

Eye (2005), *Bird Boat* (2006) and *Headless* (2008) are recurring characters in Martin's practice, each with their individual and evolving stories, characteristics and messages.

These characters, alongside others, form a personal lexicon that won't necessarily be obvious to the viewer. Beyond their bold, dramatic impact, they offer insight into hidden layers of meaning within the works that speak to how Martin has always used her drawing to work through personal demons and challenges, from the privacy of her childhood bedroom to the public space of the museum.

Martin's time in Japan led to her preference for pen and ink, which unlike graphite cannot be erased – once the mark is made you have to live with it, including any mistakes. What is noticeable about Martin's methodology is that, in order to facilitate the freedom to respond spontaneously, she adheres to quite strict parameters and rules, such as predominantly using black ink; being loyal to a selection of Lumocolor permanent markers made by Staedtler; and always choosing medium-sized tips. She attributes this to the fact that the arts in Japan remain predominantly craft-based practices, in which individuals learn techniques and use prescribed tools that are passed down through generations. 'Mastering' a discipline is premised on precise codes and rules – even if these are then interpreted and individualised later.

As a legacy of her time in Japan, many of Martin's works are still made in a very public manner, live in front of an audience, with each drawing containing an intimate resonance to the particular time or place of its creation. Music and performance remain core to her practice, specifically rhythm and repetition. She has recently

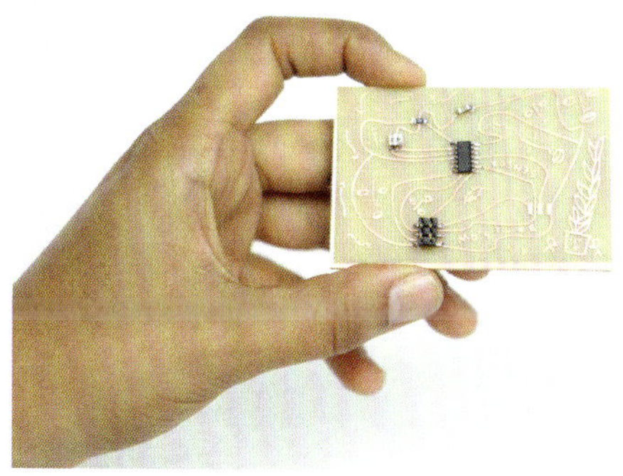

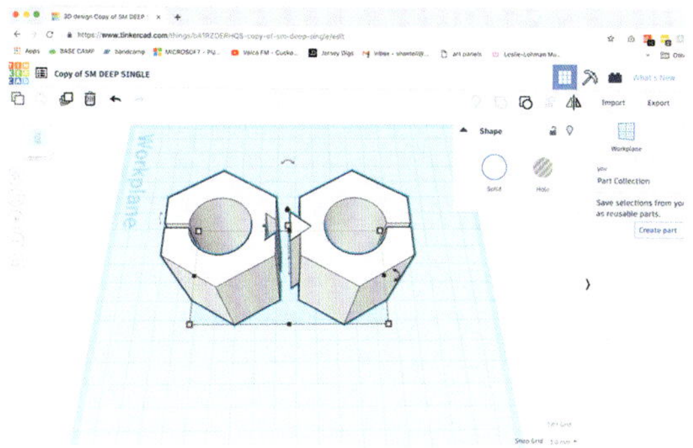

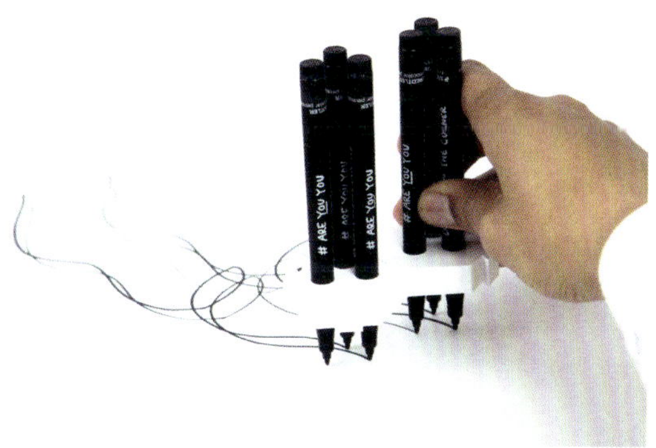

Top to bottom: Milled printed circuit board (PCB) created in collaboration with Jonathan Bobrow at MIT Media Lab, Cambridge, MA, in 2014–15; Screenshot of Tinkercad webapp showing work in progress on Martin's modular *Connectors* (2016) at Pier 9, San Francisco; *Connectors* in action with six Staedtler markers.

started to create music, mainly on the piano, partly inspired by her collaboration with Kendrick Lamar in 2016 for Art Basel Miami Beach. This 75-minute performance saw the two working simultaneously to produce a performative artwork captured on video. Lamar began the set using a beat-making machine to build the rhythm, then Martin came in to start drawing on a blank canvas as Lamar continued to collage different sounds, both working in tandem until they had realised a unique work of art. Since then, Martin has started to develop her own musical and spoken-word performances, extending the language element of her practice to become another form of live improvisation, in which she will offer anecdotes about her early upbringing and memories, riffing off words and questions offered by the audience.

Having firmly established her signature style, Martin is always curious to take it apart and test it with different technologies and situations. She does this through two activities. The first of these is taking part in residencies and projects with research institutes and teaching organisations. The second is undertaking commissions with commercial companies to produce customised merchandise. It is relatively unusual to find an artist pursuing these two avenues in parallel, as they are usually seen as mutually exclusive – an artist either follows the commercial path of responding to a brief, or a non-profit route of academic research. However, this separation is largely due to perceived rather than inherent differences. In both contexts there are set criteria, but also the freedom to interpret and to assert an individual artistic identity onto the output. Martin approaches both activities with equal enthusiasm – despite a tendency among certain elements of the art world to look down on the commercial sector, the idea of an artist remaining removed from commerce is in itself a privileged one.

In 2014, Martin became a research affiliate and artist in residence at MIT Media Lab in Cambridge, Massachusetts, lecturing there and using its facilities over a prolonged period. Over the next year, she collaborated with Jonathan Bobrow, an artist programmer and research assistant there, to make a functioning printed circuit board from scratch. The idea behind the project was to approach the circuit board in a different way – not just optimising its efficiency, but paying attention to the way it looked by creating a new design for this normally hidden element. They milled a custom-made copper plate with a Martin-drawn design for the traces that connected the components, creating a work of art that is also a functional tool.

A fascination with technology drives Martin to investigate the component parts of a drawing: how long are the lines; how long

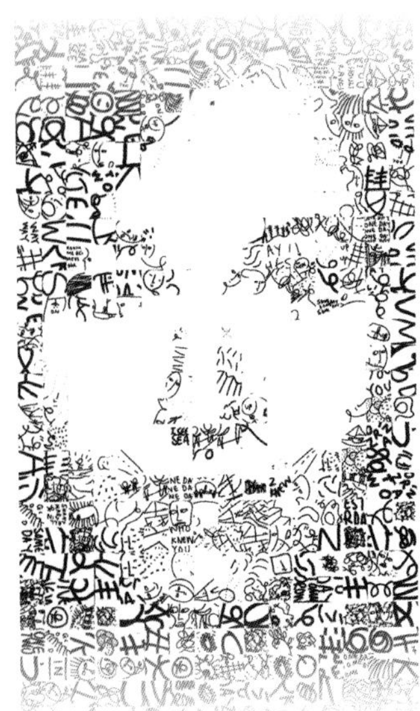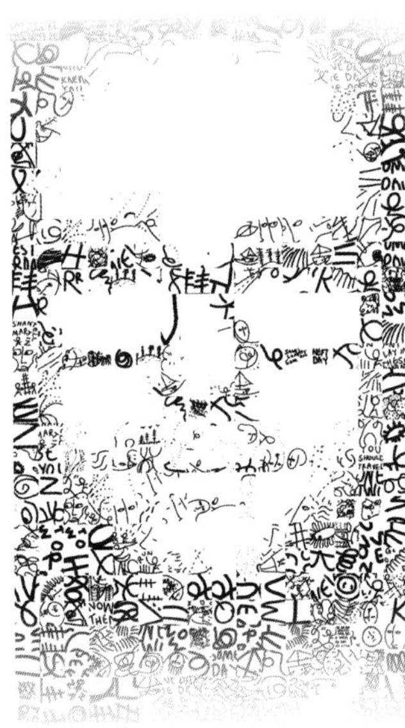

did it take; what are the angles; what is the mass of negative space; what effect can different tools have. Having started as a VJ, reliant on technology to make her work seen and available, Martin has continued to explore new technologies to develop tools that allow her to expand her practice. For example, as part of her 2016 residency at Autodesk's Pier 9 Workshop in San Francisco, she began using its design and fabrication resources to prototype new drawing implements. Utilising computer-aided design (CAD) software and 3D printers, Martin designed an adaptable kit of parts that can be assembled to create a multipart tool that allows the user to draw with two, three or even six pens at a time. Simple enough to be constructed and operated by children, it has been made available by Martin in the form of seven new open-source designs, which can be 3D-printed in resin plastic.

Martin has also collaborated with Zach Lieberman, an artist and researcher, on several occasions to develop and use open-source digital technology to create new works that exist online. In 2015, they created an algorithm code for an interactive photo exhibition *WE ARE... #facesintech* at the annual Grace Hopper Celebration, a gathering of women technologists organised by digital community AnitaB.org. This code created portraits of the women who visited and took part in the conference by creating outlines of their faces, and automatically filling these with a collage of Martin's drawings, producing a unique likeness of each individual.

In 2018, Martin was invited to experiment at Google Creative Lab, New York, with a new augmented-reality app created with Google's ARCore technology, which has been developed from open-source experiments. This app allows individuals to create line drawings in augmented reality, and was used by Martin to make a virtual drawing that appears in three-dimensional space, simply by drawing on her smartphone.

In the commercial sector, Martin also works in a collaborative way, exemplified by her partnership with interior design Kelly Wearstler. They spent months exchanging ideas and sample pieces before working together to create a joint capsule collection that launched with a successful exhibition at Wearstler's store in Los Angeles in 2014. This mutually appreciative partnership resulted in a number of original objects, such as chairs, ottomans, marble pieces and leather jackets, and the store's windows were also customised with Martin's characteristic line drawings for the collection's launch.

At the 2018 edition of Salone del Mobile, Milan's premier design fair, Martin undertook a more straightforward commission for the iconic jewellery brand Tiffany & Co. to launch its new home collection. The firm invited female artists from across the globe, including Martin, Marilyn Minter, Laurie Simmons and Anna-Wili Highfield, to create installations around the concept of the greenhouse for its store in the Piazza del Duomo. Each of the artists was given a beautifully wrought miniature greenhouse made of sterling silver, copper and glass, and invited to make this objet d'art their own, adapting it to create a piece to be placed in one of the store's windows. The commission allowed Martin to work on a scale that contrasted with her usual room-sized installations. Martin was interested in the selection of a relatively new motif – the modern greenhouse – by a company known for its adherence to traditional craft-based objects and techniques developed over centuries. Martin customised her greenhouse with line drawings and adapted objects that represented her own quest to perfect her craft – drawing – in pursuit of self-discovery.

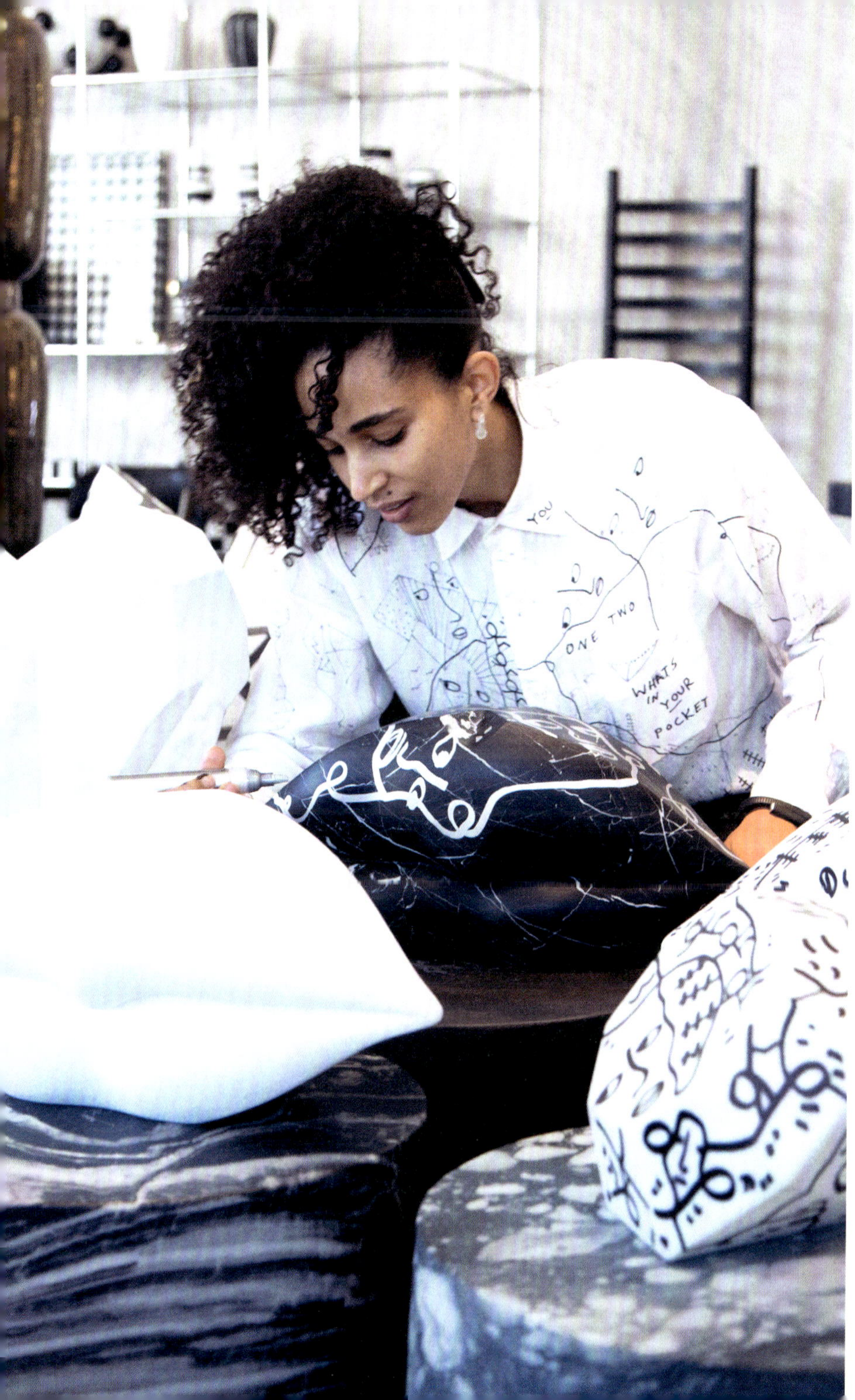

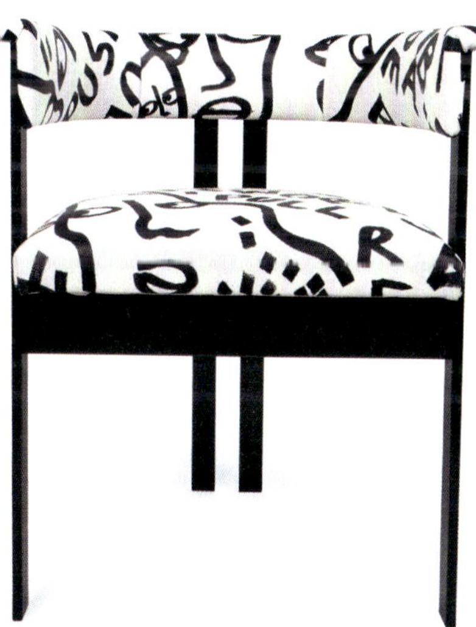

Customised Elliot Chair, 2014. Ink on leather on metal frame, 69 x 57.2 x 47 cm (27 x 22 ½ x 18 ½ in). Collaboration with Kelly Wearstler.

DRAW ON EVERYTHING

'Don't Hide in the Corner'

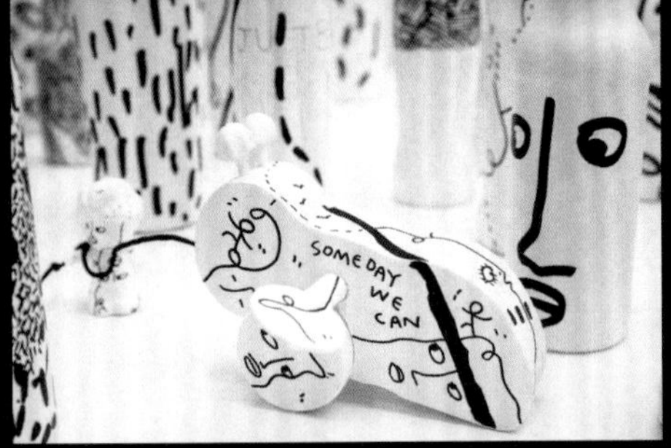

Above and opposite: Details of Martin's installation for the exhibition *Someday We Can* in the Sculpture Court, Albright-Knox Art Gallery, Buffalo, NY, 2017.

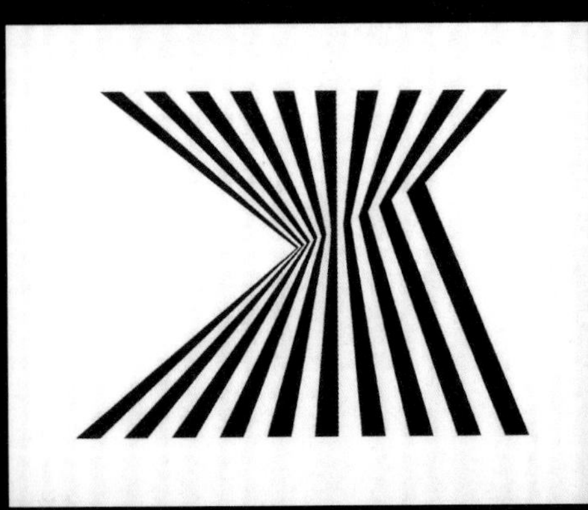

Bridget Riley, *Untitled (Fragment 1/7)*, 1965.
Screenprint on Perspex, 67.3 x 83.8 cm
(26 ½ x 33 in). Tate, London. Purchased 1970.

Just as Martin seeks to expand the range and application of her drawing practice, so she seeks to diversify the surfaces upon which she draws. Whether working with objects or on a public wall, she sees her interventions as a way to instil these surfaces with a new life or to rethink our relationship with a place or item. For her 2017 solo exhibition *Someday We Can* at the Albright-Knox Art Gallery, Buffalo, New York, Martin took over the Sculpture Court to create an immersive installation comprising toys, bottles and miscellaneous objects presented on a table sculpture, in front of a large wall drawing. The objects, which were covered in gesso and customised individually by Martin, included some personal memorabilia – some brand new, some ten or fifteen years old – alongside toys given to her by nieces or nephews, or donated by US company Fisher-Price, as well as bottles in various shapes and sizes. Overall, the energy and playfulness of the surrounding drawn environment made a dazzling, slightly overwhelming first impression, pushing audiences away as they attempted to take in the composition as a whole. But then, as viewers were drawn to look closer at the table installation, they started to recognise familiar objects or toys that they or their children also had, making their experience of the work more accessible. The installation therefore operated on different focal ranges, as well as on different planes – horizontal and vertical. What unified the work was the simplicity of the palette, completely devoid of colour, a defining characteristic of the majority of Martin's work. She comments:

> There has definitely been a lot of black and white in my work, and that's for a few reasons. It's very simple and it's very calming, and it's quite difficult at the same time. What I do is I draw and I create a line, but to create a line that is recognisably you, or is confidently you, takes a lot of practice and a lot of time. With black-and-white work you can see that, you can see the hard work within that. And you also create the space for possibility when people see the work.

In using such as simple palette, Martin is in the company of artists such as the British painter Bridget Riley, whose adherence to just one or two colours for each painting makes her early Op-art works graphically striking and instantly recognisable. New York-based artist Julie Mehretu also uses minimal colour in her drawings and paintings to place emphasis on her own lexicon of individual characters and calligraphic marks that, in a different way to Martin's, offer signifiers for social as well as political references. There is

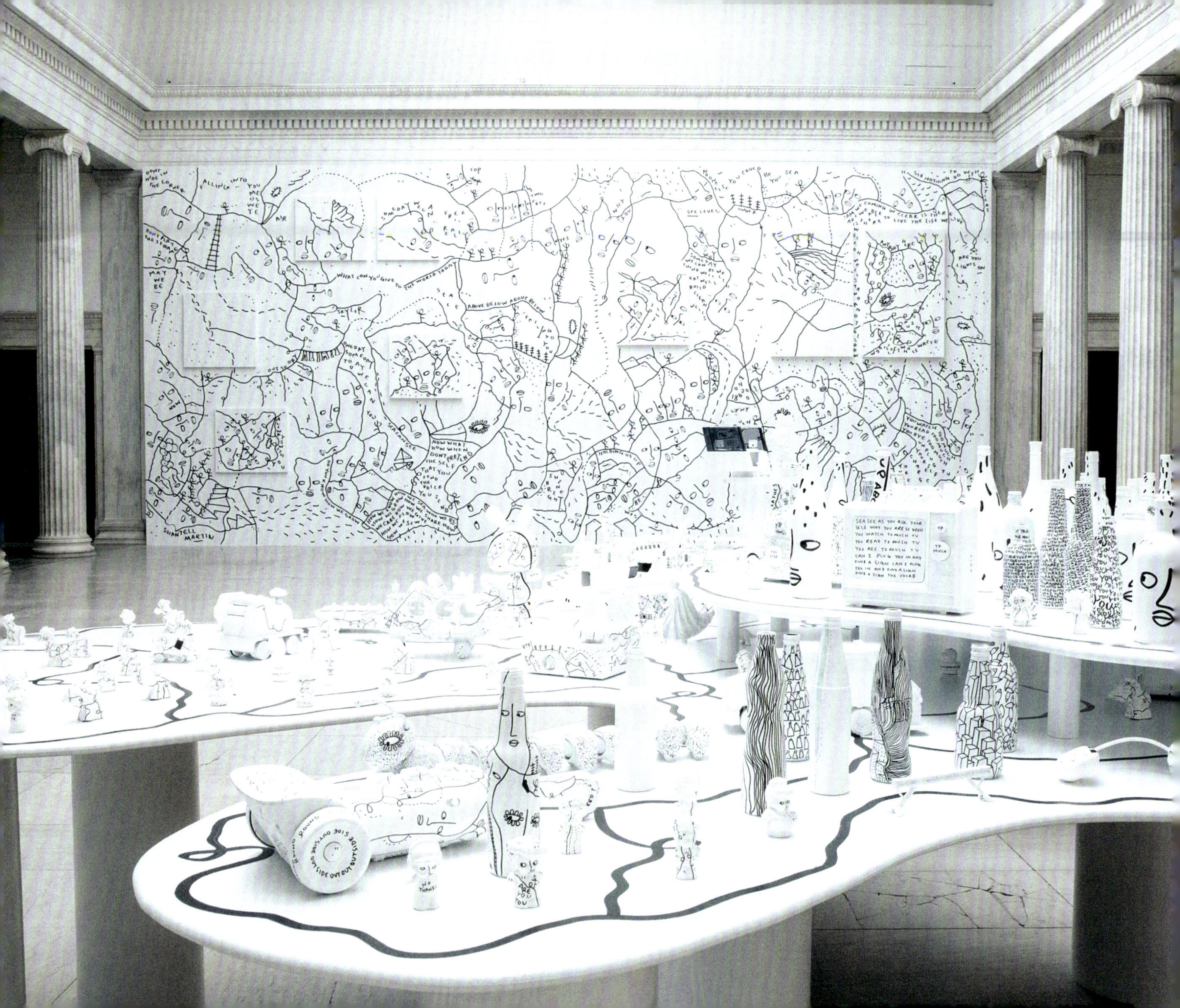

also a kinship in how the two artists use mark-making to create hermetic spaces, or indeed their own worlds, rather than to represent a specific location or history, and the activity of drawing is central to this ambition for both of them. Mehretu comments: 'The structure, the architecture, the information and visual signage that goes into my work changes in the context of what's going on in the world and impacting me. Then there's this other subconscious kind of drawing, this other activity that takes place, that is interacting with everything that is changing, and it's the relationship between the two that really pushes me.'[9]

At the same time as the exhibition *Someday We Can,* Martin created a permanent outdoor mural in Buffalo entitled *Dance Everyday*. It was the first time the gallery had commissioned an artist to make a dual project in this way. Covering a 60-metre (200-foot) wall with her characteristic drawings, including dashes, blips and faces in profile, Martin also added written affirmations such as 'reach', 'shine', and 'yes we can'. The work reminds the surrounding community, who will live with it in perpetuity, that positive action can result in transformational change for good. She states that 'the lines and the words are the same thing, they have the same importance as anchors sprinkled out across the drawing... there is this common positive theme within the words... So they are almost like seeds.'

At San Francisco's Chandran Gallery in 2017, Martin again took the opportunity to offer positive messaging throughout her environmental installations. She commented, 'The title of the show, *Charge Your Self*, is about taking time for yourself... about making sure that the input has good intention, that you're doing what you love, that what you do will give you energy.' The exhibition included site-specific wall drawings, canvas works, objects and editions, and, at the opening, Martin used the way she incorporates language within her practice as the basis for an interactive drawing performance, which included both music and spoken word. In an interview for *Juxtapoz* magazine, Martin was asked if she preferred to draw on her own or in front of an audience, to which she replied:

If I draw by myself, it tends to be more detailed and dreamy, but perhaps a little bit more realistic things might seep in there. I enjoy drawing with an audience because you're exposing the creative process, which I don't think we expose

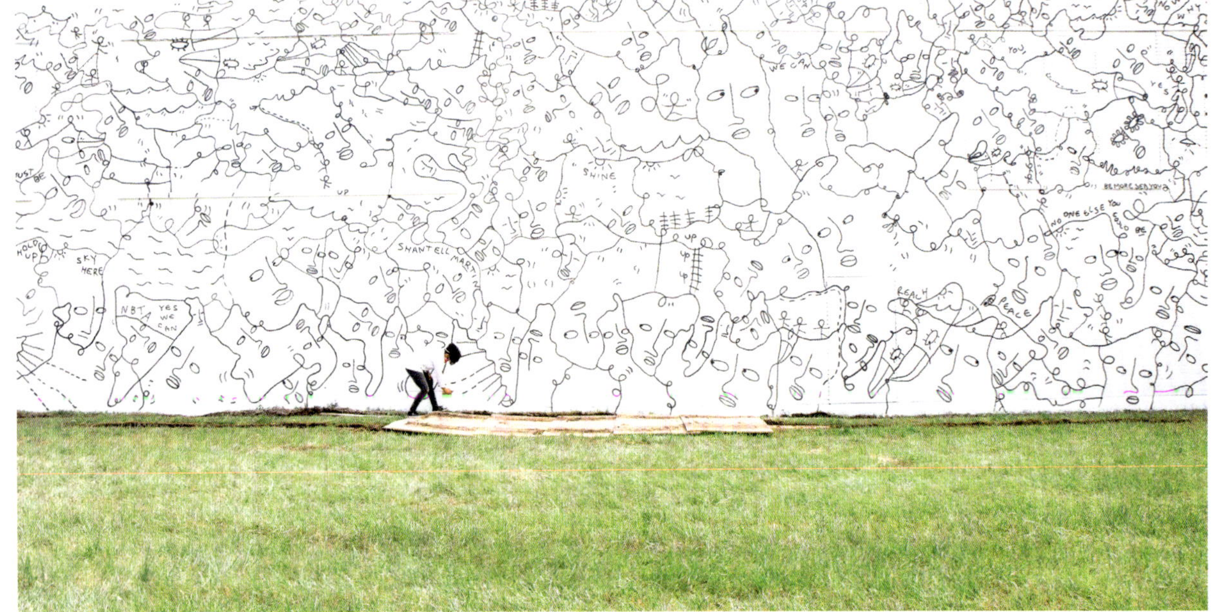

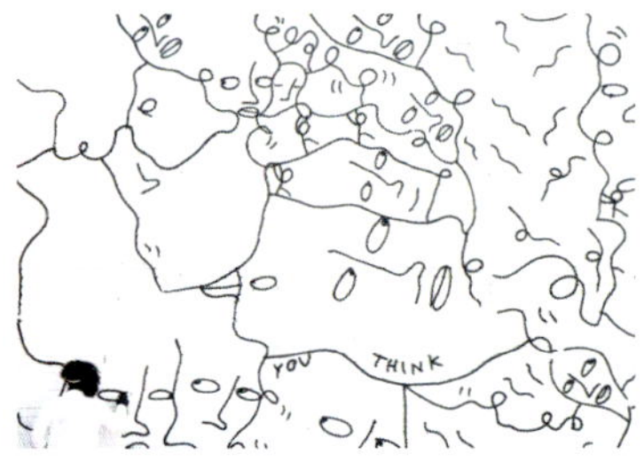

Left and above: Martin at work on *Dance Everyday* (2017) at the former Houdaille Industries Plant, Buffalo, NY, in June 2017. The mural was commissioned as part of her exhibition *Someday We Can* at the Albright-Knox Art Gallery, Buffalo, NY.

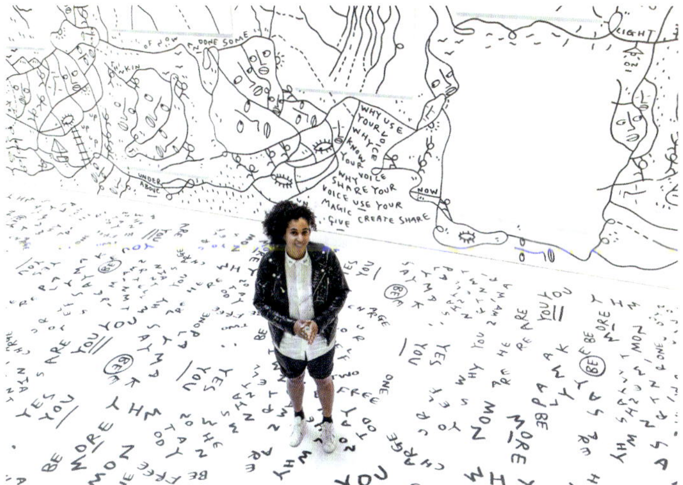

Martin in the middle of her installation for
the exhibition *Charge Your Self*, Chandran
Gallery, San Francisco, July 2017.

or share enough. The audience becomes a part of the work
and the experience, which makes it more relevant to that
time and place, and the audience. I'm very good at distract-
ing myself, so if I was alone, I would end up watching Netflix
rather than working, but if people are watching me, I have
that pressure. It puts me in a position where I don't have
time to think about what I'm doing, I've just gotta do it. And
that's a good space to be in, where you don't let your mind
wander or let insecurity sink in, or try to be anyone else.
You just have to go with it.[10]

Another artist celebrated for working live, in this case on the
streets of New York during the 1980s, is Keith Haring, who also
discussed the experience:

I was learning, watching people's reactions and interactions
with the drawings and with me and looking at it as a phenomenon. Having this incredible feedback from people, which is
one of the main things that kept me going so long, was the
participation of the people that were watching me and the
kinds of comments and questions and observations that were
coming from every range of person you could imagine, from
little kids to old ladies to art historians.[11]

Like Haring, a proportion of Martin's work is realised outside in a
public space. The location and context of the work affects its out-
come – for example she might come up with a list of key words that
resonate with that place or space, which then reverberate throughout the work. Again, Haring describes a similar phenomenon:

The context of where you do something is going to have
an effect. The subway drawings were, as much as they were
drawings, performances. It was where I learned how to
draw in public. You draw in front of people. For me it was
a whole sort of philosophical and sociological experiment.
When I drew, I drew in the daytime, which meant there were
always people watching. There were always confrontations,
whether it was with people that were interested in looking
at it, or people that wanted to tell you that you shouldn't be
drawing there.[12]

Perhaps these connections between the two artists are no coincidence. New York seems to emit an energy and an openness that
encourage individuals to create their own way of doing things.
Compared to London, which tends to operate within a defined
set of codes and networks – especially in the art world – Martin
appreciates the transparency and positive attitude displayed in
the US towards those who seek to forge an independent path.

One of Martin's largest outdoor works was *Don't Hide* from
2017, a giant mural in downtown Denver covering 650 square
metres (7,000 square feet) of walls, pavements, columns and other
surfaces in the city centre. The work was so large that Martin used
a skateboard to move around the piece while drawing it, to the
amusement of passers-by. Like many of her works, it now only
exists in the form of photographic documentation. 'Don't Hide' is
a phrase that can be found across Martin's work, for example in a
collection of sneakers and clothing for Puma. It originated as the
message 'Don't Hide in the Corner', which is one of those seeds
Martin puts in her work so that they might grow as an idea. She
says of the role of this particular message:

I put that in there as a reminder to myself initially to get out,
as a reminder to put stuff in the world. Left to my own devices
I'd rather just hide and be by myself and not engage with
anyone. So these words, 'Don't Hide in the Corner', is like
'get out there', show yourself, create things.[13]

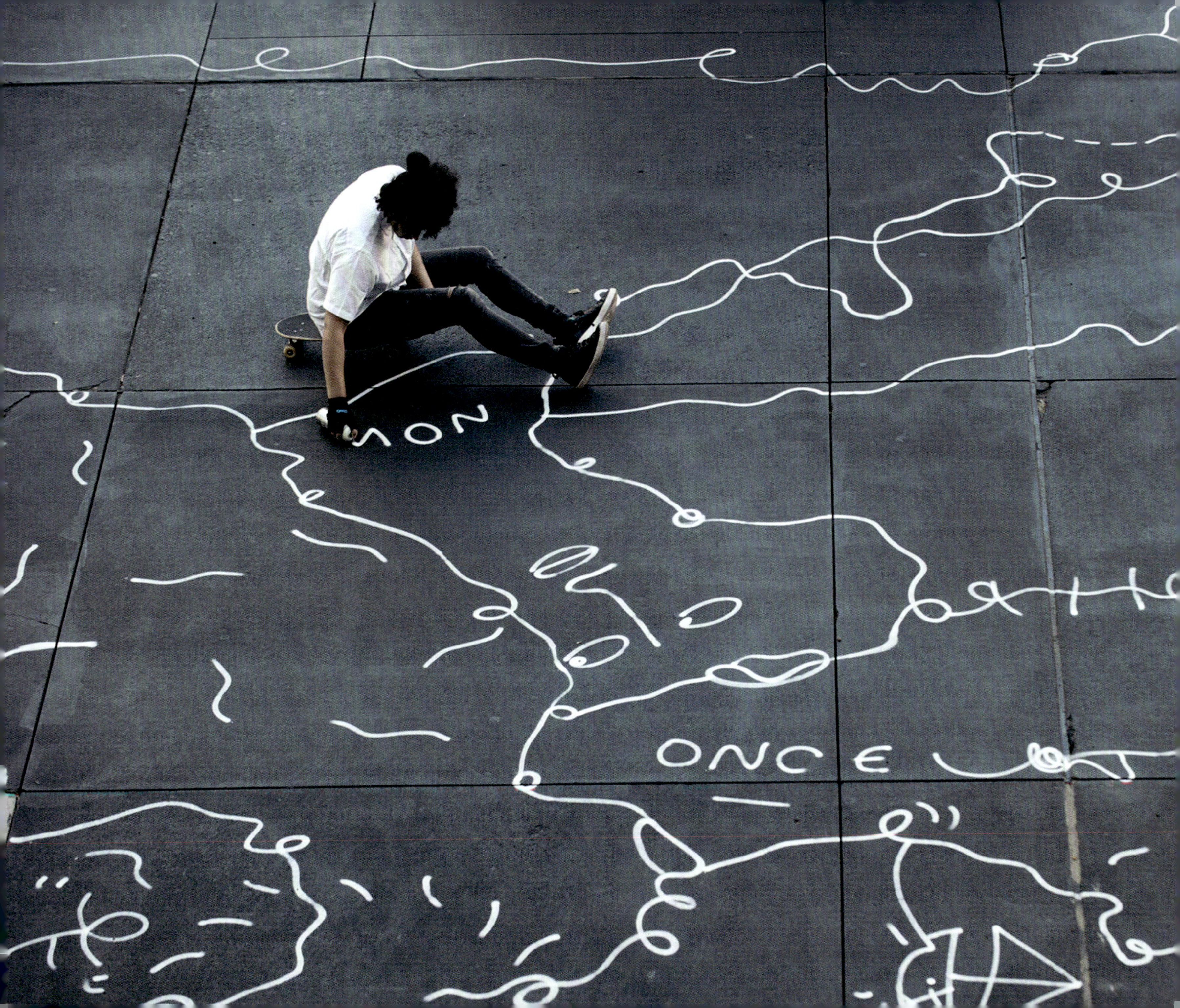

MON
ONCE

YOU ARE YOU

Martin uses her drawing as a means to share personal moments through the process of making, and to progress her quest to understand how identity can be articulated. She comments, 'With all the clichés about drawing, you have to look at it as the most fundamental gift that is given as a child. Sometimes people don't take it seriously enough because everyone can do it. But it has been and is very personal to me as it has enabled me to think through bigger questions and darker times.'[14] Generously sharing both process and creative energy with her audience, Martin responds in her work to a common struggle to express who we are. Having used drawing to develop her own language to express and understand what has made her who she is today, Martin has a genuine motivation and energy to share that potential with others, which in turn is why people respond so positively to her work.

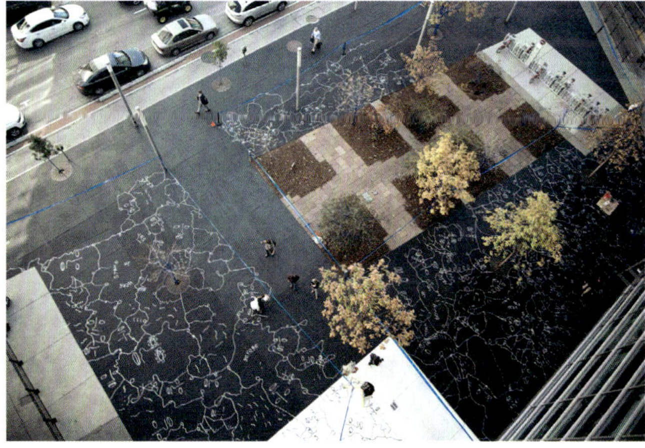

Opposite and above: Martin using a skateboard to complete *Don't Hide* (2017), and a bird's-eye view of work in progress, taken from Colorado Convention Center, Denver, in October 2017.

1 This and other short quotes by Martin are taken from her website <https://shantellmartin.art/> and have been approved by the artist.
2 Paul Klee, 'Contributions to a Theory of Pictorial Form, Lecture Notes from the Bauhaus at Weimar and at Dessau', *Paul Klee Notebooks, Volume One: The Thinking Eye*, ed. Jurg Spiller (London: Lund Humphries, 1961), p. 105.
3 Robert L. Herbert, Eleanor S. Apter and Elise K. Kenny (eds.), *The Société Anonyme and the Dreier Bequest at Yale University: A Catalogue Raisonné* (New Haven and London: Yale University Press, 1984), p. 376.
4 Cornelius Cardew, 'A Scratch Orchestra: A Draft Constitution', *The Musical Times*, vol. 110, no. 1516 (June 1969), p. 617.
5 See <https://www.youtube.com/watch?v=PbL9vr4Q2LU>.
6 Shantell Martin, *Wave: A Journey Through the Sea of Imagination for the Adventurous Colorist* (New York: TarcherPerigree, 2016)
7 Midori Matsui, *The Age of Micropop: The New Generation of Japanese Artists*, exhibition catalogue (Mito: Contemporary Art Gallery, Art Tower Mito, 2007), p. 9.
8 Midori Matsyu, *Ryoko Aoki*, exhibition guide (Los Angeles: Hammer Museum, 2005), n.p.
9 Quoted in Lawrence Chua, 'Julie Mehretu', *Bomb*, no. 91 (Spring 2005), p. 25.
10 Quoted in 'Installation Views of Shantell Martin's Immersive "Charge Your Self" Exhibition @ Chandran Gallery', *Juxtapoz* (14 July 2017), <https://www.juxtapoz.com/news/installation/installation-views-of-shantell-martin-s-immersive-charge-your-self-exhibition-chandran-gallery-w-video/>.
11 Jason Rubell, 'Keith Haring: The Last Interview', *Arts Magazine*, vol. 65, no. 1 (September 1990), p. 59.
12 Ibid.
13 'Exploring Philosophy, Design, Business, Art and Tech with Shantell Martin', *New York Said Podcast*, episode 100 (29 May 2018), <https://www.newyorksaid.com/shantell-martin/>.
14 Interview with the author, December 2018.

DOT
MARTIN

SHANTELL
MARTIN

LON

COLLABORATE MORE
READ MORE TRAVEL MORE
SHARE MORE GO SEE MORE

THINKING
BRITISH
VS
ENGLISH
GO HOME
THAMESMEAD

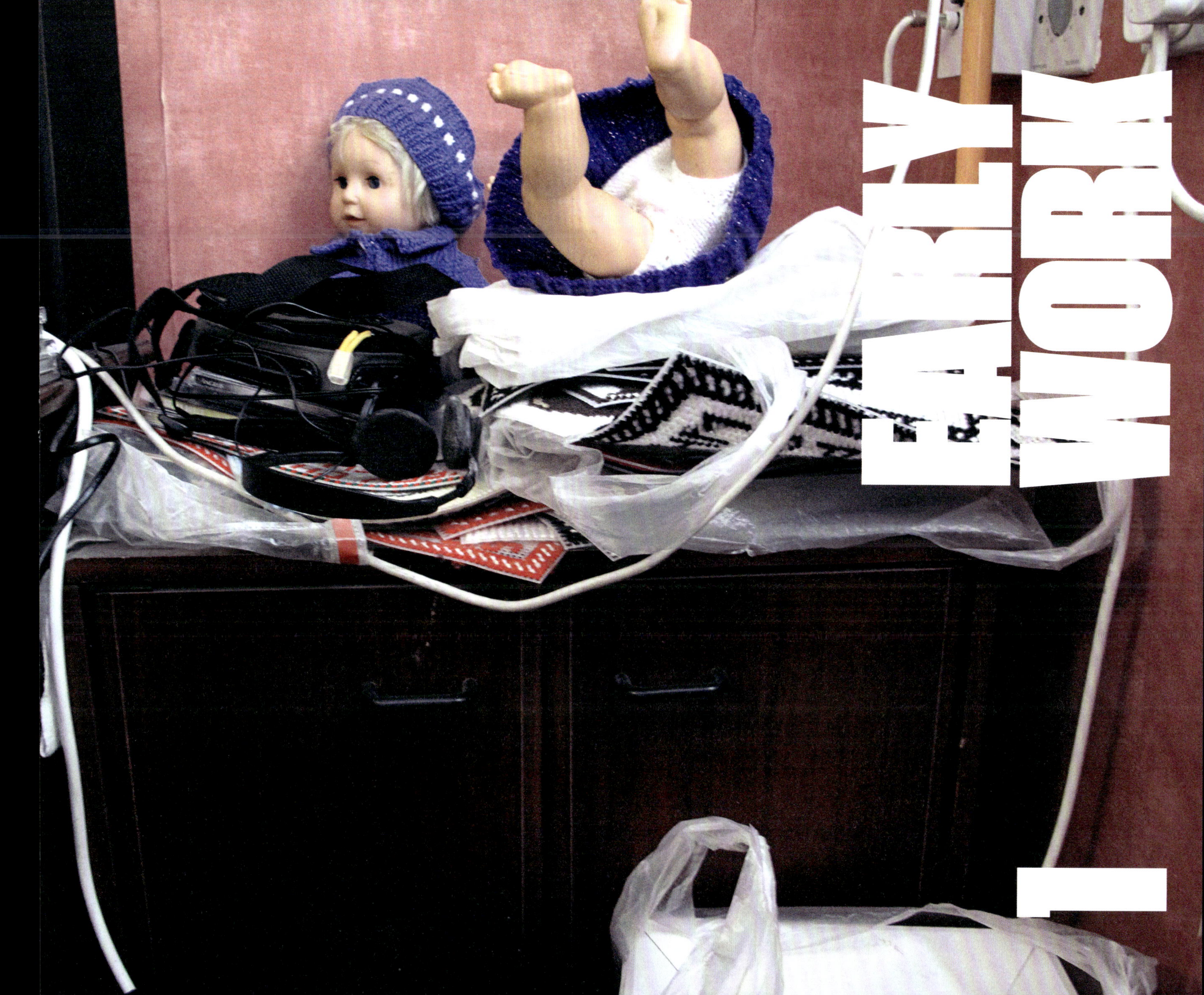
EARLY WORK
1

DEAR GRANDMOTHER

Martin's 'Dear Grandmother' collaboration began around 2002, when Martin commissioned her grandmother Dot Martin to embroider a pair of works entitled *Half White 1980* as a reflection on racial identity. The pair worked on almost a hundred needlepoints together, with Dot adding her own touches of colour or language along the way. Martin sees these works as symbolically bridging gaps of distance, generation, race and culture, creating an inclusive backdrop for artistic creation. **Clockwise from bottom left:** *Half White 1980* (2007); *Half White 1980* (2007); *Tower* (2008); *Let's Be Friends* (2009); *Love* (2008); *Lucky in Life* (2009). **Opposite:** Dot Martin at work at her home in Thamesmead, c. 2010.

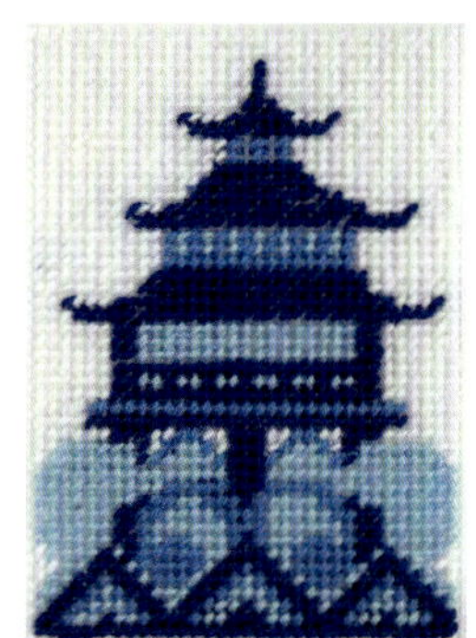

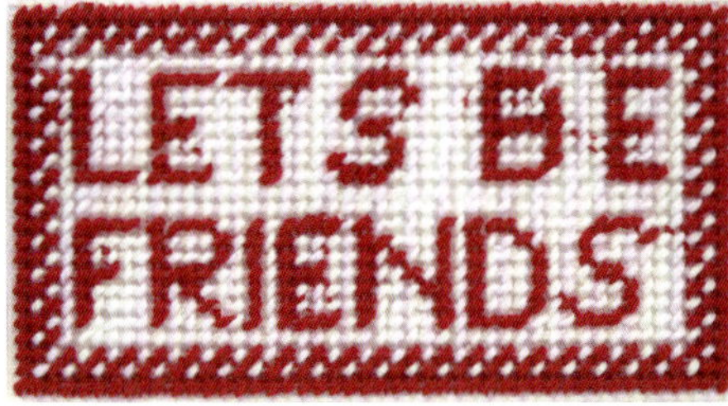

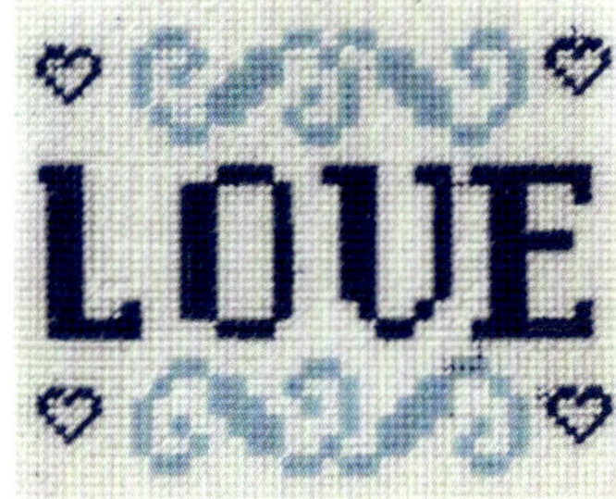

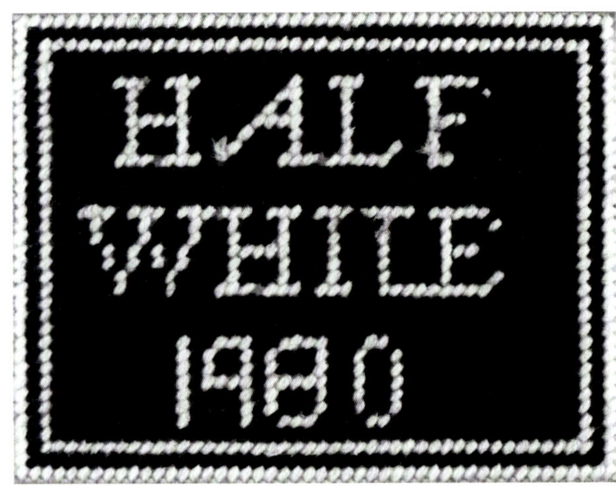

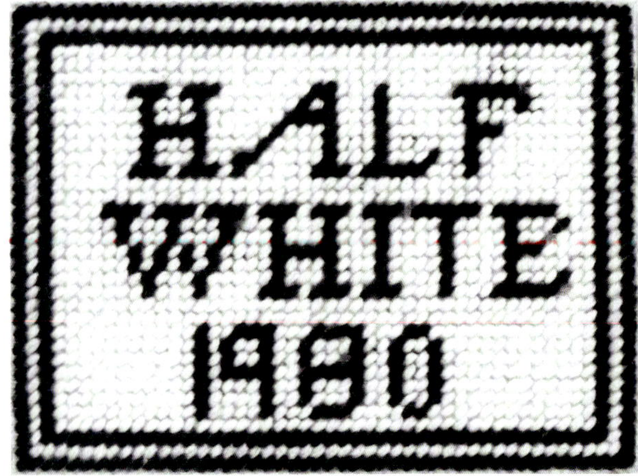

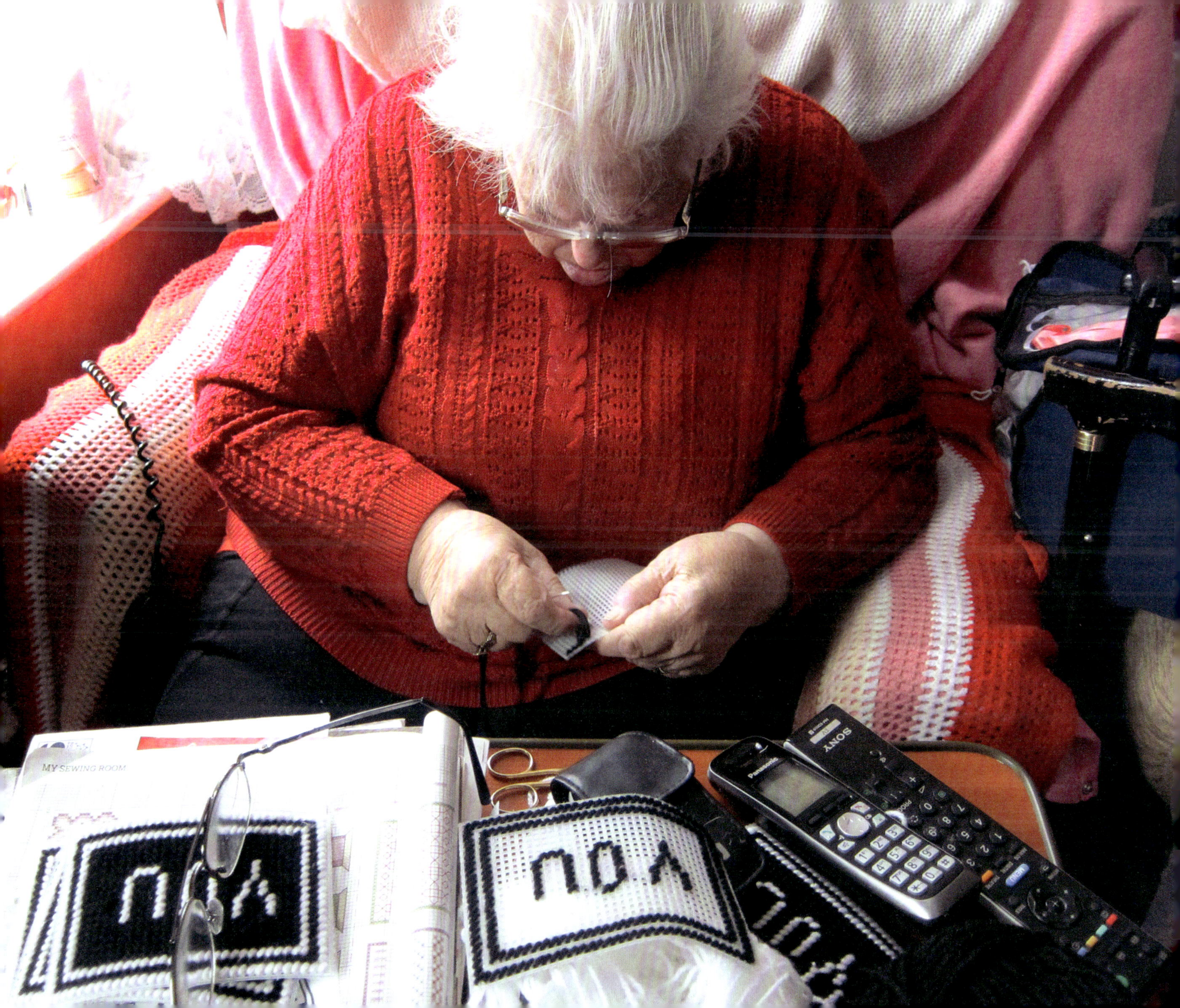

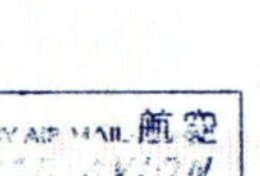

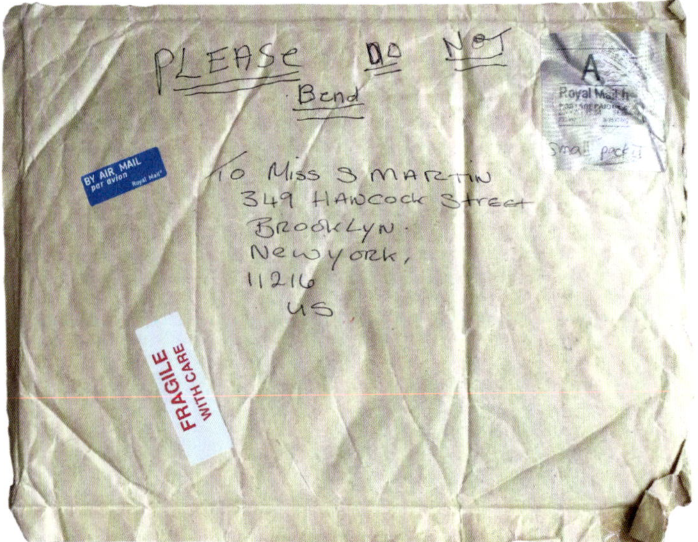

Sat 23/6/12

Mrs D Martin
110 Fieldfare RD
Thamesmead
S E 28
8- H P

Dear Shanetell
Thank you for all your photos and the newspaper yo sent me. I have given mum hers & Gemma.
Very good keep up the good work.
I'm sending you the sewing you asked for.
I wasn't sure which way you wanted it so I have sent two for you also the about my memories of you I do hope you will like them please let me know
I'm sending two Bartleys letters but I must admit I opened one by mistake. (Sorry)
Gemma is on the move again in two weeks time. cant afford the rent increase. council wont help.
I've got foot clinic. eye test and hospital 20 July. Busy month
On the 19 of July mum me are going to Hasting with the club I go to.
Well will close now
All the best Nan - Holly
xx L L L

I wanted to ask for a favour!
Remember when you made me those sewing's.
Half White [HALF WHITE 1980]. I would like to see
if you could sew another, this time.

[LOST] + [FOUND]. Both in black and
white, Maybe in
reverse colour's?

Also one more thing. I would like
to try out some other ideas by myself
So if you have any of that plastic.
black, white wool and a needle
Spare please send them
my way. I think you should
have my new address?

Hope that you are keeping
well...
take Care. lots of love
Shantell

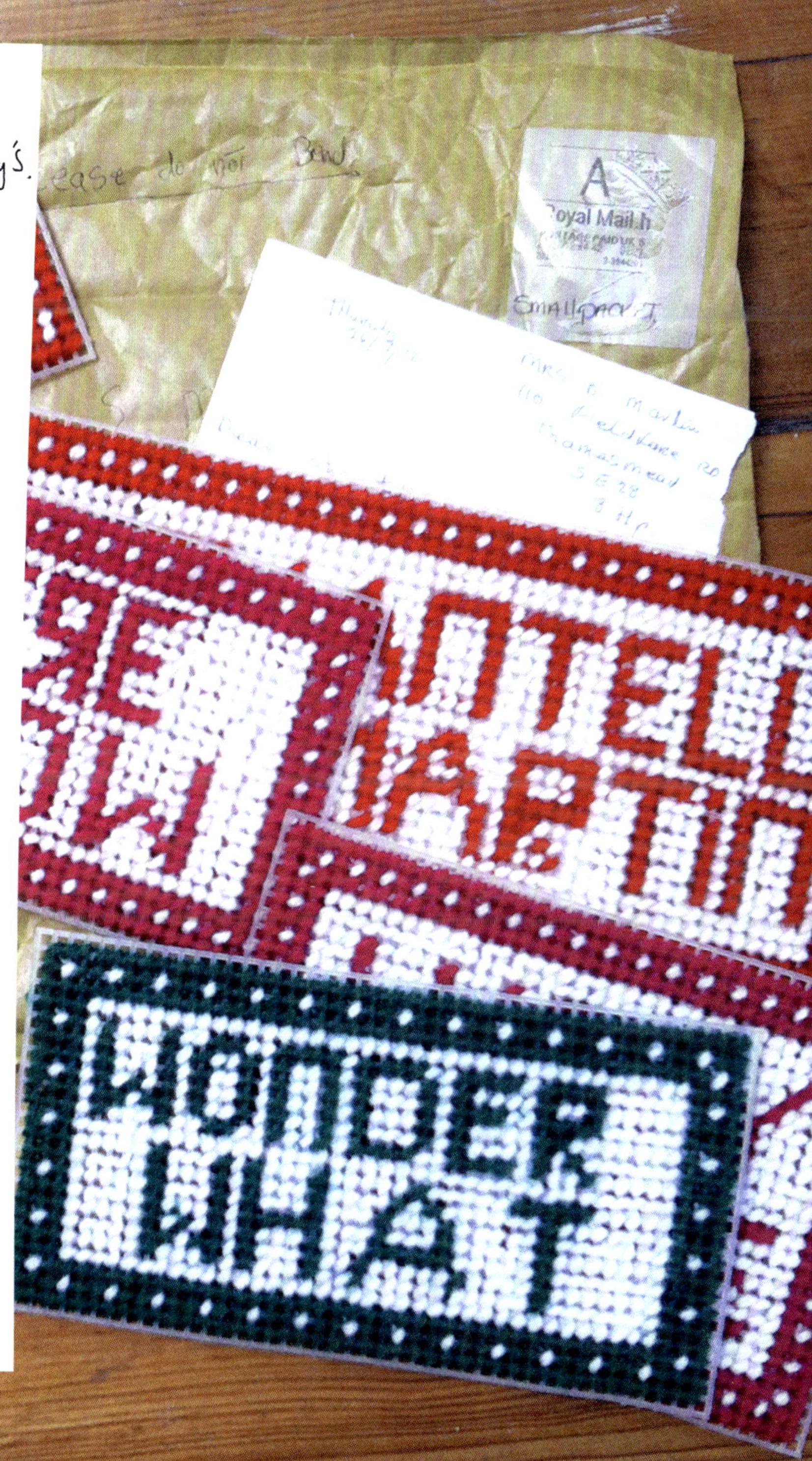

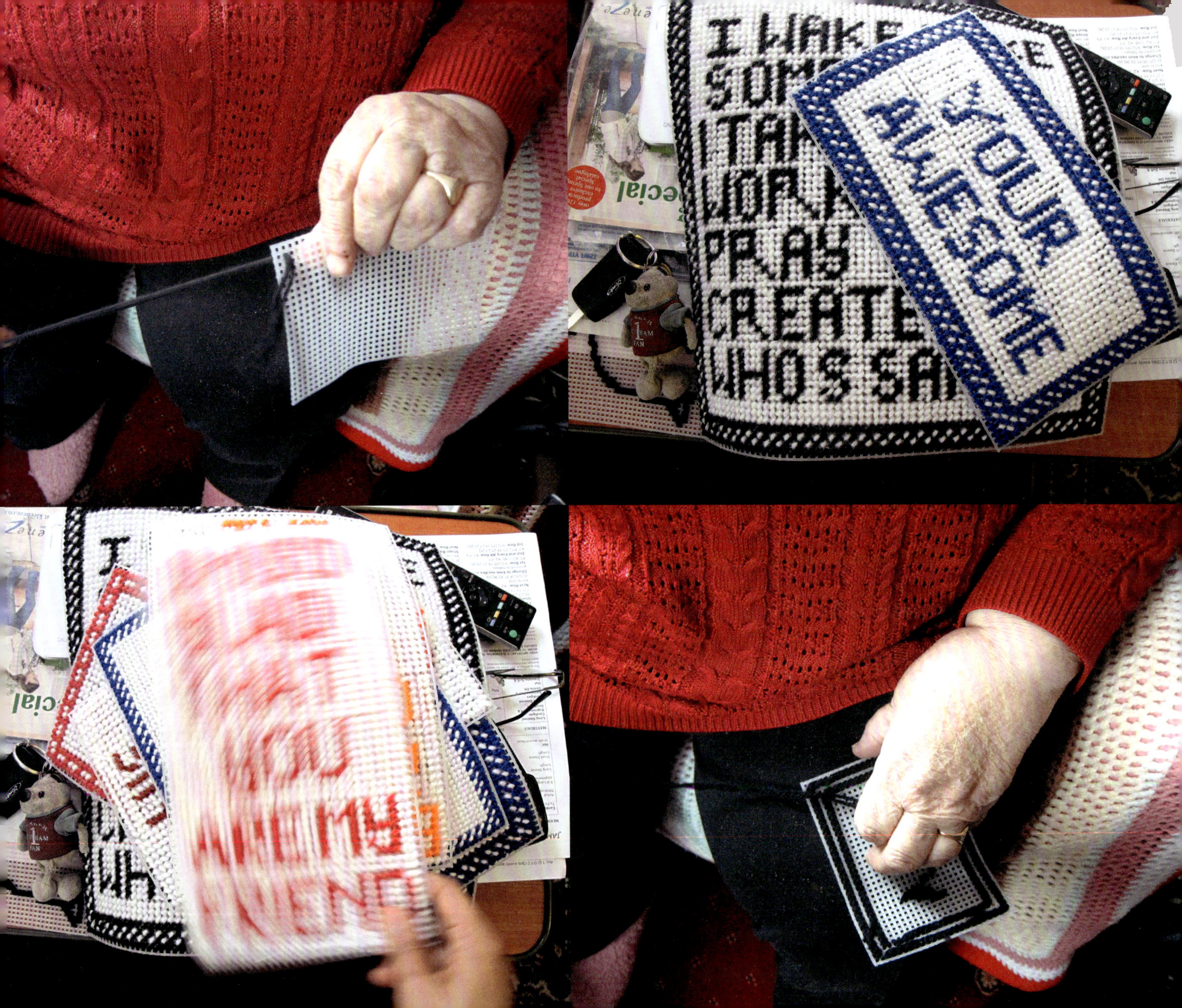
I WAKE
SOME
I TA
WOR
PRAY
CREATE
WHO S SA
YOUR AWESOME

Opposite: Dot Martin at work on the 'Dear
Grandmother' series (2002–15), c. 2010.

ENGLISH
BRITISH

Top to bottom: English (2010), British
(2010), Go Home (2009) and Come
Home (2009) needlepoints from the
'Dear Grandmother' series (2002–15).

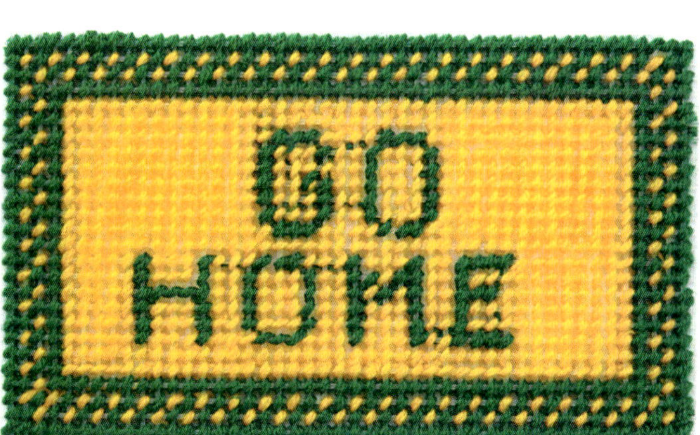
GO
HOME

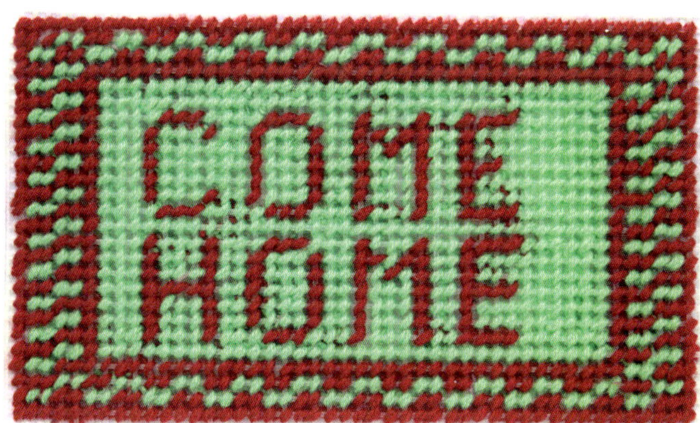
COME
HOME

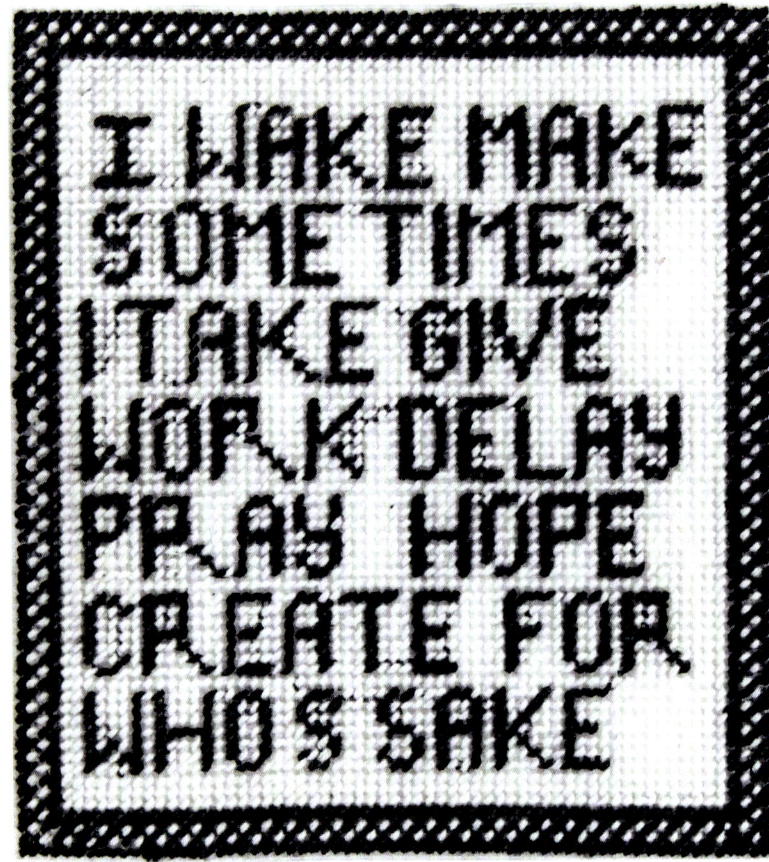

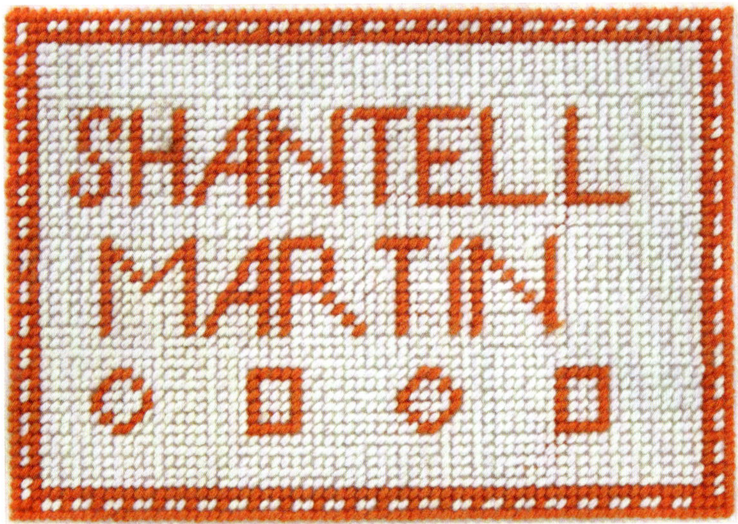

Clockwise from bottom left: *Who You Are* (2010), *I Wake* (2010), *Shantell Martin* (2007), *Me* (2010) and *You* (2010) needlepoints from the 'Dear Grandmother' series (2002–15).

Opposite: Works from the series piled up at Dot Martin's home in Thamesmead, 2013.

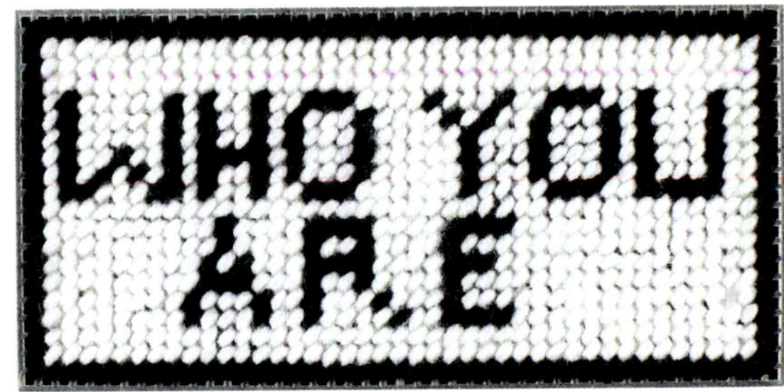

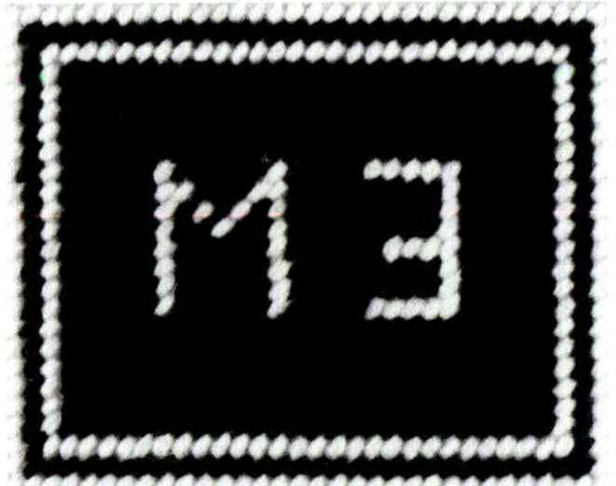

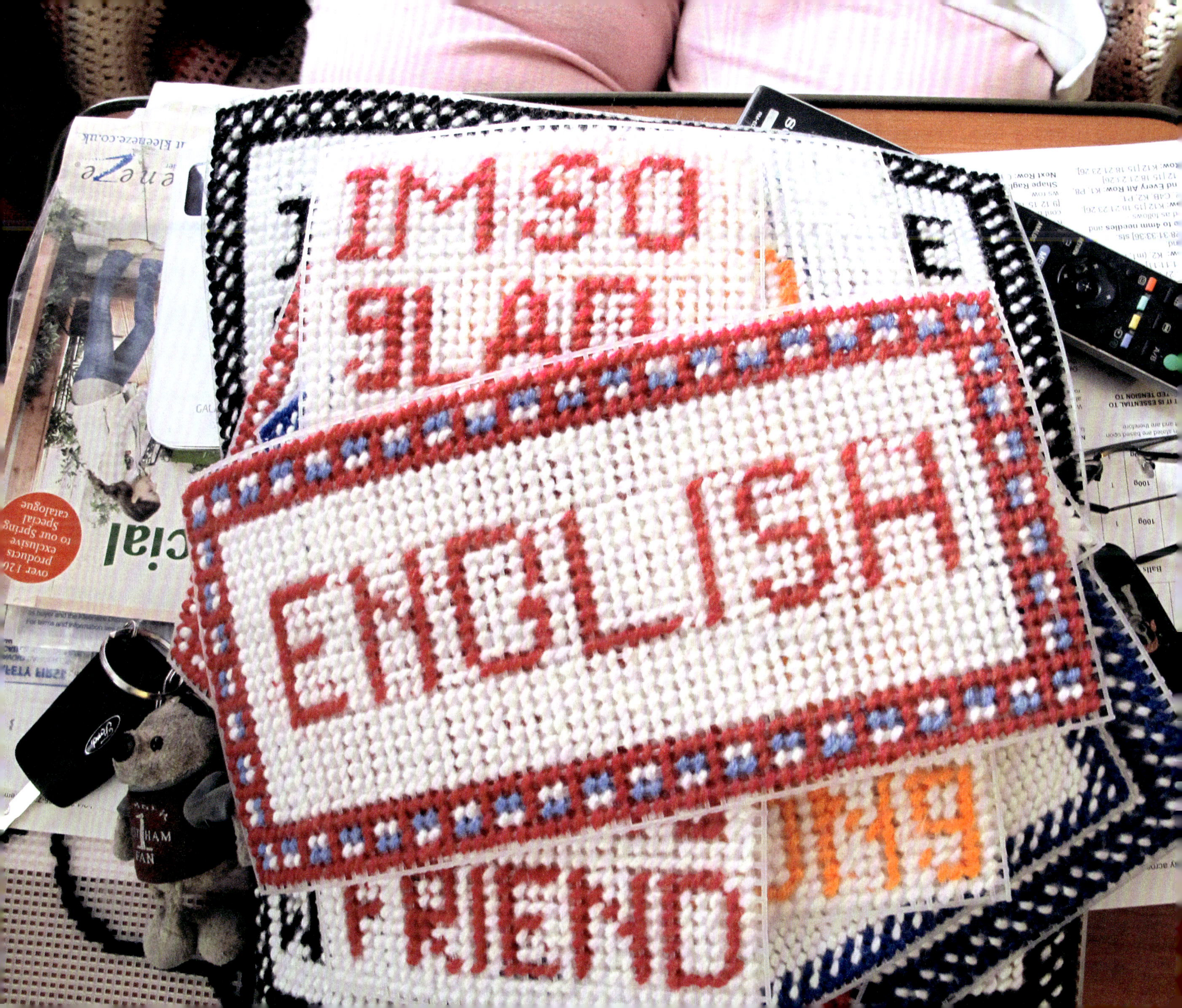

I'M SO
ENGLISH
FRIEND

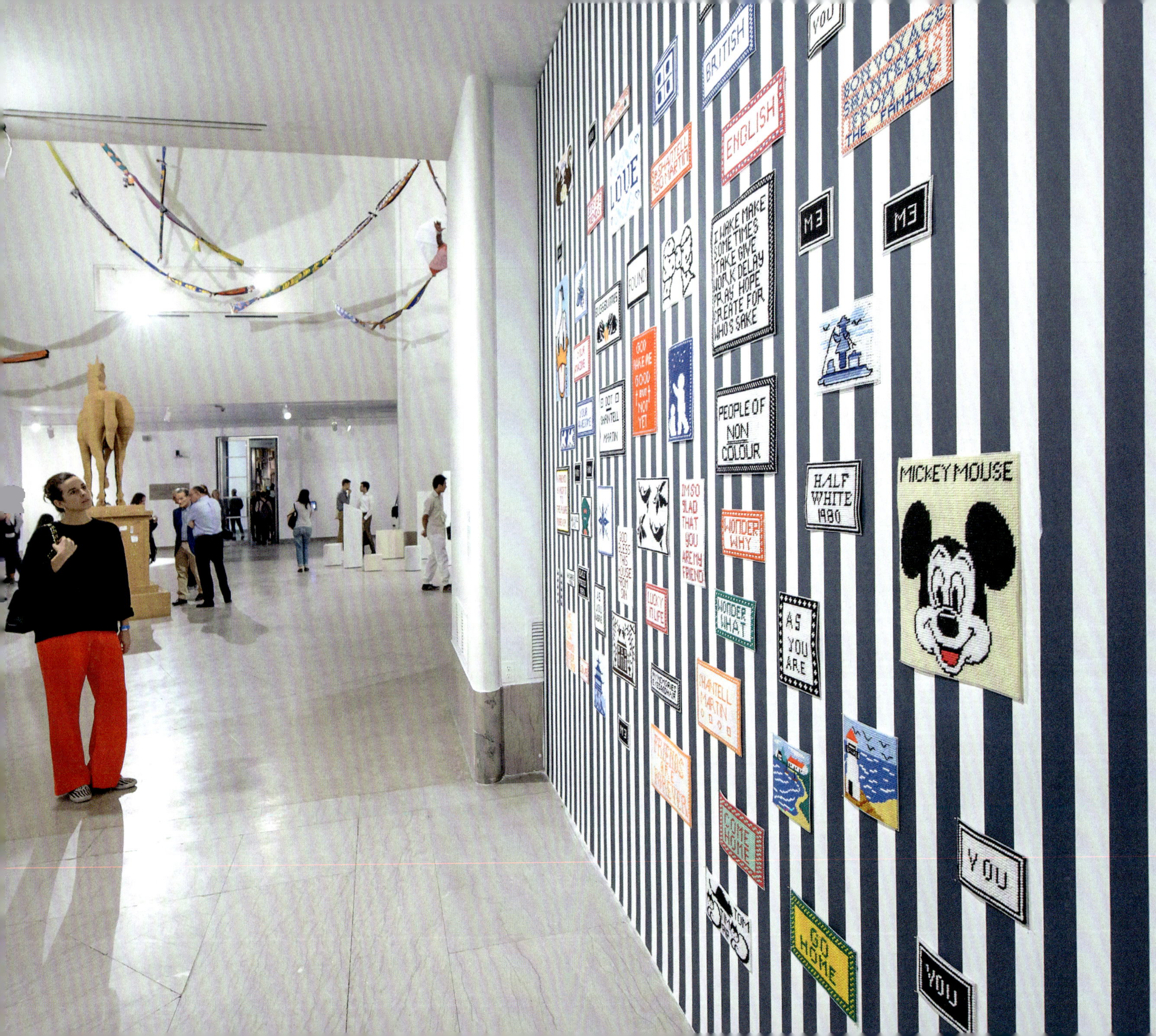

BRITISH
ENGLISH
YOU
BON VOYAGE
LOVE
ME
ME
PEOPLE OF
NON
COLOUR
HALF
WHITE
1980
MICKEY MOUSE
WONDER
WHY
WONDER
WHAT
AS
YOU
ARE
GO
HOME
YOU
YOU

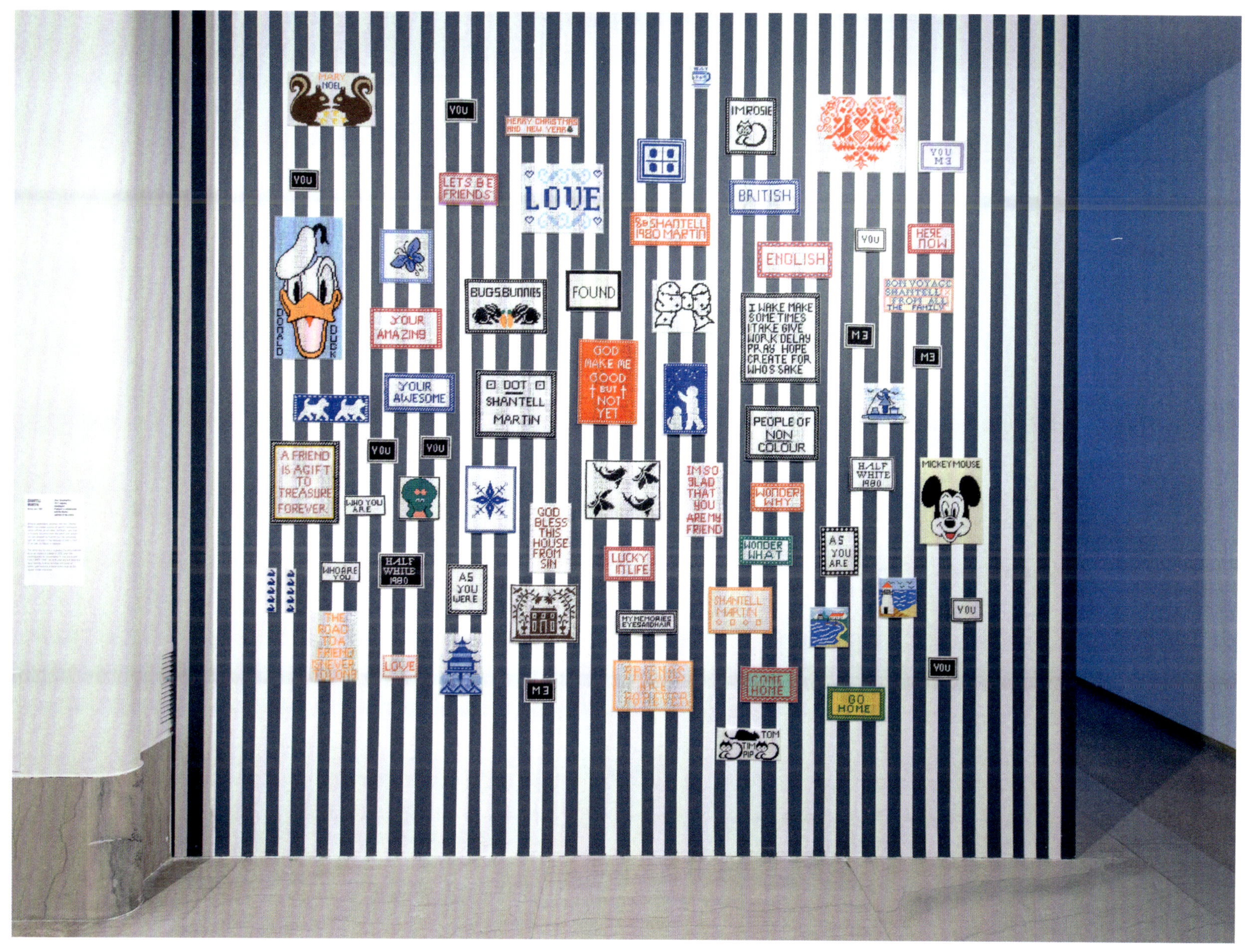

The 'Dear Grandmother' series (2002–15) in the *Crossing Brooklyn* exhibition at the Brooklyn Museum, New York, 2014. The installation was inspired by the curators' visit to Martin's flat, when the works were laid out on her black-and-white bedsheets.

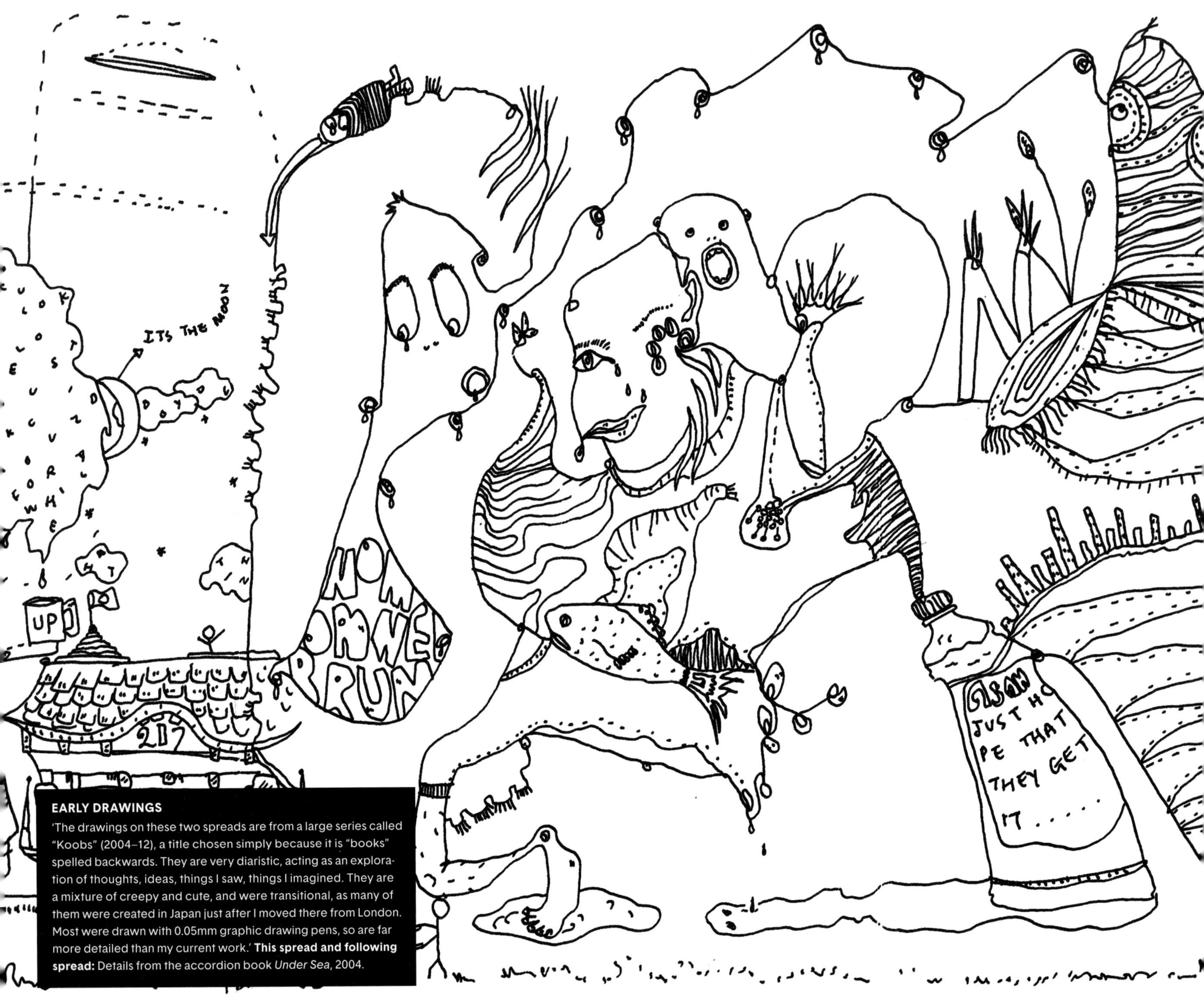
ITS THE MOON
UP
NOW ORWELL RUM
JUST HOPE THAT THEY GET IT . . . . .

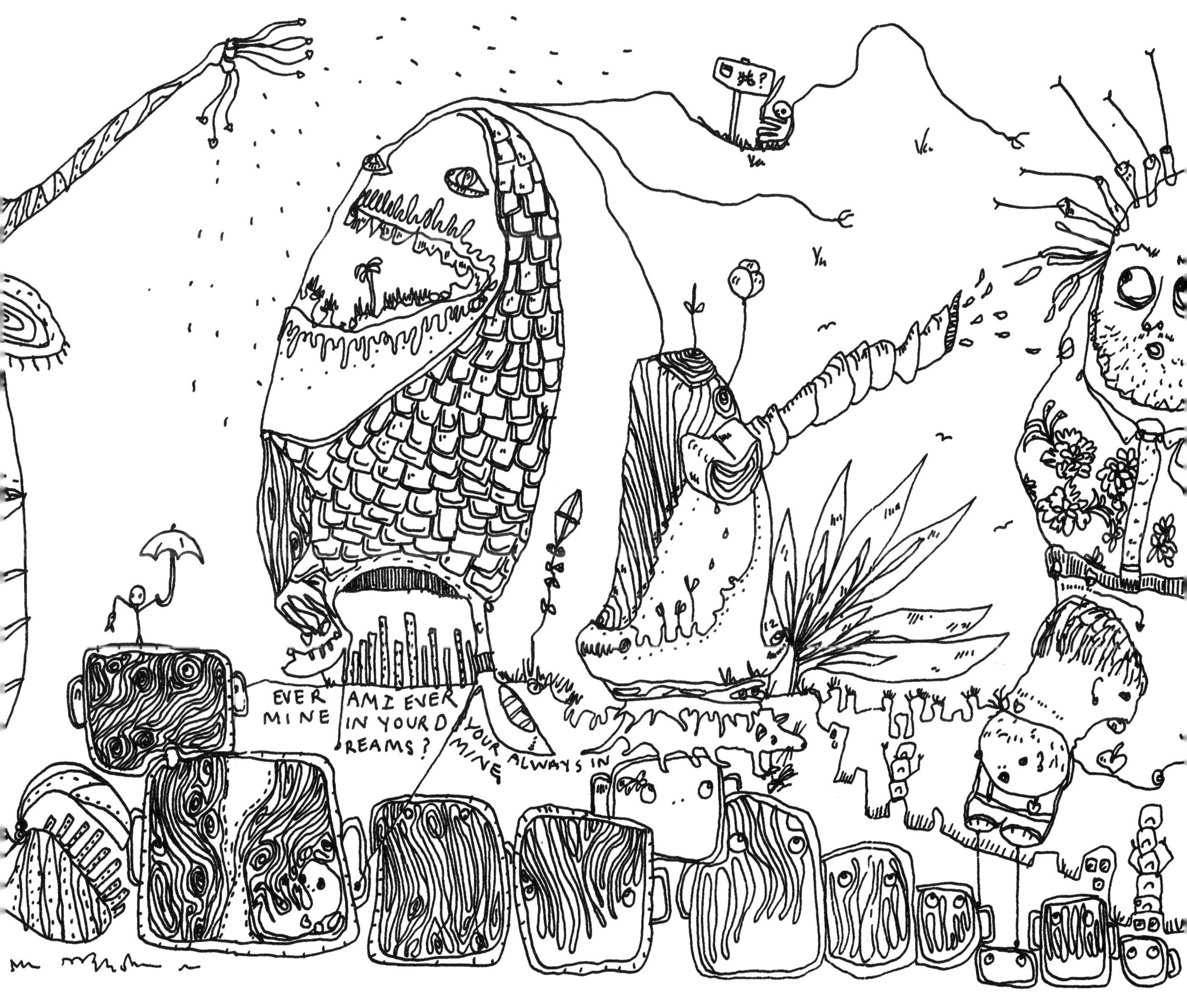
EVER MINE
AM I EVER IN YOUR DREAMS?
YOUR ALWAYS IN MINE

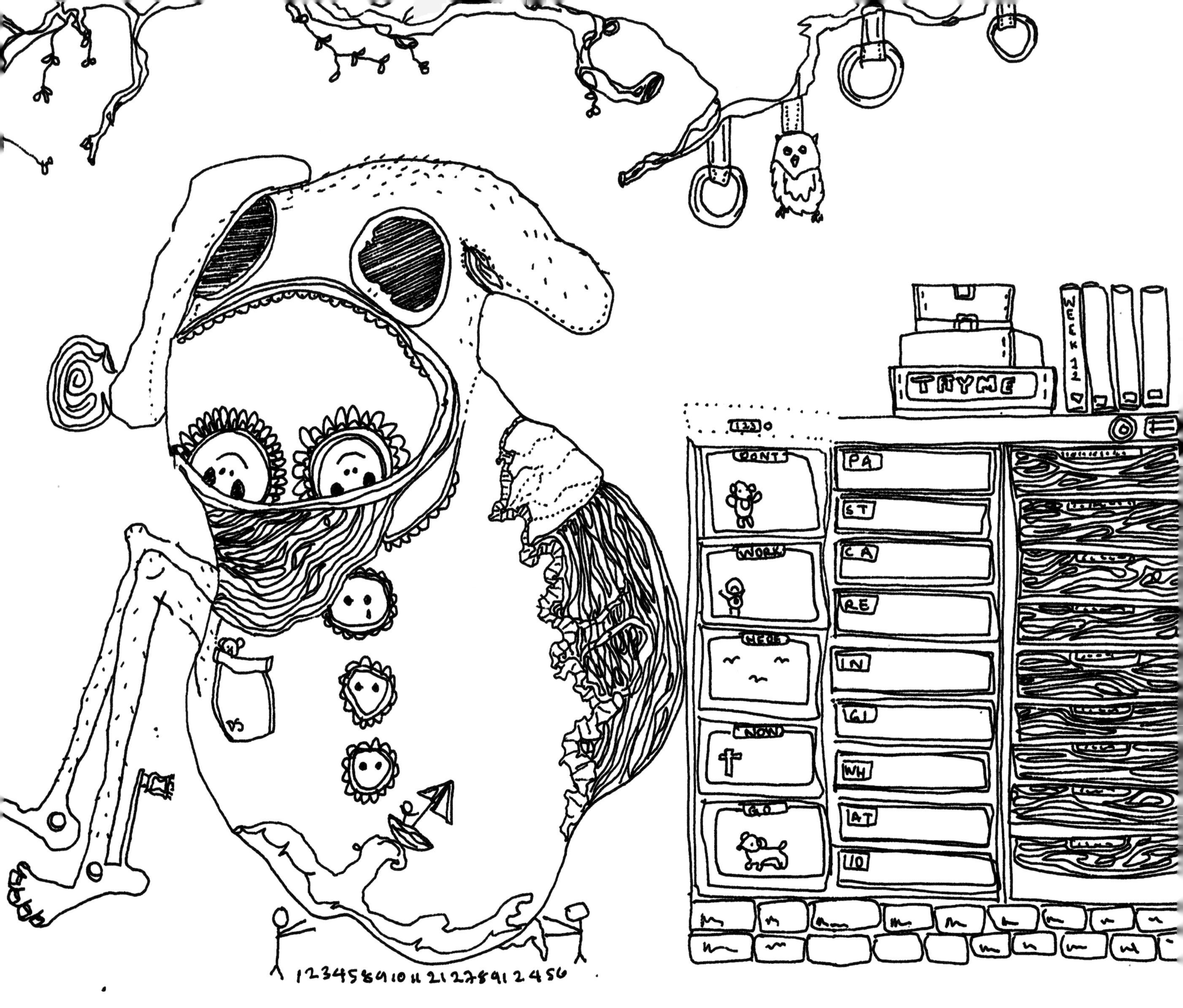

TRYME
WEEK 11
123 0
PANT
WORK
NEST
NOW
GO
PA
ST
CA
RE
IN
GI
WH
AT
10
1 2 3 4 5 8 9 10 11 21 2 7 8 9 1 2 4 5 6

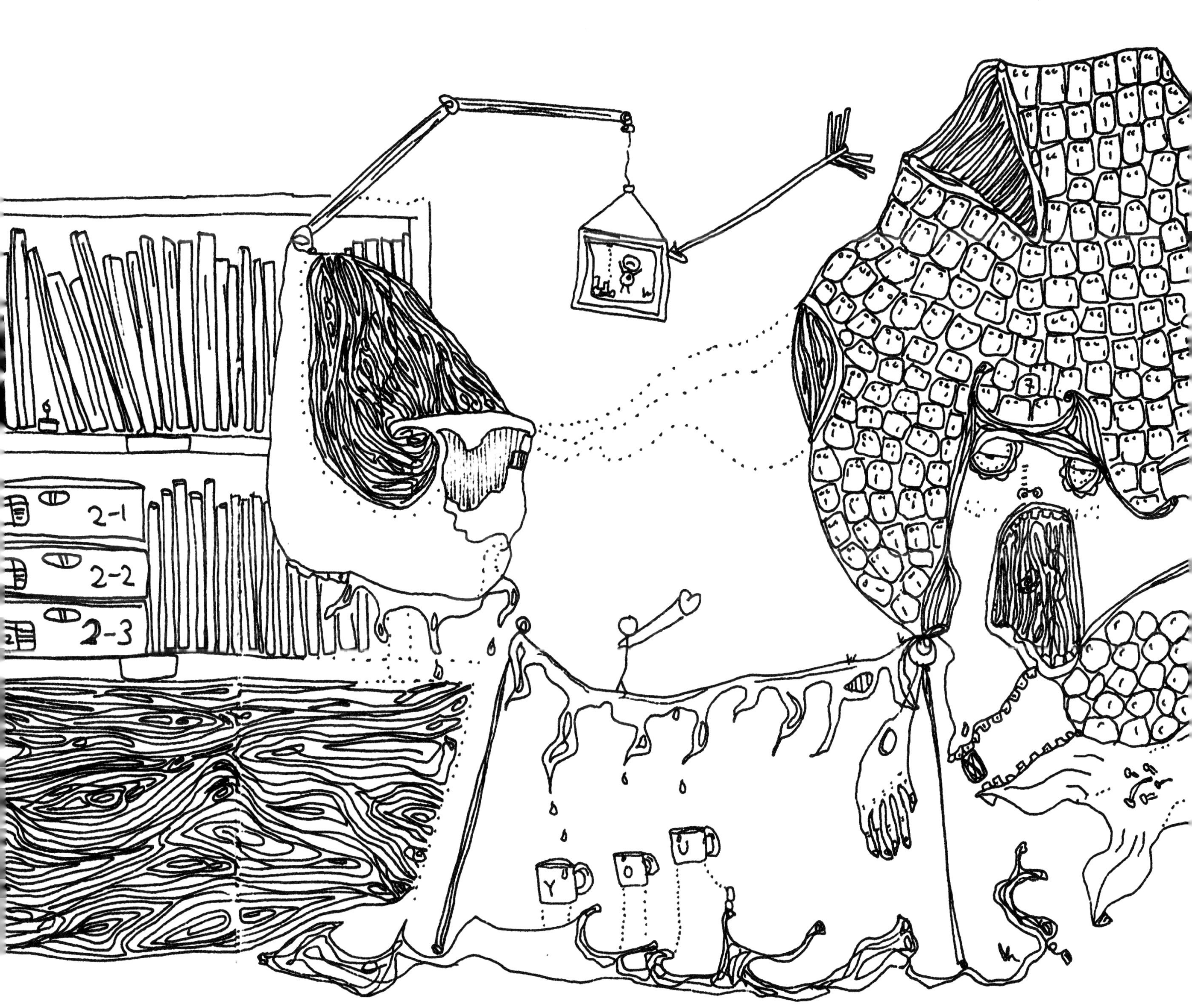

2-1
2-2
2-3

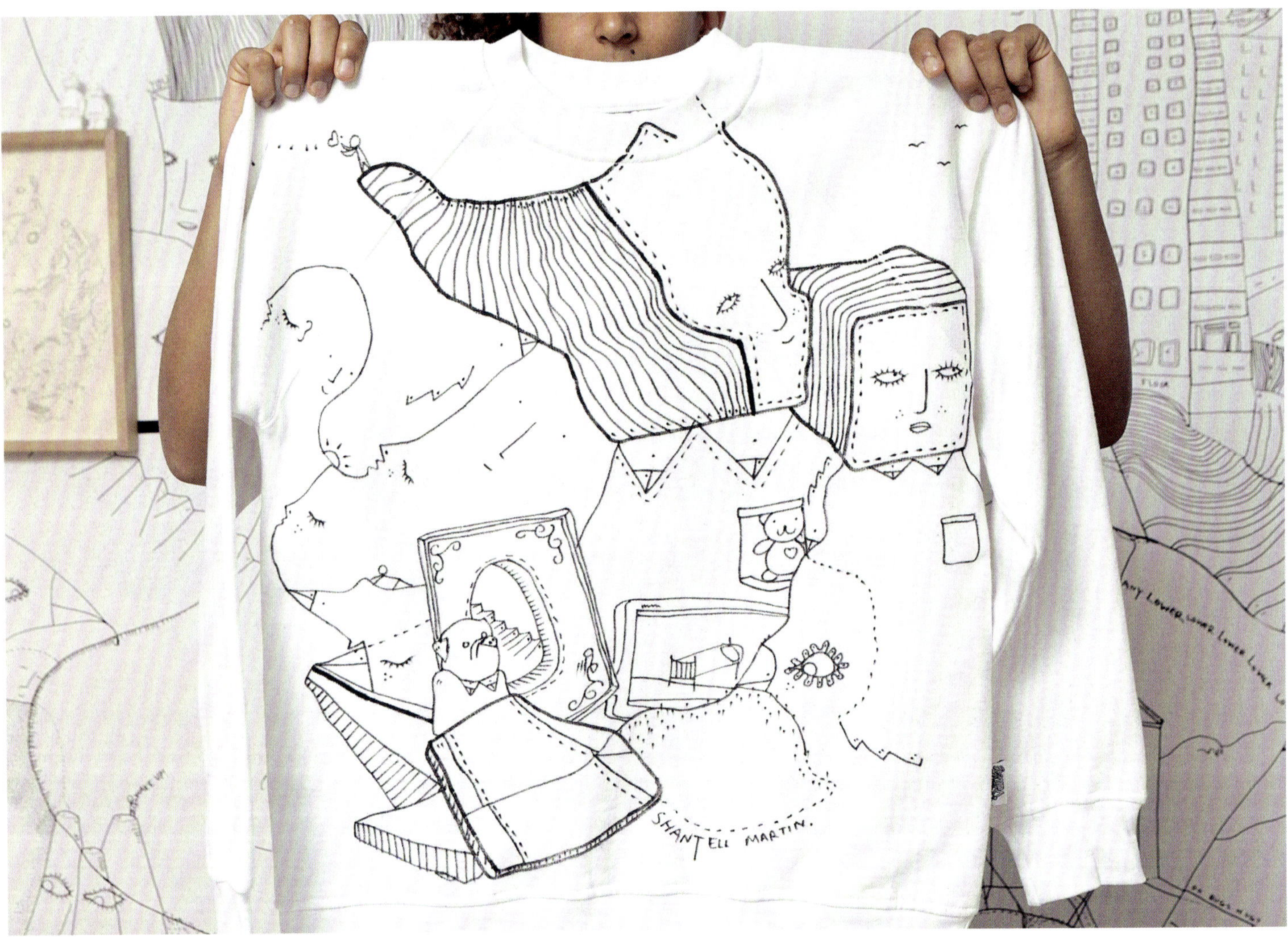

HAND-DRAWN SWEATERS

In 2012, Martin created a striking collection of hand-drawn sweaters, each one unique and able to function as a piece of art or as clothing, or even in both roles. The sweater's owner has the choice whether to hang their garment on a wall, thus treating it as an artwork and preserving it in perpetuity, or to put in on and wear it out (in both senses). Bridging the gap of engagement between her art and her audience in this manner remains a fundamental ambition in Martin's practice. **This spread:** Martin with examples from the collection in the bedroom at her studio in Bed-Stuy, Brooklyn, 2012. **Following spread:** Behind-the-scenes and final images from the photoshoot for the collection in the main studio at Bed-Stuy, 2012.

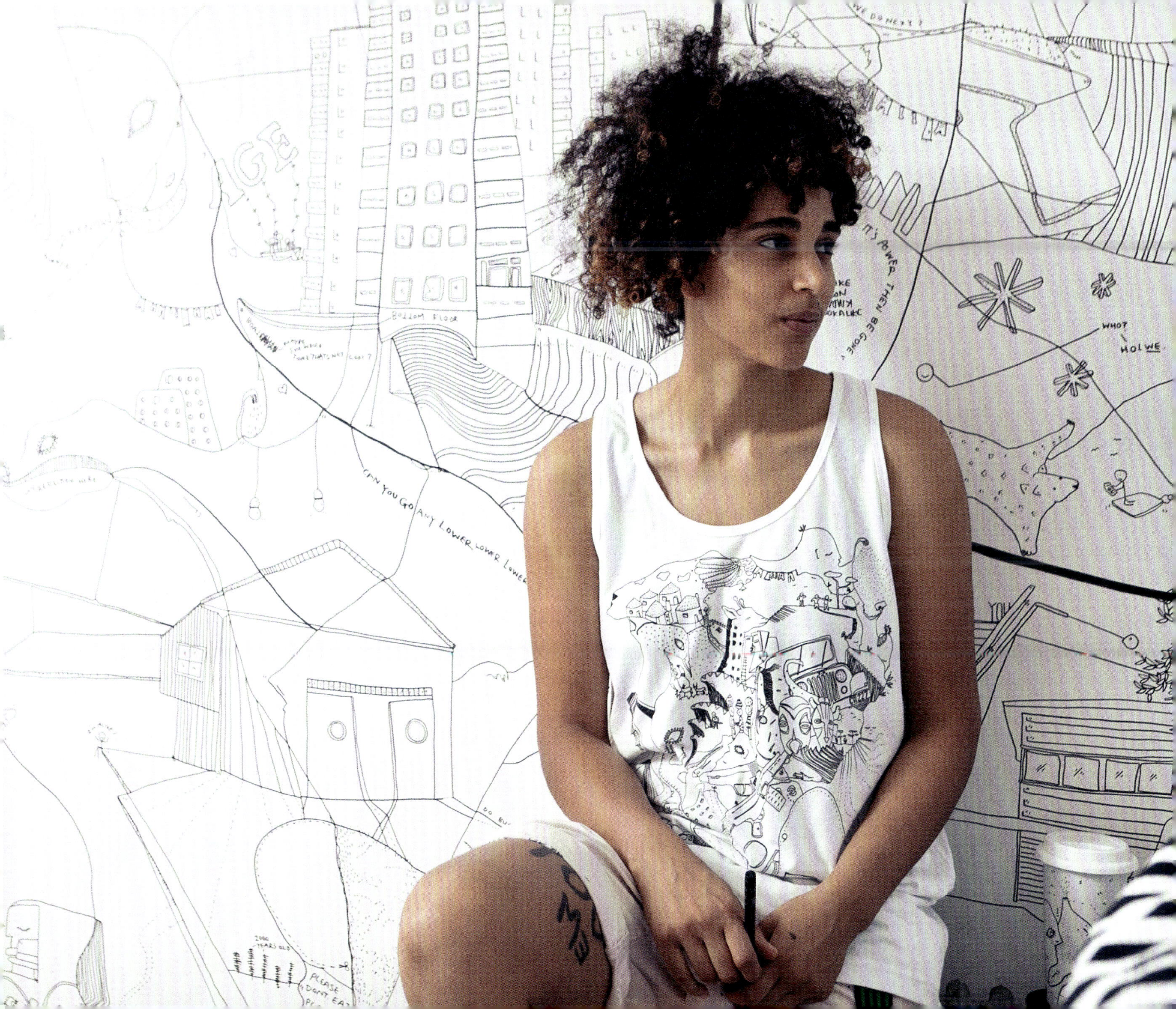

BOTTOM FLOOR
CAN YOU GO ANY LOWER LOWER LOWER
WHO?
HOLWE
PLEASE DON'T EAT
2000 YEARS OLD

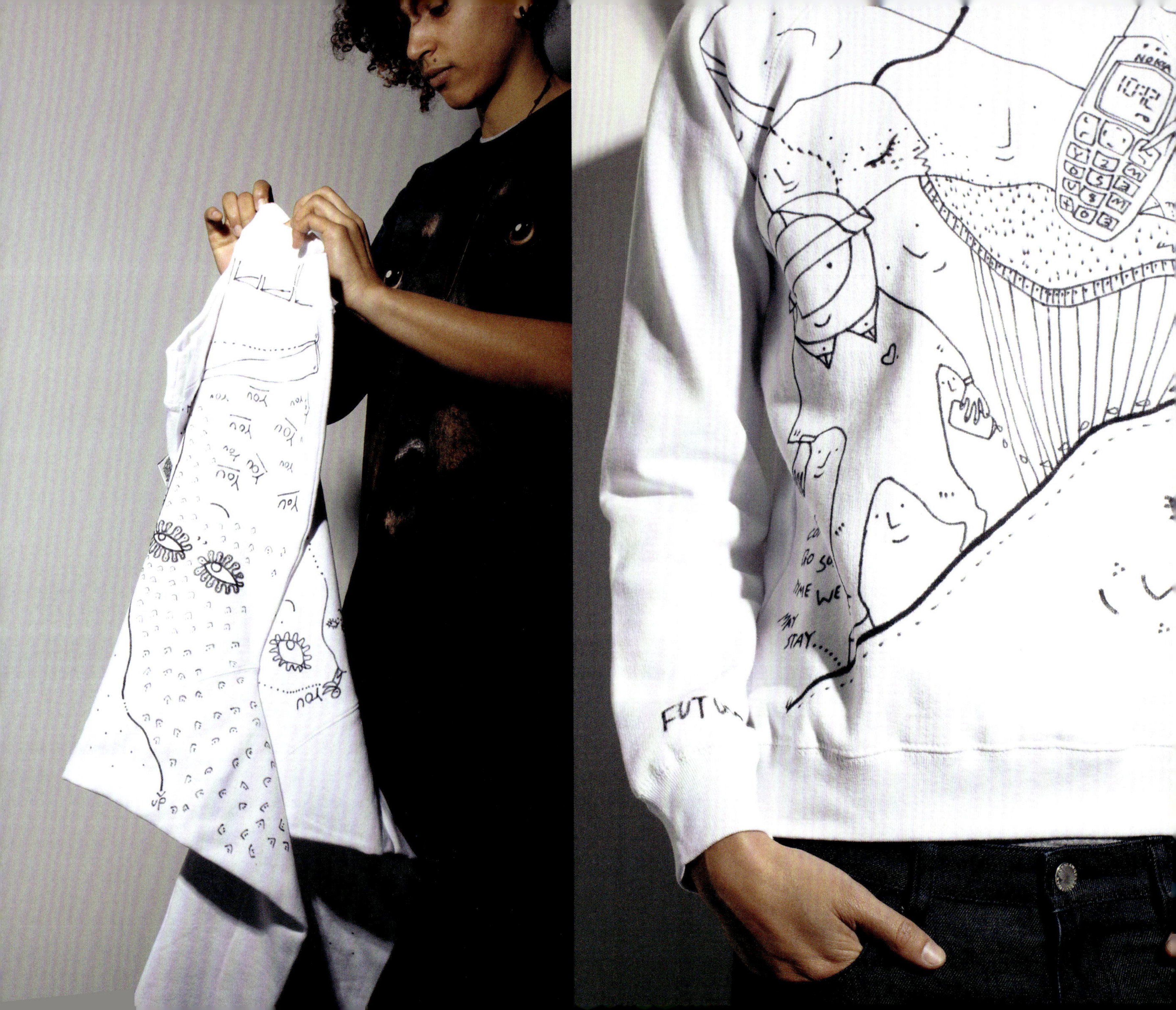
NOKIA
YOU
YOU
YOU
YOU
YOU
YOU
YOU
GO SO
TIME WE
STAY
FUT

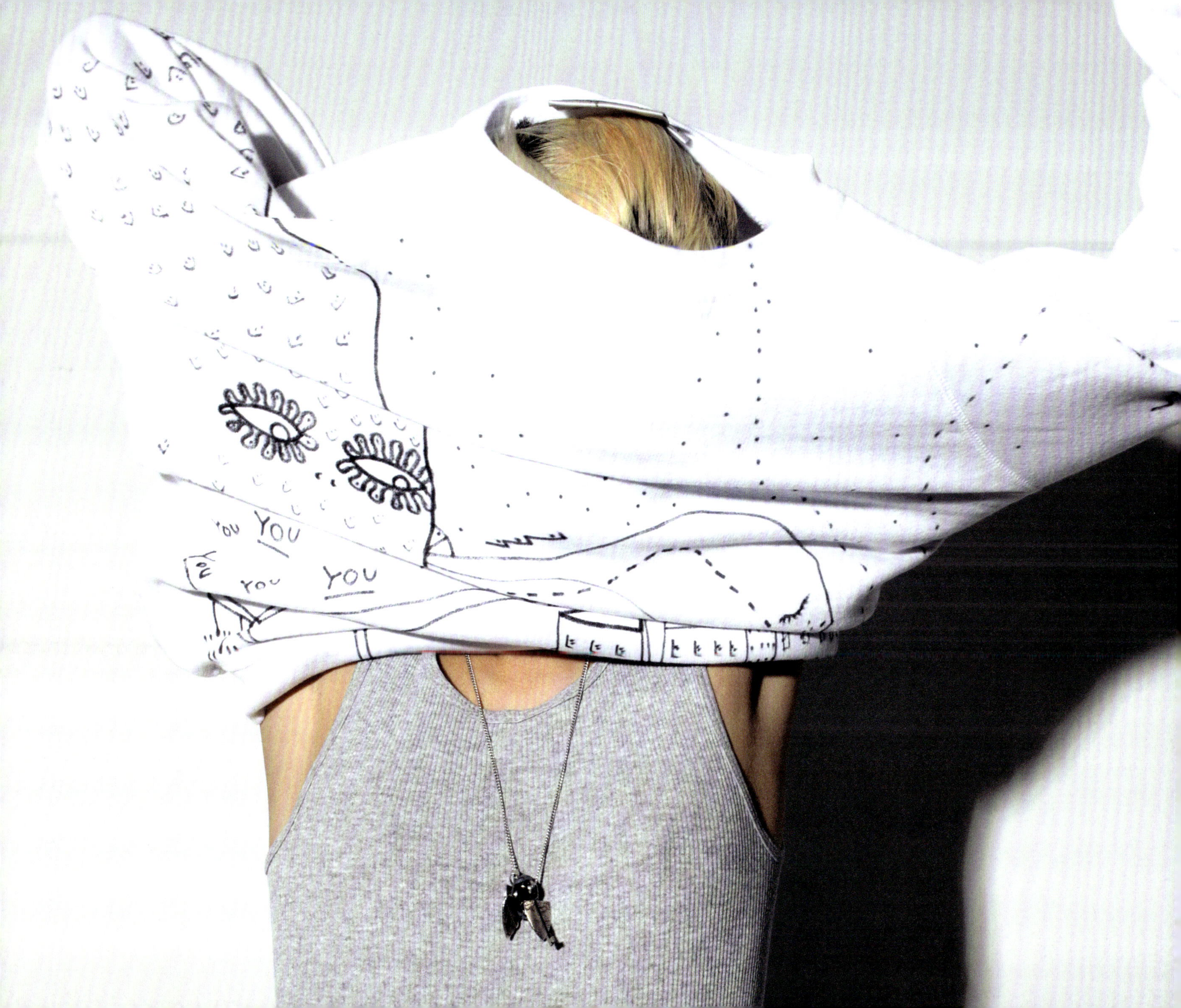
YOU
YOU
YOU
YOU

PENS HAVE TAKEN ME ALL AROUND THE WORLD.

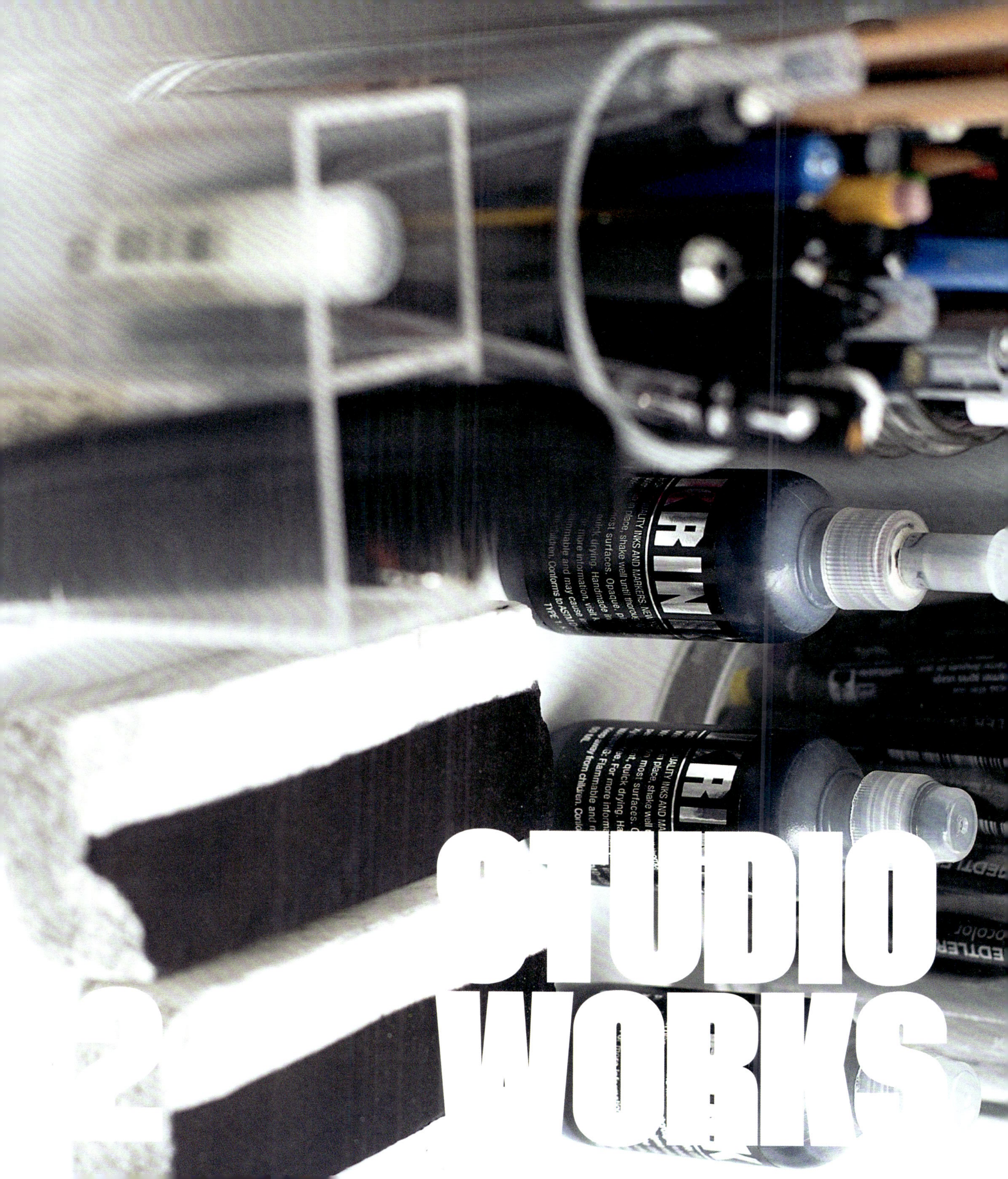

STUDIO
WORKS

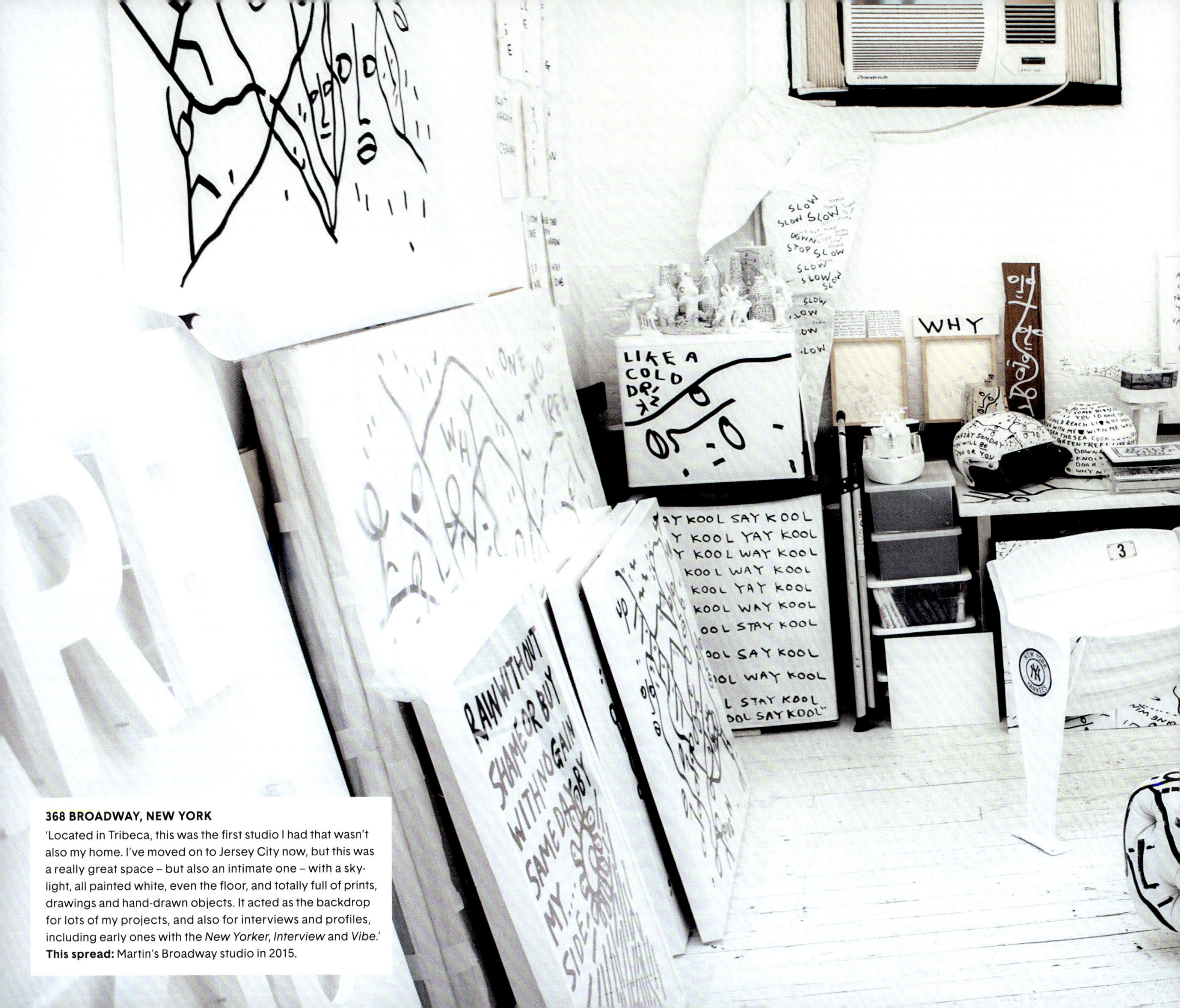

368 BROADWAY, NEW YORK

'Located in Tribeca, this was the first studio I had that wasn't also my home. I've moved on to Jersey City now, but this was a really great space – but also an intimate one – with a skylight, all painted white, even the floor, and totally full of prints, drawings and hand-drawn objects. It acted as the backdrop for lots of my projects, and also for interviews and profiles, including early ones with the *New Yorker*, *Interview* and *Vibe*.' **This spread:** Martin's Broadway studio in 2015.

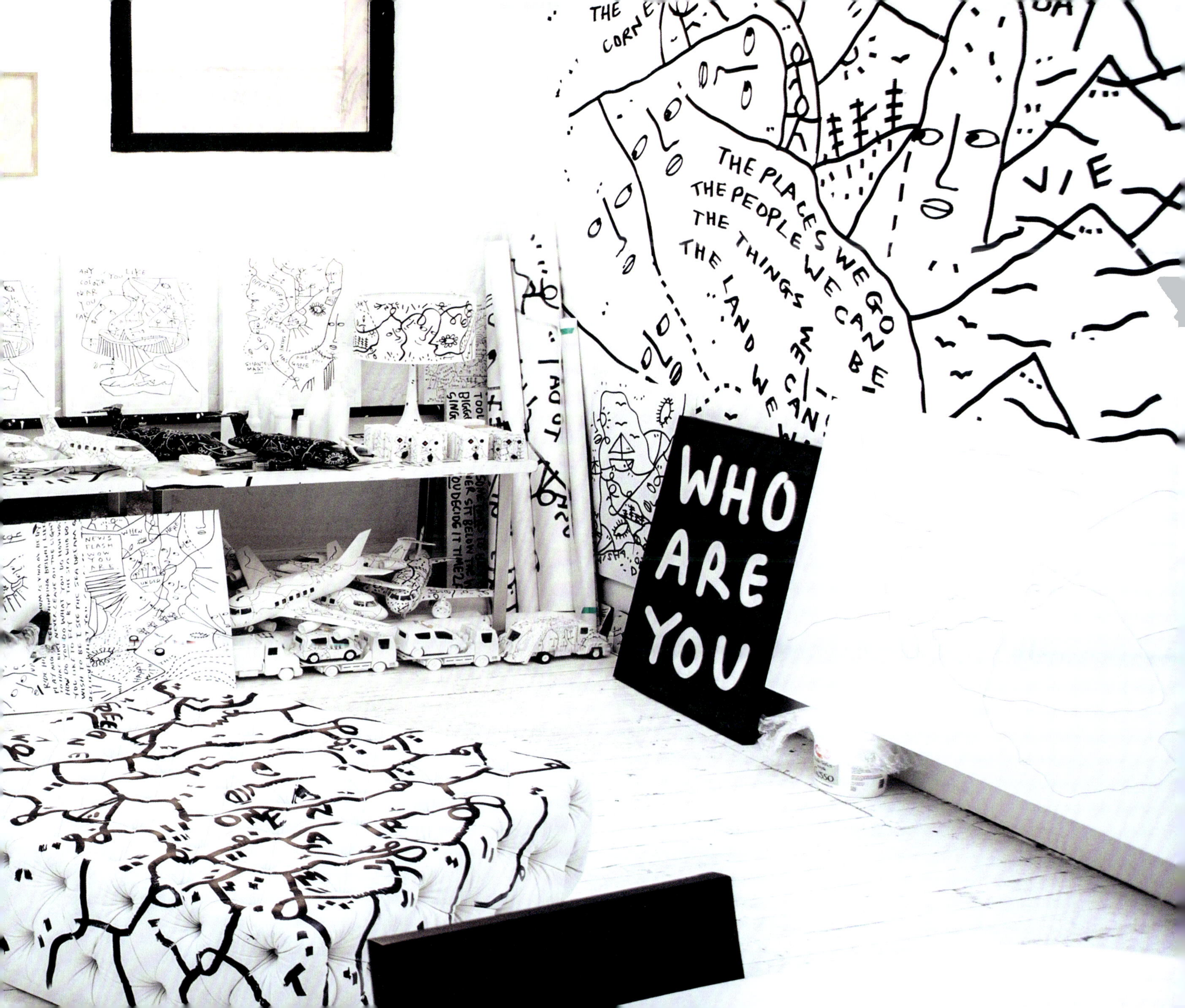

THE PLACES WE GO
THE PEOPLE WE CAN BE
THE THINGS WE CAN
THE LAND WE CAN
WHO ARE YOU

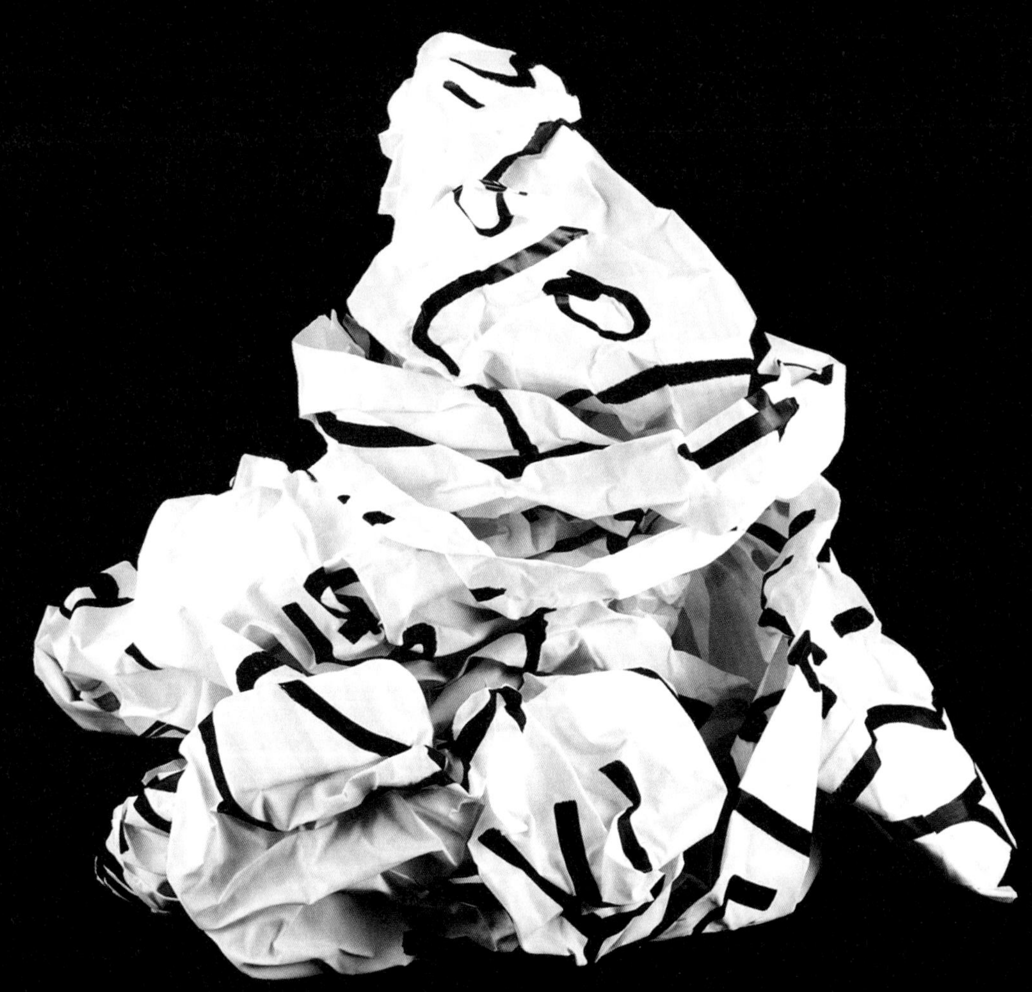

Scrunched, 2013.
Ink on paper.

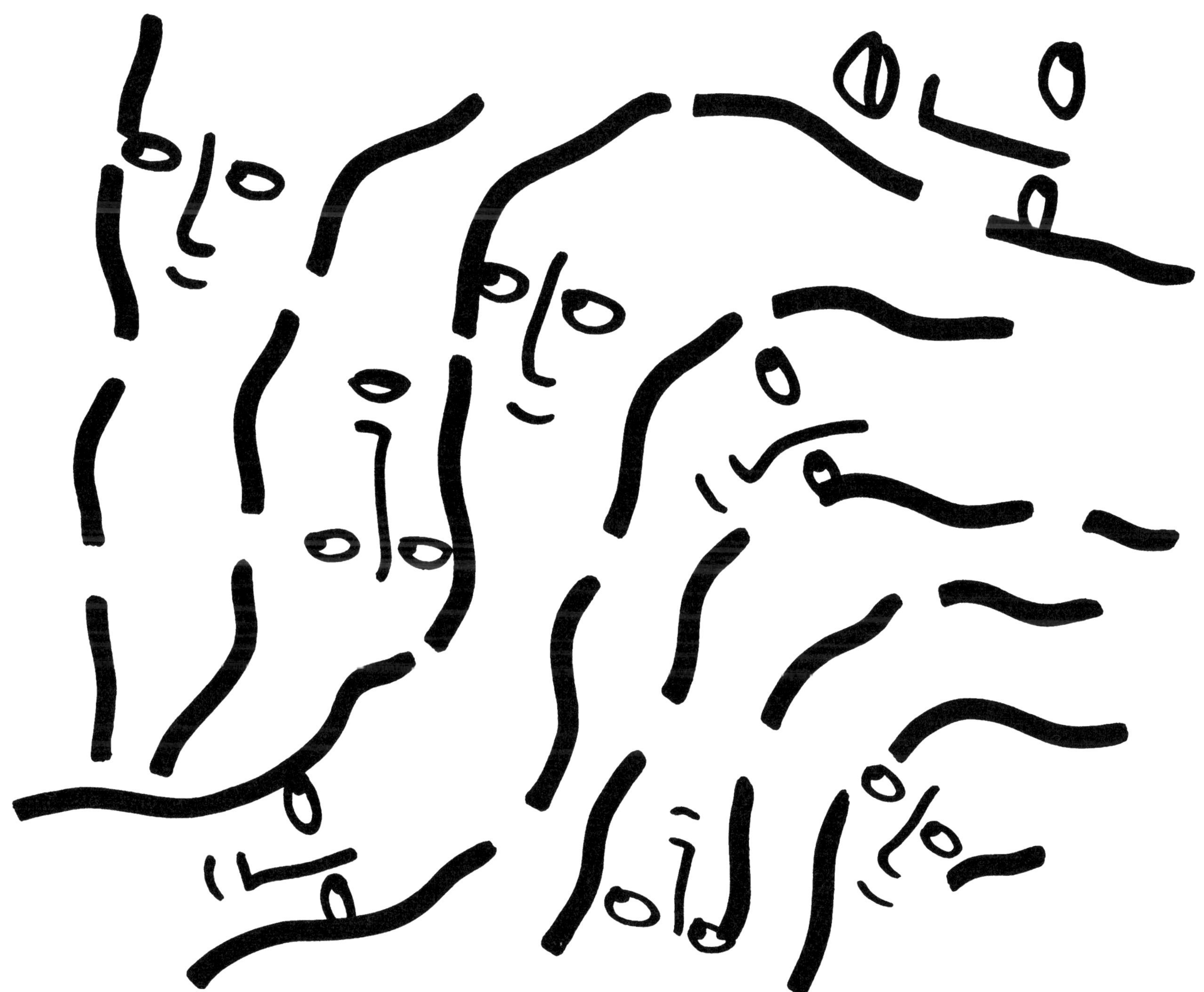

Garden Faces, 2012.
Ink on paper.

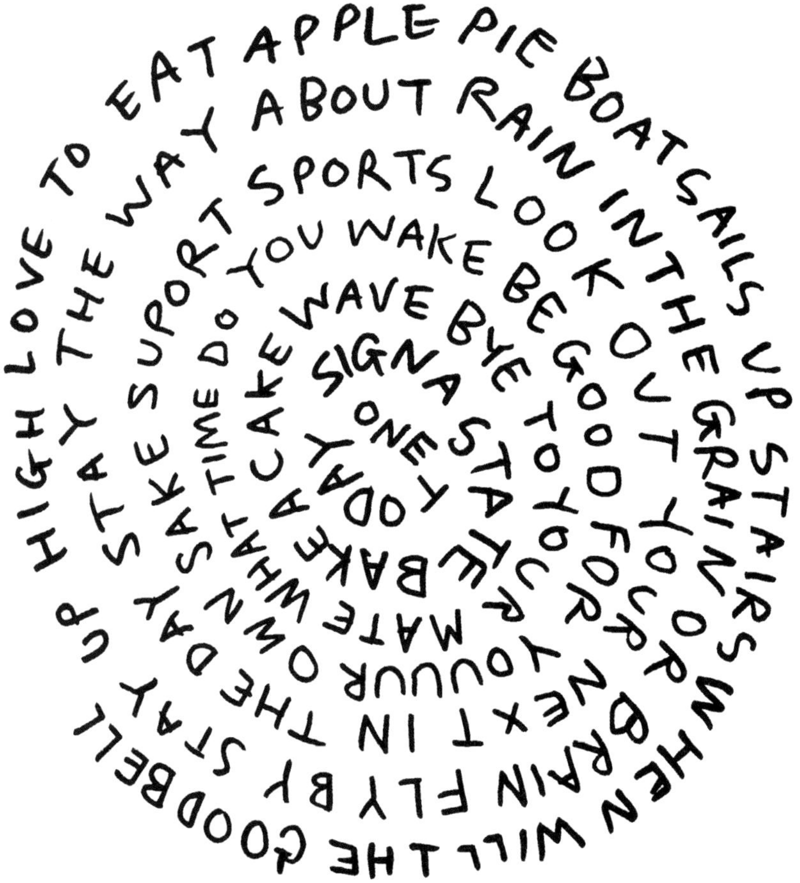

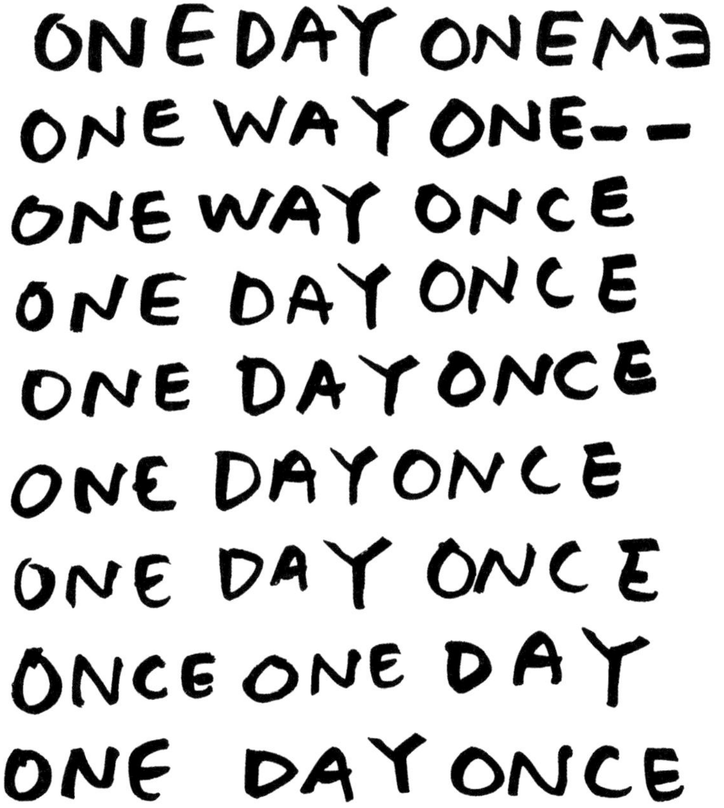

Ramblings
'I call this collection of ink-on-paper pieces "Ramblings" (2012–13). They're an exercise in stream-of-consciousness drawings and writings, a celebration of spontaneity and being in the present.' **Left to right:** *Eat Apple Pie*, 2013; *One Day Once*, 2012; *Who You Knew*, 2013; *Gone Alone*, 2013.

SAVE BEES NO ONE ELSE I WE COULD BE.
BECOME ME YOU WE DRINK MORE
BUT GIVE MORE THINK FLIGHT MORE
WE WILL WE TAKE BE MORE
SAVE THE SKY WE CAN WE MIGHT
SOMETIME TREES SAVE AND
WE TOUCH HOLD OF THE
WE TAKE HOLD ONE DAY
SOMEDAY SOMEDAY ONE DAY
FREE OR IN NEED THREE
FREE OR IN NEED SOME
BE MORE JUST BE MORE
WHO KNEW
WHO YOU
NEW

HOW MUCH DO YOU NEED
WE ASK AS I SCRATH MY KNEE
DO YOU REALLY HOW
WHAT YOU DO NOT SEA TAKE IT
ALL IN AND DON'T EVER COME
TO ME REAL STEAK OLD SOLD LEFT
BELIEVE WHAT COME ME OLD
EN NEW GOLDEN GOLD
BLUE GONE GONE
ALONE
ONE TWO FREE FREE REALLY
DO YOU BE BELIEVE
ONE

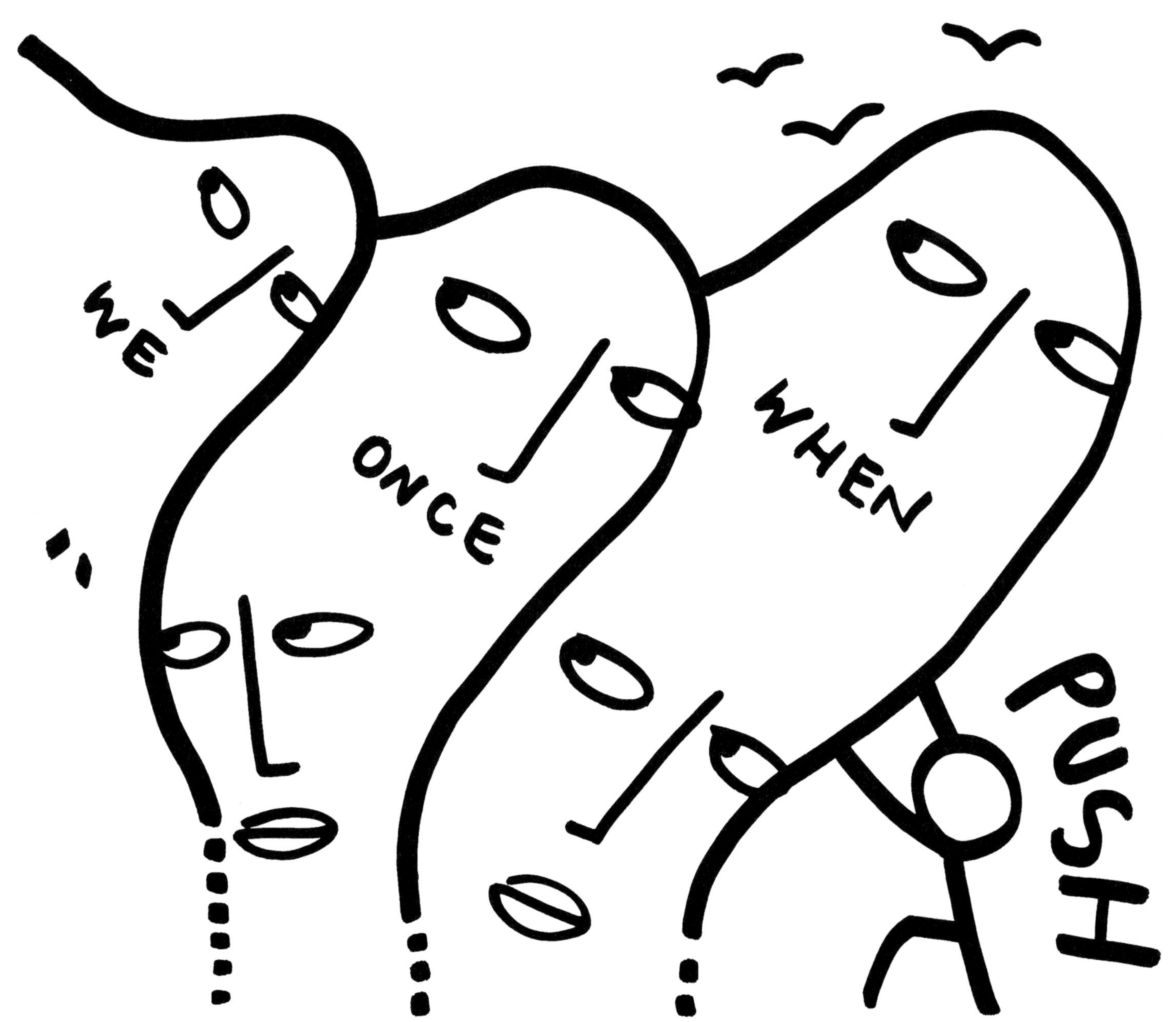

We Once When Push, 2013.
Ink on paper.

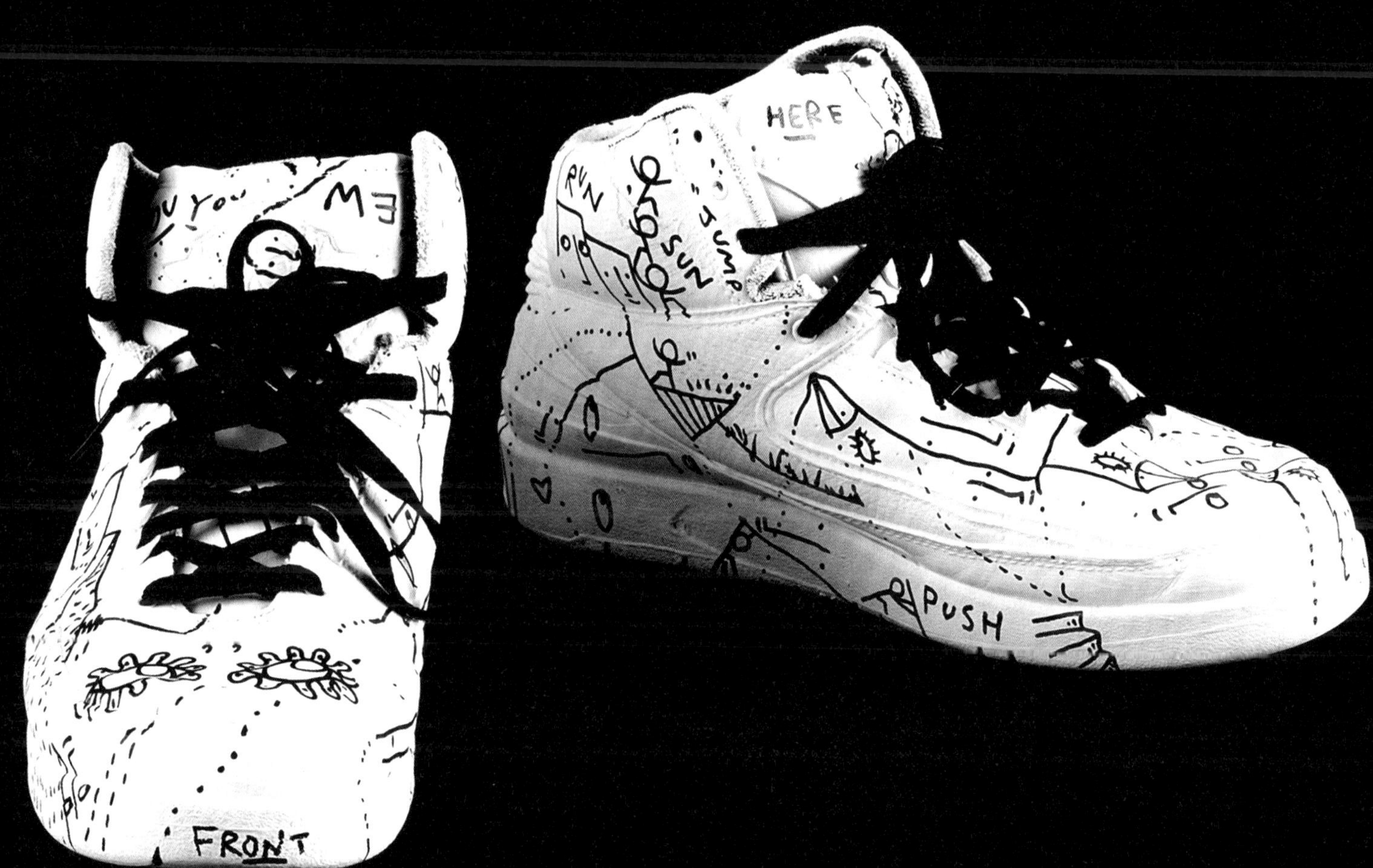

Air Jordans, 2013.
Ink on sneakers.

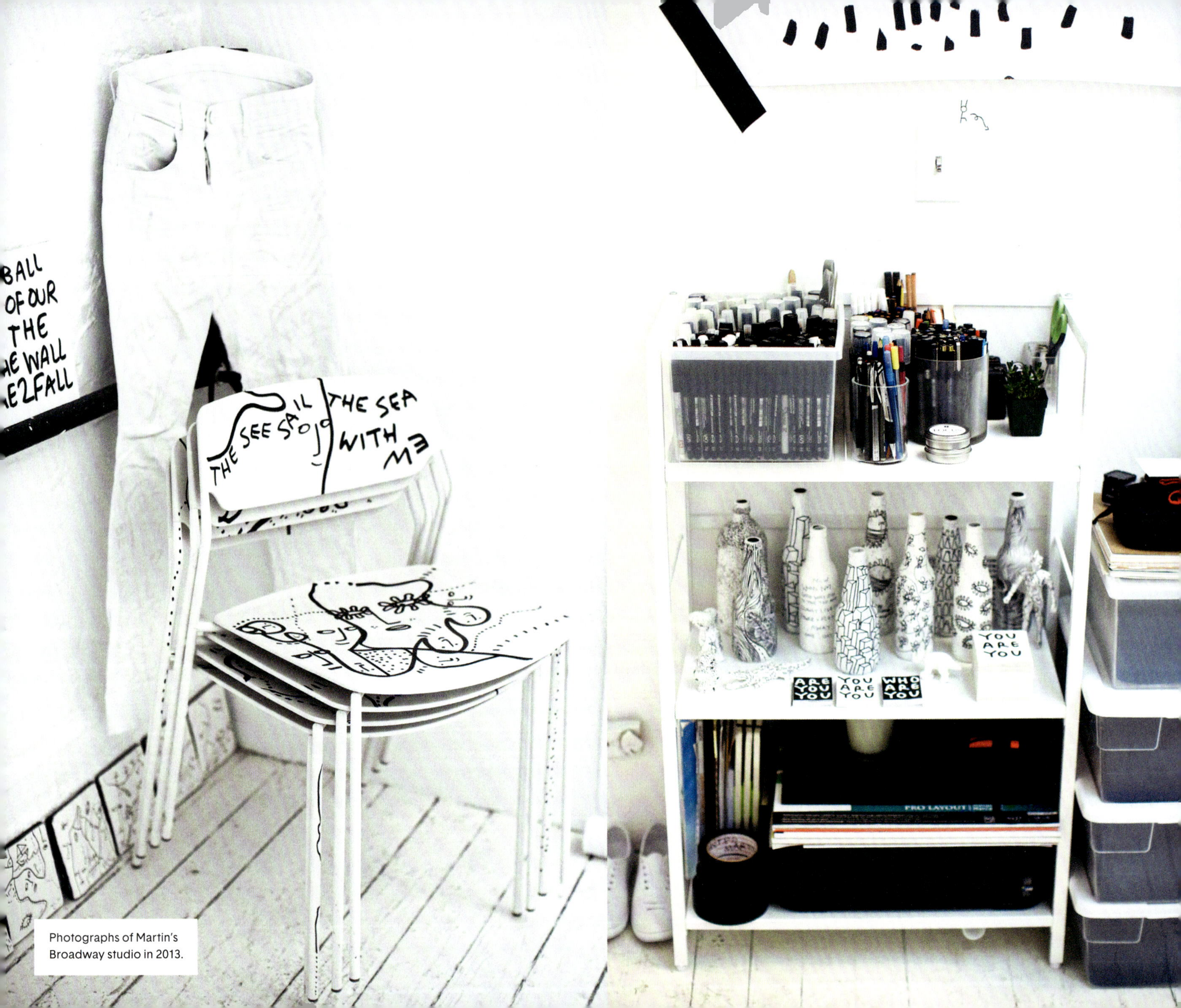

Photographs of Martin's Broadway studio in 2013.

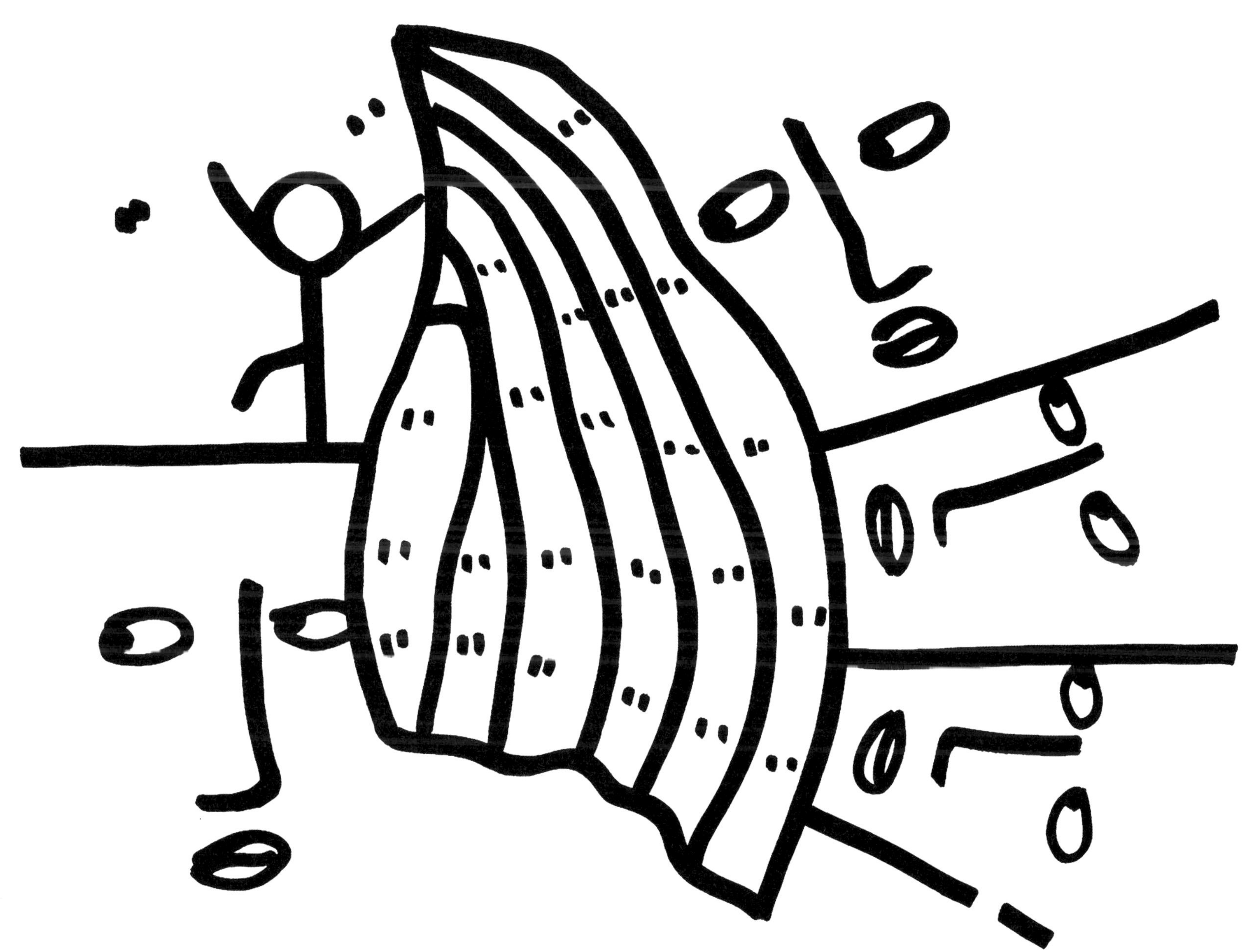

Four Faces, 2013.
Ink on paper.

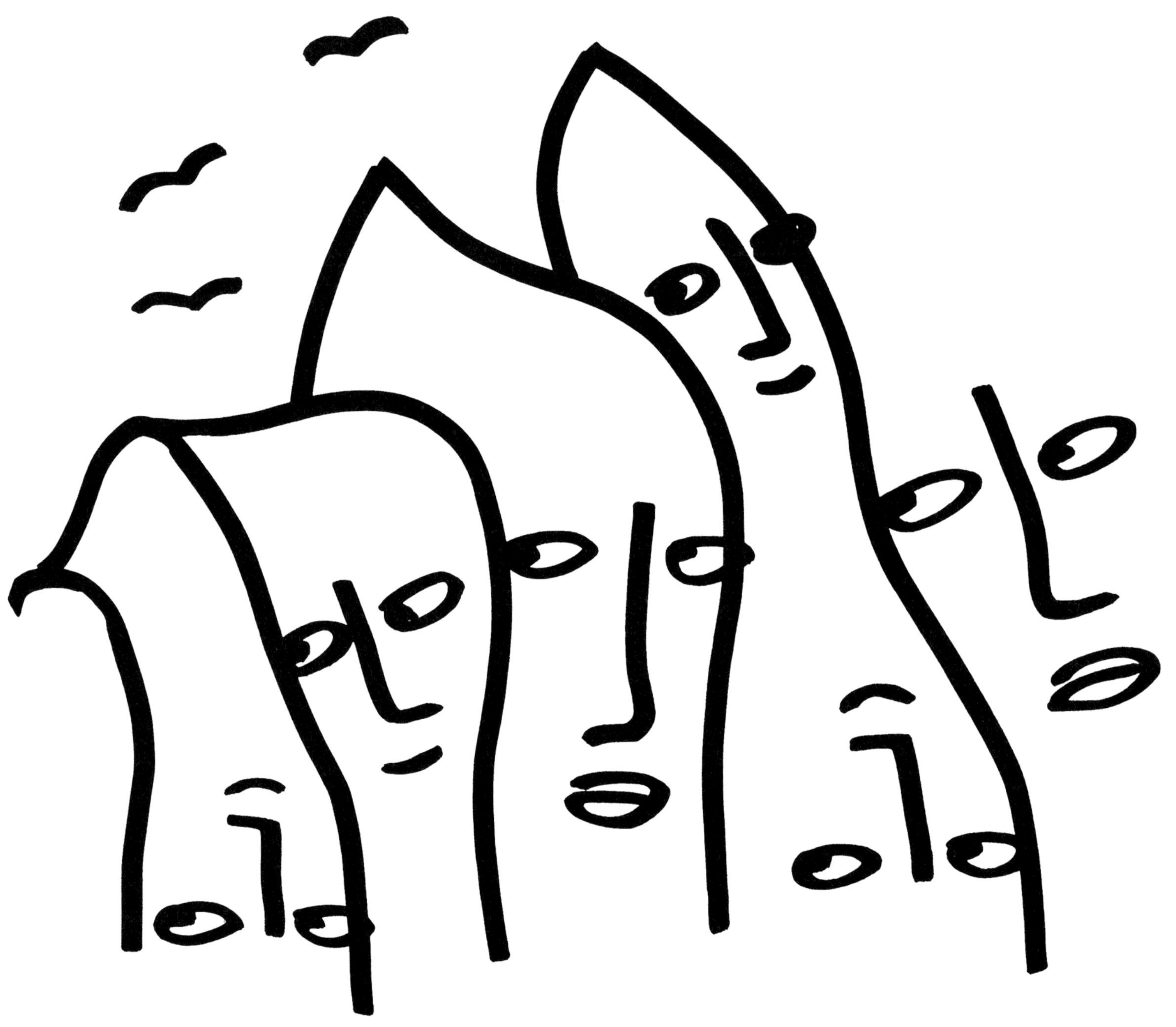

Six Faces, 2014.
Ink on paper.

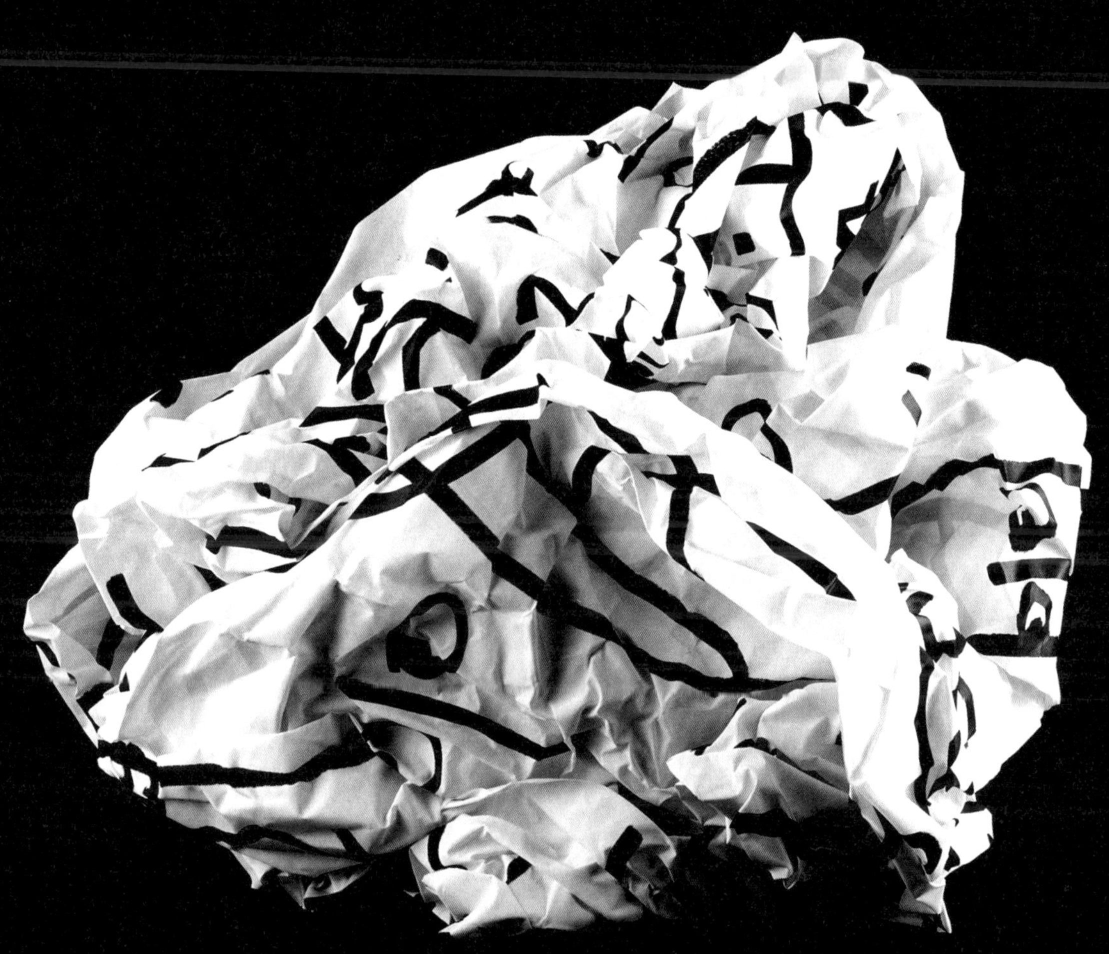

Scrunched, 2013.
Ink on paper.

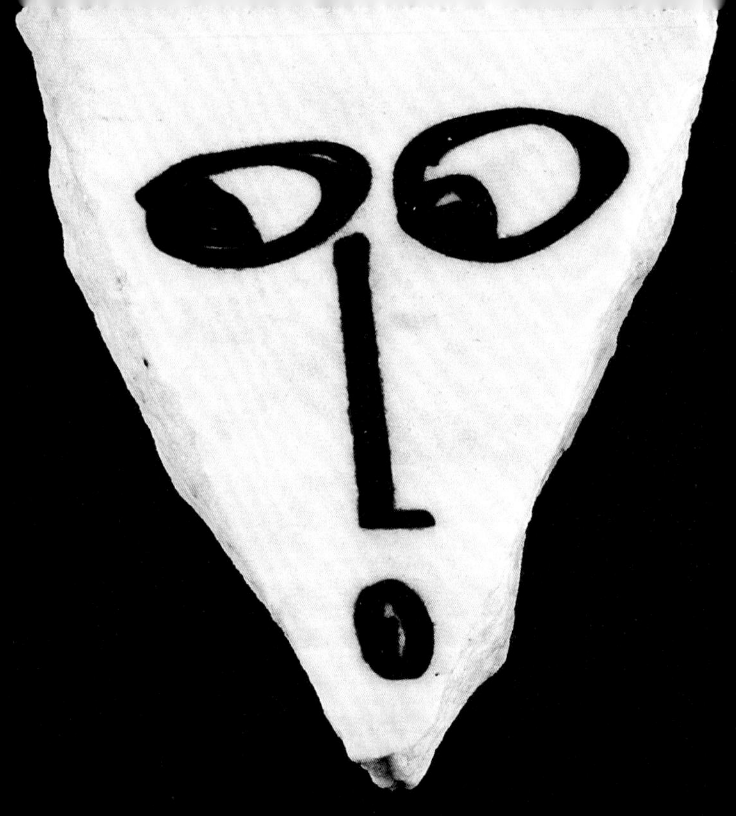
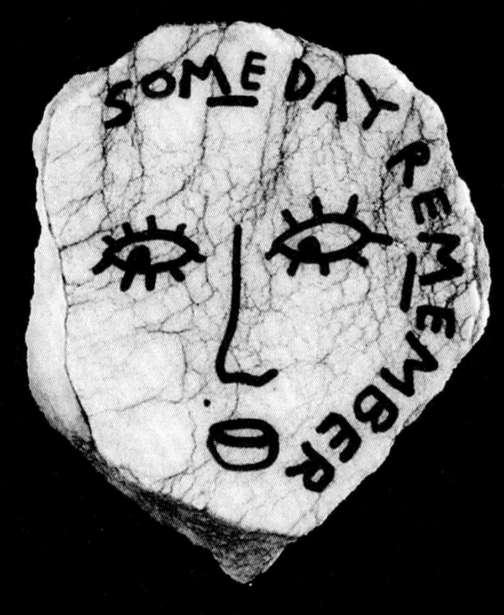

Marble Heads

'In late 2012, I visited my friend and collaborator Stefan
Daiberl in North Florida. While there, he took me to a
marble yard, and I took home as many scraps as possible
to work with, which eventually became this collection
called "Marble Heads" (2013–14).' **Left:** *Marble Head*, 2013.
Right: *Marble Head: Someday Remember Me*, 2013.

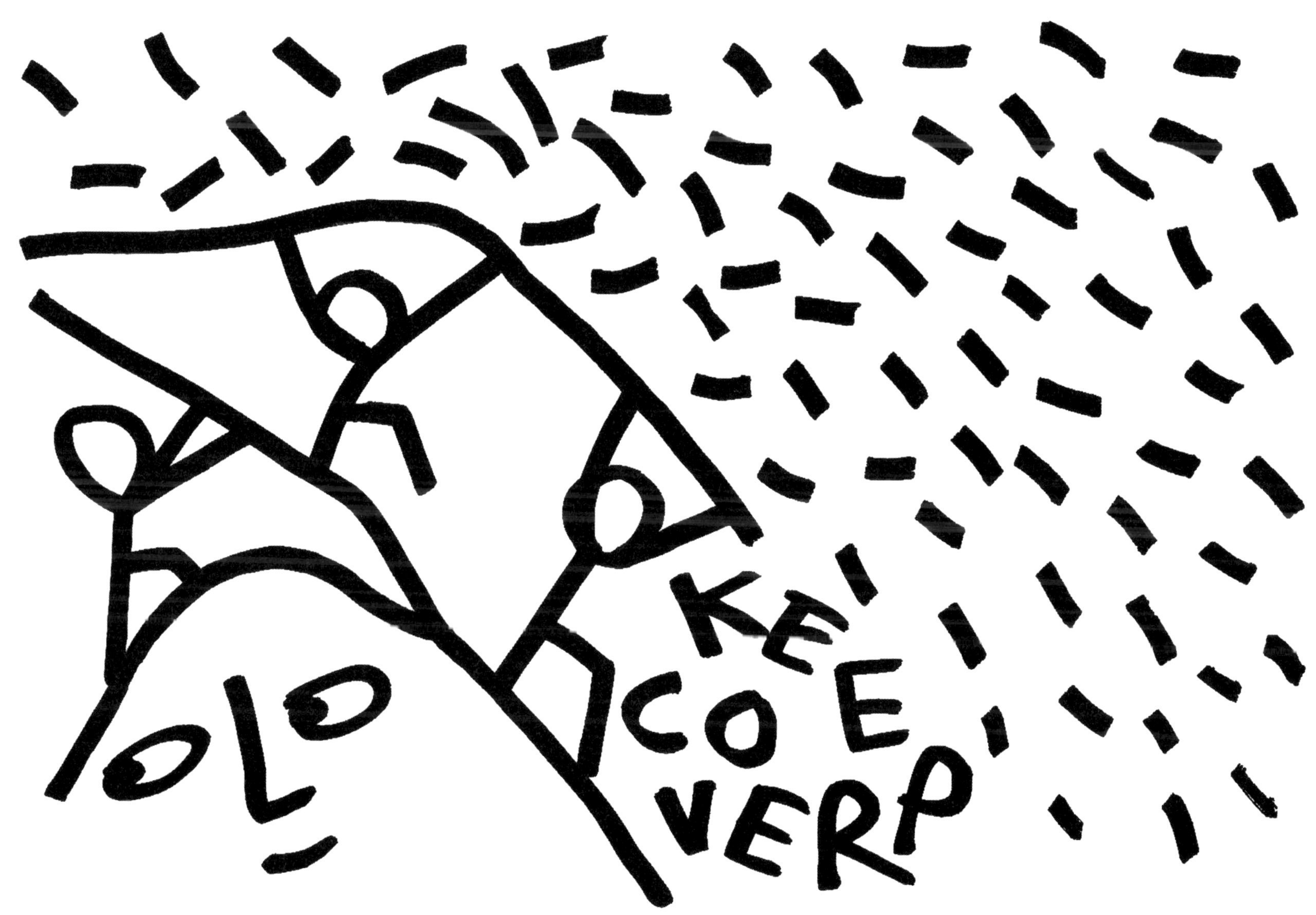

Keep Cover, 2013.
Ink on paper.

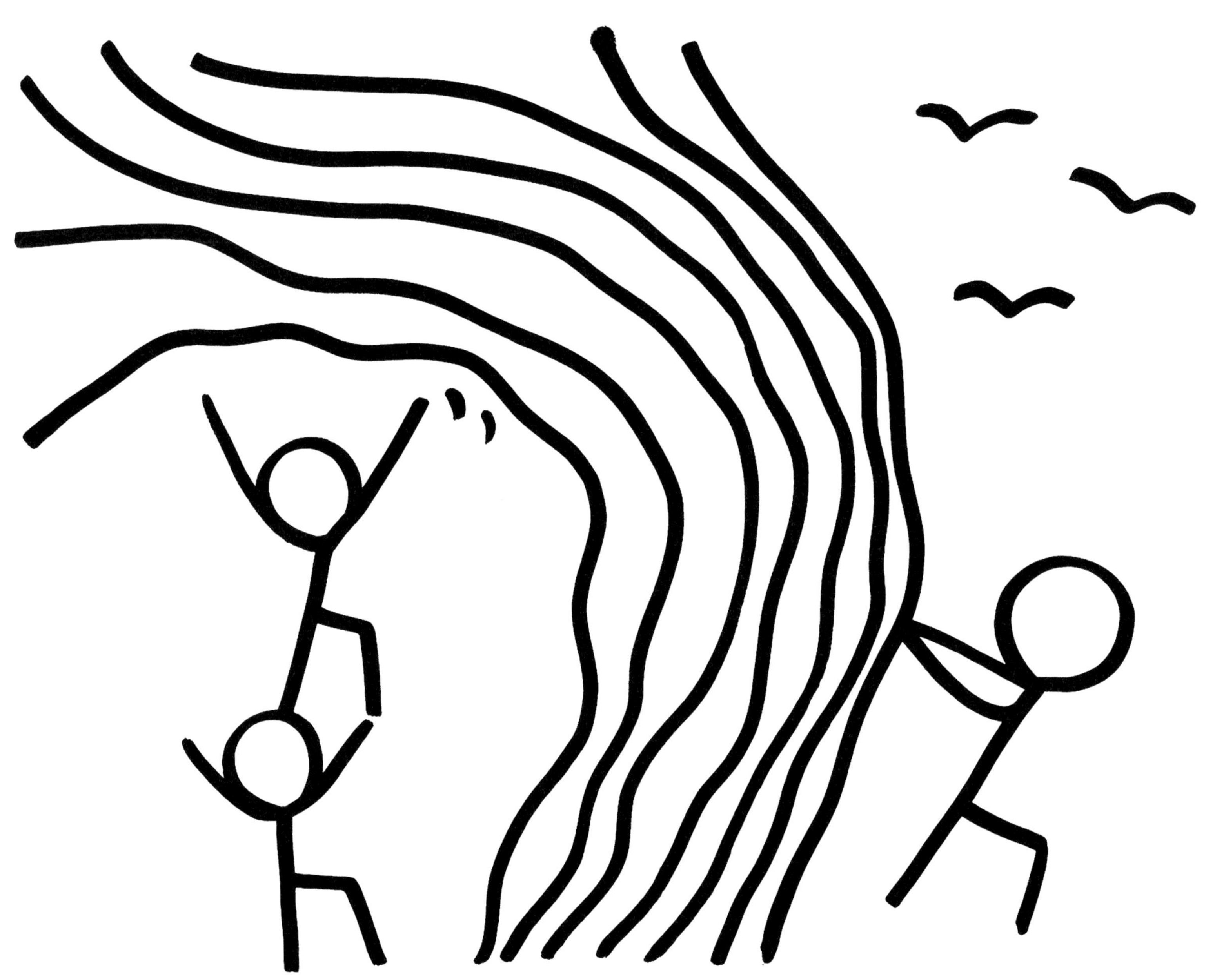

Pull and Hold, 2014.
Ink on paper.

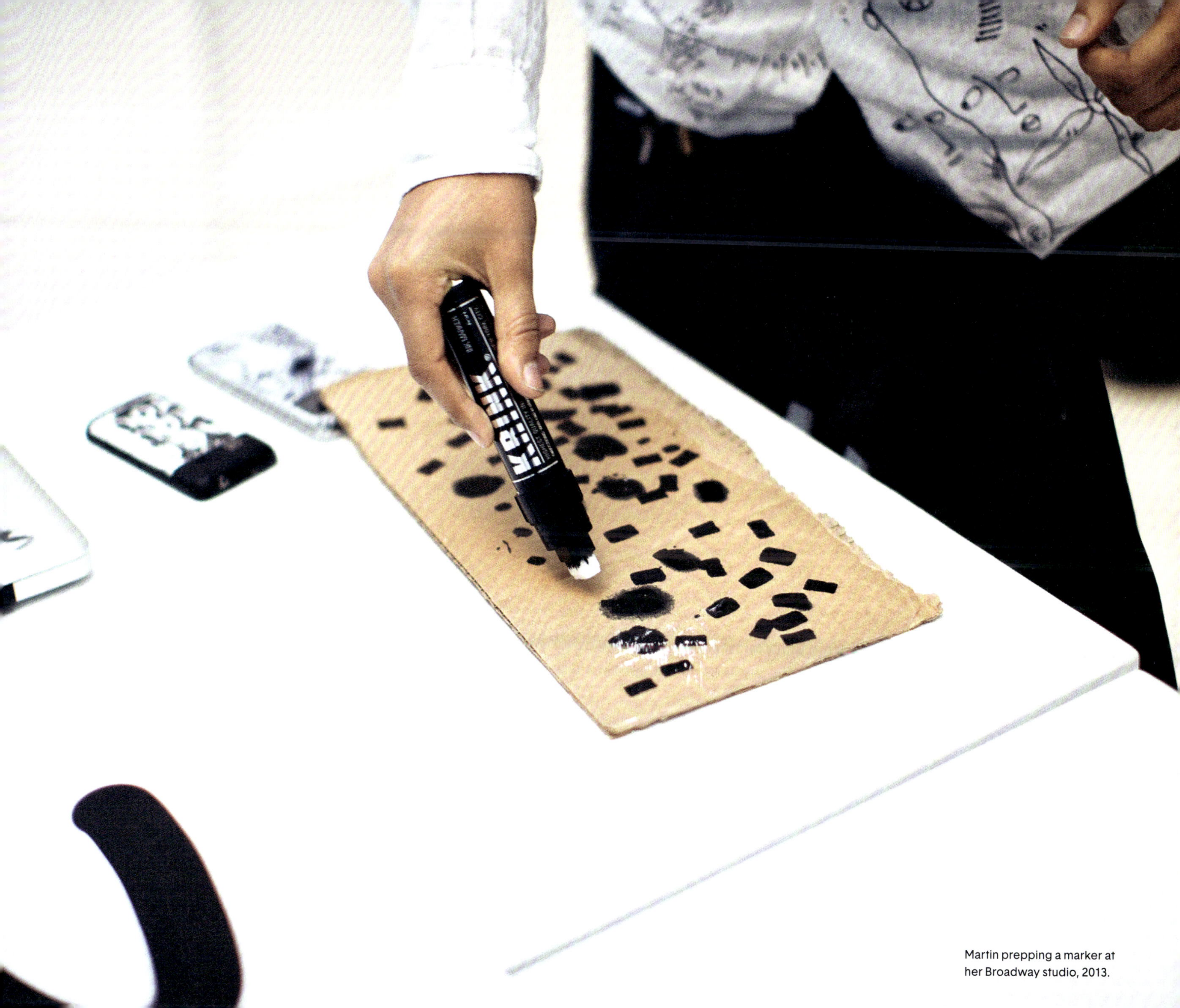

Martin prepping a marker at
her Broadway studio, 2013.

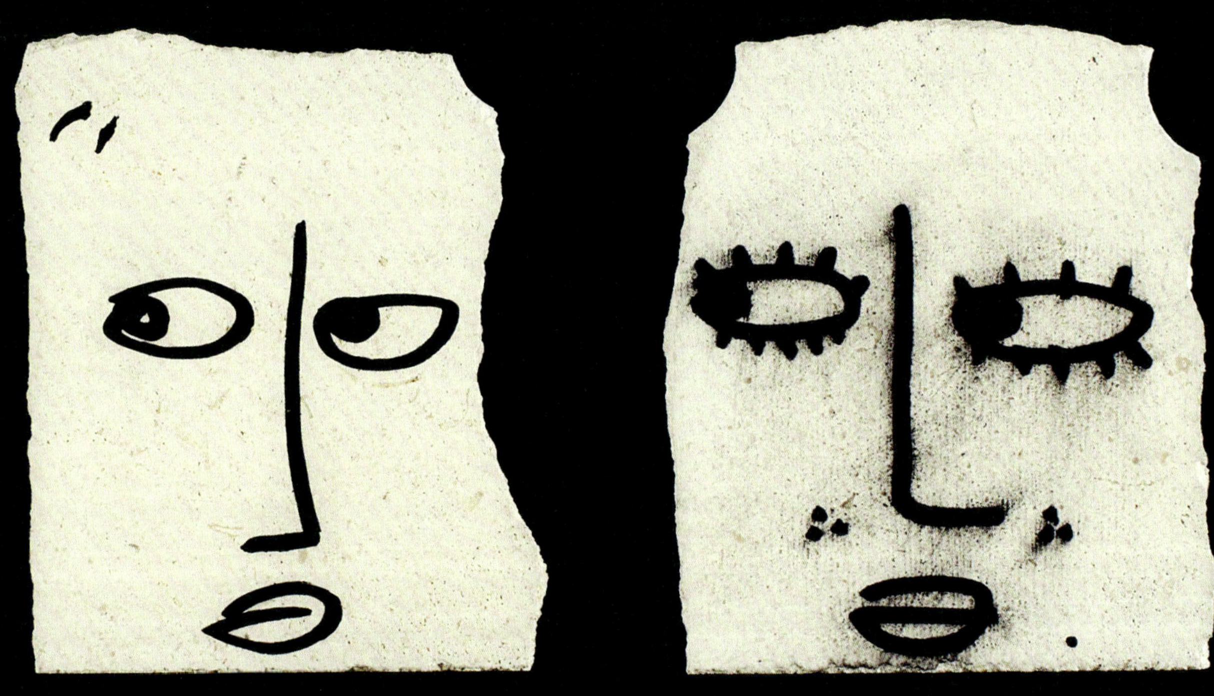

Left: *Marble Head*, 2013.
Right: *Marble Head*, 2013.
Ink on found marble.

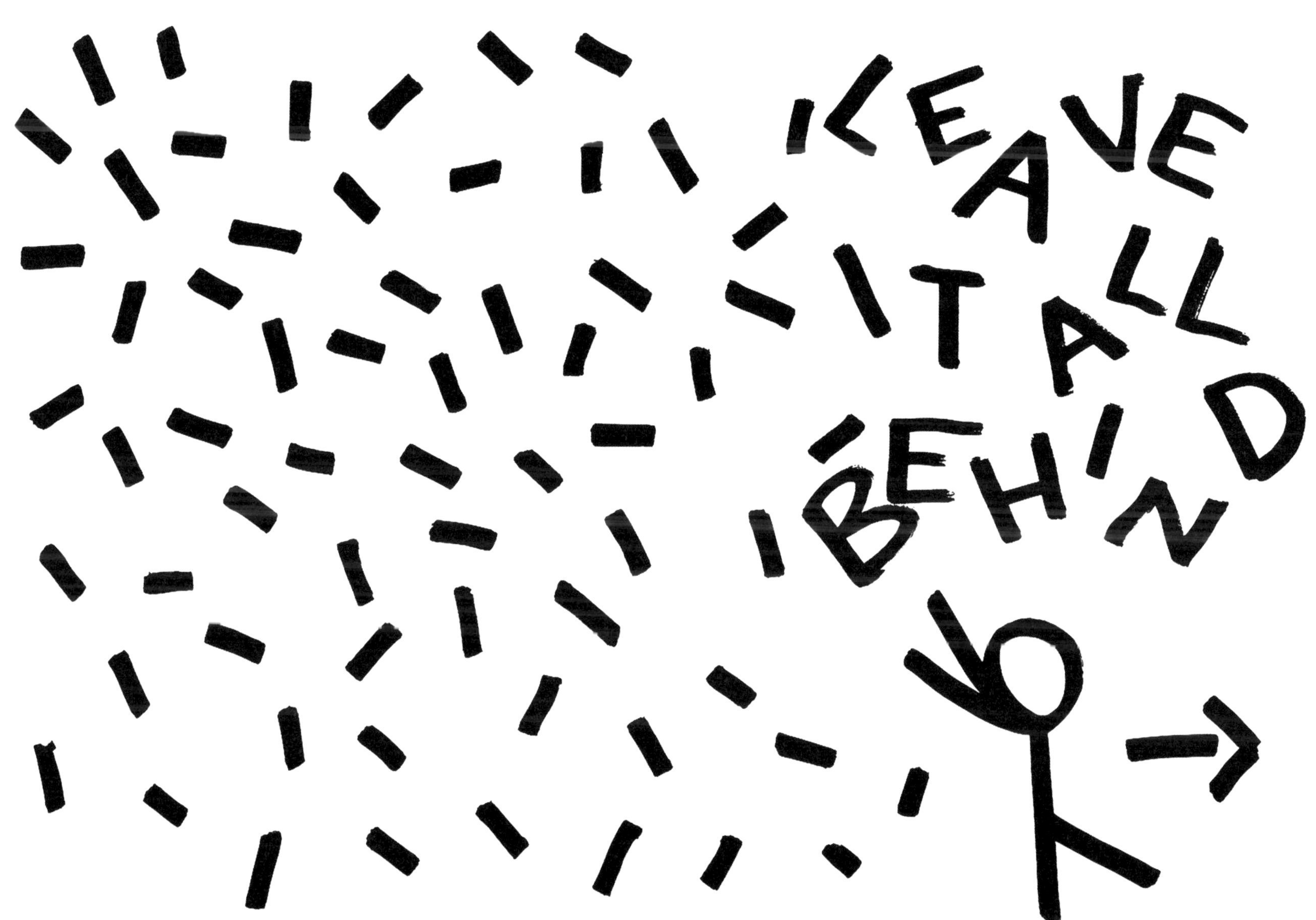

Leave It All Behind,
2013. Ink on paper.

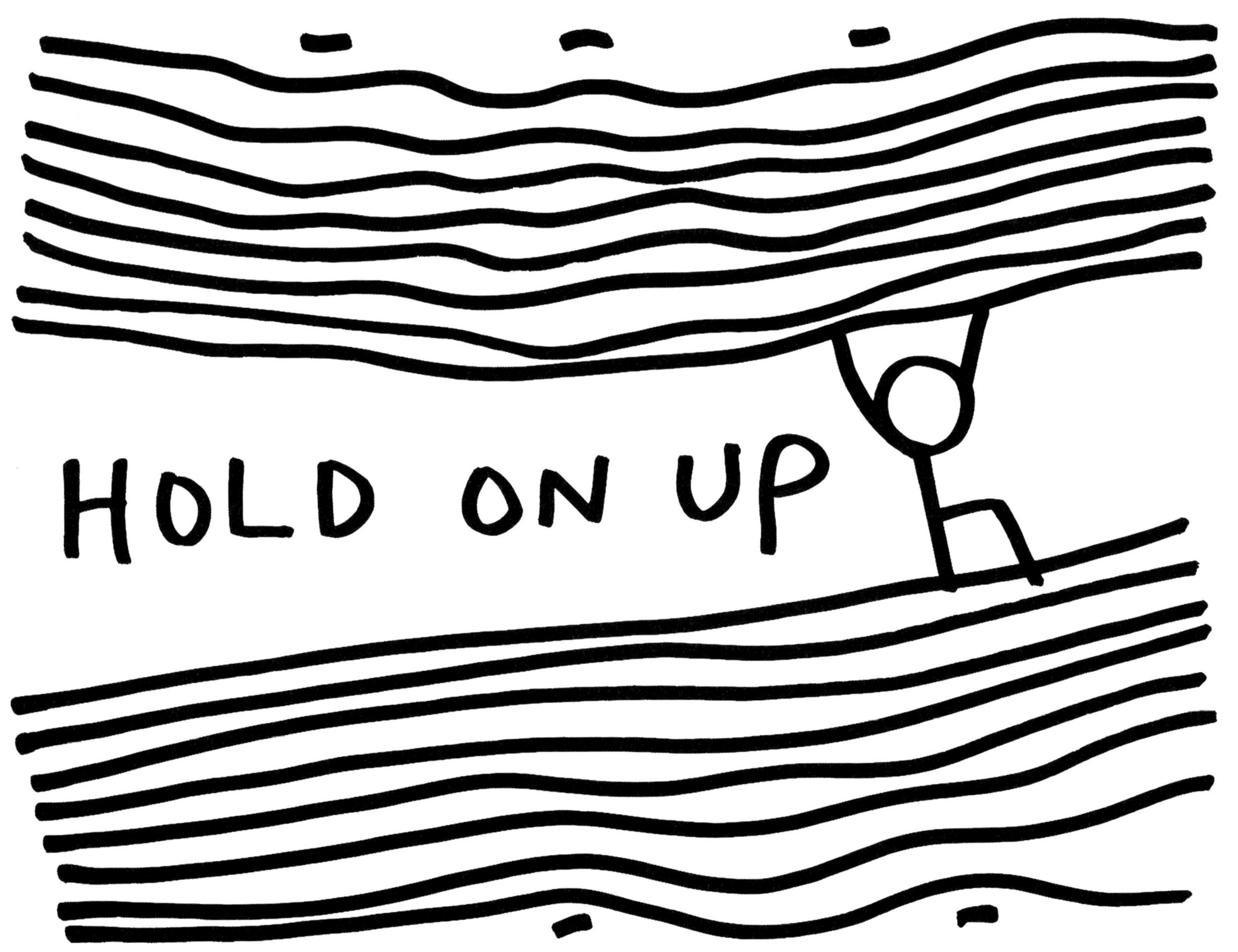

Hold On Up, 2014.
Ink on paper.

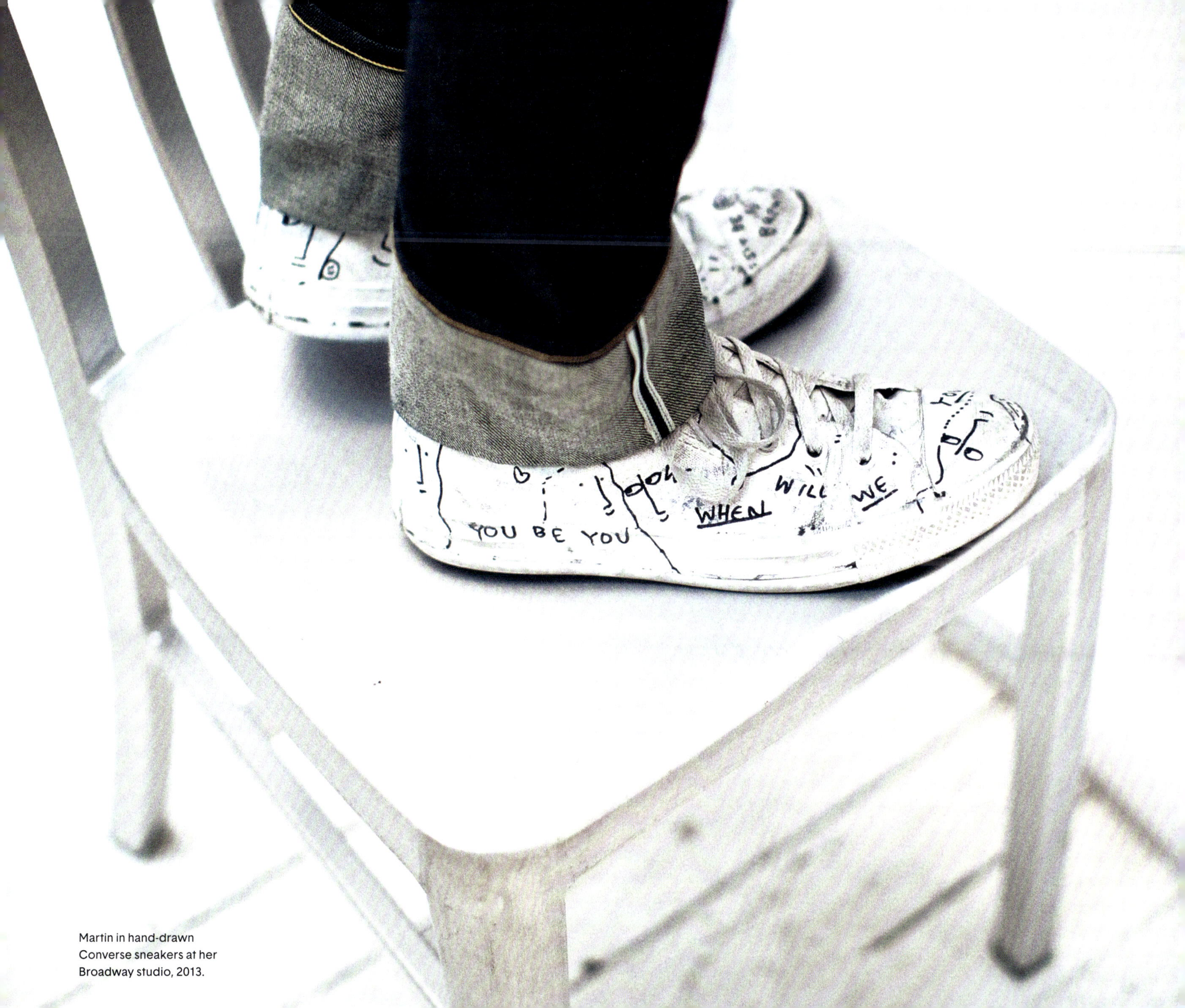

Martin in hand-drawn
Converse sneakers at her
Broadway studio, 2013.

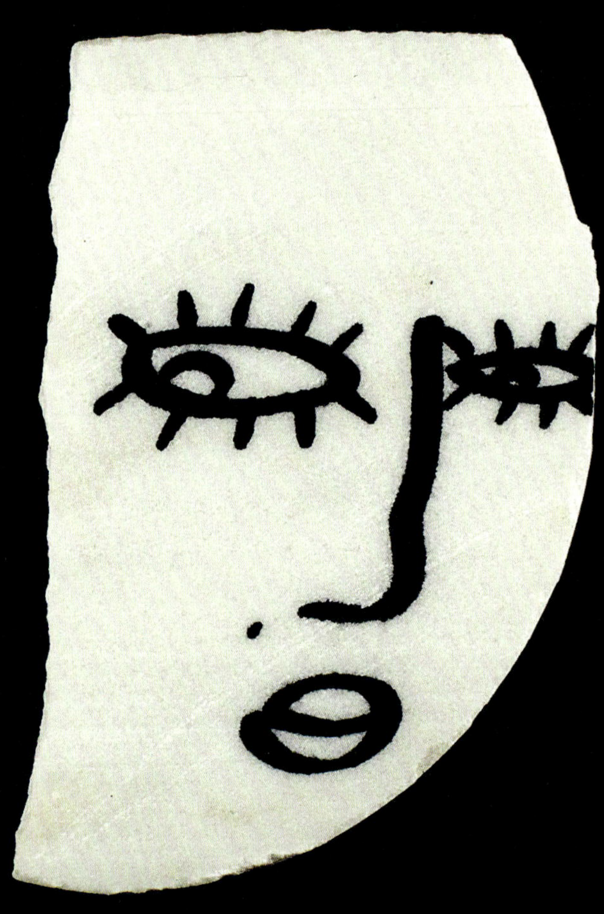

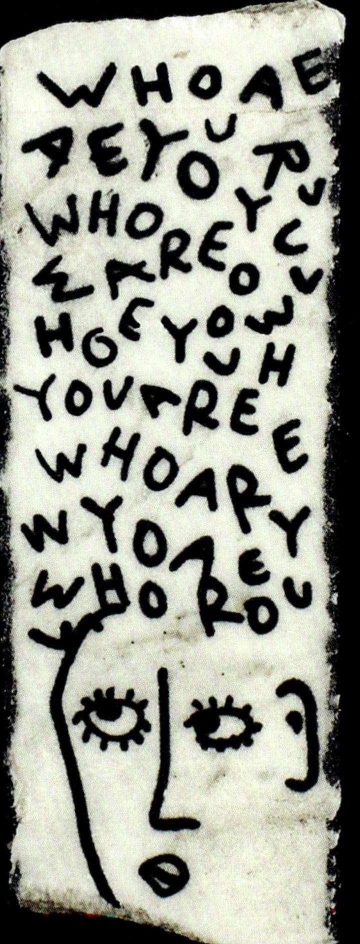

Left: *Marble Head: Open Eyes*, 2013.
Right: *Marble Head: Who Are You*,
2013. Ink on found marble.

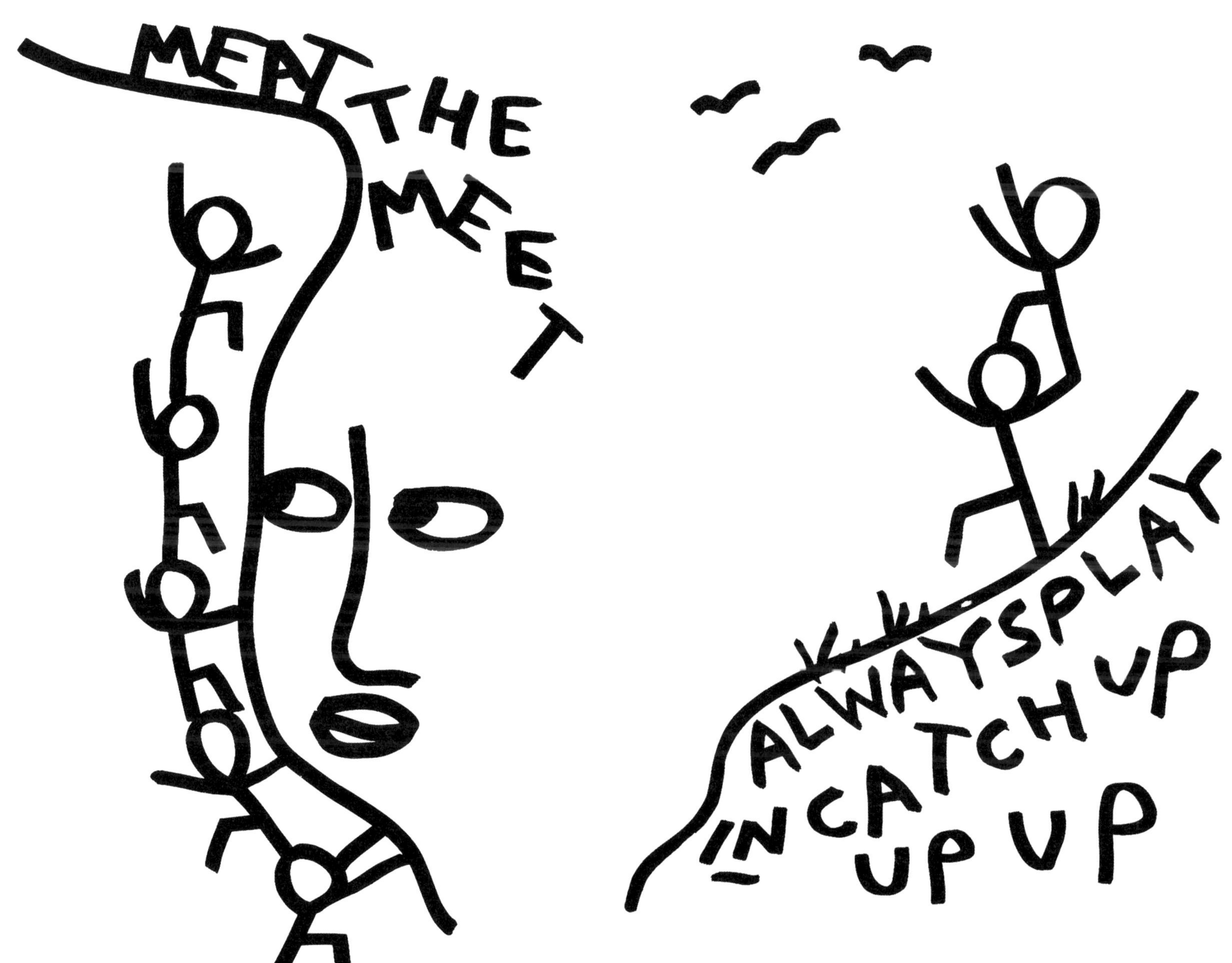

Left: *Meat the Meet*, 2013.
Right: *Always Playing*, 2014.
Ink on paper.

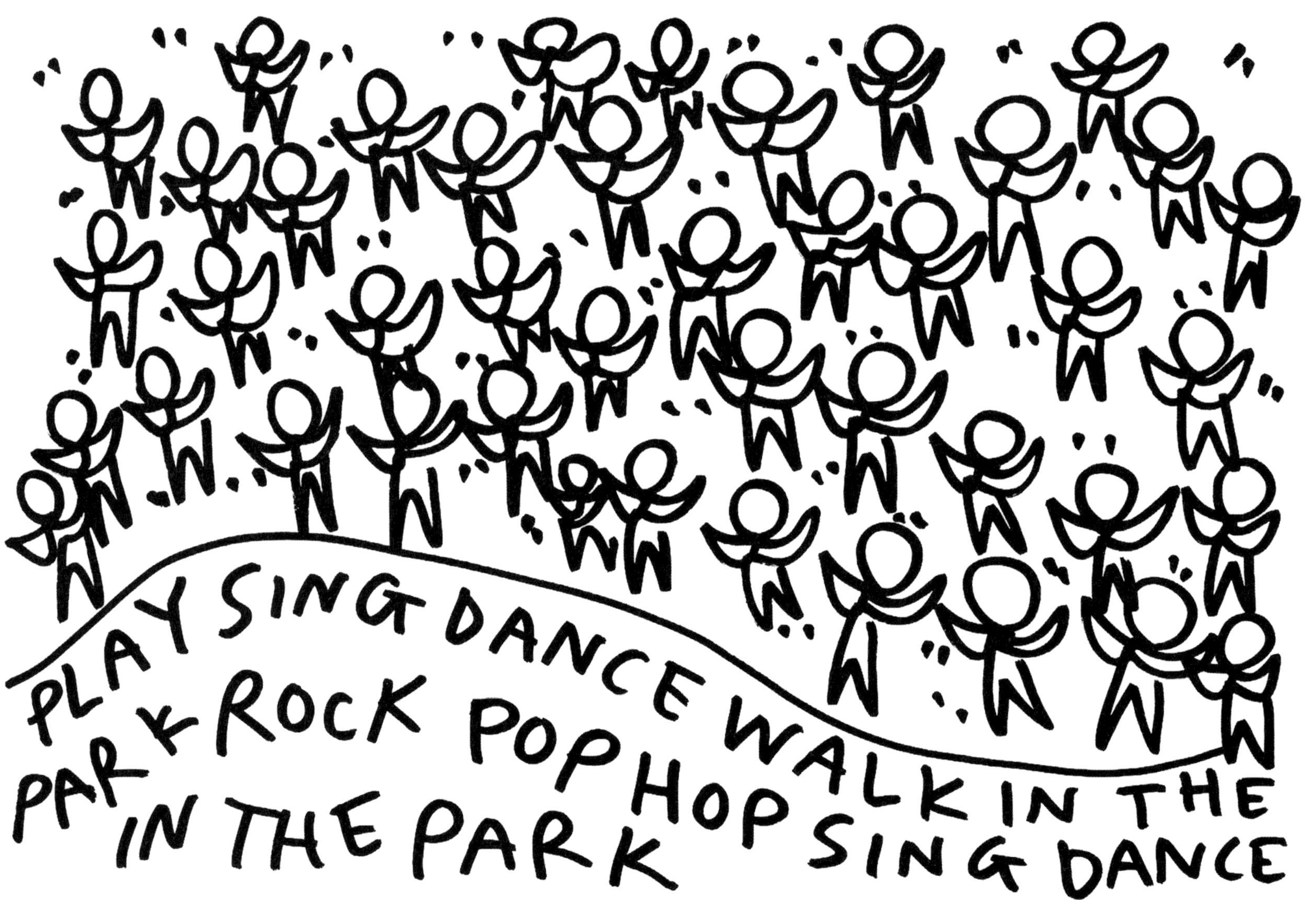

Play Sign Dance, 2013.
Ink on paper.

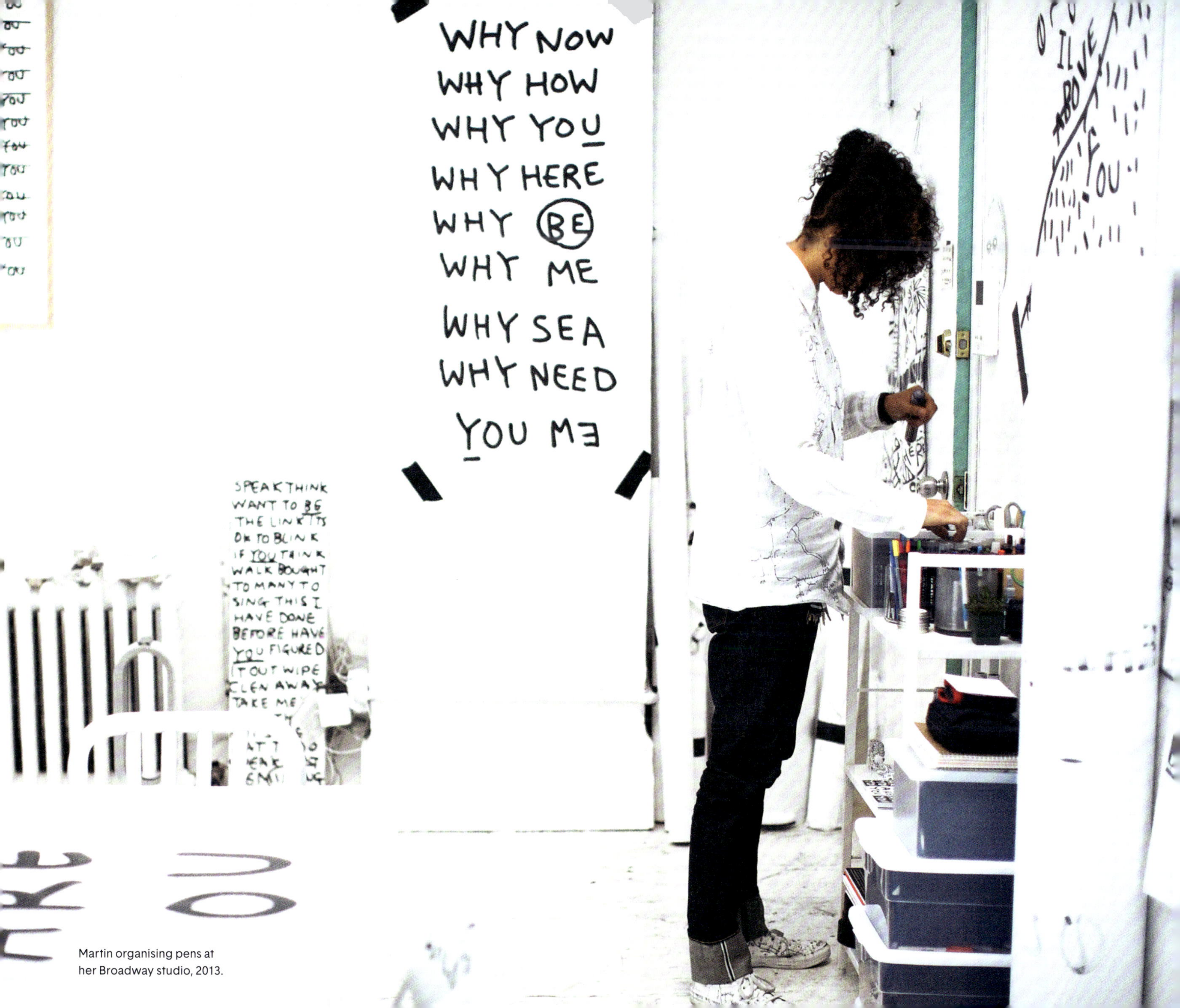

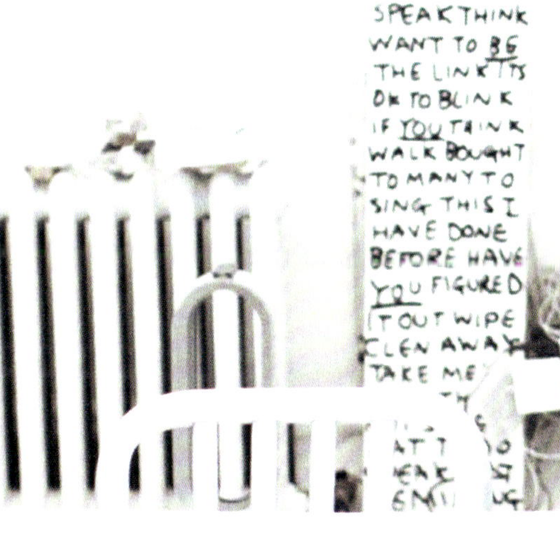

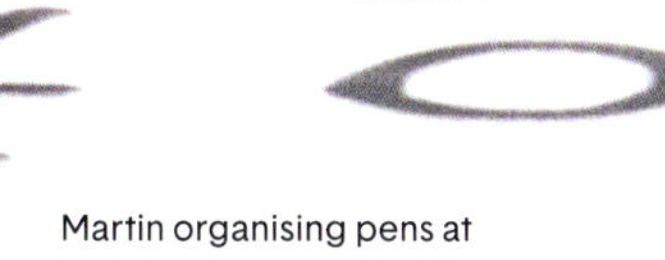
Martin organising pens at
her Broadway studio, 2013.

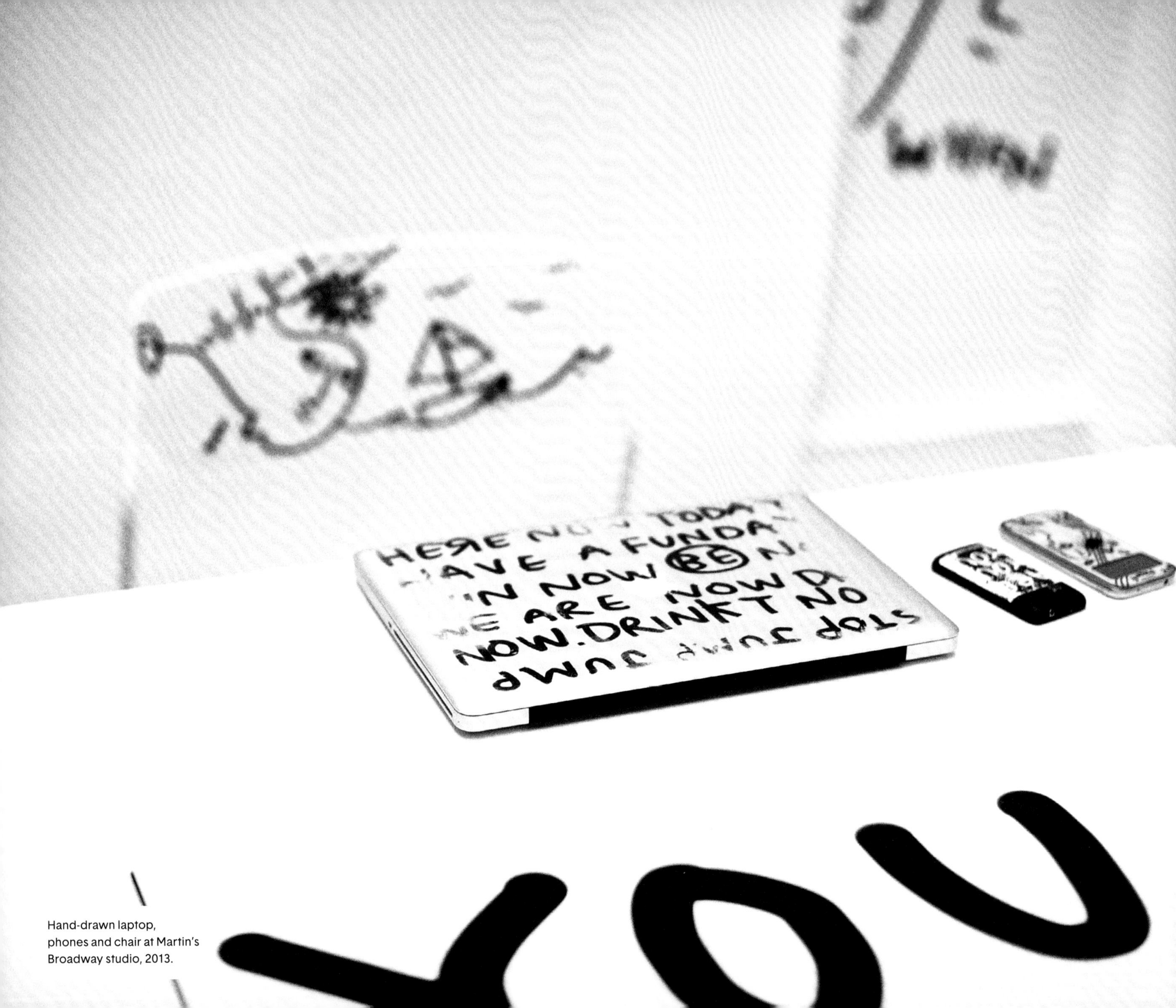

Hand-drawn laptop,
phones and chair at Martin's
Broadway studio, 2013.

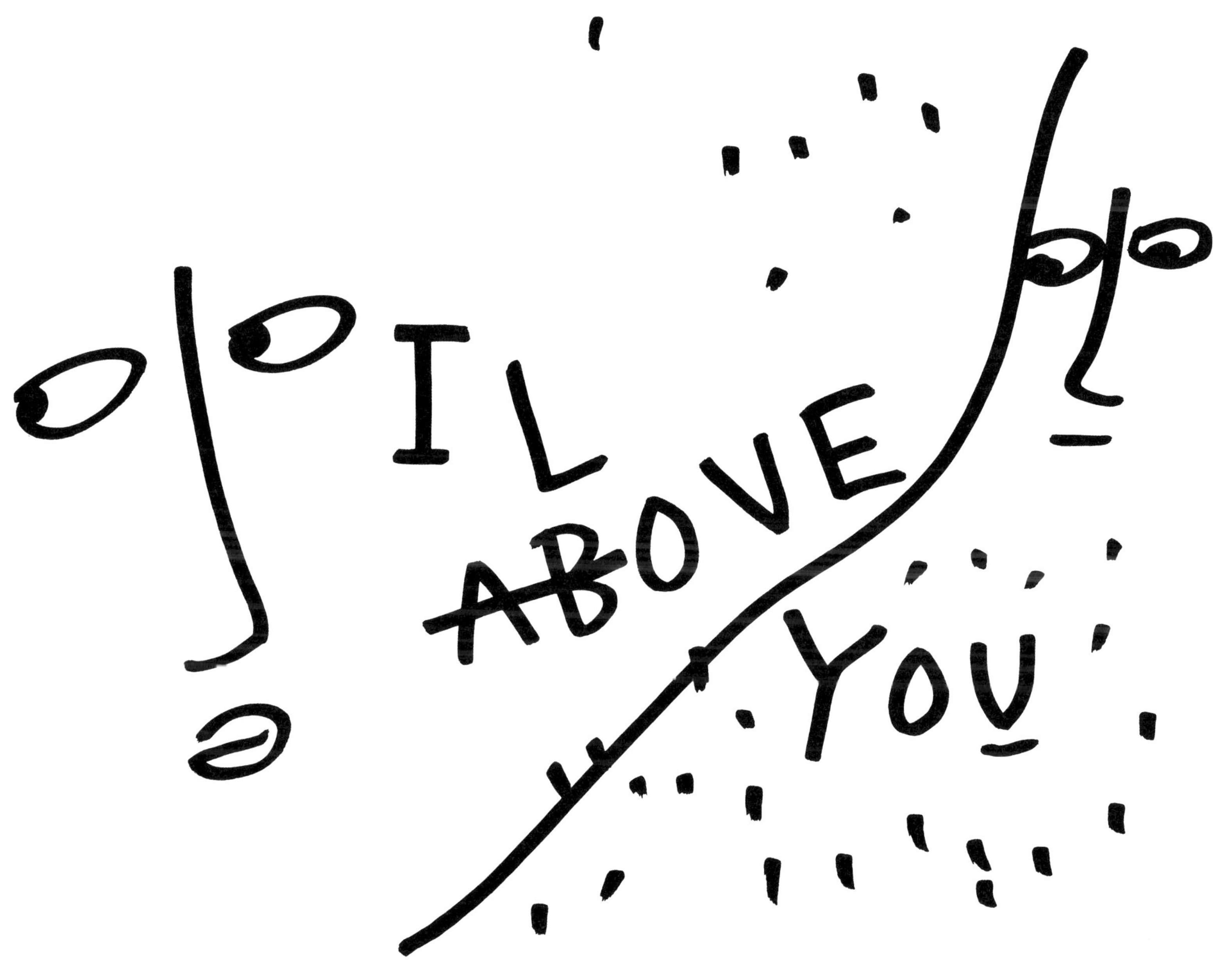

I Love You, 2014.
Ink on paper.

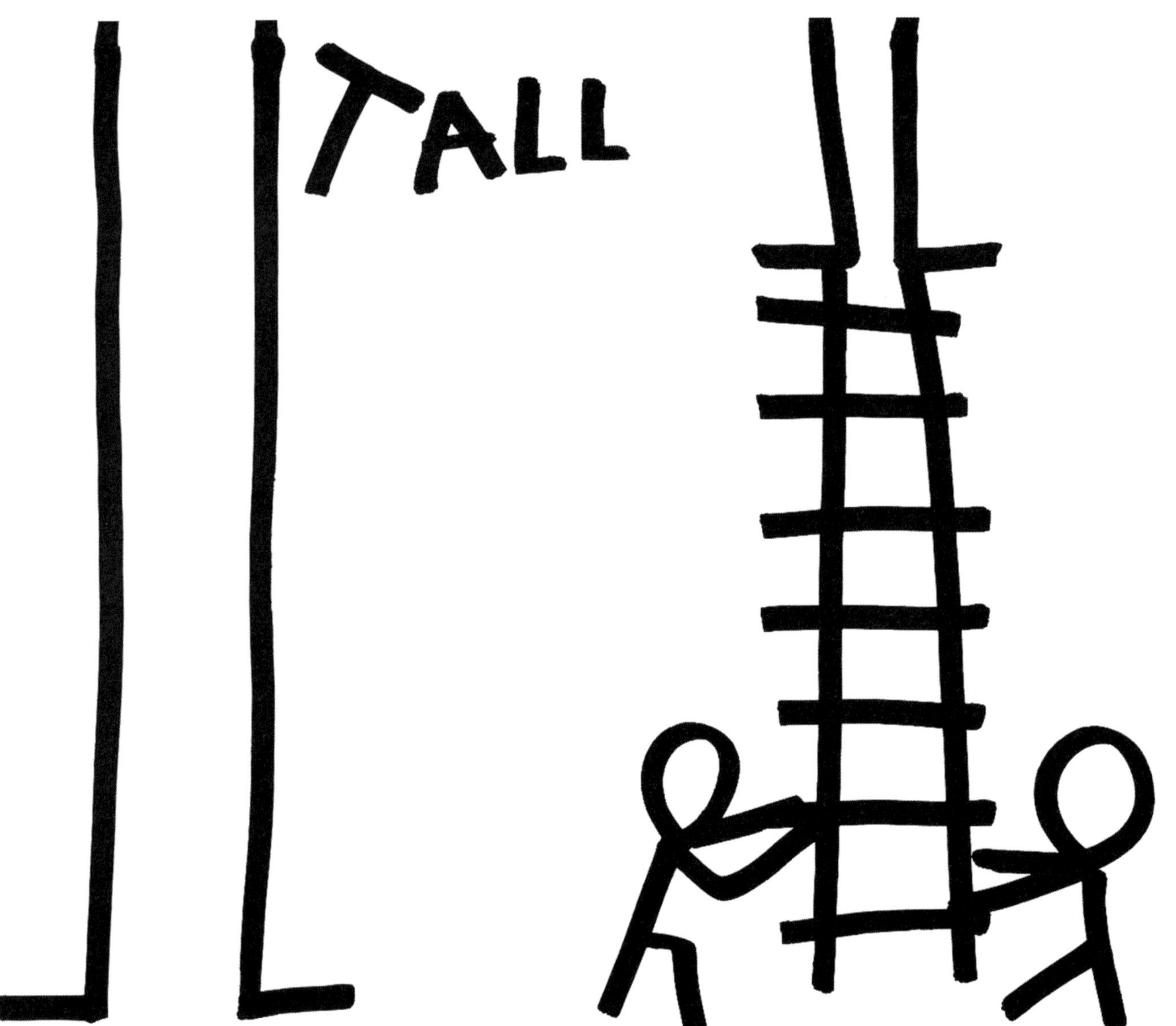

Tall, 2013.
Ink on paper.

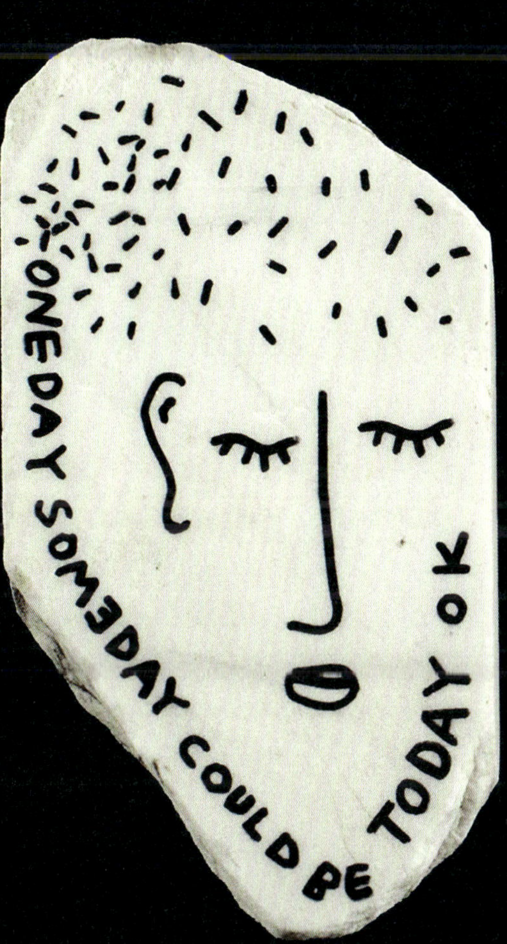

ONE DAY SOMEDAY COULD BE TODAY OK

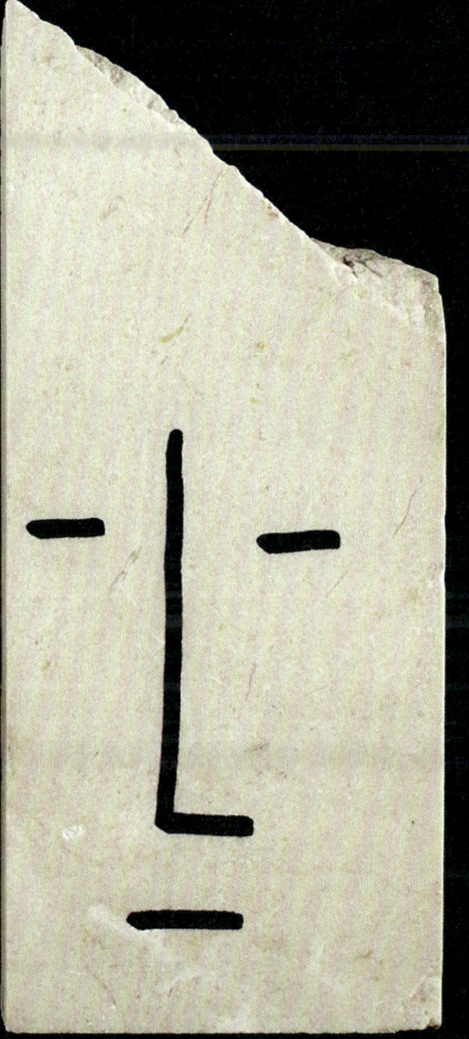

Left: *Marble Head: One Day Someday Could Be Today*, 2013.
Right: *Marble Head: Closed Eyes*, 2013. Ink on found marble.

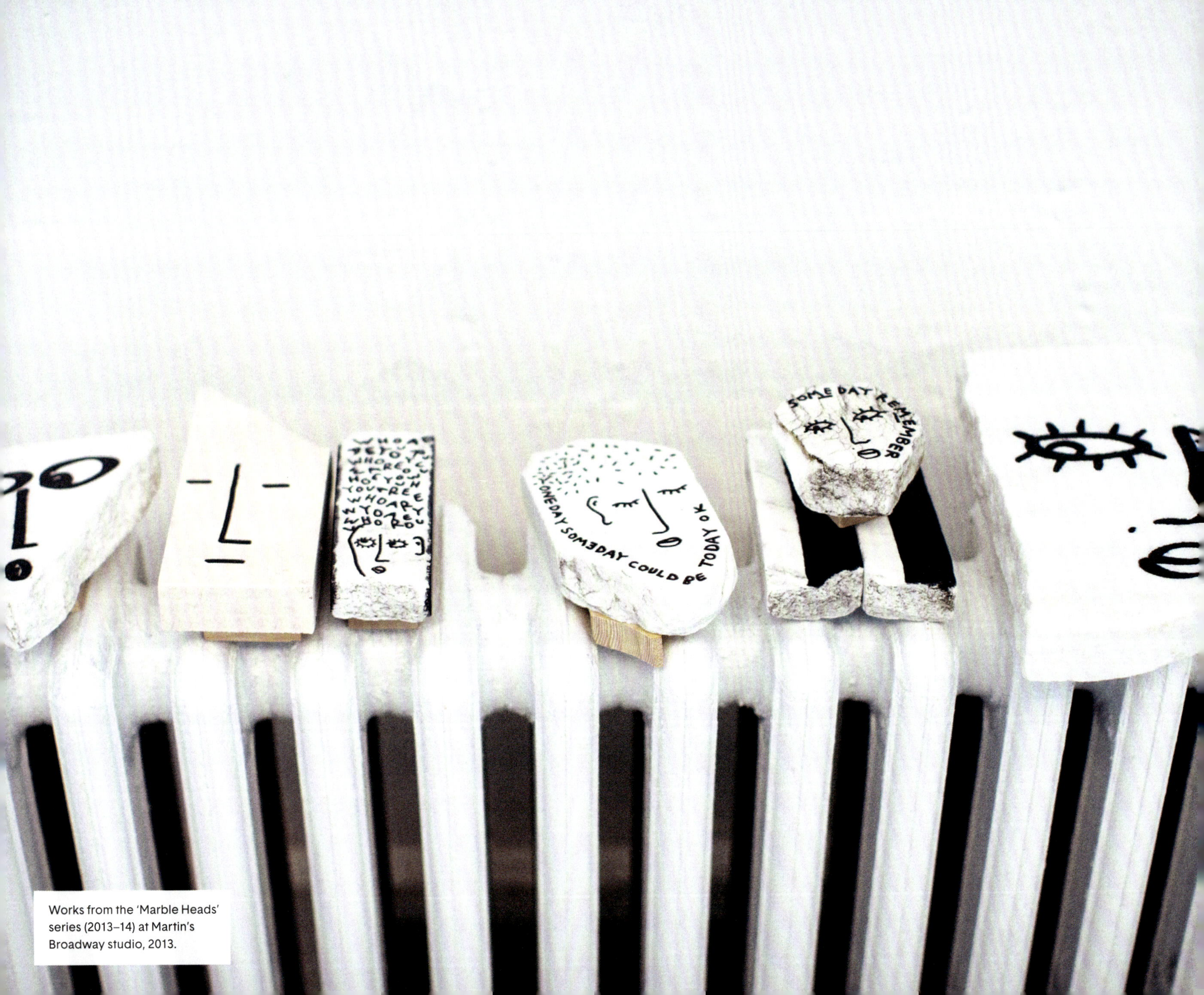

Works from the 'Marble Heads' series (2013–14) at Martin's Broadway studio, 2013.

WHY NOW
WHY HOW
WHY YOU
WHY HERE
WHY BE
WHY ME

WHY SEA
WHY NEED
YOU ME

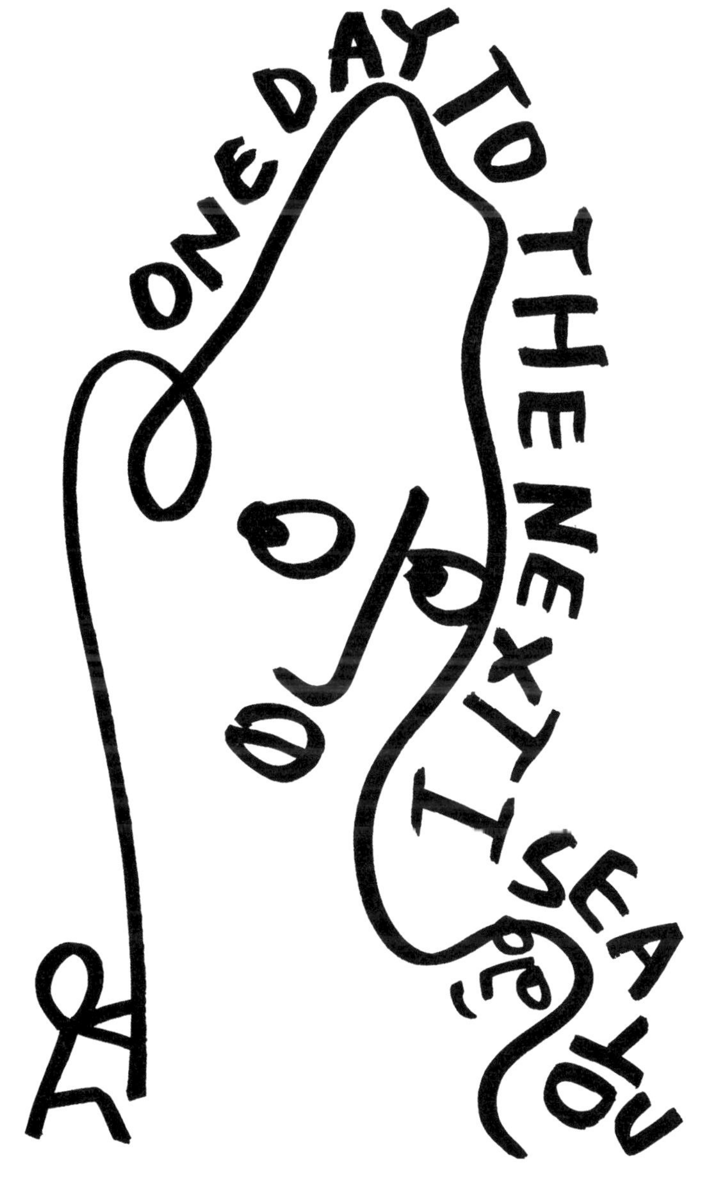

Left: *Why Now*, 2013.
Right: *One Day to the Next*,
2014. Ink on paper.

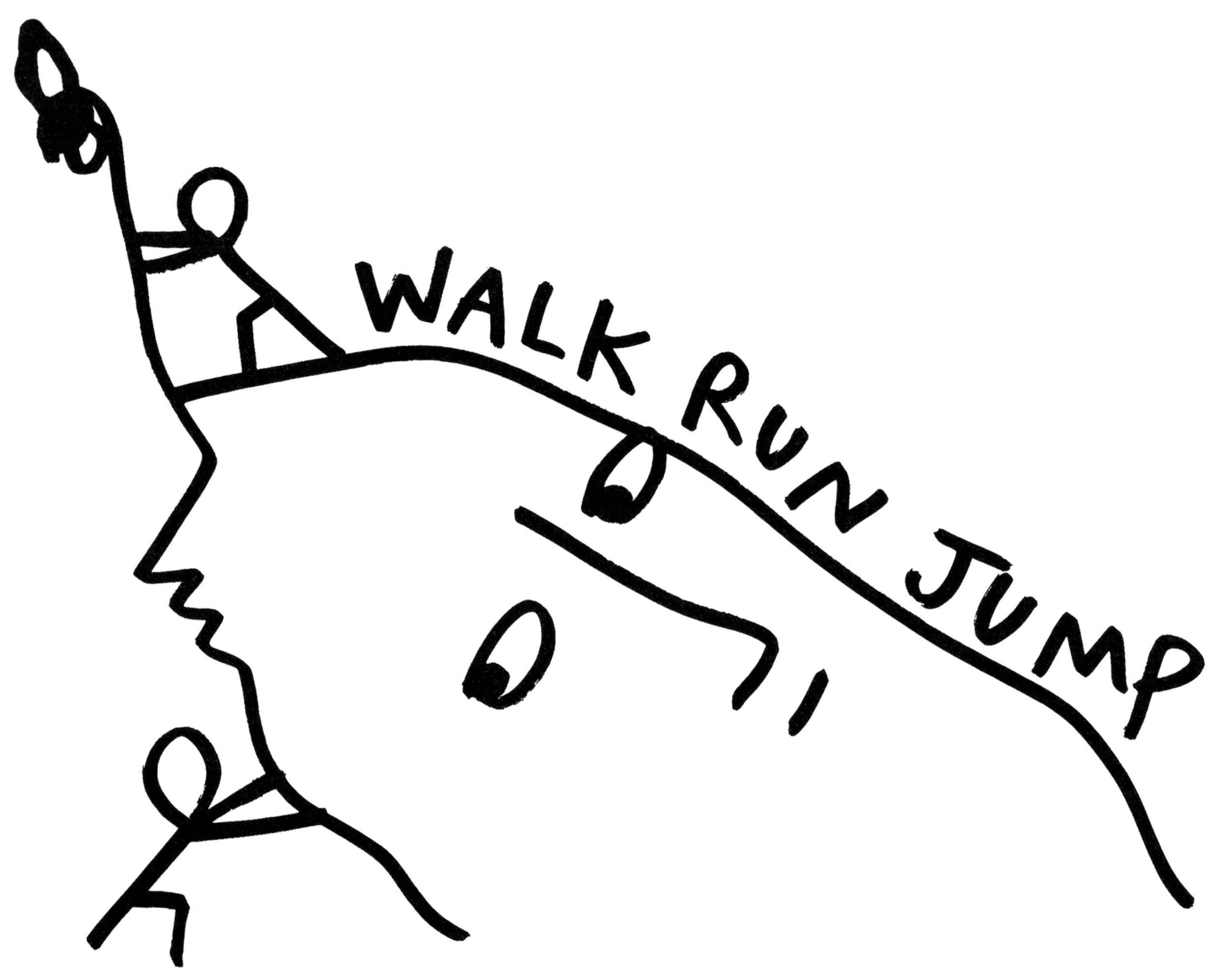

Walk Run Jump, 2014.
Ink on paper.

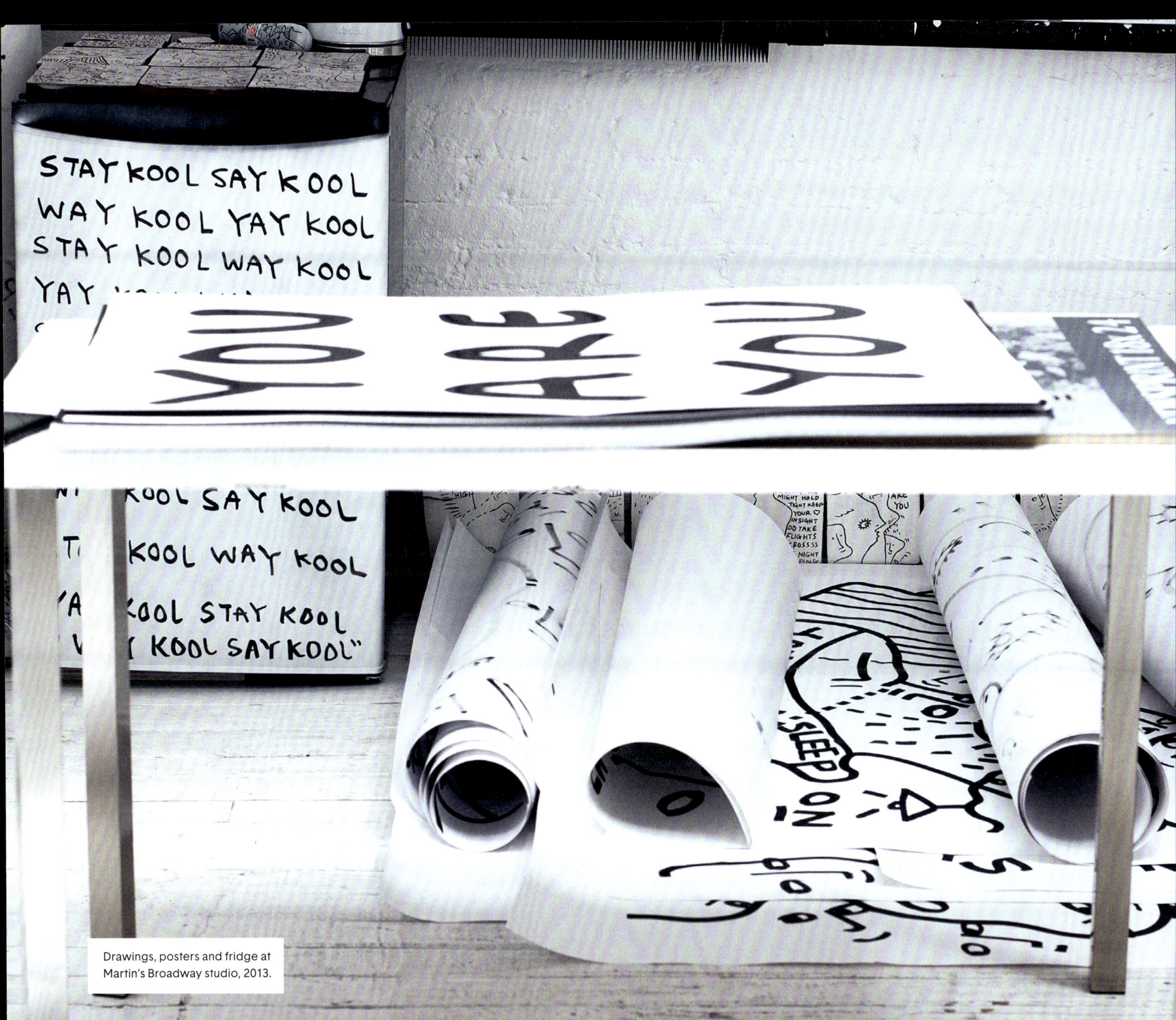

Drawings, posters and fridge at
Martin's Broadway studio, 2013.

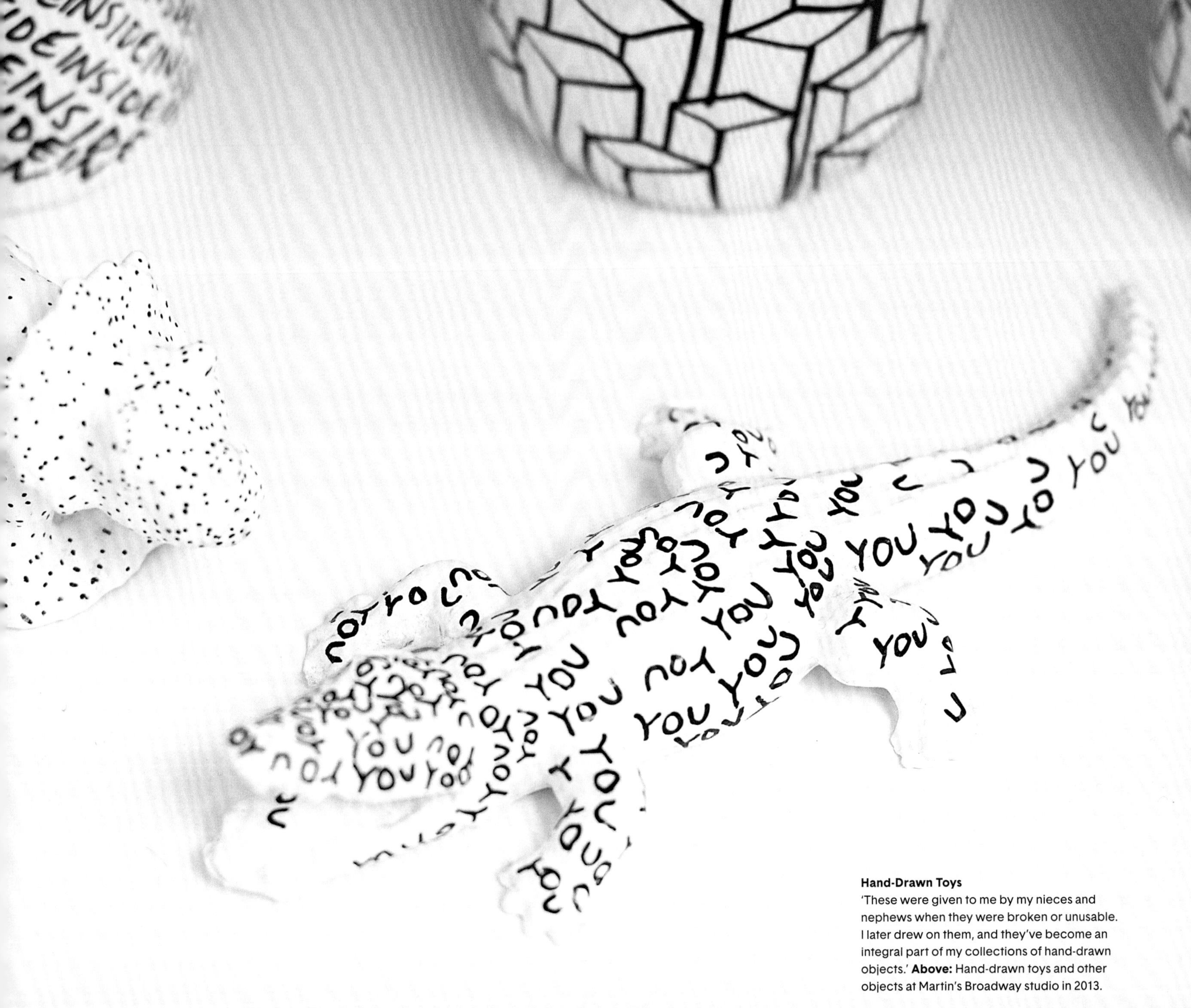

Hand-Drawn Toys
'These were given to me by my nieces and nephews when they were broken or unusable. I later drew on them, and they've become an integral part of my collections of hand-drawn objects.' **Above:** Hand-drawn toys and other objects at Martin's Broadway studio in 2013.

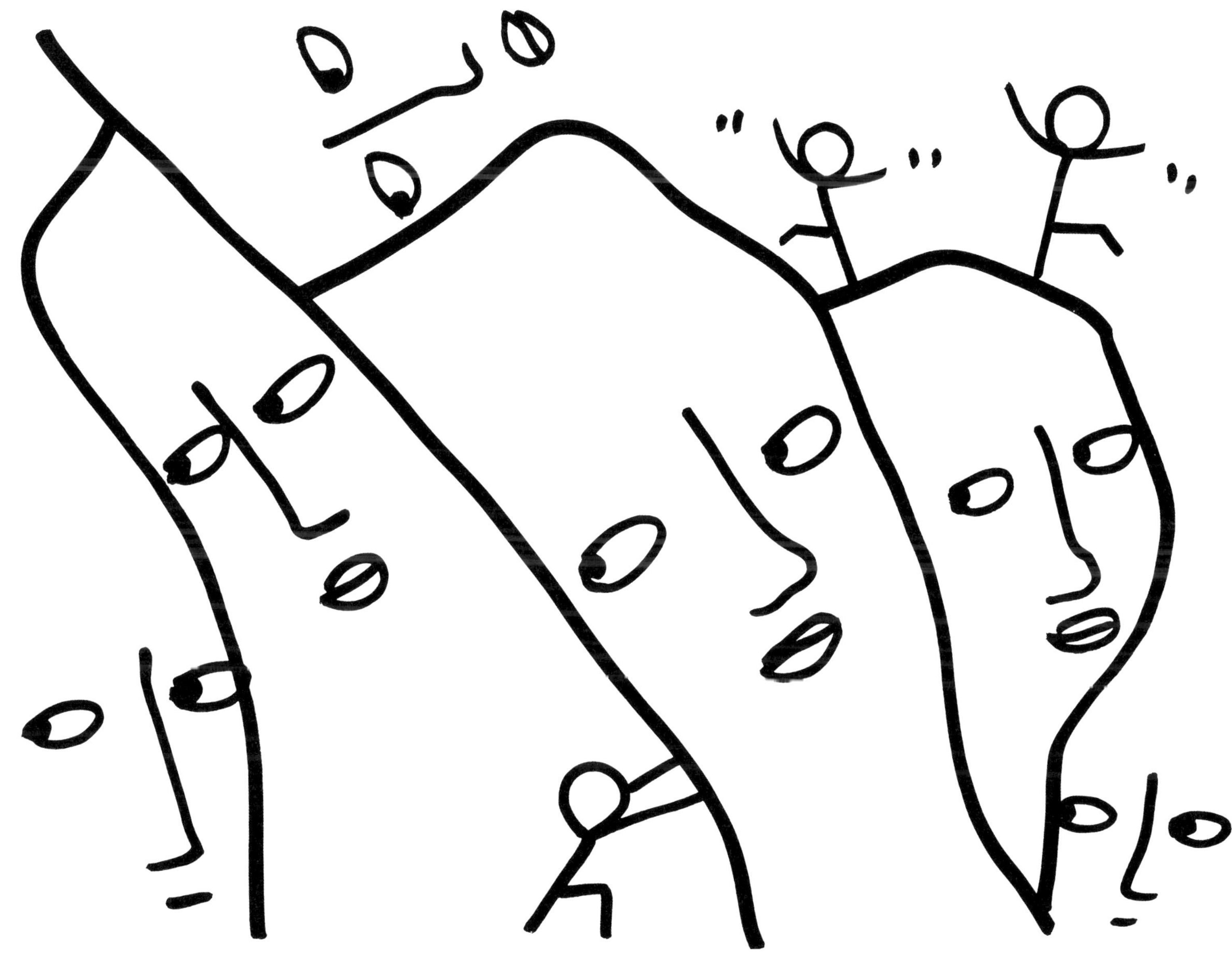

Six Faces, 2012.
Ink on paper.

All You, 2013.
Ink on vellum.

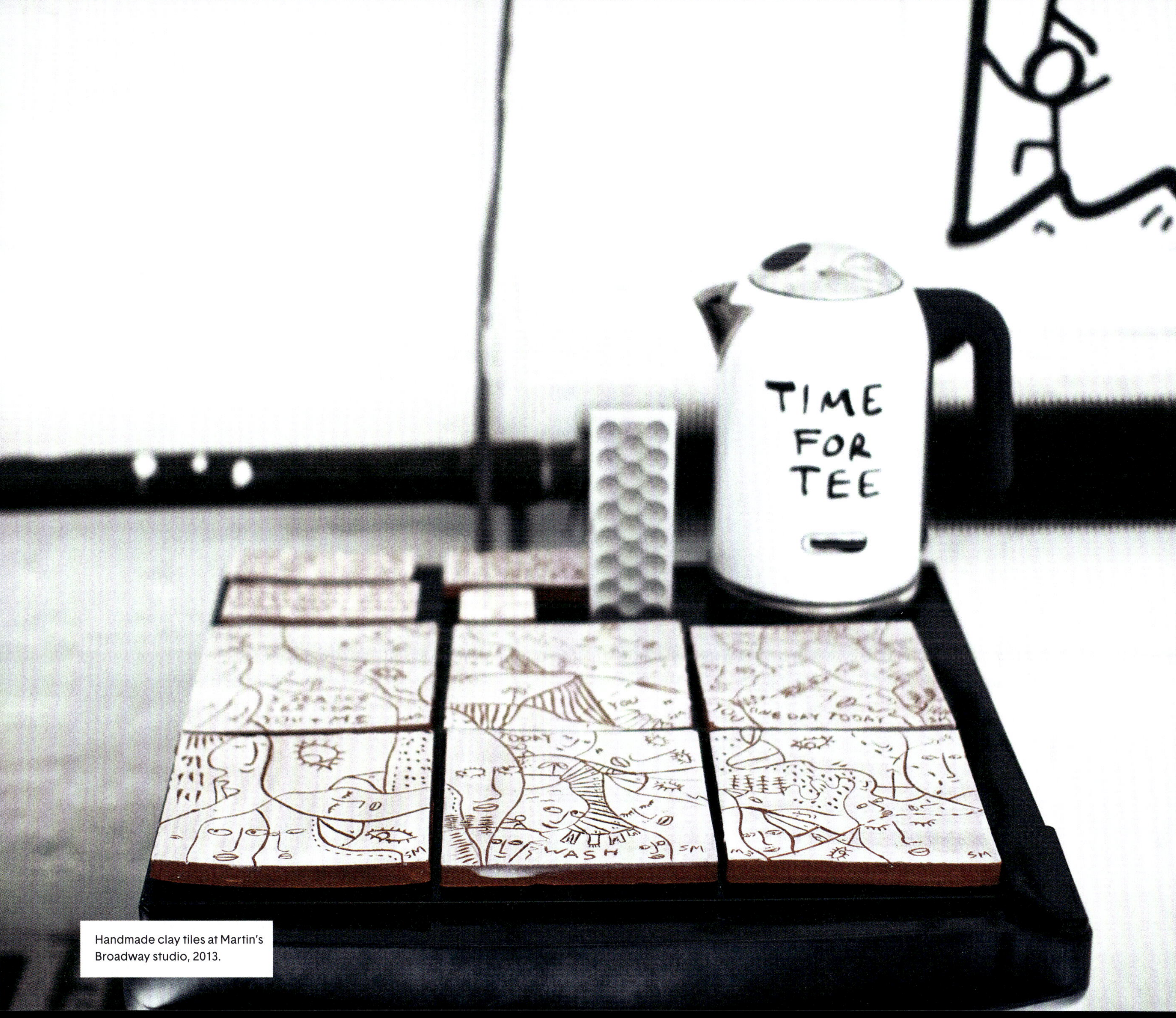

Handmade clay tiles at Martin's Broadway studio, 2013.

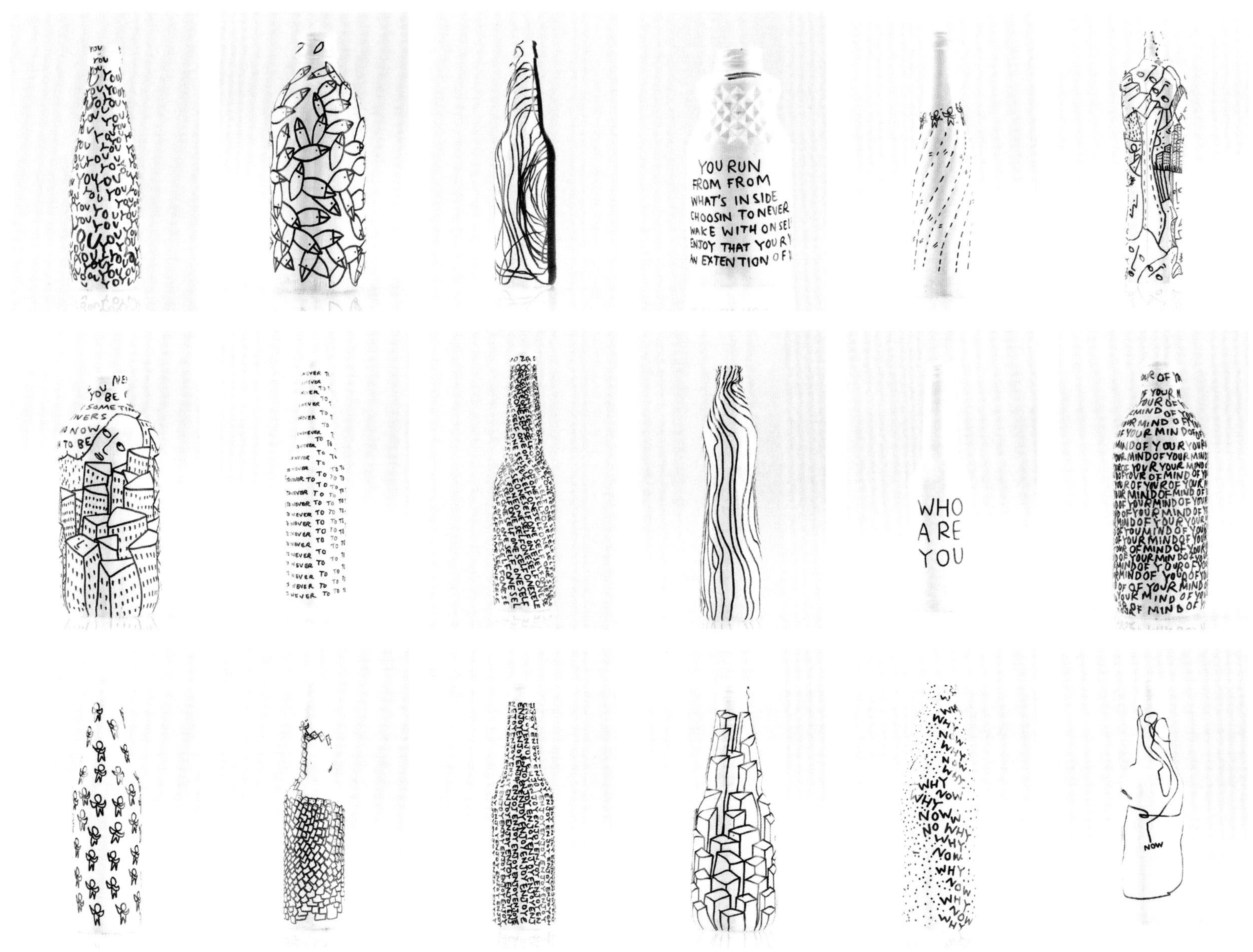

Above: Hand-drawn bottles,
2012–13. Ink and gesso on glass.
Opposite: Hand-drawn toys, 2012.
Ink and gesso on plastic.

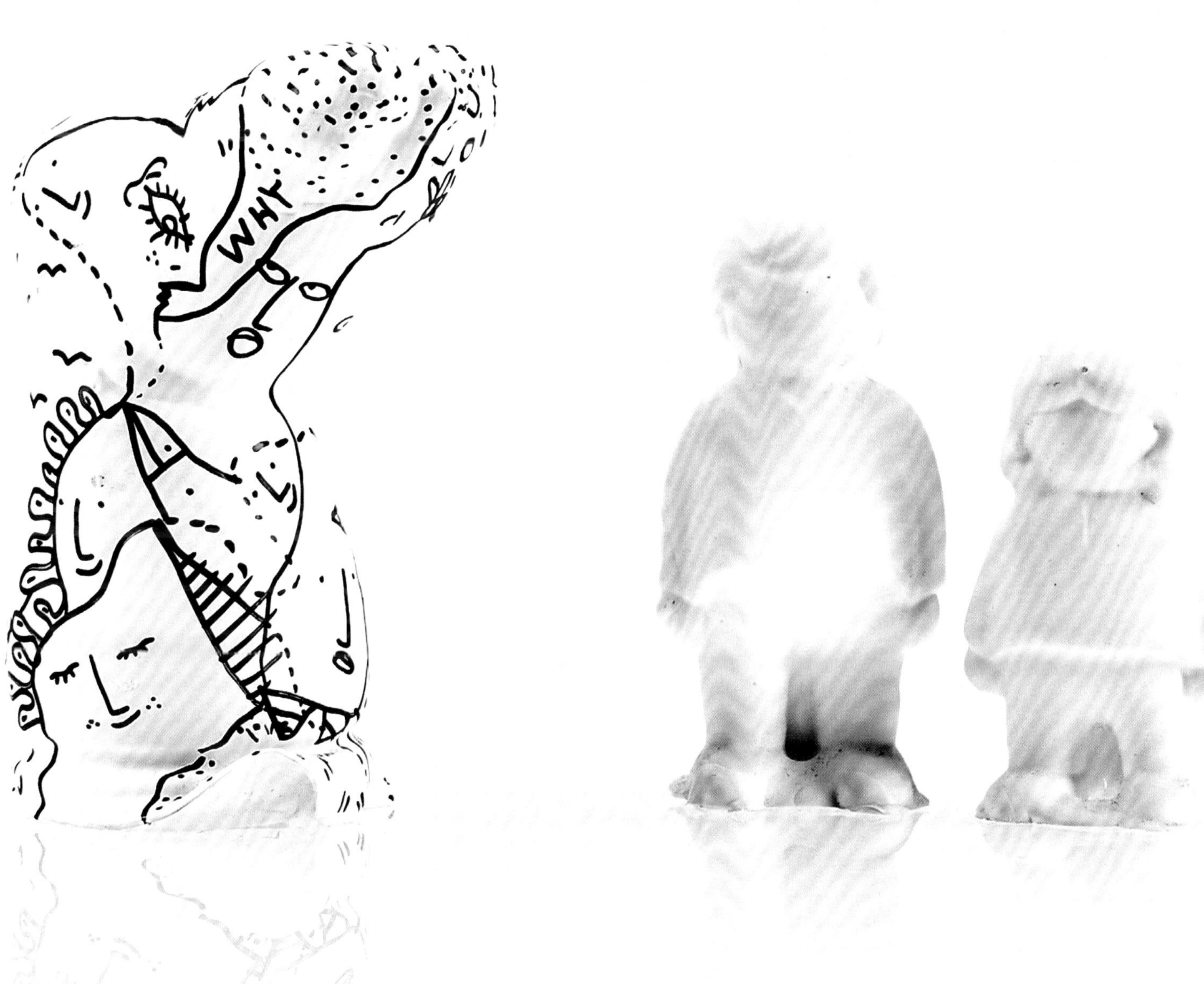

WHY

EAT WELL
DRINK WELL
HELP BUILD
CLEAN WELLS

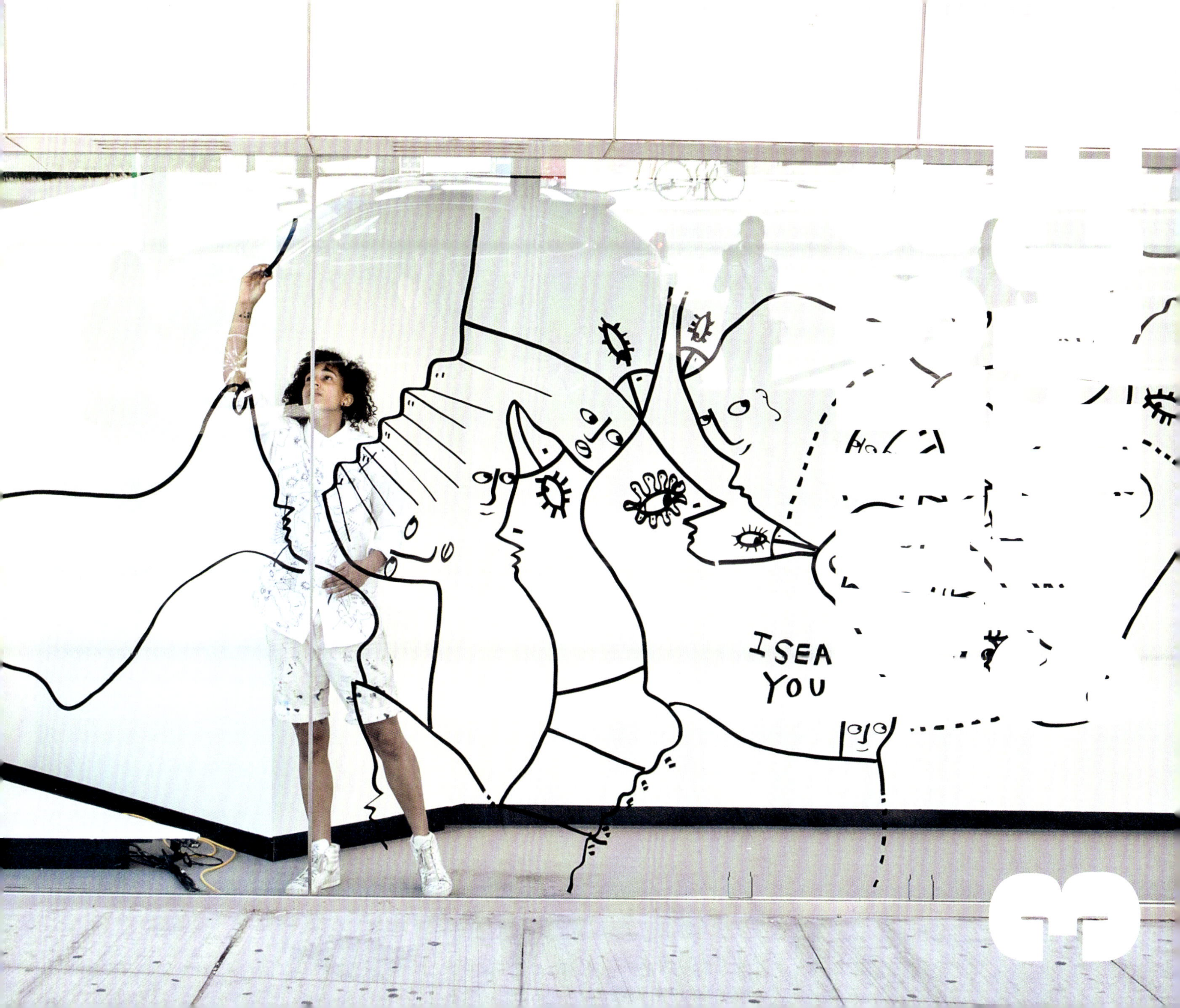
I SEA
YOU

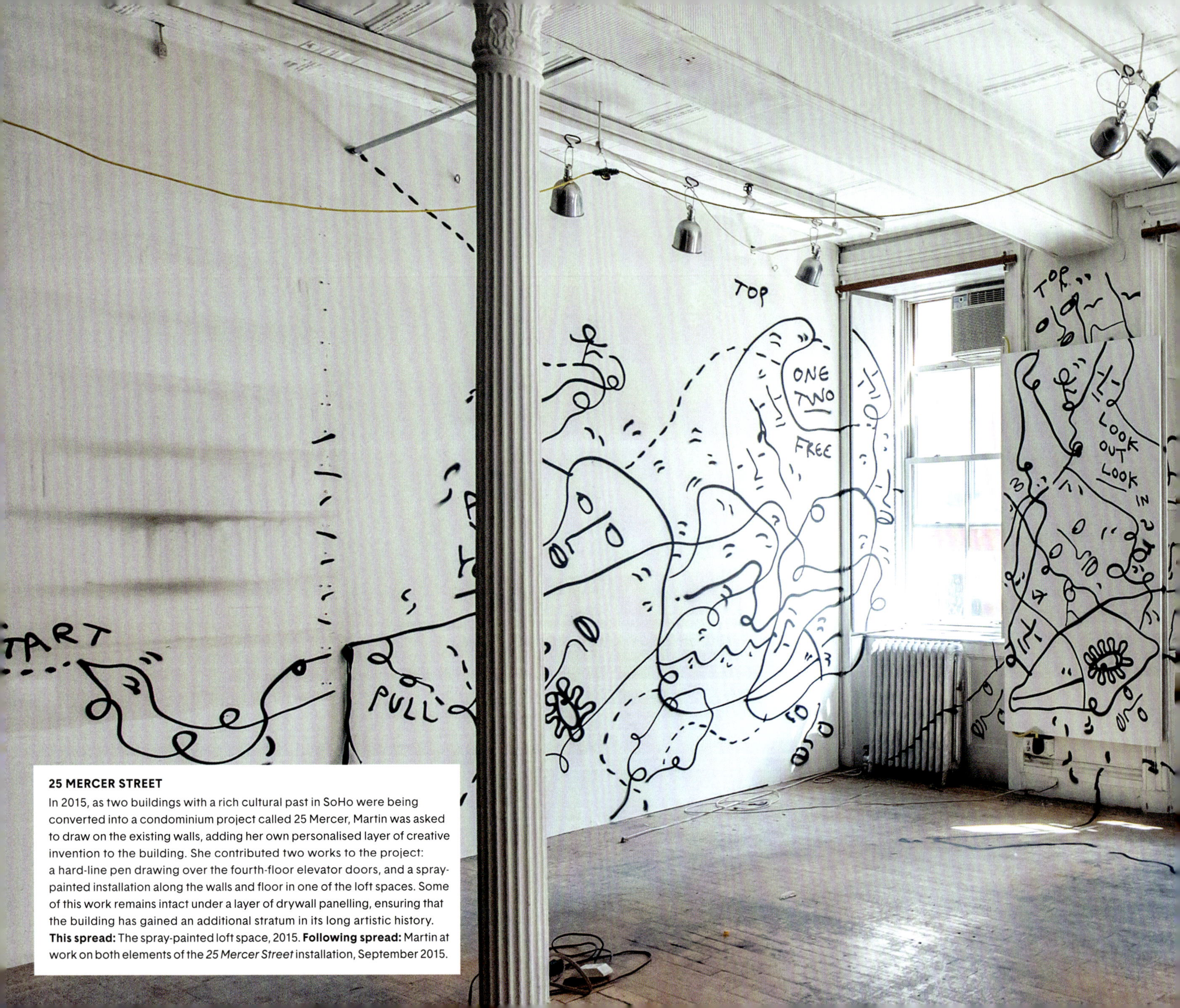

25 MERCER STREET

In 2015, as two buildings with a rich cultural past in SoHo were being converted into a condominium project called 25 Mercer, Martin was asked to draw on the existing walls, adding her own personalised layer of creative invention to the building. She contributed two works to the project: a hard-line pen drawing over the fourth-floor elevator doors, and a spray-painted installation along the walls and floor in one of the loft spaces. Some of this work remains intact under a layer of drywall panelling, ensuring that the building has gained an additional stratum in its long artistic history.
This spread: The spray-painted loft space, 2015. **Following spread:** Martin at work on both elements of the *25 Mercer Street* installation, September 2015.

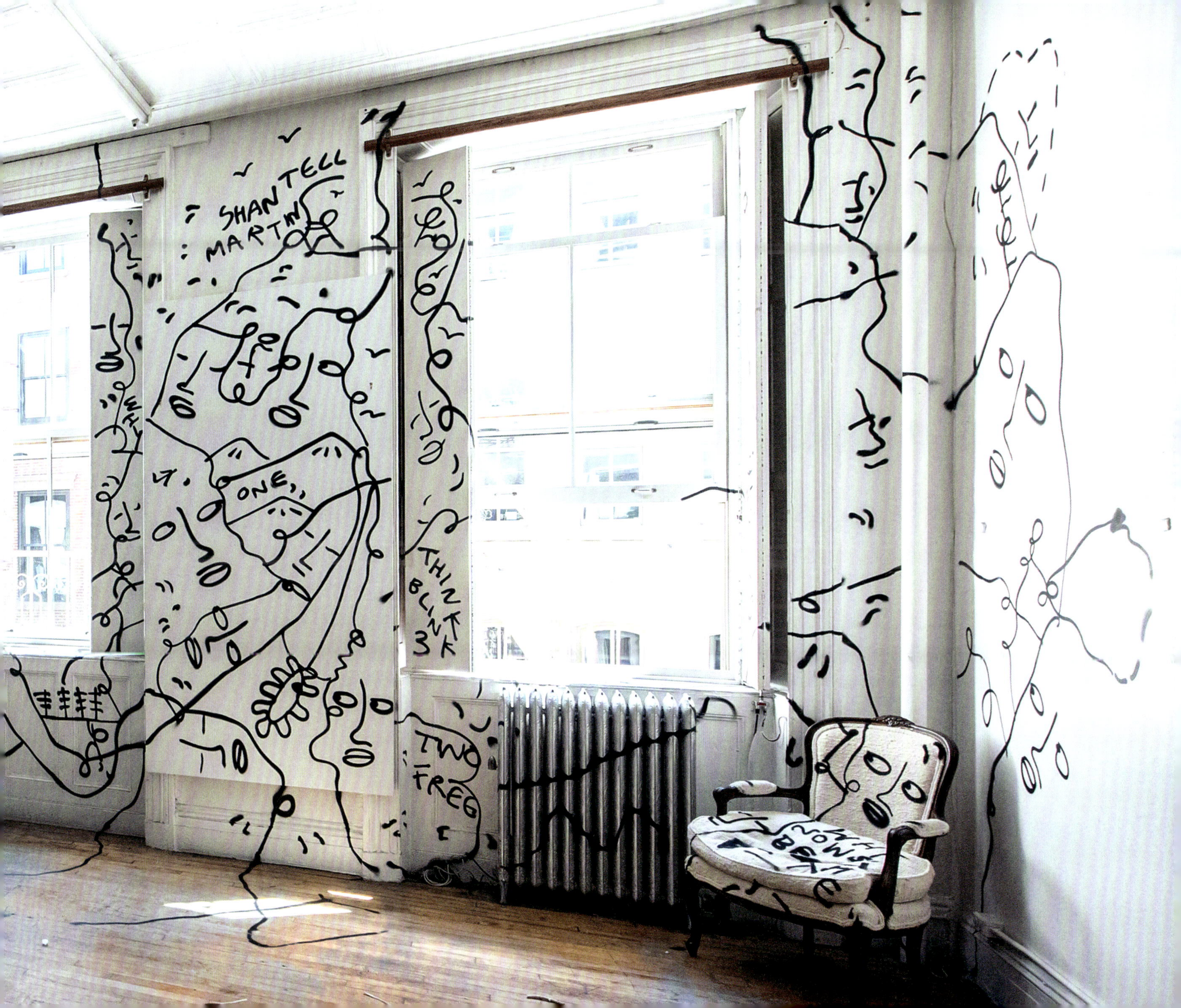

SHANTELL
MARTIN
ONE
THINK
BLINK
3
TWO
FREG

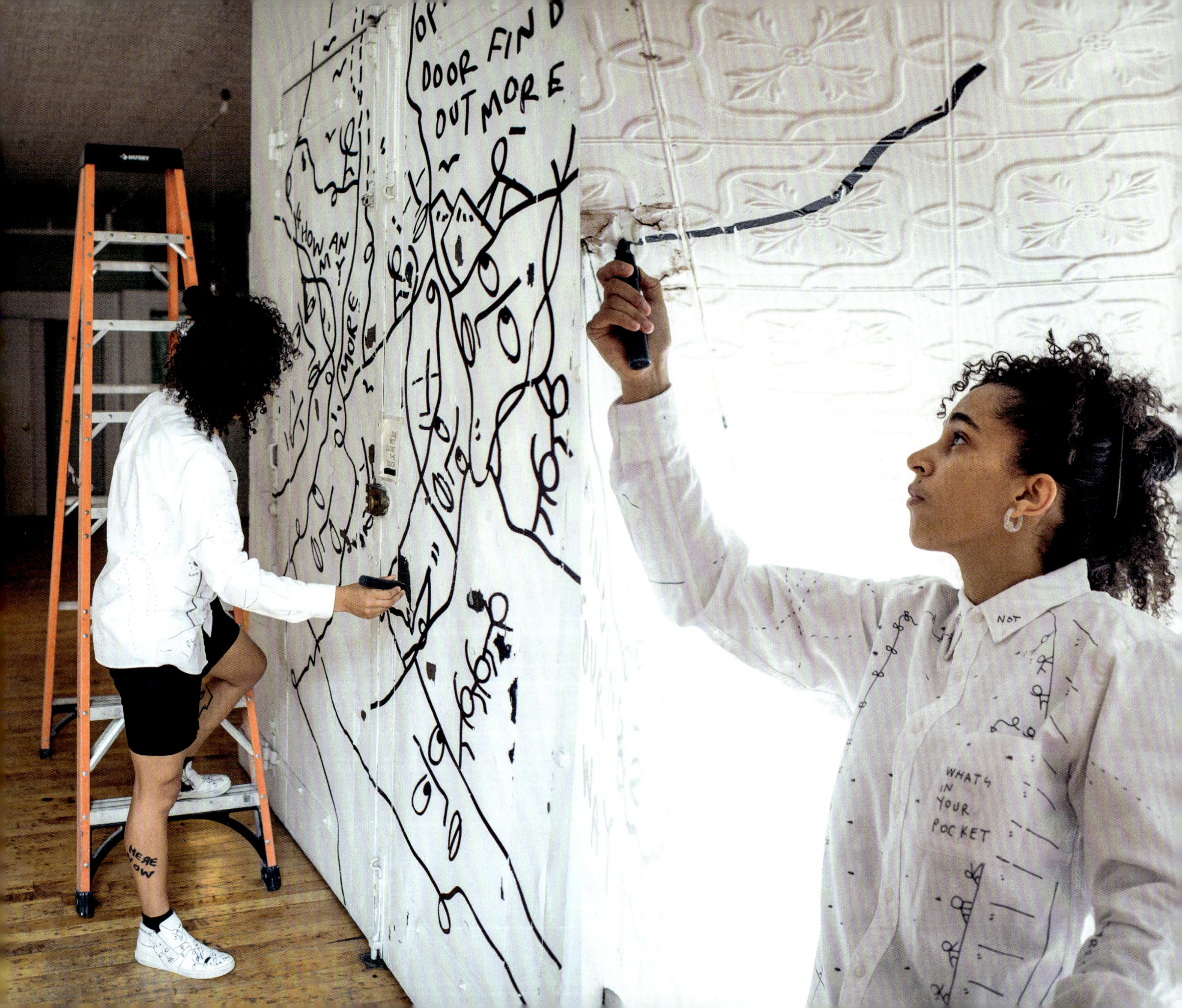
DOOR FIN D
OUT MORE
HOW MANY
MORE
WHATS
IN
YOUR
POCKET
NOT
HERE
NOW

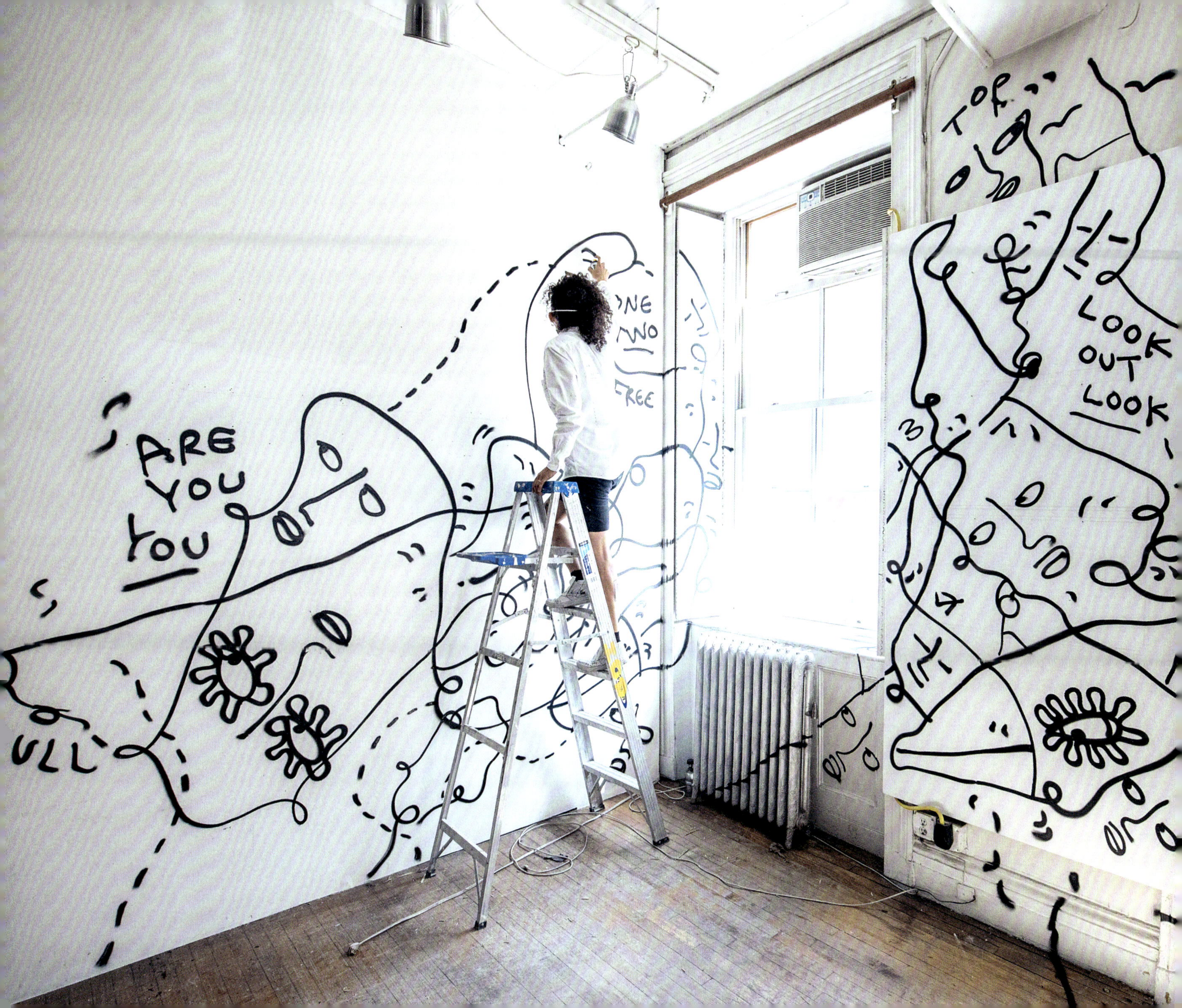

ARE
YOU
YOU
ULL
ONE TWO
FREE
TOP
LOOK
OUT
LOOK

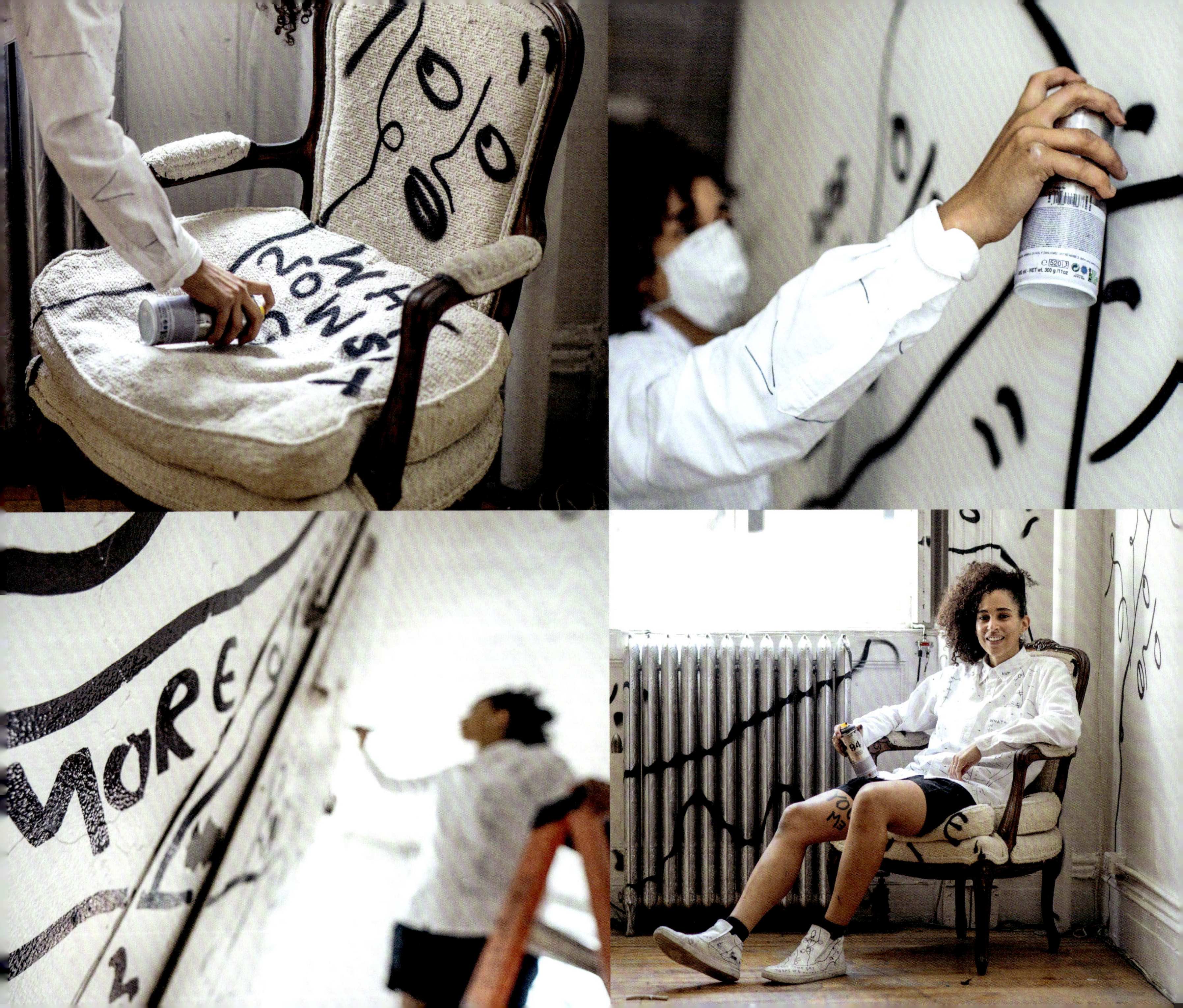

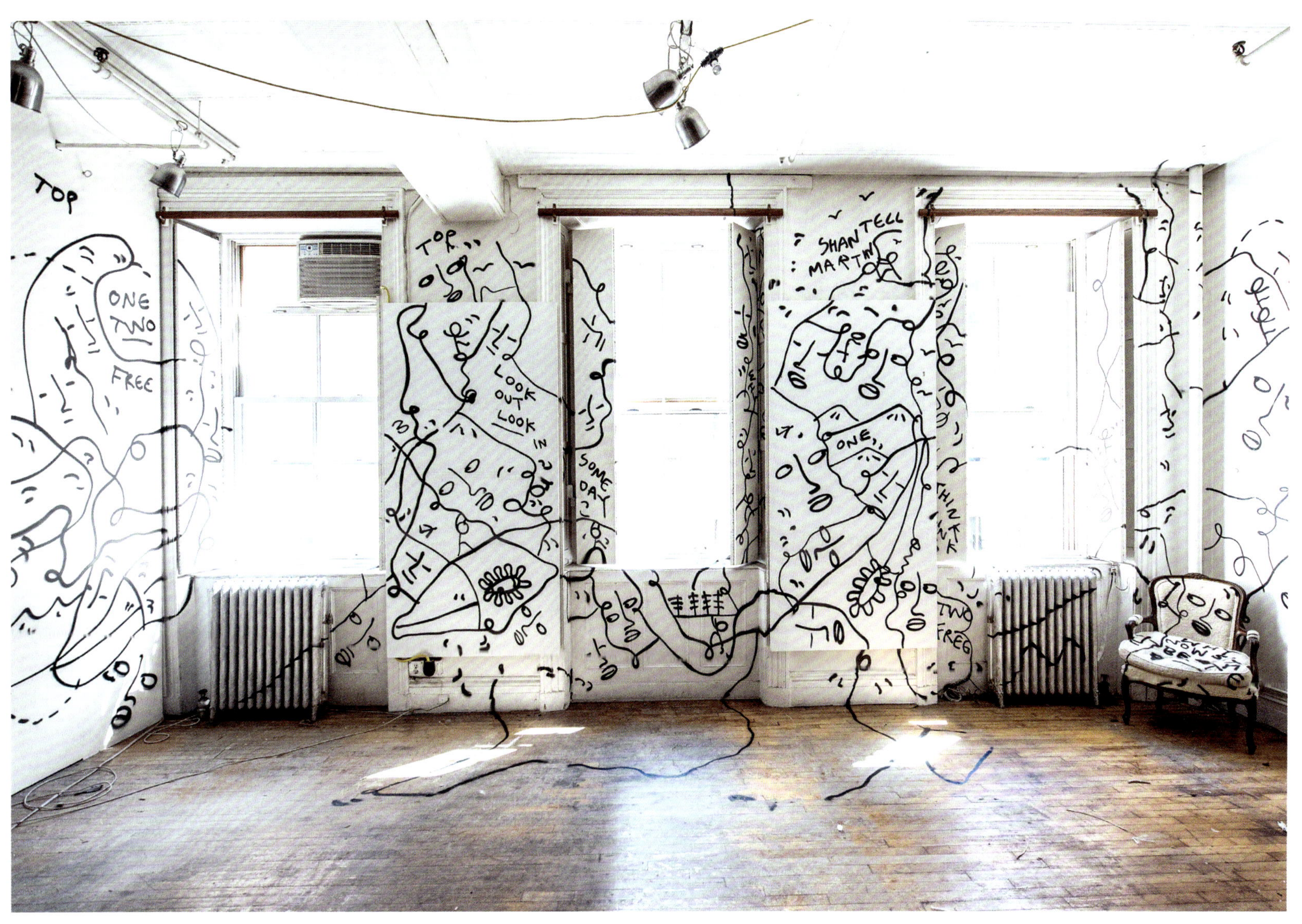

Above: The completed loft for *25 Mercer Street*, Soho, New York, 2015. **Opposite:** Martin at work on the installation in September 2015.

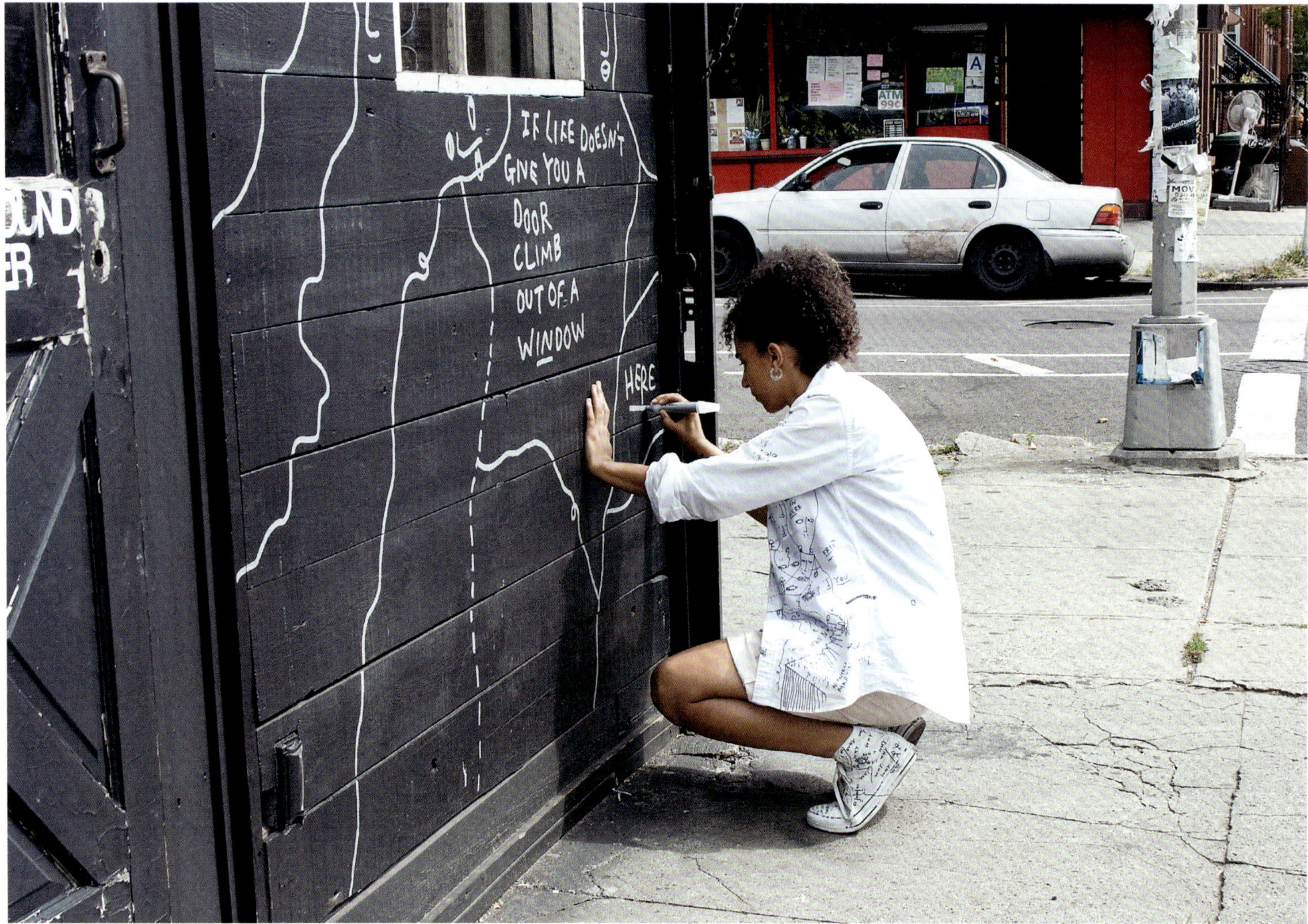

SARAGHINA

In 2013, Martin was commissioned by Edoardo Mantelli, the owner of Saraghina – one of the best pizza places in the up-and-coming Bed-Stuy neighbourhood of Brooklyn – to appropriate its black-painted wooden exterior as a canvas. The resulting mural in silver marker became something of a local icon, acting as Martin's homage to Brooklyn, where she used to live and work. Inscribed underneath a window on one of the building's flanks, one of her pithy insights – 'If life doesn't open a door, climb out of a window' – is still visible. **This spread and following spread:** Martin drawing on the facade of Saraghina, Brooklyn, in September 2013.

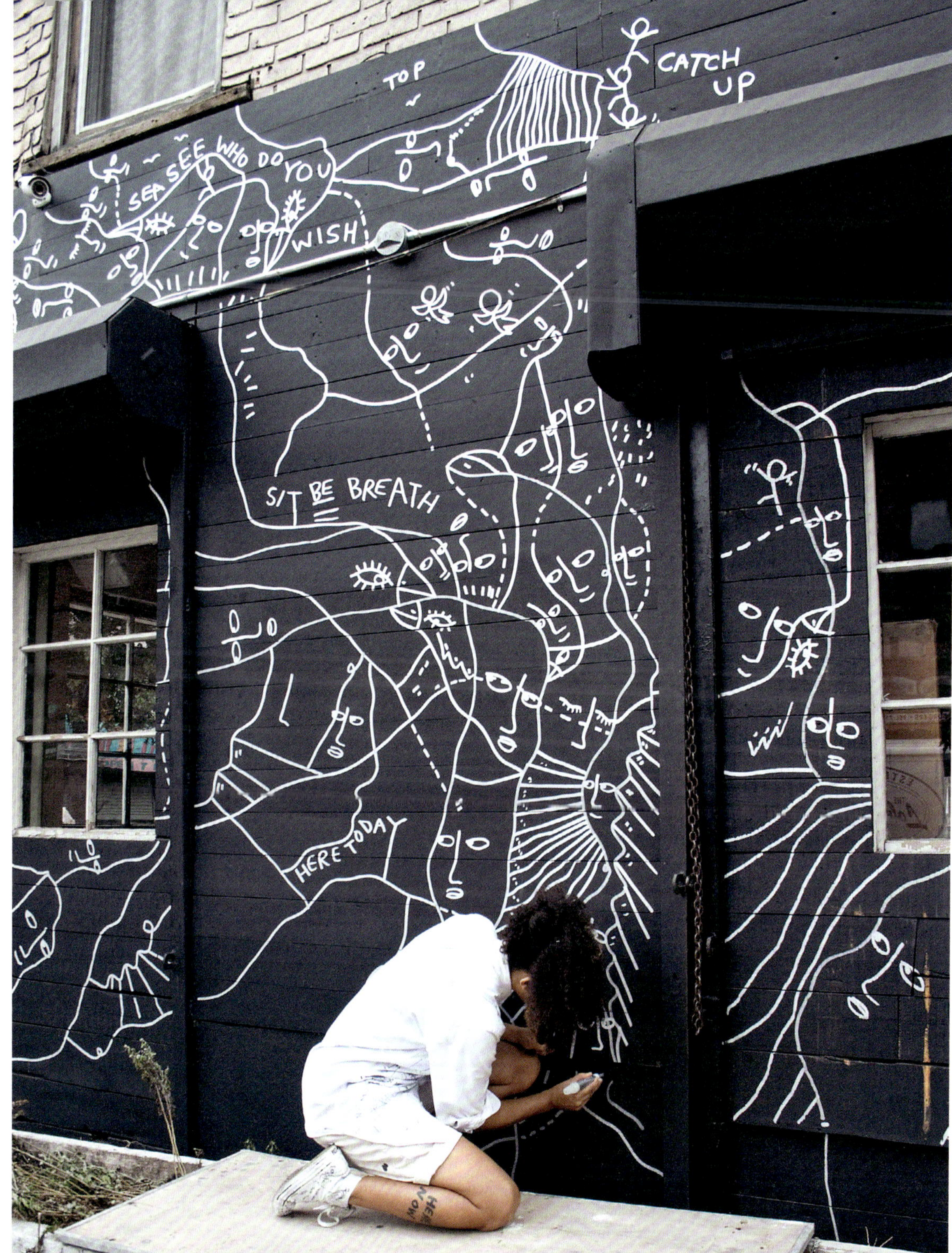
TOP
CATCH UP
SEA SEE WHO DO YOU
WISH
SIT BE BREATH
HERE TODAY

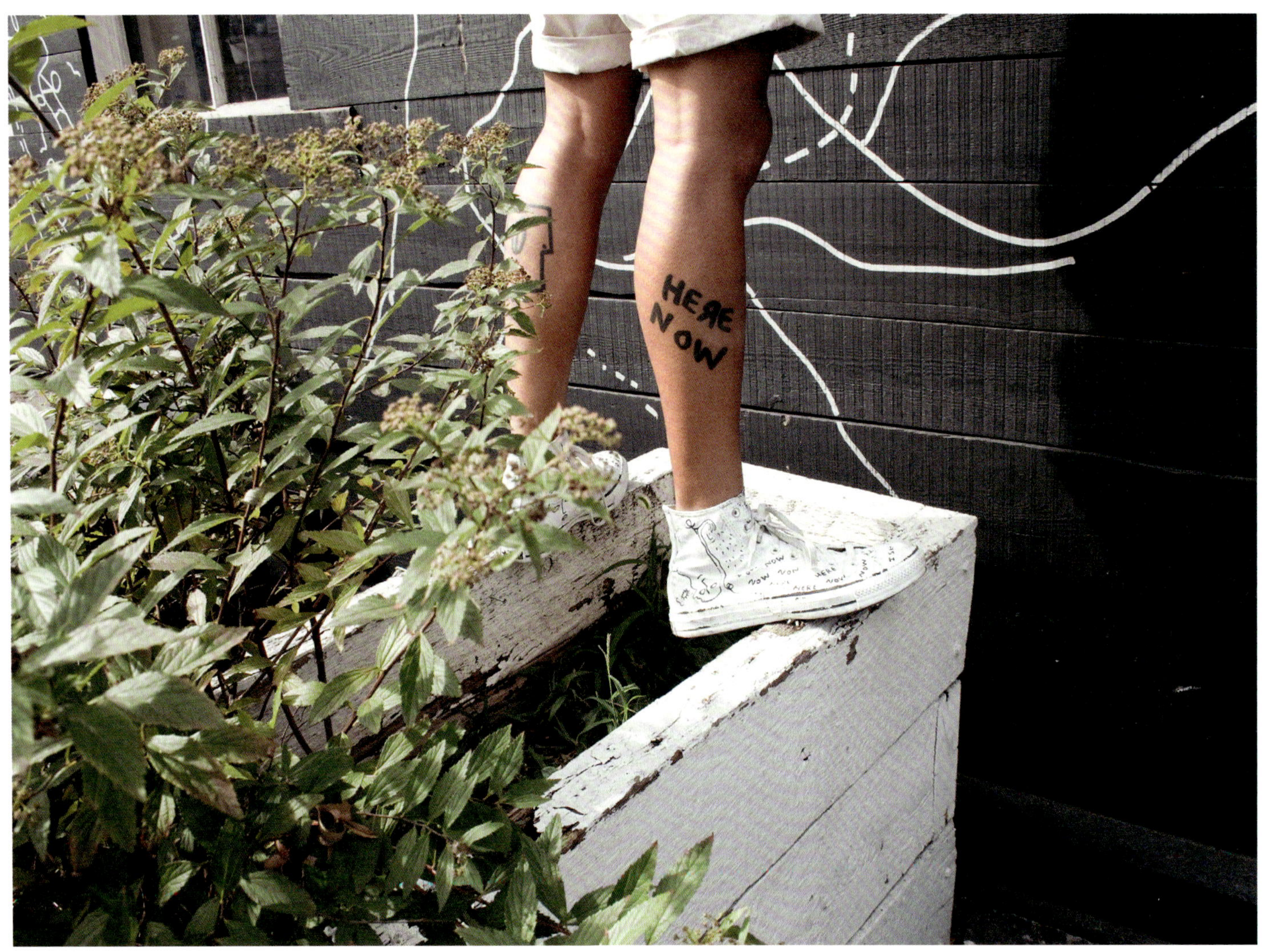

HEяE
N OW

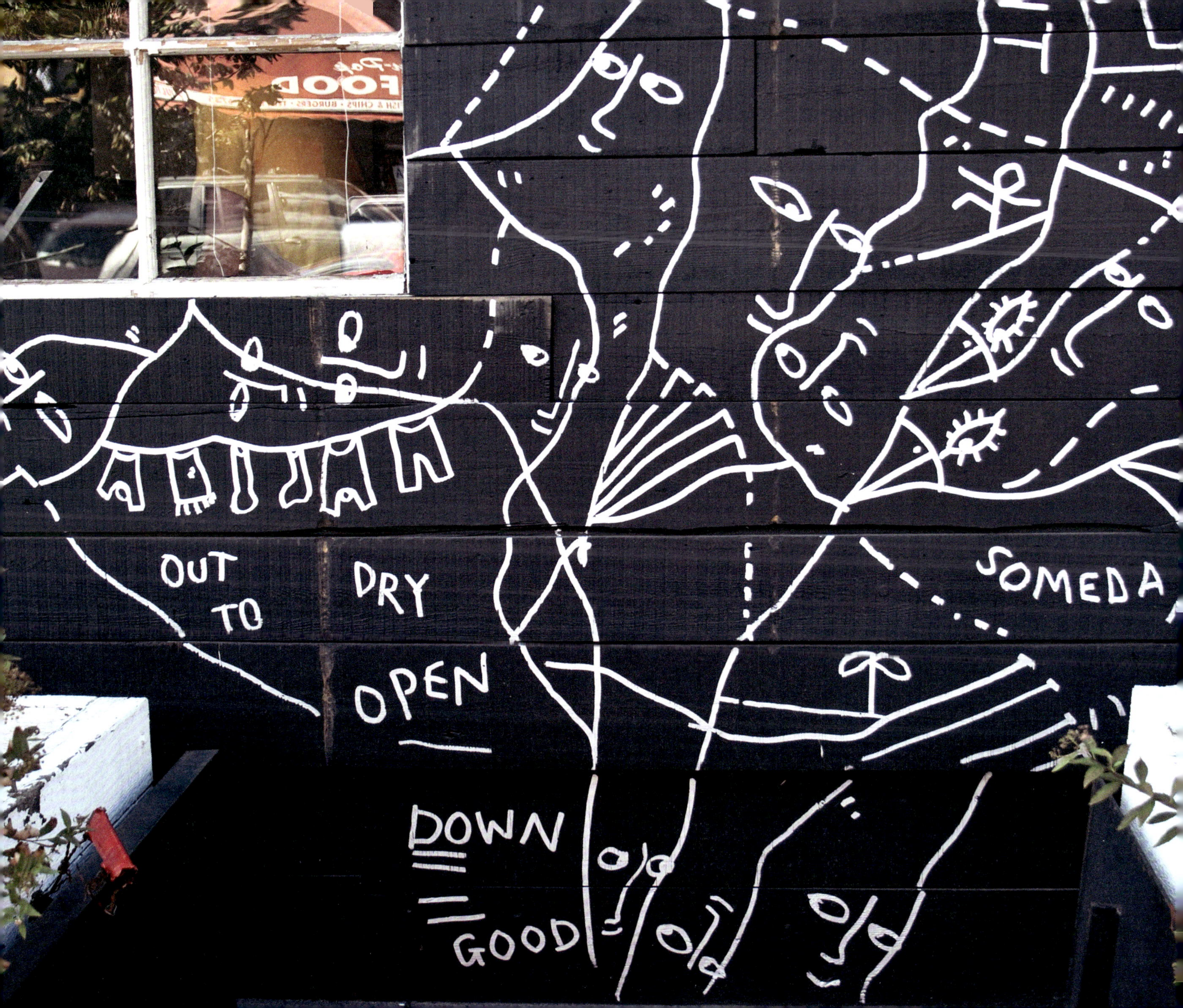
FOOD
OUT TO DRY
SOMEDA
OPEN
DOWN
GOOD

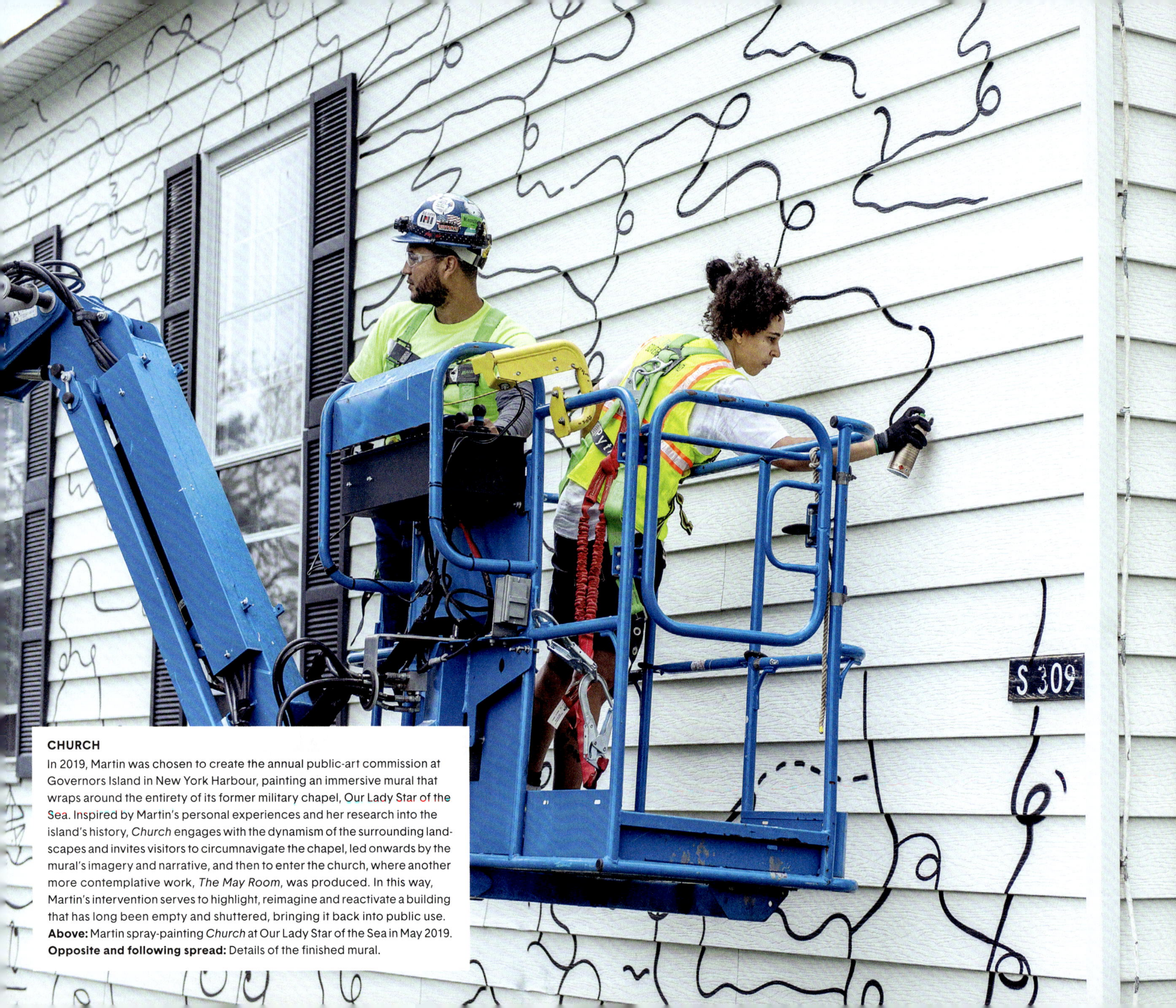

CHURCH

In 2019, Martin was chosen to create the annual public-art commission at Governors Island in New York Harbour, painting an immersive mural that wraps around the entirety of its former military chapel, Our Lady Star of the Sea. Inspired by Martin's personal experiences and her research into the island's history, *Church* engages with the dynamism of the surrounding landscapes and invites visitors to circumnavigate the chapel, led onwards by the mural's imagery and narrative, and then to enter the church, where another more contemplative work, *The May Room*, was produced. In this way, Martin's intervention serves to highlight, reimagine and reactivate a building that has long been empty and shuttered, bringing it back into public use.
Above: Martin spray-painting *Church* at Our Lady Star of the Sea in May 2019.
Opposite and following spread: Details of the finished mural.

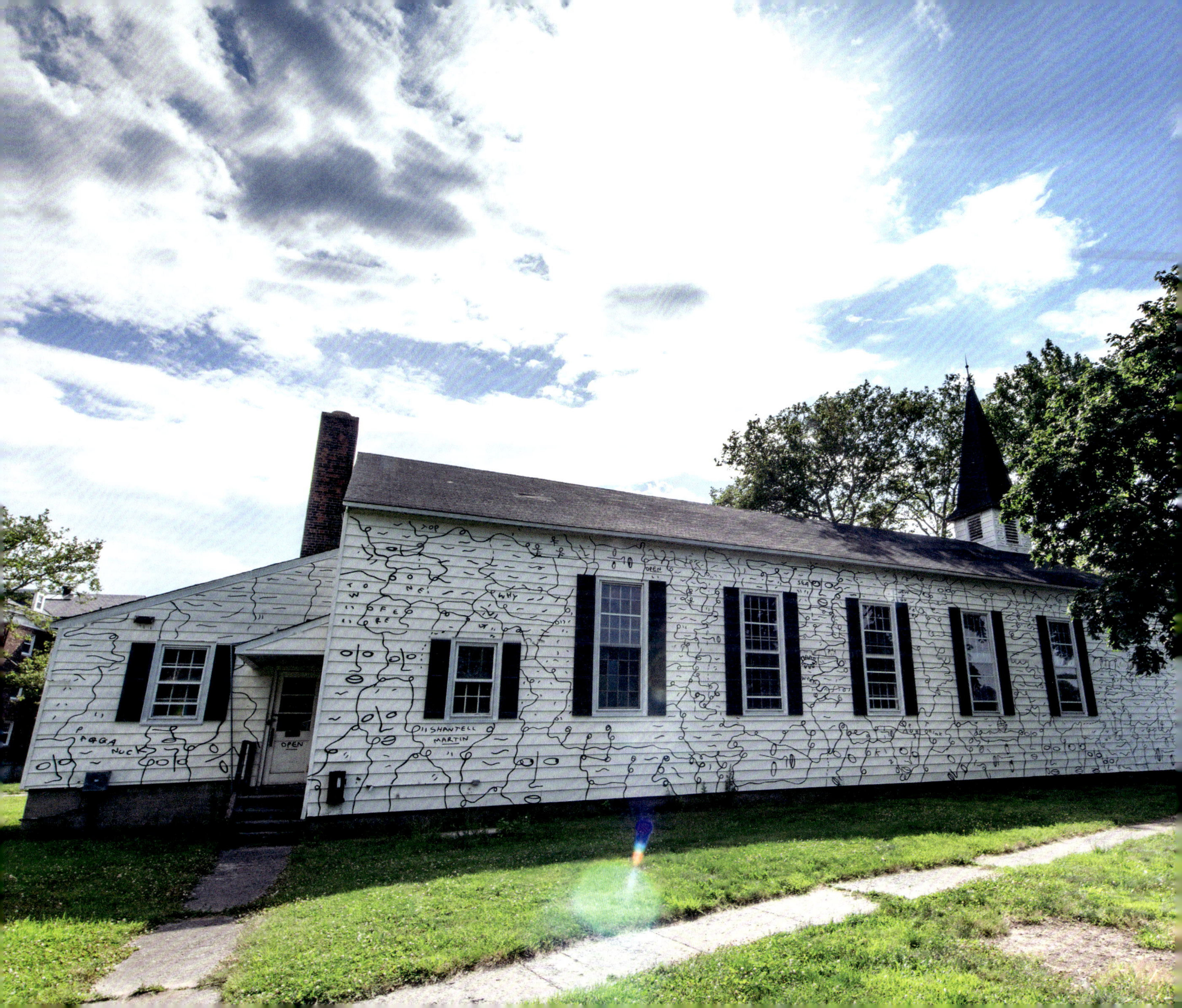
TOP
ONE
TWO
WHY
OPEN
OPEN
SHANTELL
MARTIN
PAGA
NUCK

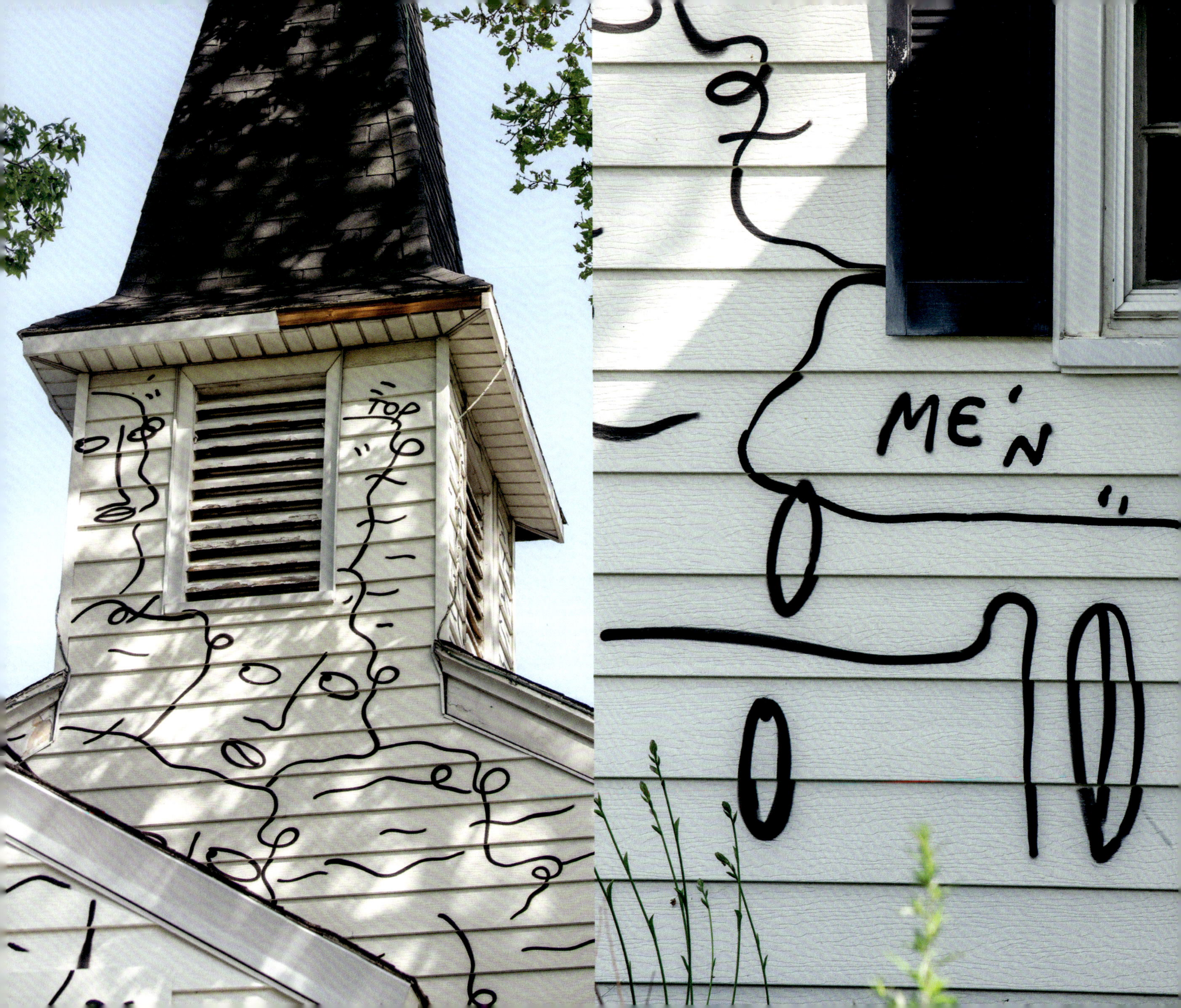

ME'N

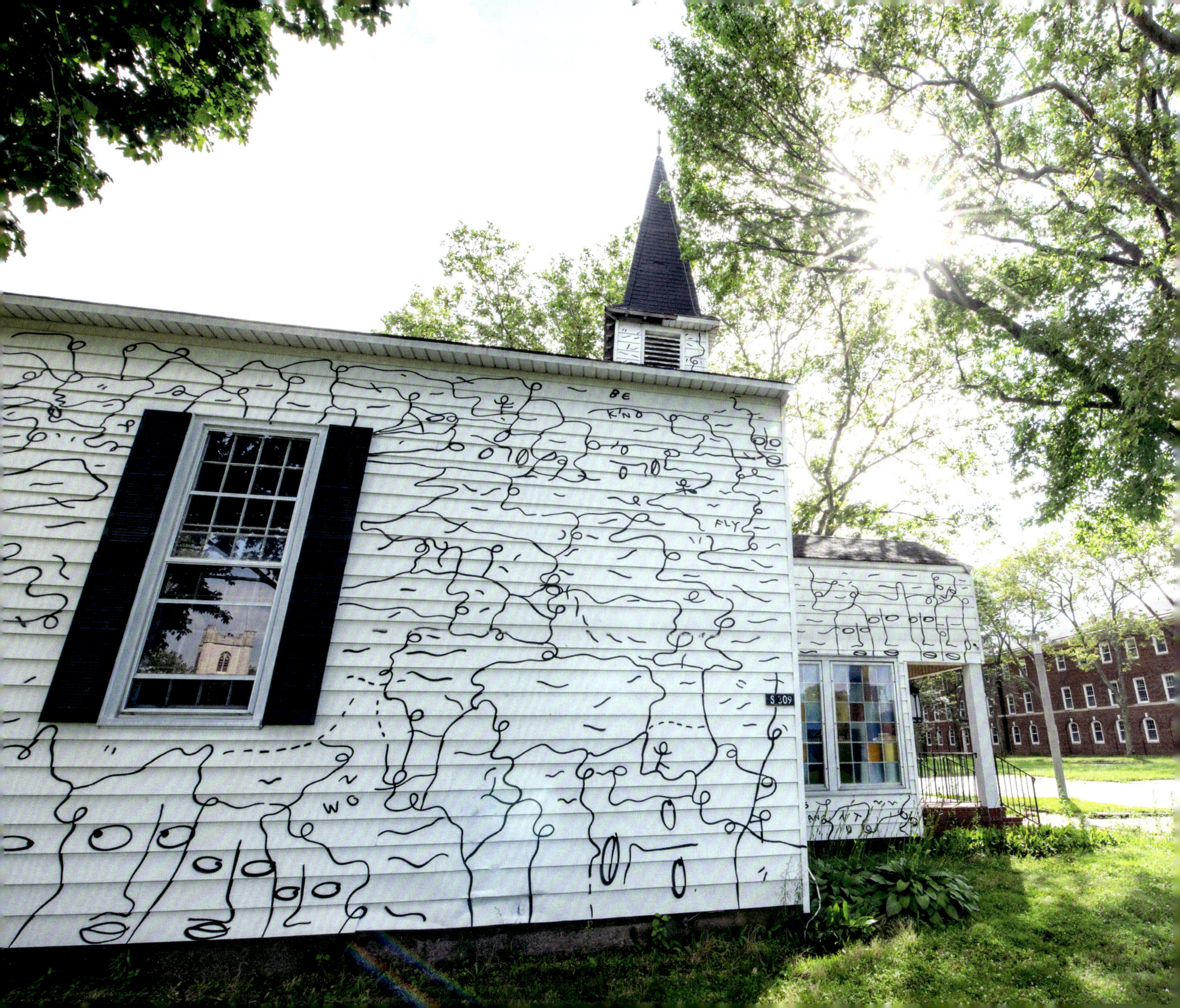

BE
KIND
FLY
S 309

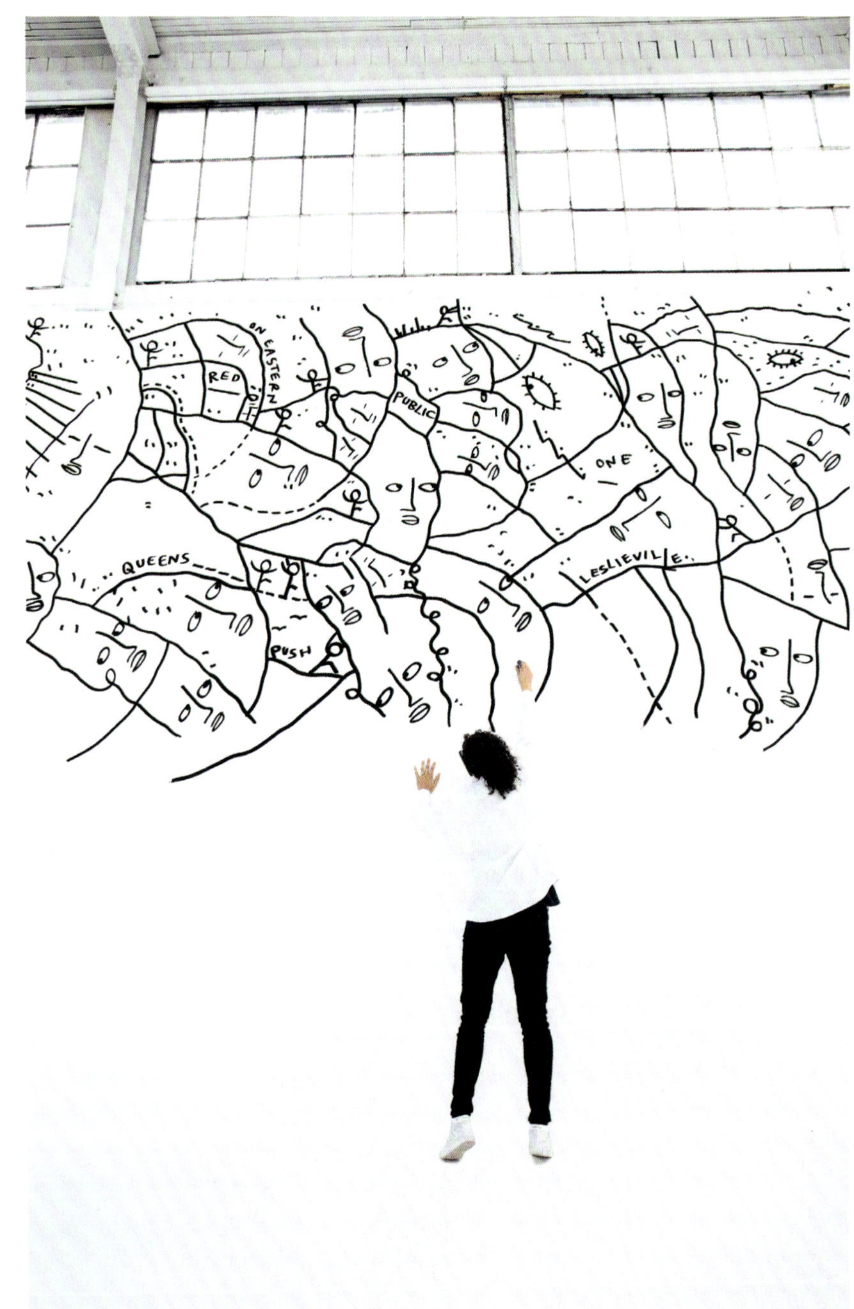

NIAGARA FALLS

For an event in 2015 at District 28, Toronto, held to announce the launch of Saks Fifth Avenue in Canada, Martin was invited to create an immersive experience for the city's cultural community. The resulting installation, *Niagara Falls*, included a large, enveloping mural covering the walls and floor, in which Toronto landmarks and neighbourhoods were referenced. During the course of the evening, this work was then personalised to include the names of guests, while Martin also gave a live-drawing performance and presented a custom collection of hand-drawn clothes, including a black leather jacket that has since become a staple of her wardrobe.

This spread and following spread: Martin at work on *Niagara Falls* in November 2015.

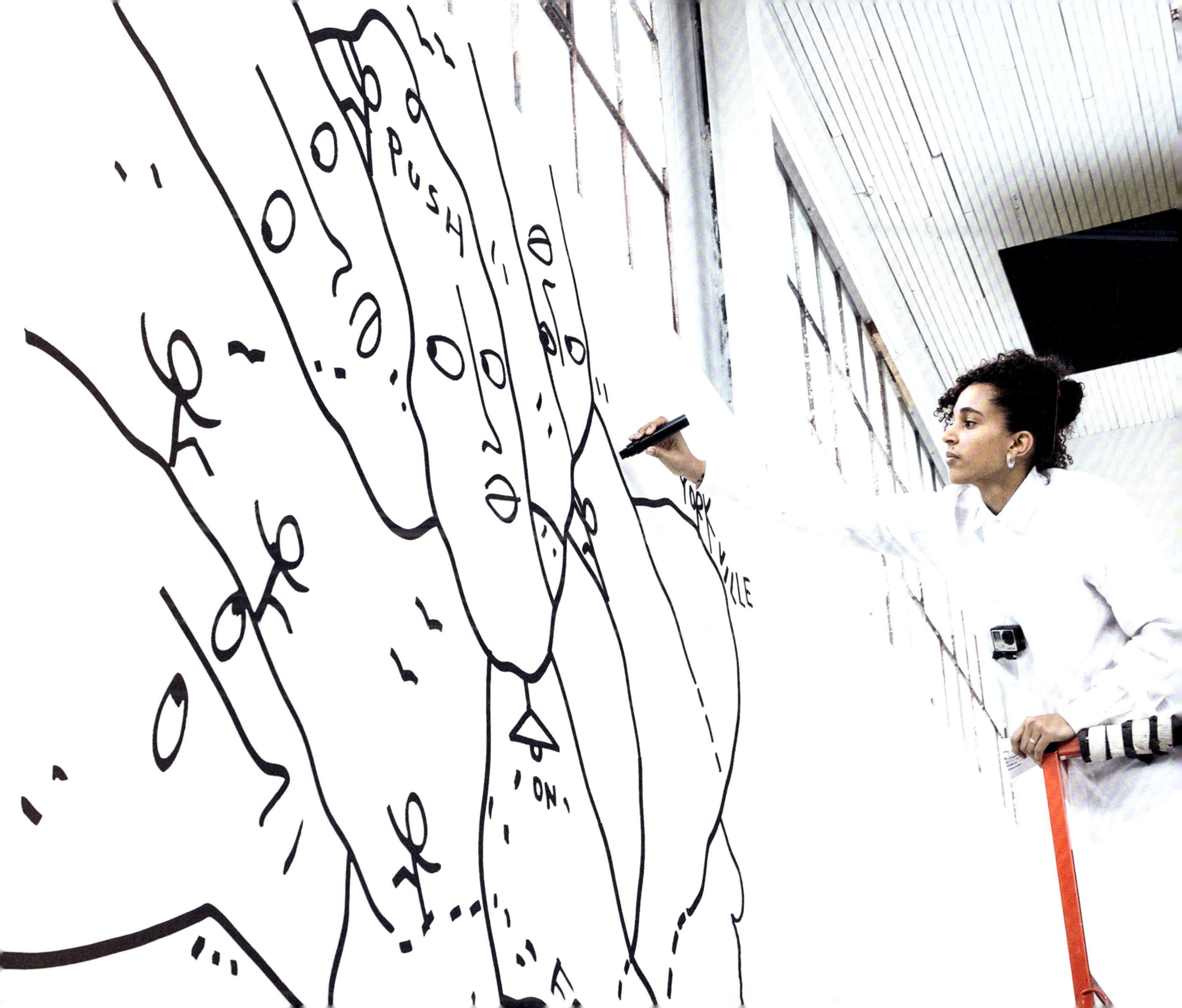

PUSH
ON
YORKVILLE

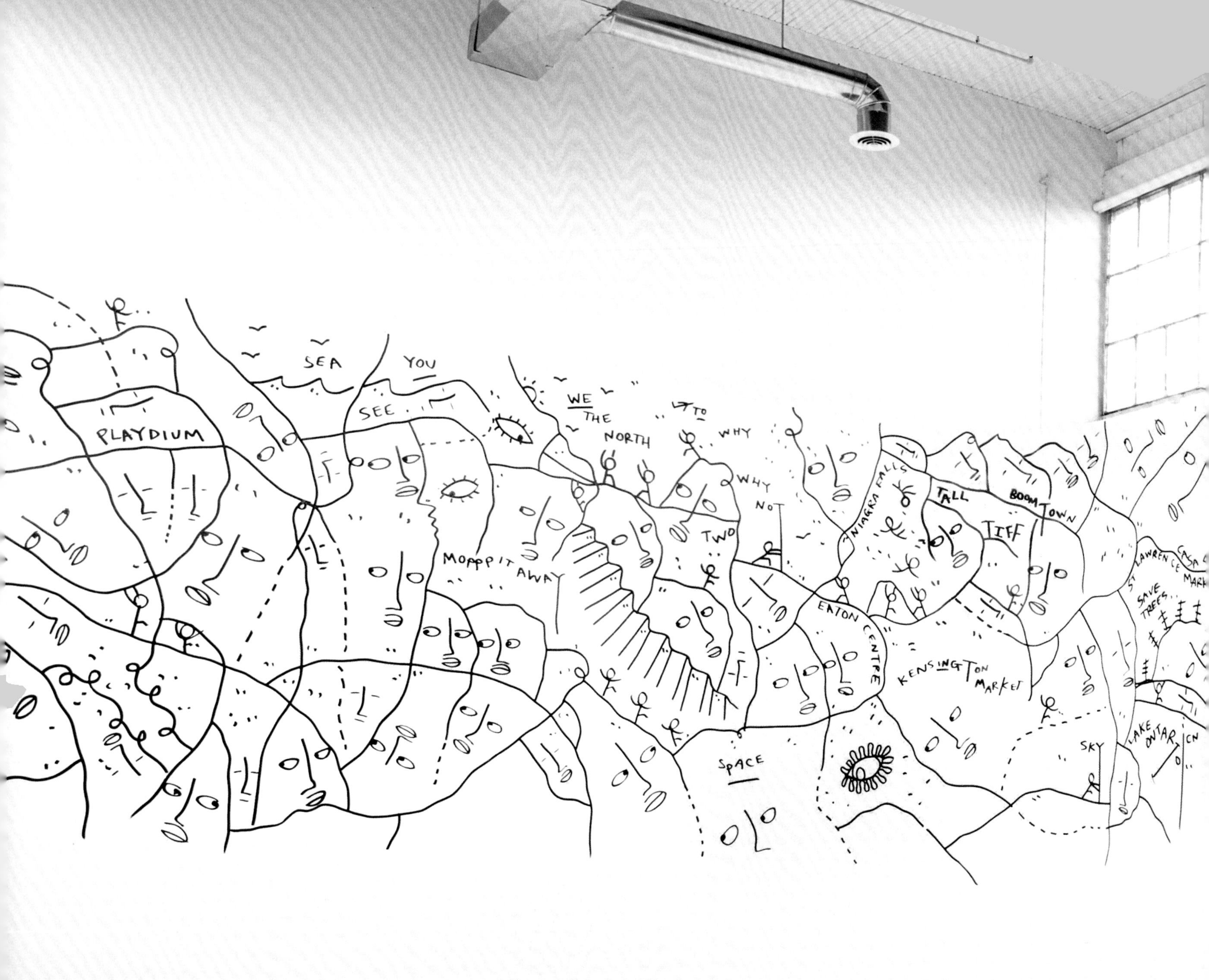

PLAYDIUM
SEA
YOU
SEE
WE
THE NORTH
TO
WHY
WHY NOT
TWO
MOPPP IT AWAY
NIAGRA FALLS
TALL
TIFF
BOOM TOWN
ST LAWRENCE MARKET
SAVE TREES
CASA
EATON CENTRE
KENSINGTON MARKET
SPACE
SKY
LAKE ONTARIO
CN

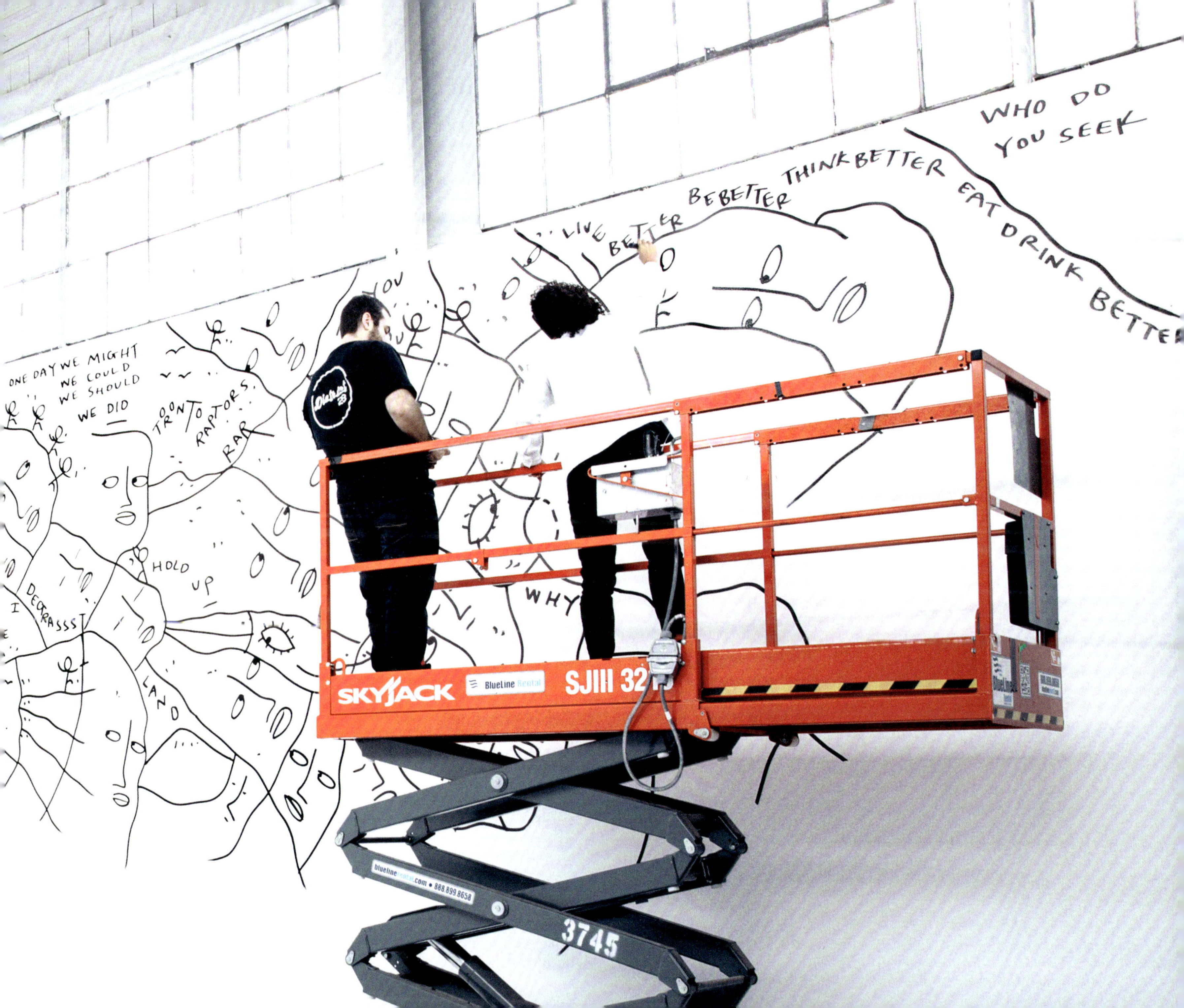

WHO DO YOU SEEK
LIVE BETTER BE BETTER THINK BETTER EAT DRINK BETTER
ONE DAY WE MIGHT WE COULD WE SHOULD WE DID
TORONTO RAPTORS RAR
HOLD UP
I DEGRASSS
LAND
WHY
SKYJACK
BlueLine Rental
SJIII 32
blueline-rental.com • 888.899.8658
3745

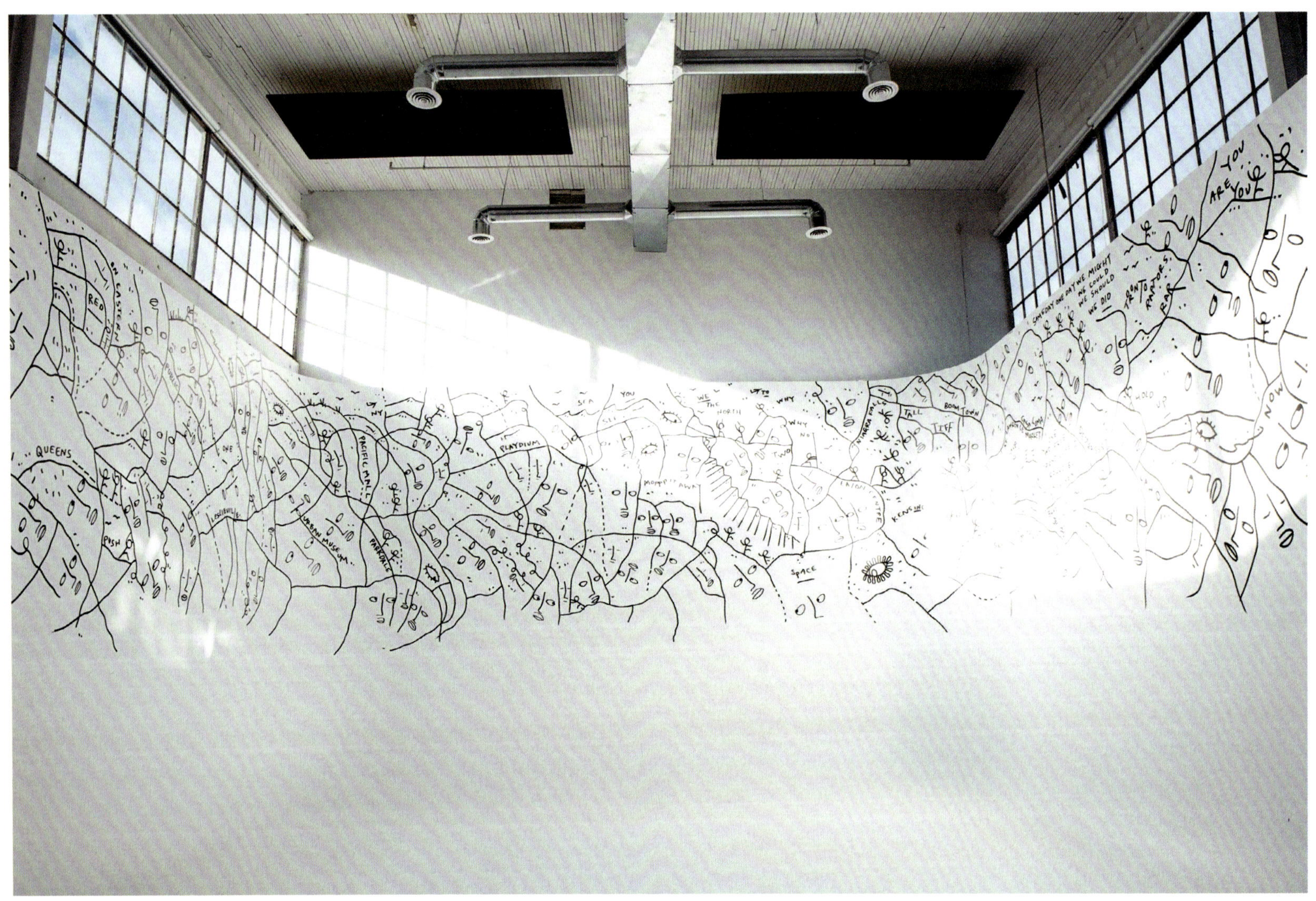

Above: The finished *Niagara Falls* mural
at District 28, Toronto, 2015.
Opposite: Martin at work on *Niagara
Falls* in November 2015.

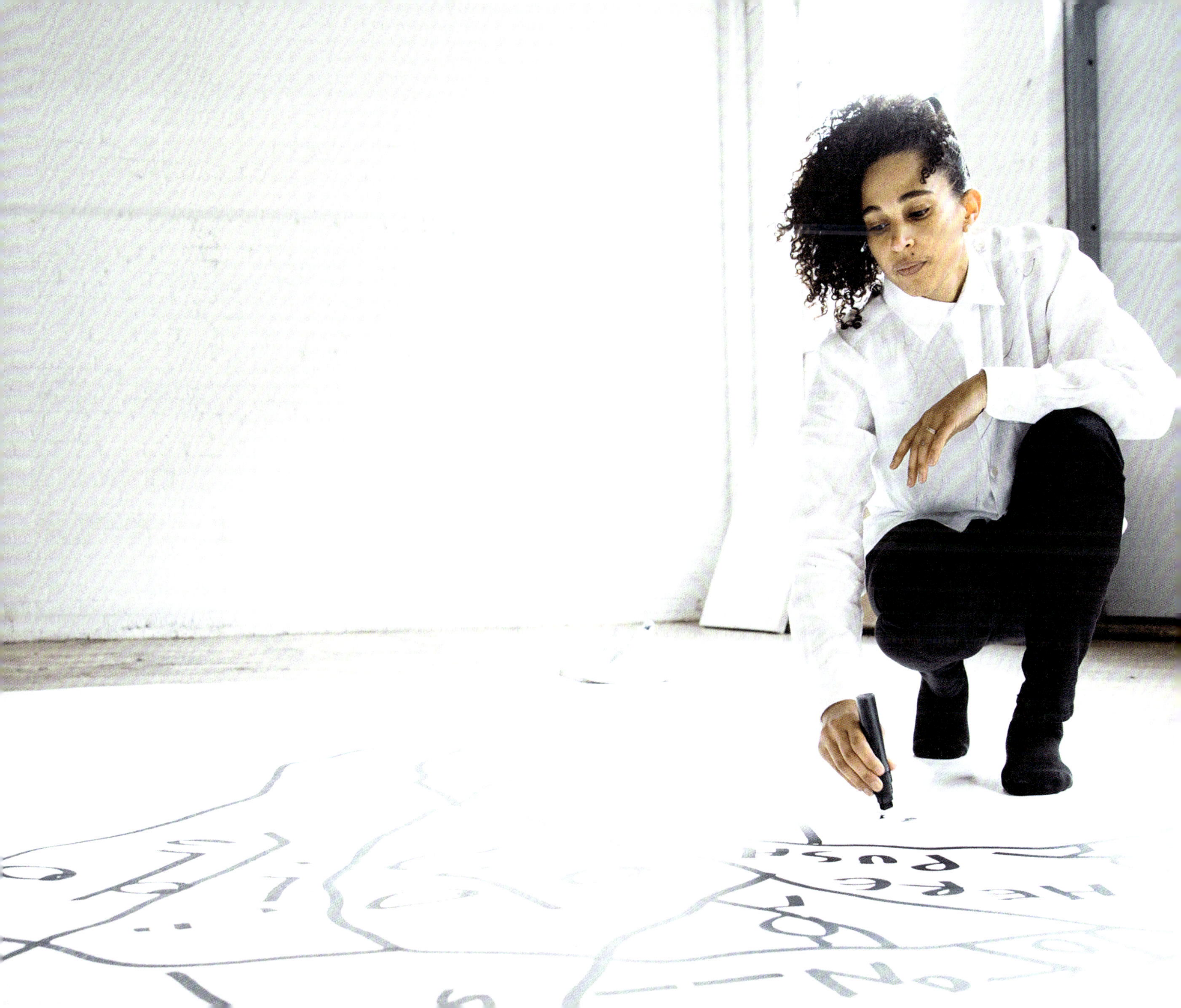

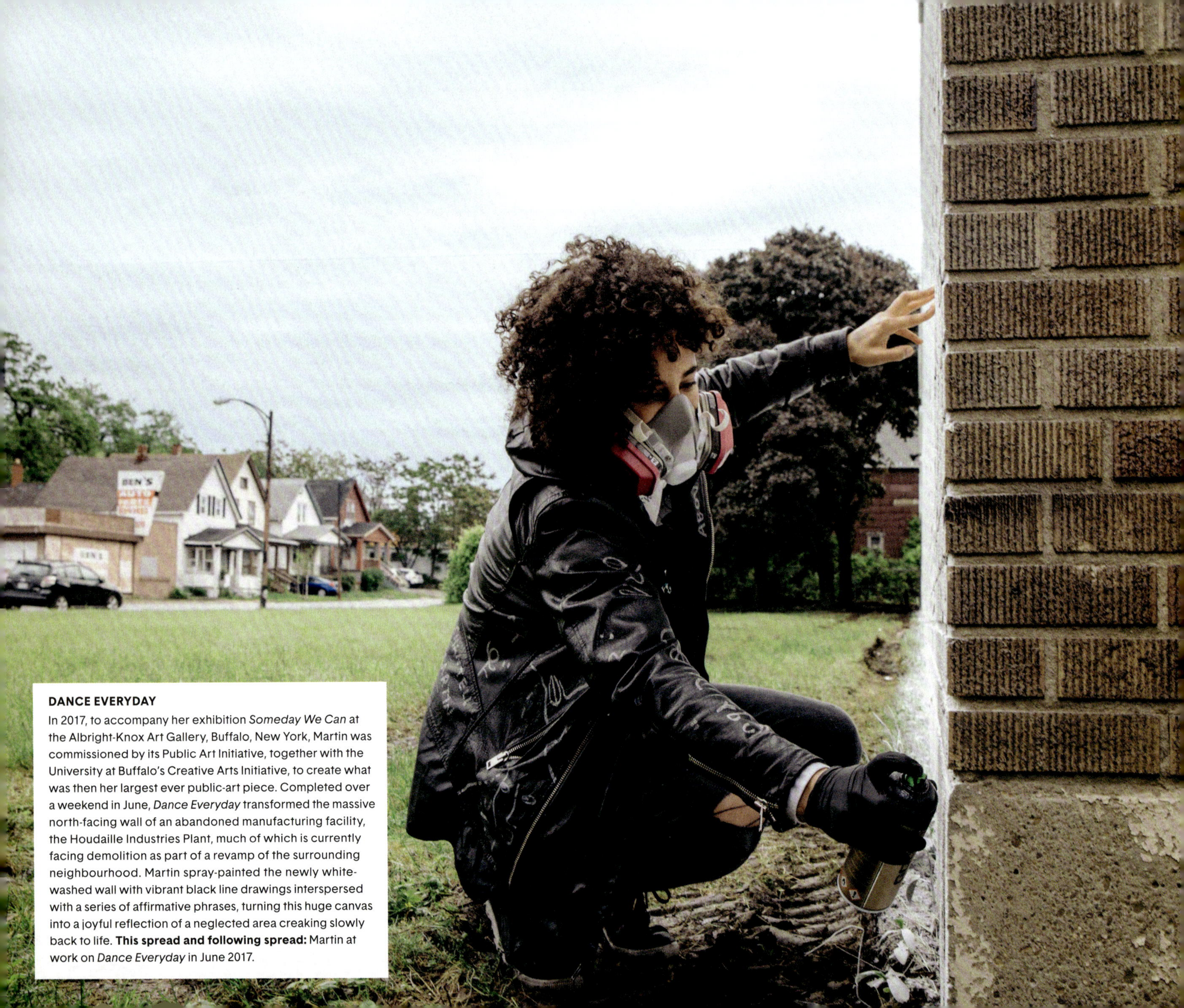

DANCE EVERYDAY

In 2017, to accompany her exhibition *Someday We Can* at the Albright-Knox Art Gallery, Buffalo, New York, Martin was commissioned by its Public Art Initiative, together with the University at Buffalo's Creative Arts Initiative, to create what was then her largest ever public-art piece. Completed over a weekend in June, *Dance Everyday* transformed the massive north-facing wall of an abandoned manufacturing facility, the Houdaille Industries Plant, much of which is currently facing demolition as part of a revamp of the surrounding neighbourhood. Martin spray-painted the newly white-washed wall with vibrant black line drawings interspersed with a series of affirmative phrases, turning this huge canvas into a joyful reflection of a neglected area creaking slowly back to life. **This spread and following spread:** Martin at work on *Dance Everyday* in June 2017.

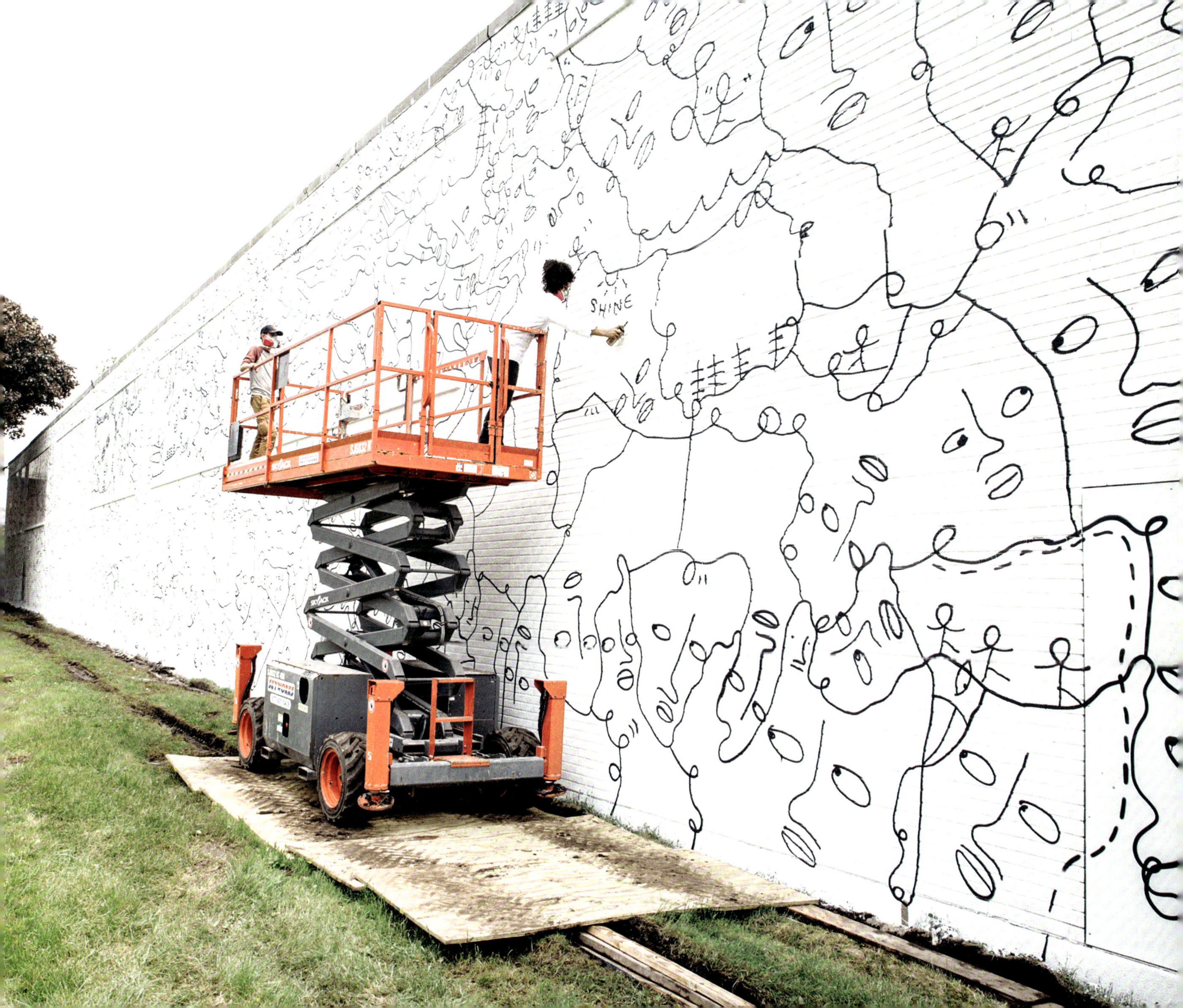

SHINE

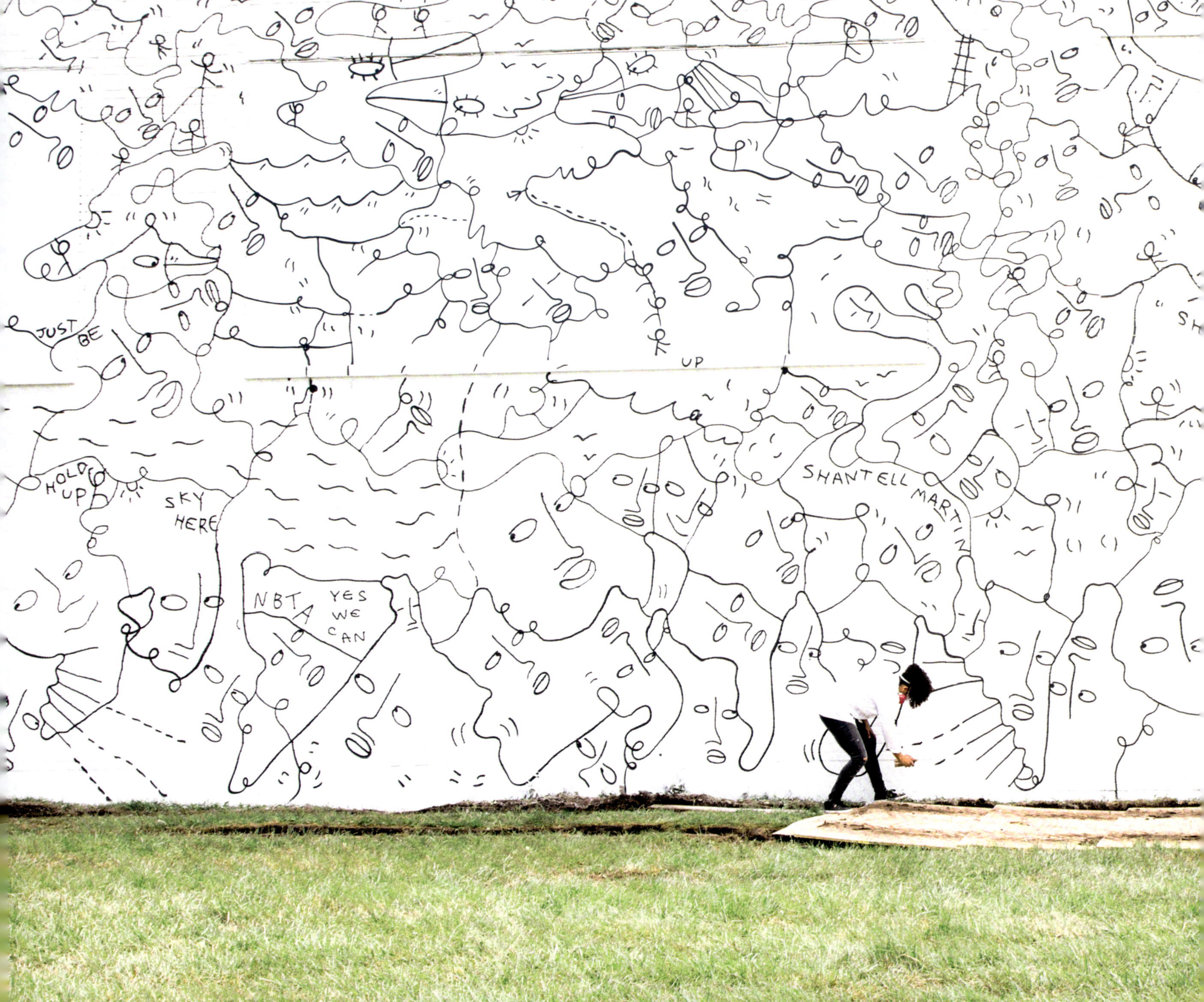

JUST BE
HOLD UP
SKY HERE
NBTA
YES WE CAN
UP
SHANTELL MARTIN

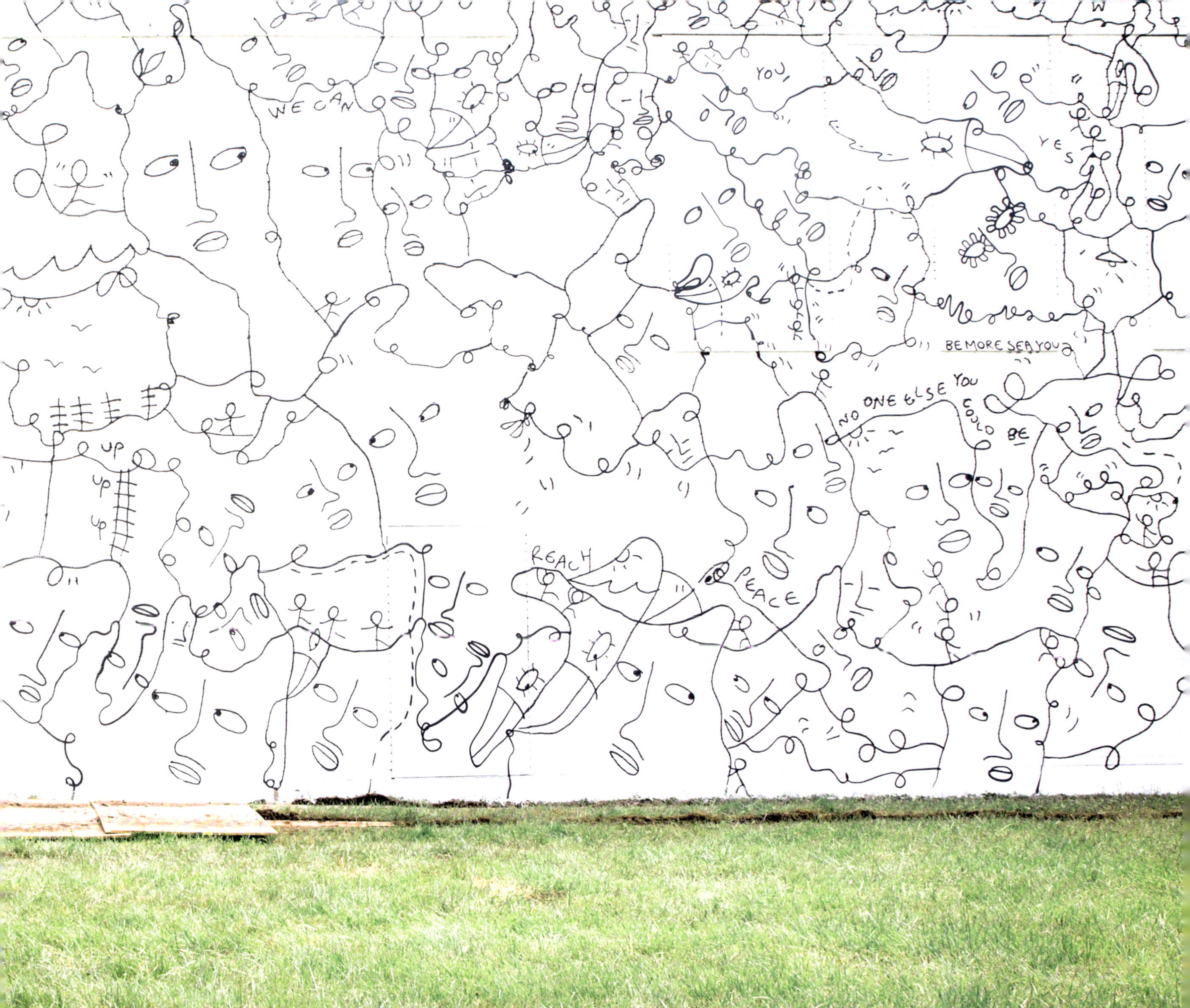

WE CAN
YOU
YES
BE MORE SEA YOU
NO ONE ELSE YOU COULD BE
UP
UP
UP
REACH
PEACE
W

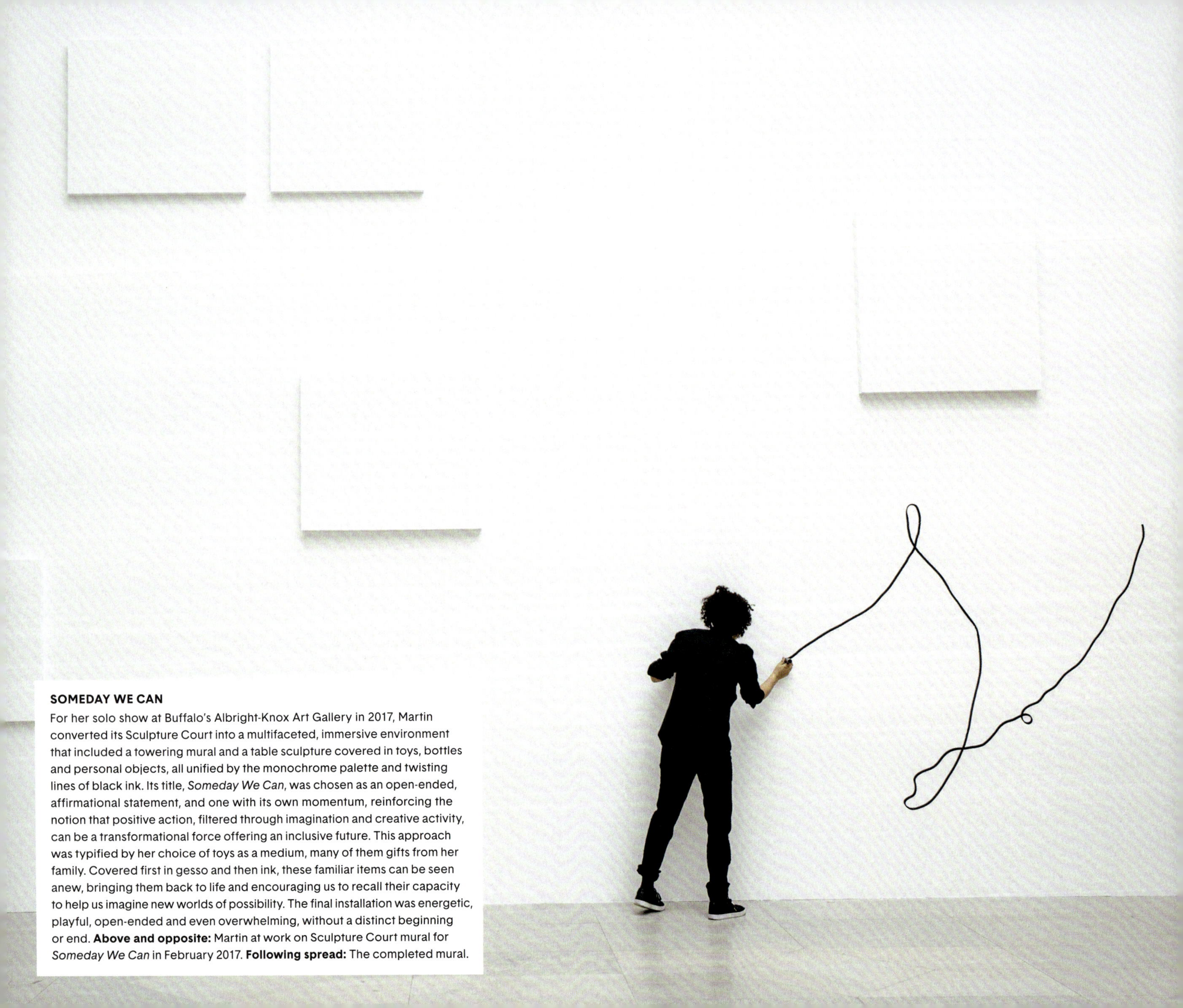

SOMEDAY WE CAN

For her solo show at Buffalo's Albright-Knox Art Gallery in 2017, Martin
converted its Sculpture Court into a multifaceted, immersive environment
that included a towering mural and a table sculpture covered in toys, bottles
and personal objects, all unified by the monochrome palette and twisting
lines of black ink. Its title, *Someday We Can*, was chosen as an open-ended,
affirmational statement, and one with its own momentum, reinforcing the
notion that positive action, filtered through imagination and creative activity,
can be a transformational force offering an inclusive future. This approach
was typified by her choice of toys as a medium, many of them gifts from her
family. Covered first in gesso and then ink, these familiar items can be seen
anew, bringing them back to life and encouraging us to recall their capacity
to help us imagine new worlds of possibility. The final installation was energetic,
playful, open-ended and even overwhelming, without a distinct beginning
or end. **Above and opposite:** Martin at work on Sculpture Court mural for
Someday We Can in February 2017. **Following spread:** The completed mural.

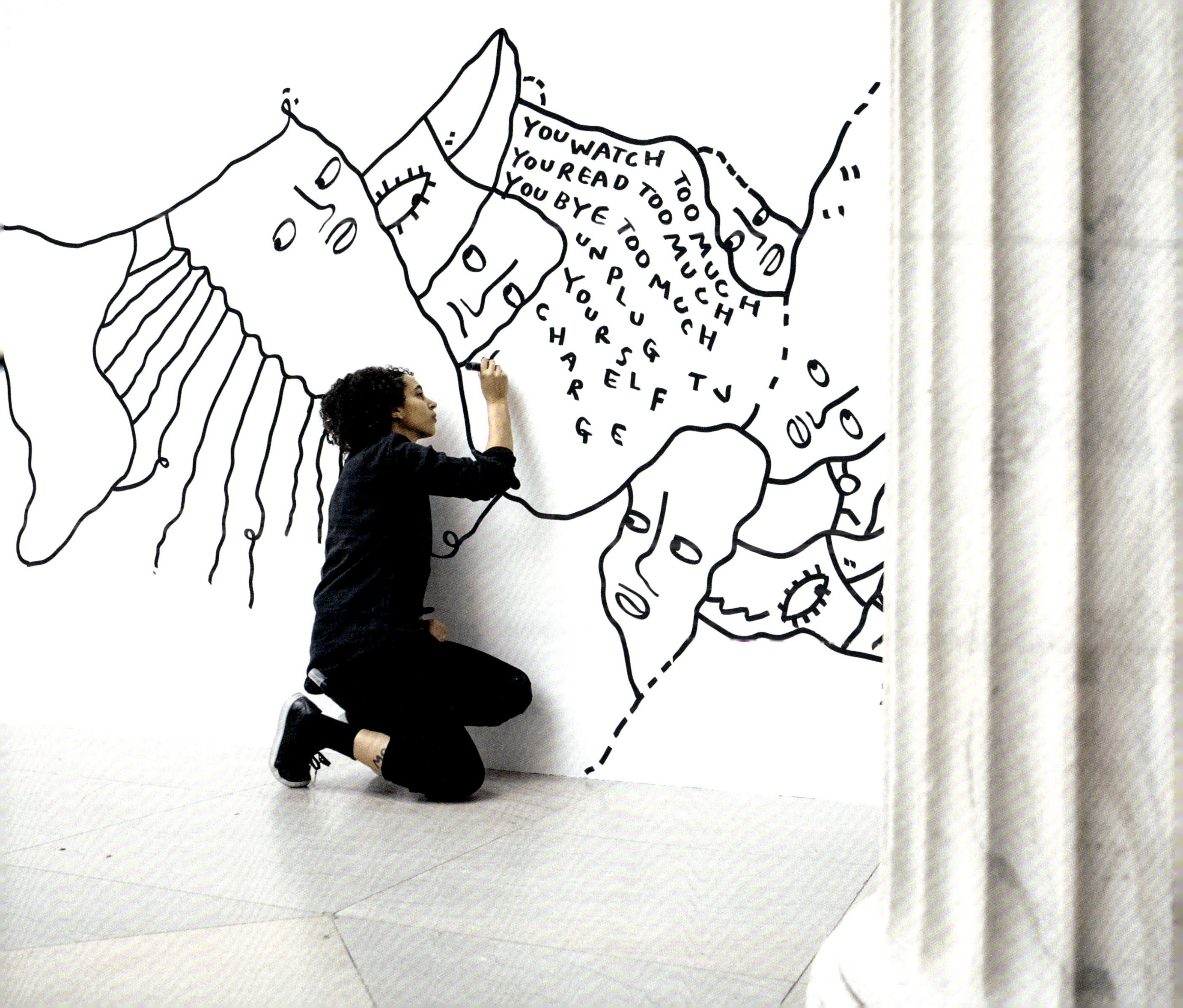

YOU WATCH TOO MUCH
YOU READ TOO MUCH
YOU BYE TOO MUCH
UN PLU G TV
YOUR S
CH ELF
A R
G
E

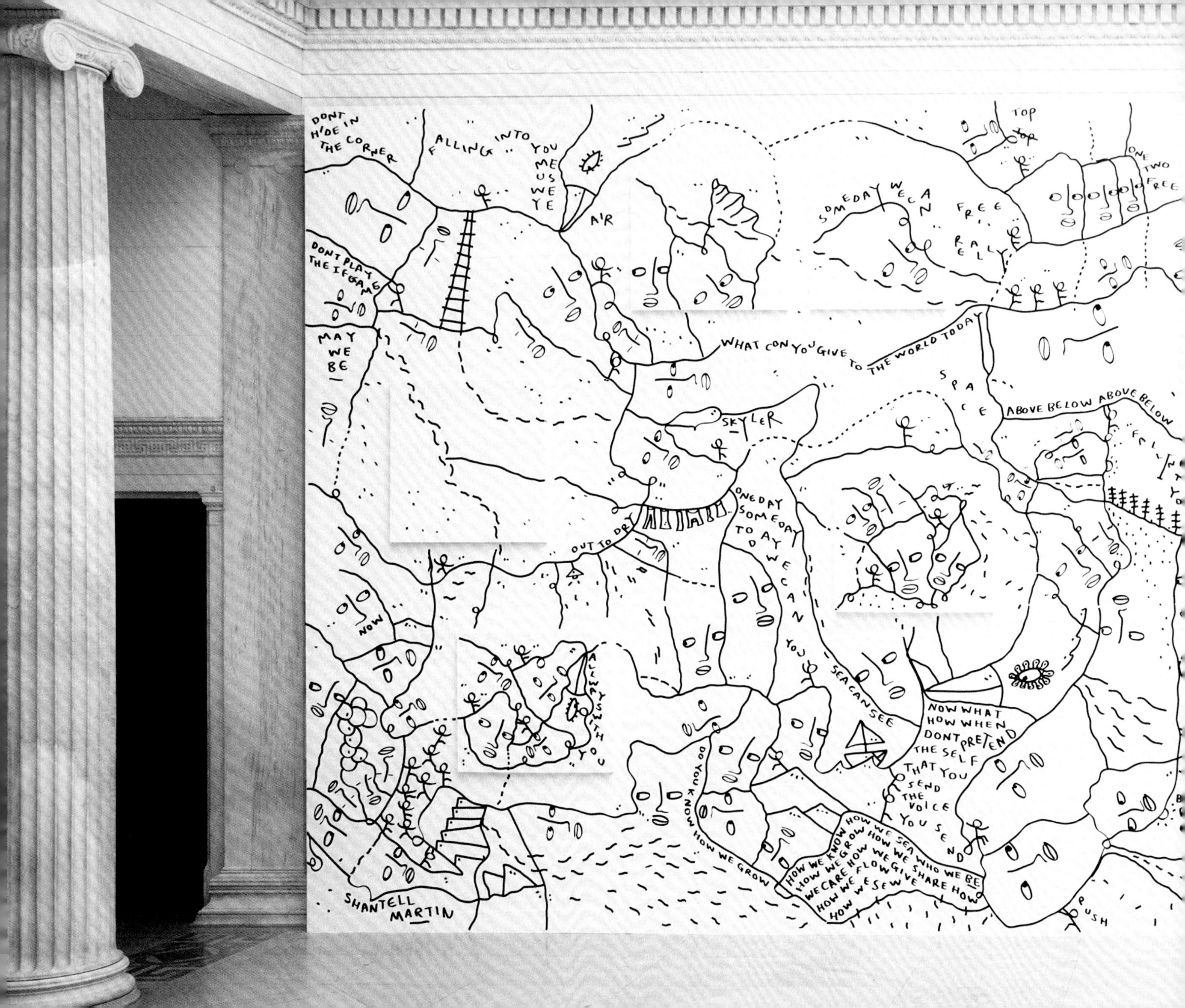

DONT HIDE IN THE CORNER
FALLING INTO YOU ME US WE YE
AIR
DONT PLAY THE IF GAME
MAY WE BE
SOMEDAY WE CAN FREE
ONE TWO FREE
TOP TOP
WHAT CON YOU GIVE TO THE WORLD TODAY
SKYLER
SPACE
ABOVE BELOW ABOVE BELOW
OUT TO DRY
ONE DAY SOMEDAY TODAY WE CAN
NOW
ALWAYS WITH YOU
SEA CAN SEE
NOW WHAT HOW WHEN DONT PRETEND THE SELF THAT YOU SEND THE VOICE YOU SEND
DO YOU KNOW HOW WE GROW
HOW WE KNOW HOW WE SEA WHO WE BE
HOW WE GROW HOW WE SHARE HOW
WE CARE HOW WE GIVE
HOW WE FLOW
HOW WE SEW
PUSH
SHANTELL MARTIN

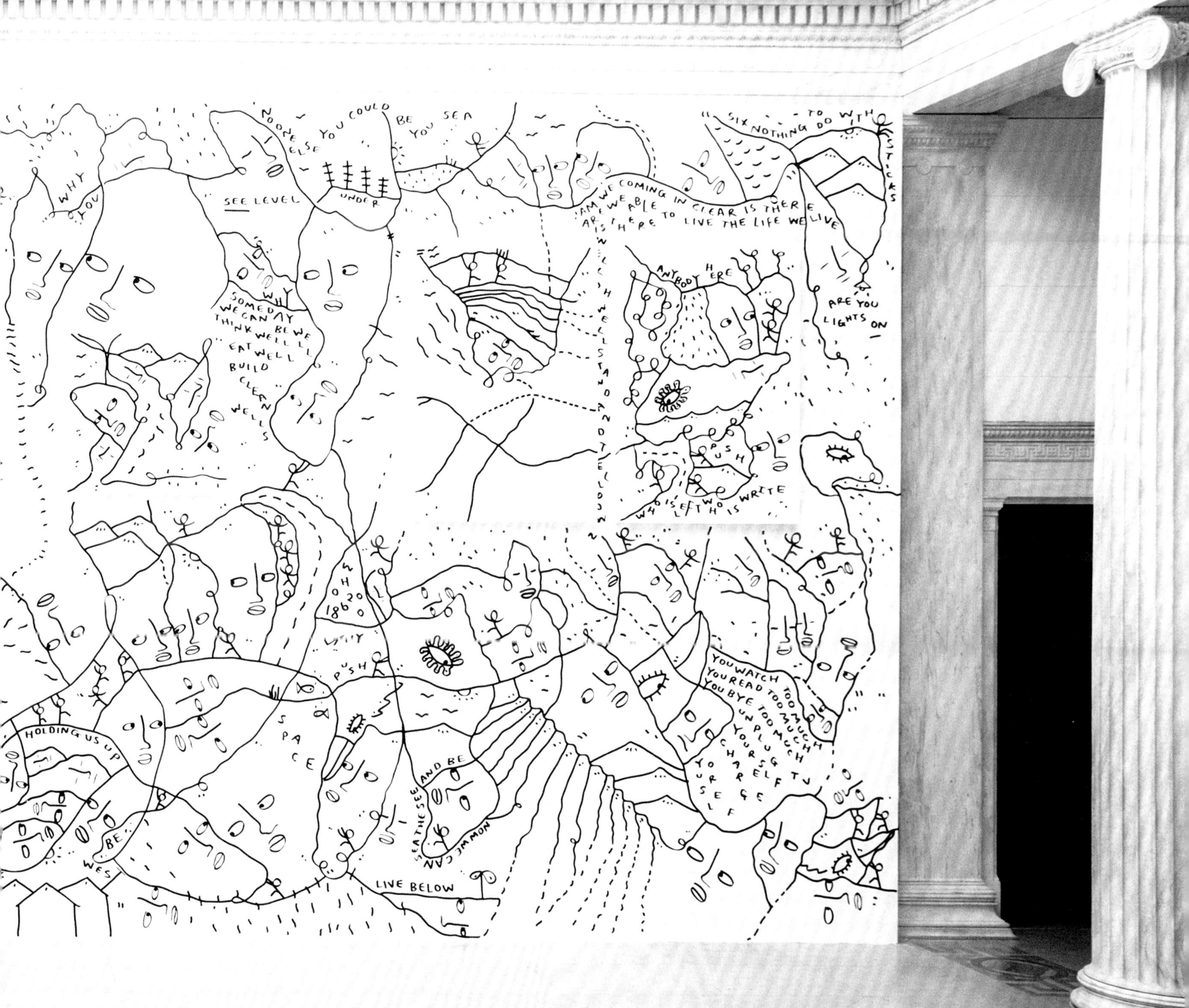

WHY YOU
NO ONE ELSE YOU COULD BE SEA YOU
SEE LEVEL UNDER
SIX NOTHING TO DO WITH STICKS
AM WE COMING IN CLEAR IS THERE
ARE WE ABLE TO LIVE THE LIFE WE LIVE
IS THERE
SOMEDAY WE CAN BE WE THINK WELL EAT WELL BUILD CLEAN WELLS
ANYBODY HERE
ARE YOU LIGHTS ON
WELL STAND AND TELL DOWN
PUSH
WHO IS LEFT WHO IS WRITE
OH H2O 1860
UTILITY PUSH
SPACE
YOU WATCH TOO MUCH YOU READ TOO MUCH YOU BYE TOO MUCH UNPLUG YOURSELF CHARGE TV YOURSELF
HOLDING US UP
BE WES
SEA THE SEA AND BE NOW WE CAN COMMON
LIVE BELOW

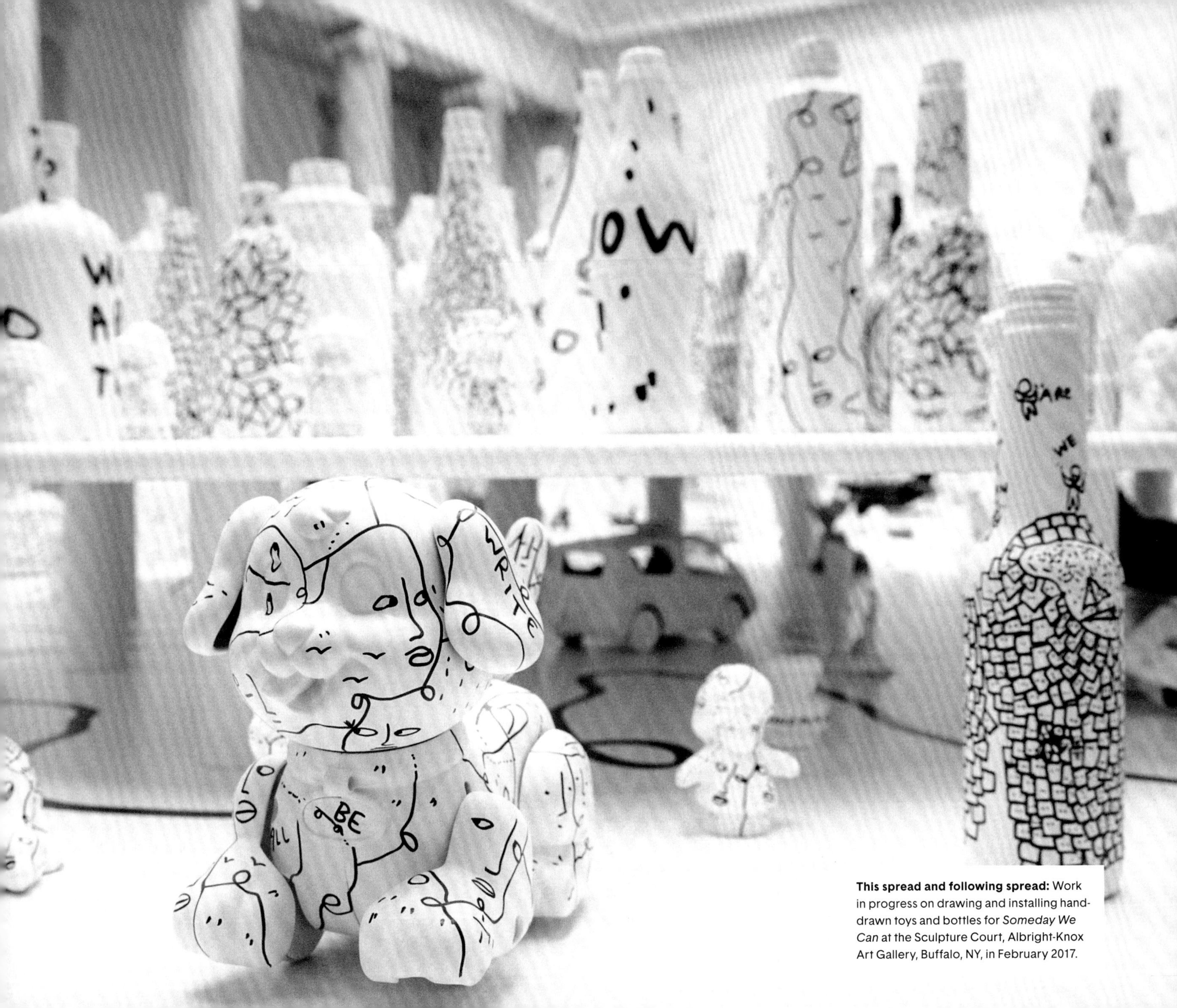

This spread and following spread: Work in progress on drawing and installing hand-drawn toys and bottles for *Someday We Can* at the Sculpture Court, Albright-Knox Art Gallery, Buffalo, NY, in February 2017.

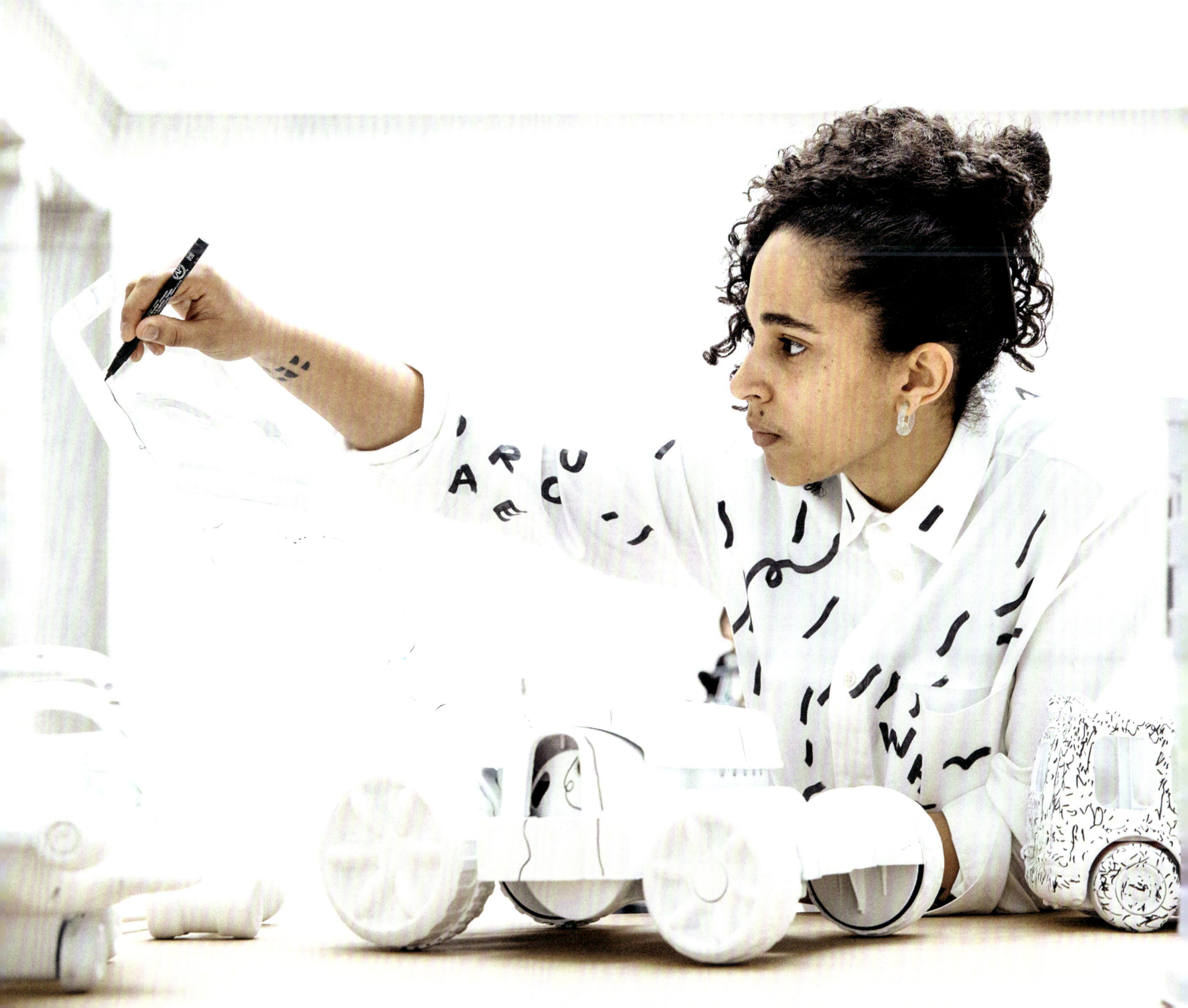

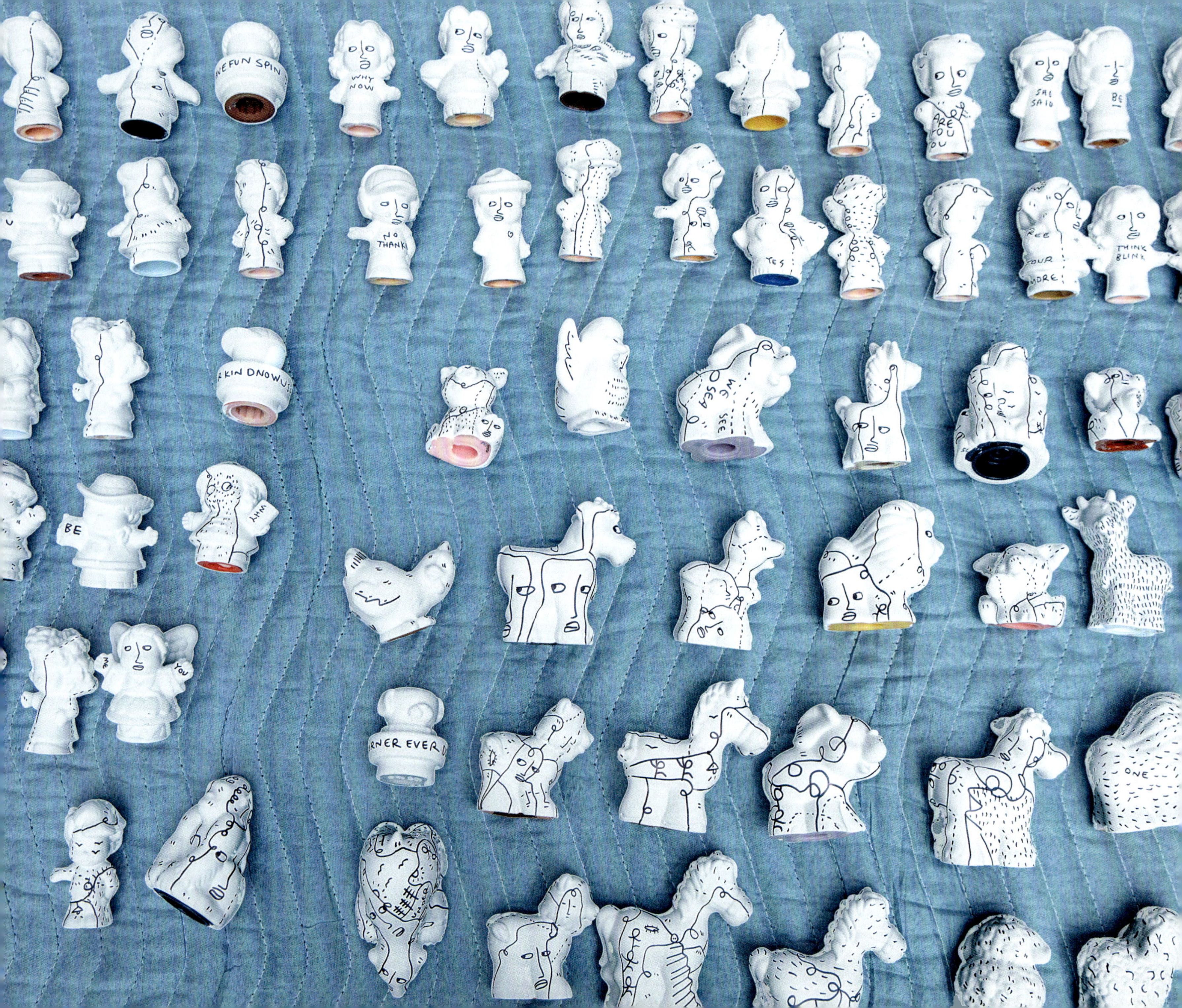

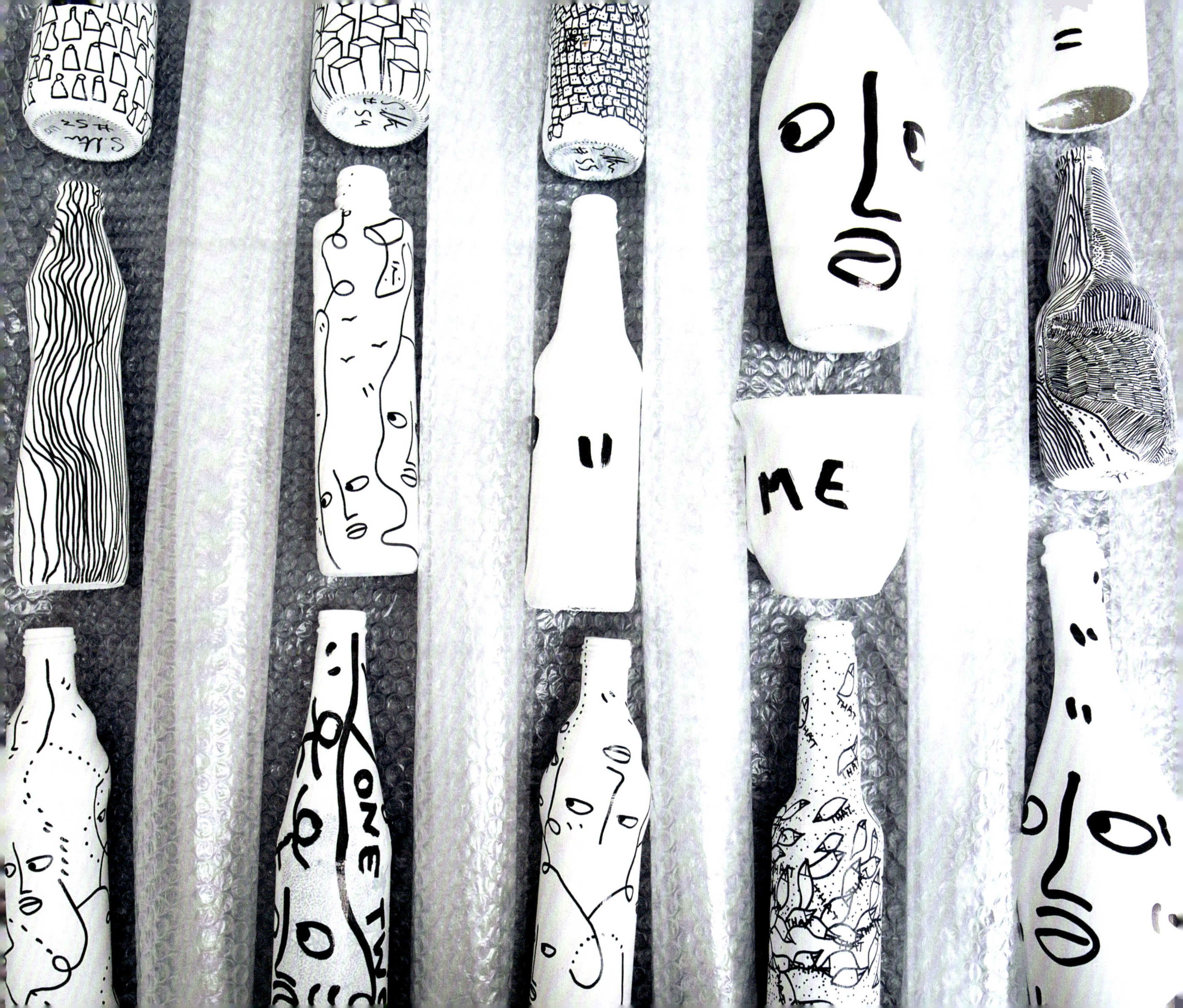
ME
ONE TWO
THAT

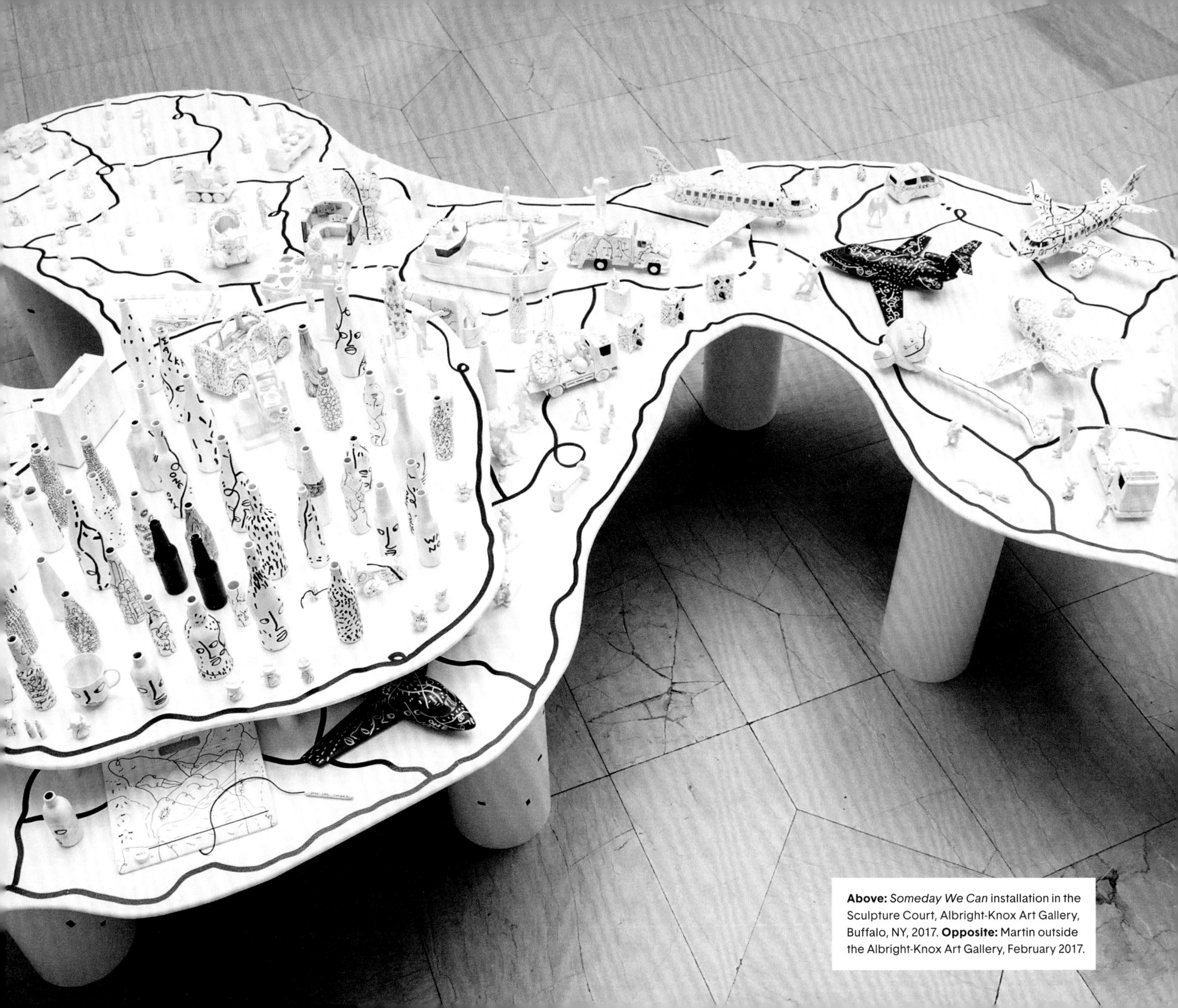

Above: *Someday We Can* installation in the Sculpture Court, Albright-Knox Art Gallery, Buffalo, NY, 2017. **Opposite:** Martin outside the Albright-Knox Art Gallery, February 2017.

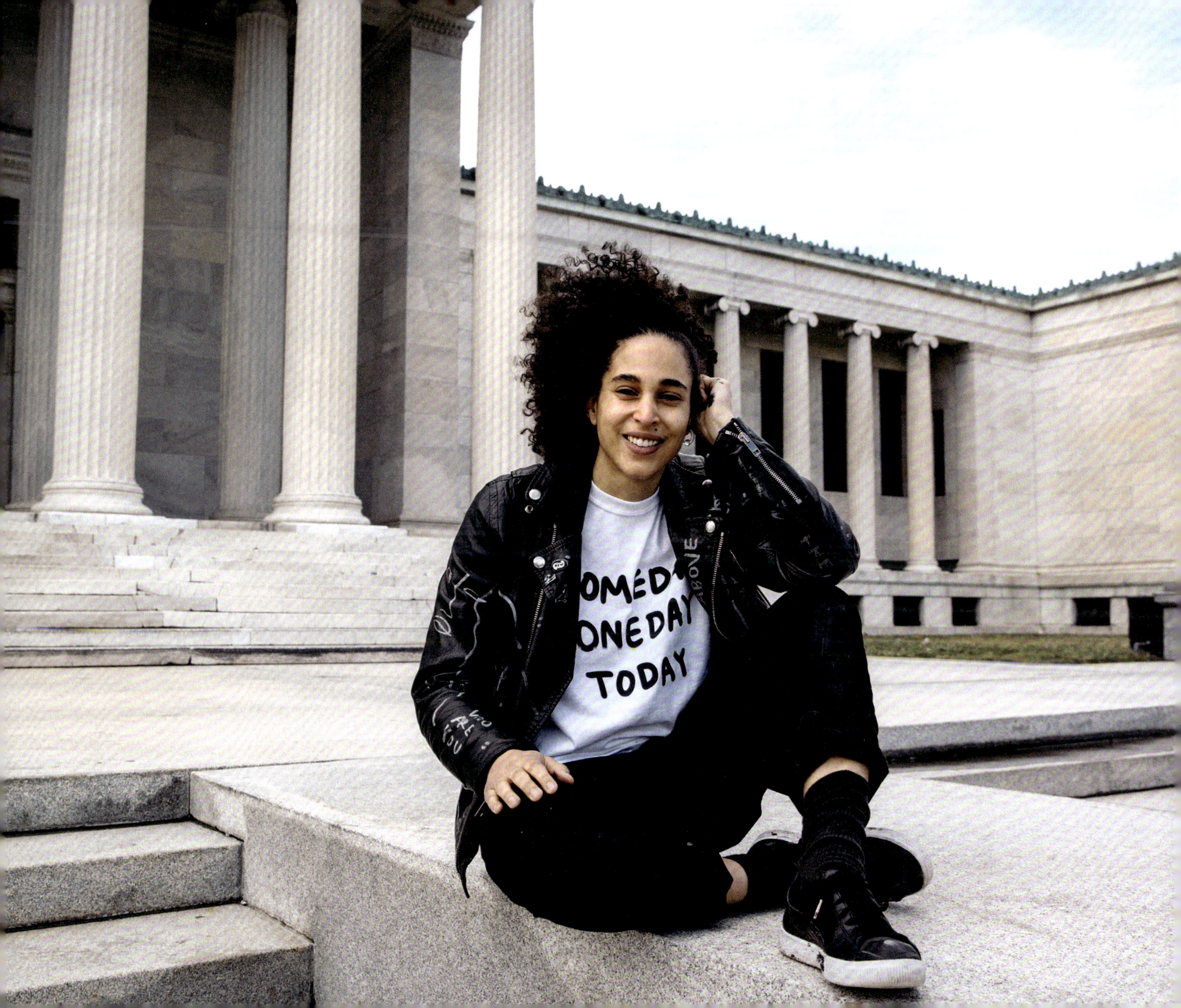
SOMEDAY
ONE DAY
TODAY

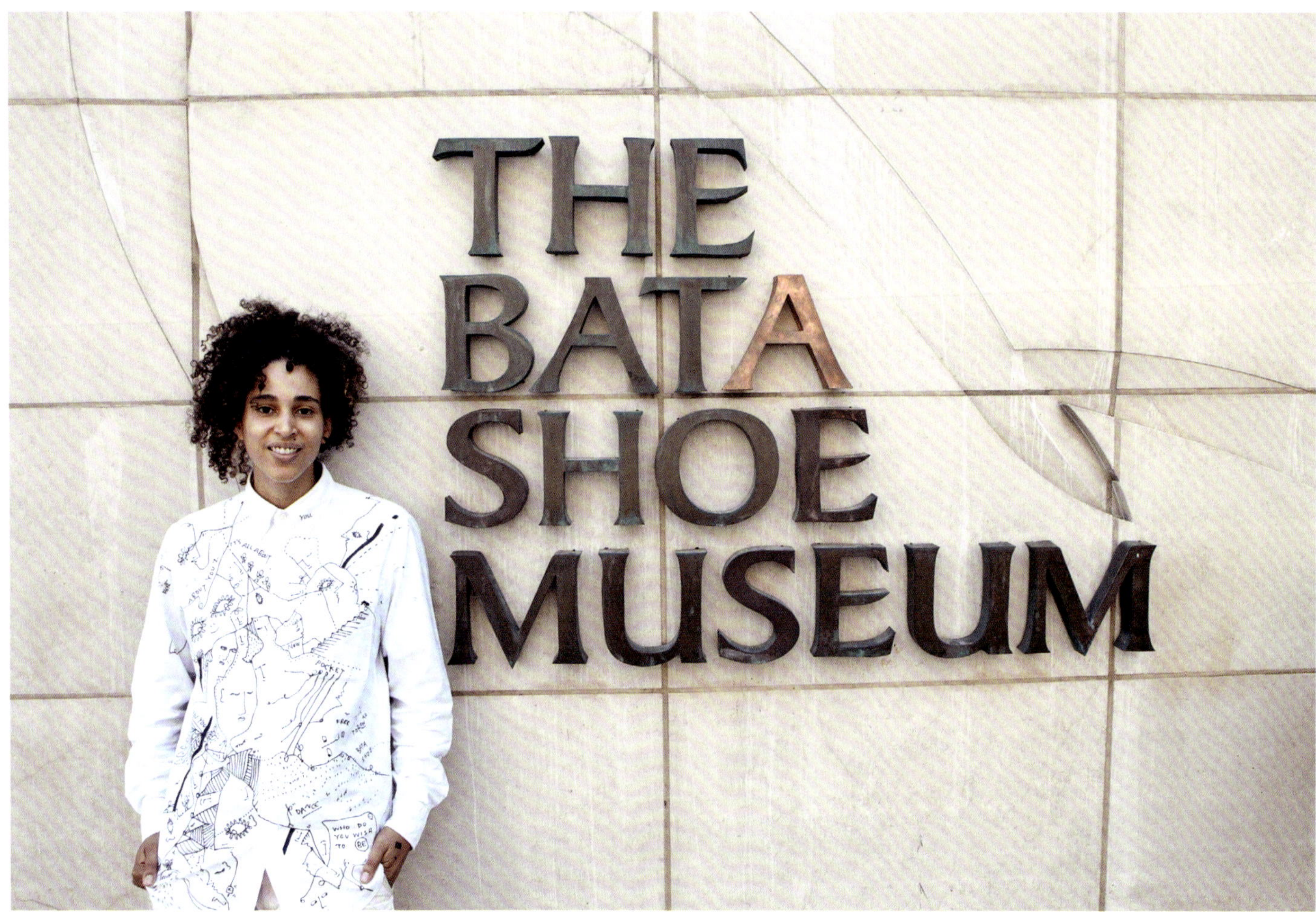

SEA YOU

In 2013, Martin created an installation to accompany the exhibition *Out of the Box: The Rise of Sneaker Culture* at the Bata Shoe Museum, Toronto, in partnership with the American Federation of the Arts. The resulting work, *Sea You*, was drawn on and behind the museum's exterior windows, and was inspired by Toronto, evoking the city's geography and its unique chill aesthetic. There was also a workshop where children were allowed to draw on other windows alongside Martin in a moment of collaboration and inclusion. A pair of her hand-drawn sneakers was exhibited in the show, which then travelled to multiple locations, including New York's Brooklyn Museum. **Above:** Martin outside the Bata Shoe Museum, July 2013. **Opposite and following spread:** Martin drawing on the museum's windows to create *Sea You*, July 2013.

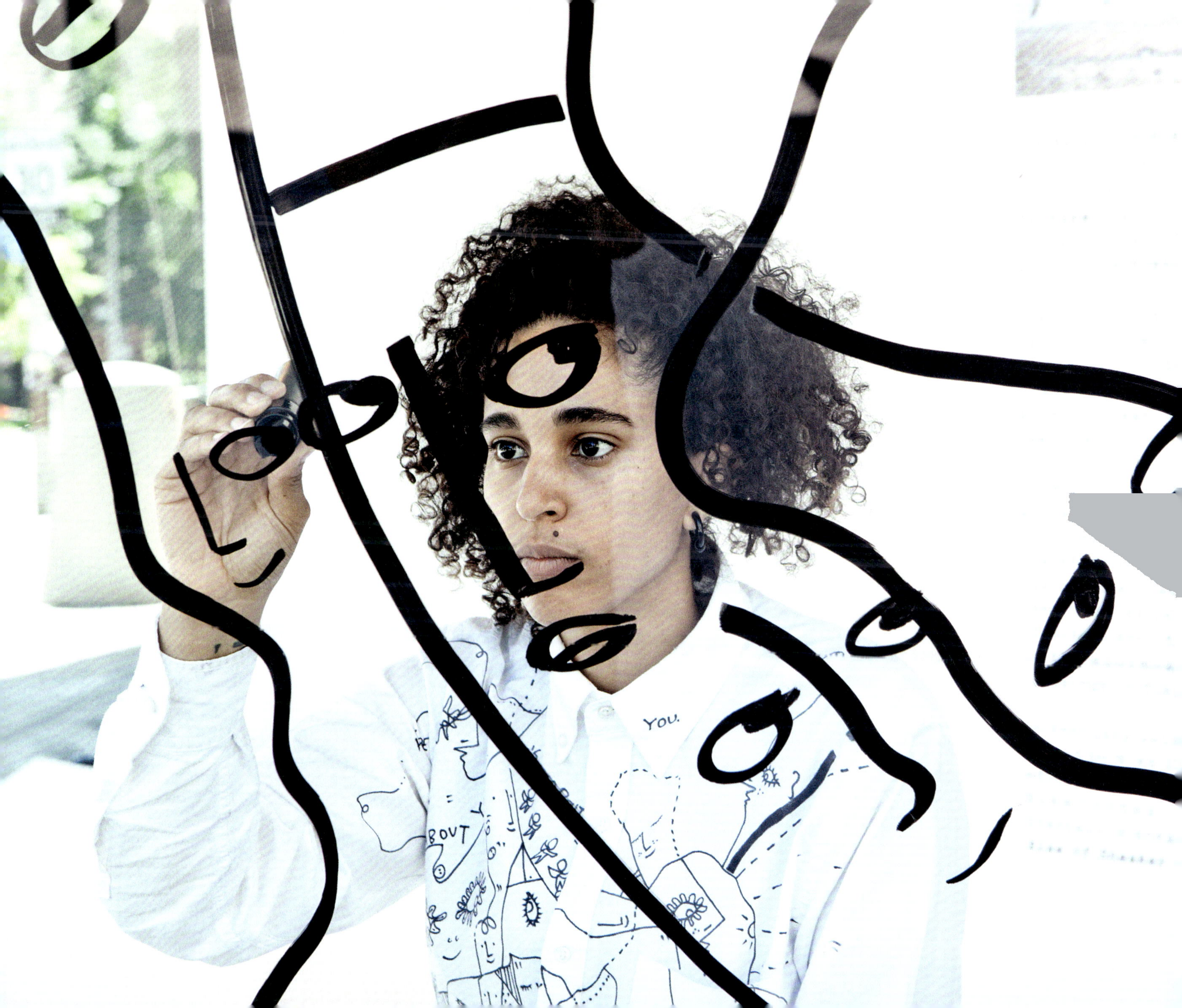

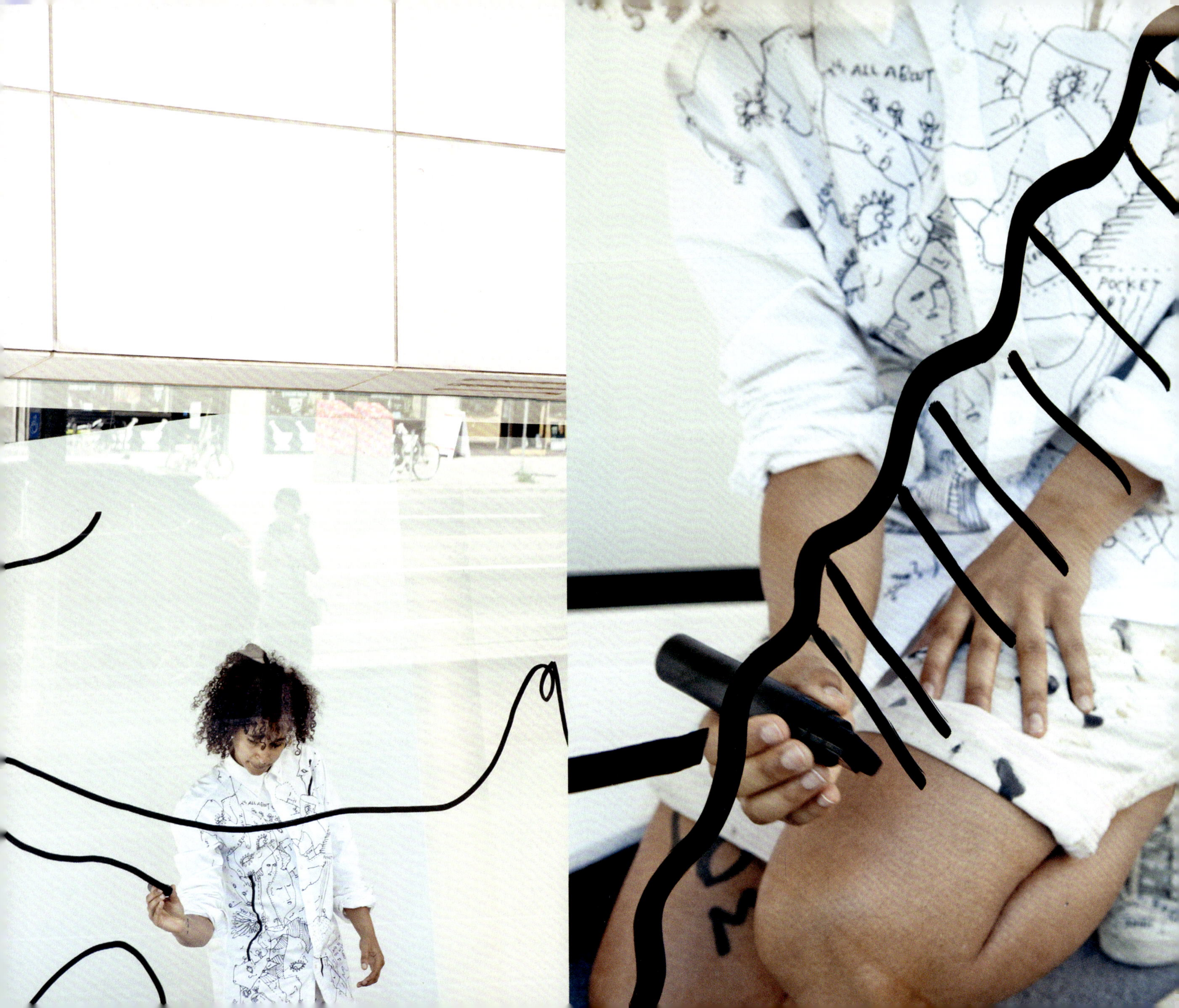

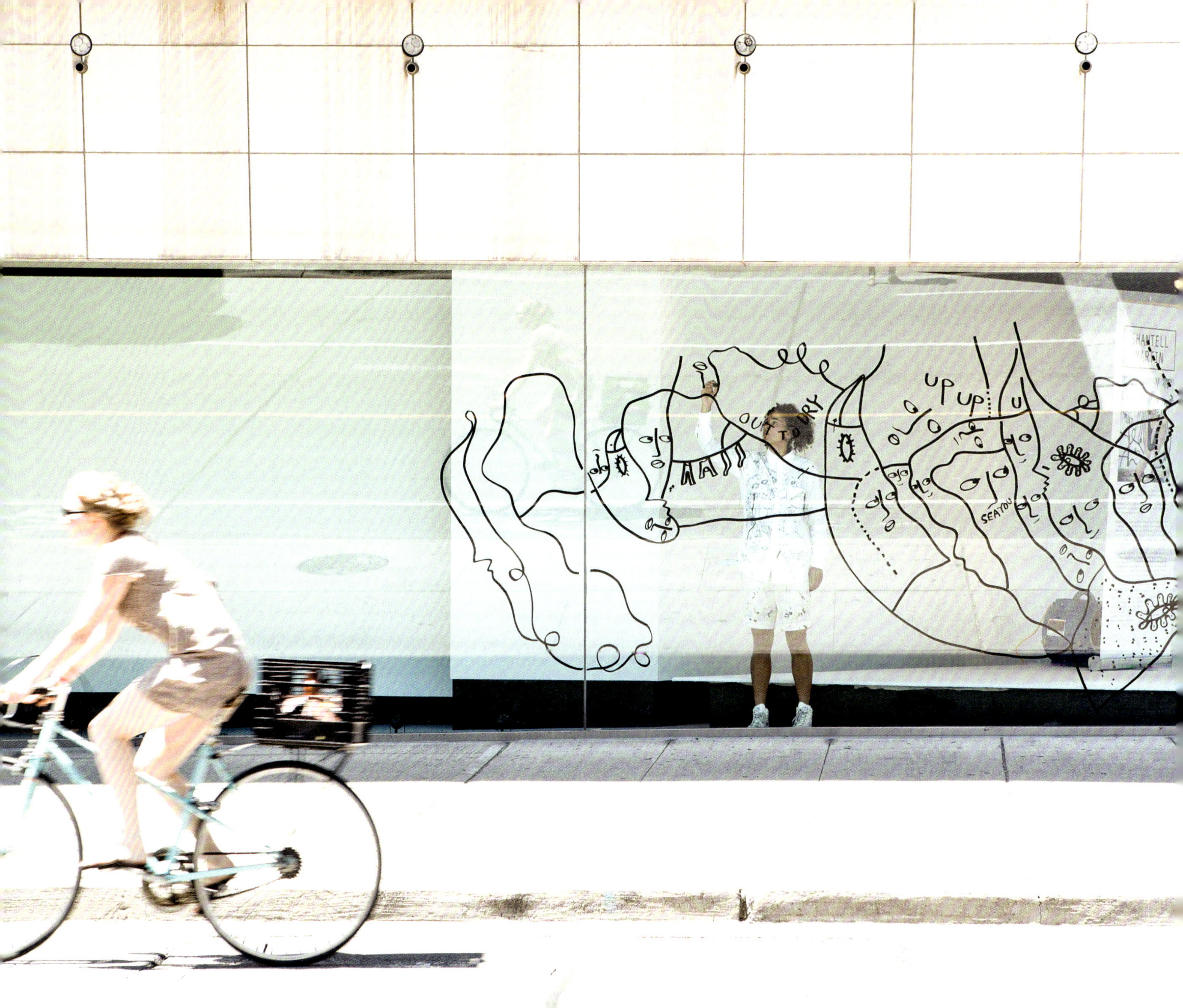

MA
OUT TO RY
UP UP
U
OLD
SEAYOU
SHANTELL
MARTIN

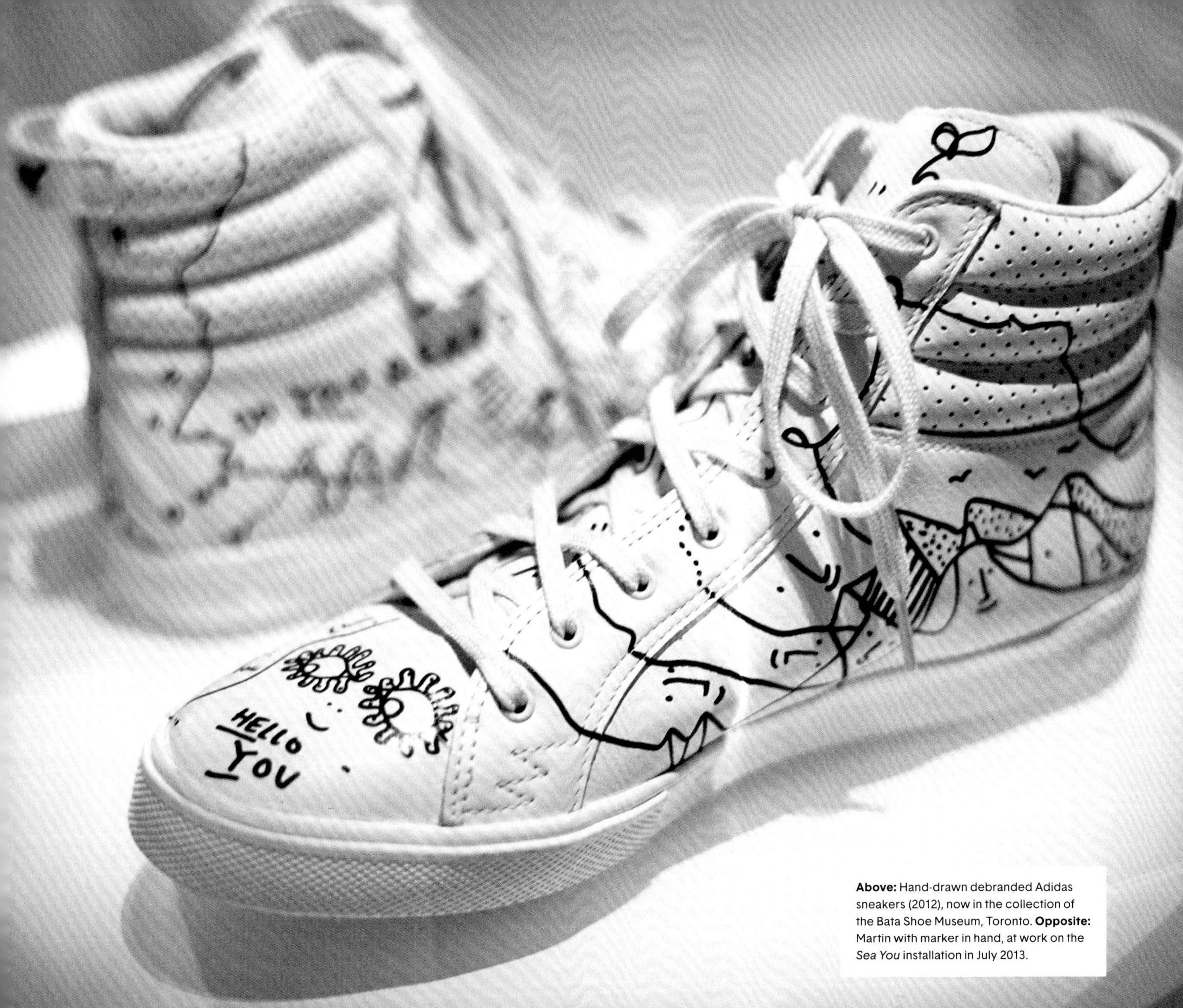

Above: Hand-drawn debranded Adidas sneakers (2012), now in the collection of the Bata Shoe Museum, Toronto. **Opposite:** Martin with marker in hand, at work on the *Sea You* installation in July 2013.

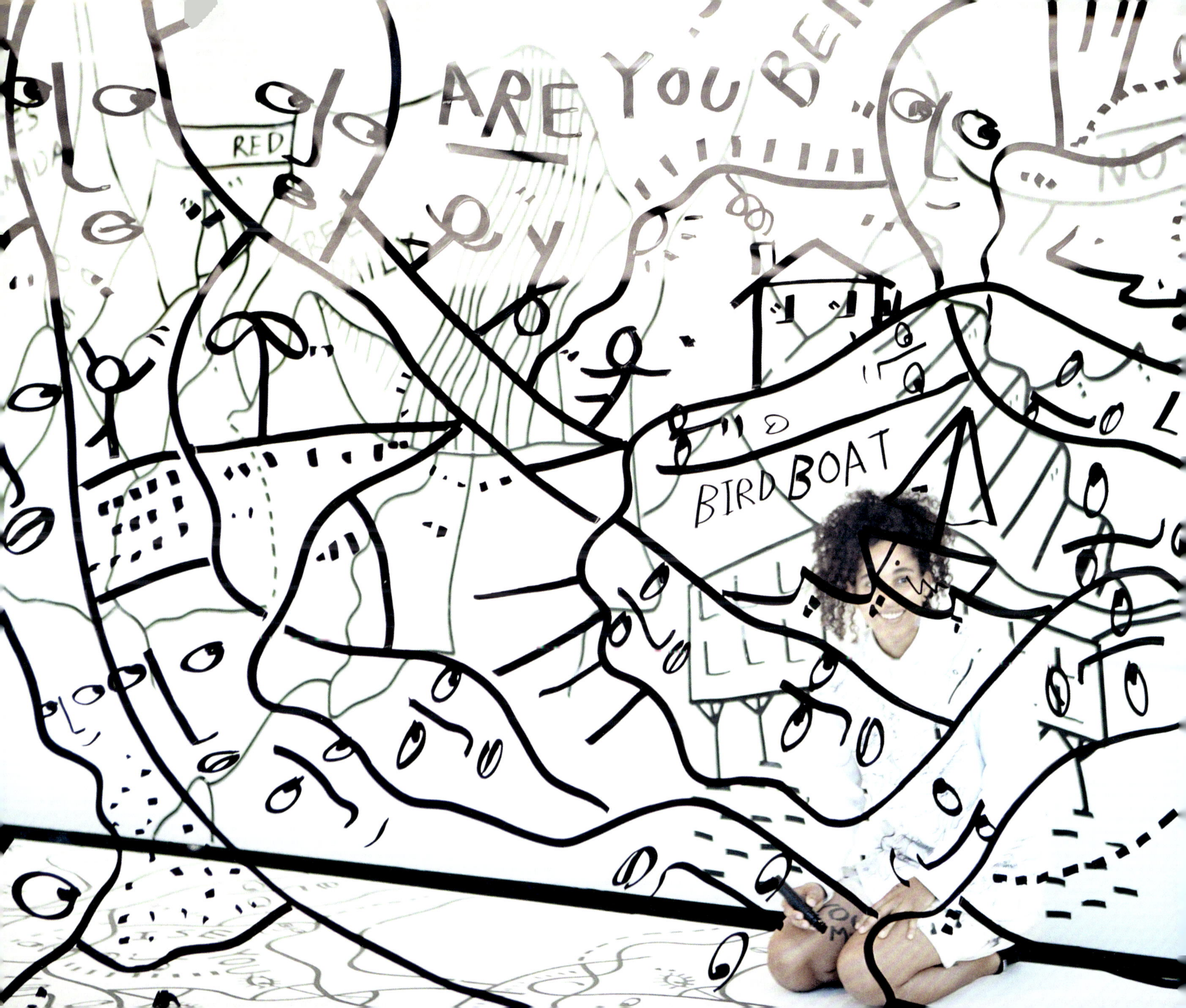

ARE YOU BE
RED
BIRD BOAT
NO

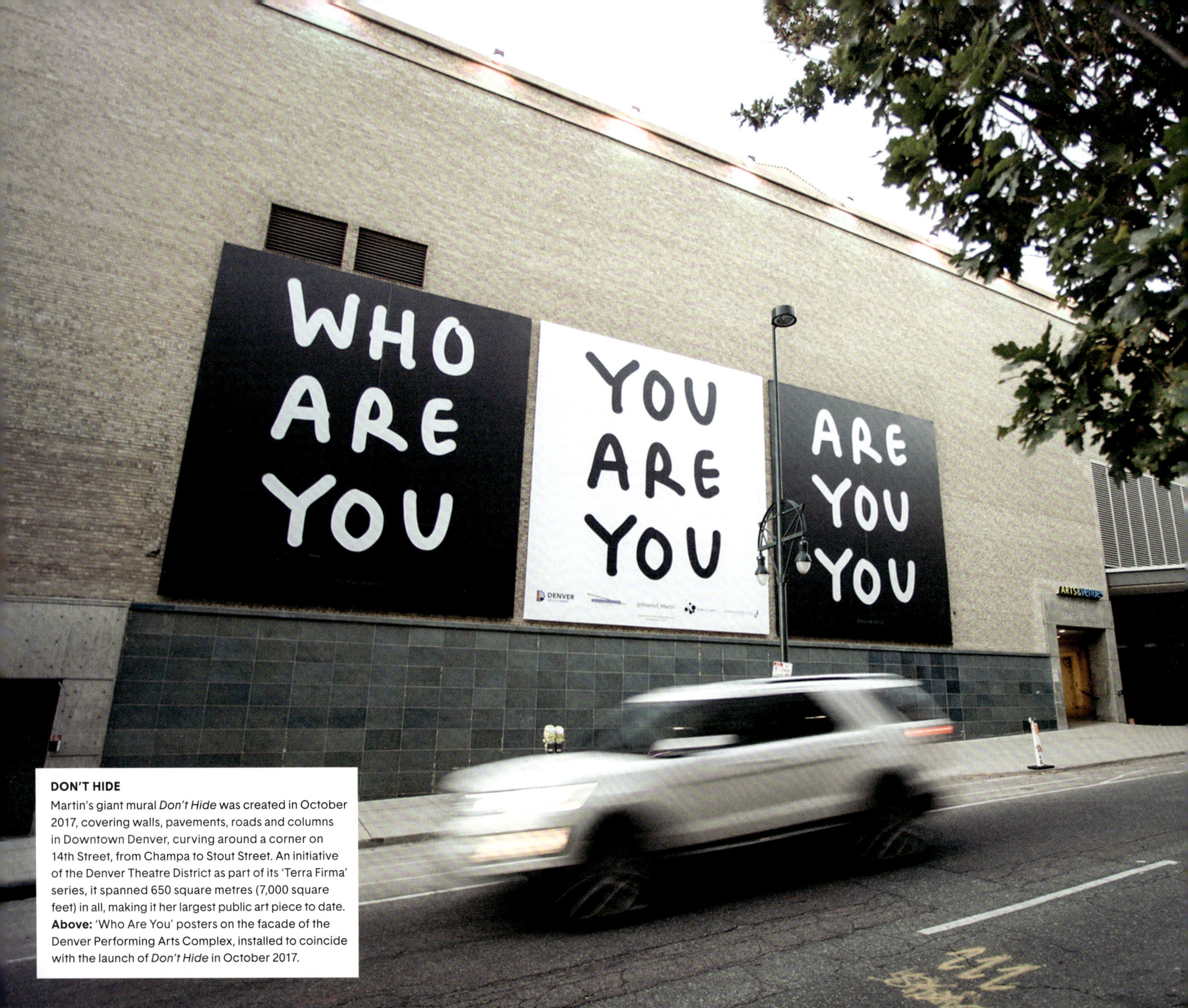

DON'T HIDE

Martin's giant mural *Don't Hide* was created in October 2017, covering walls, pavements, roads and columns in Downtown Denver, curving around a corner on 14th Street, from Champa to Stout Street. An initiative of the Denver Theatre District as part of its 'Terra Firma' series, it spanned 650 square metres (7,000 square feet) in all, making it her largest public art piece to date.

Above: 'Who Are You' posters on the facade of the Denver Performing Arts Complex, installed to coincide with the launch of *Don't Hide* in October 2017.

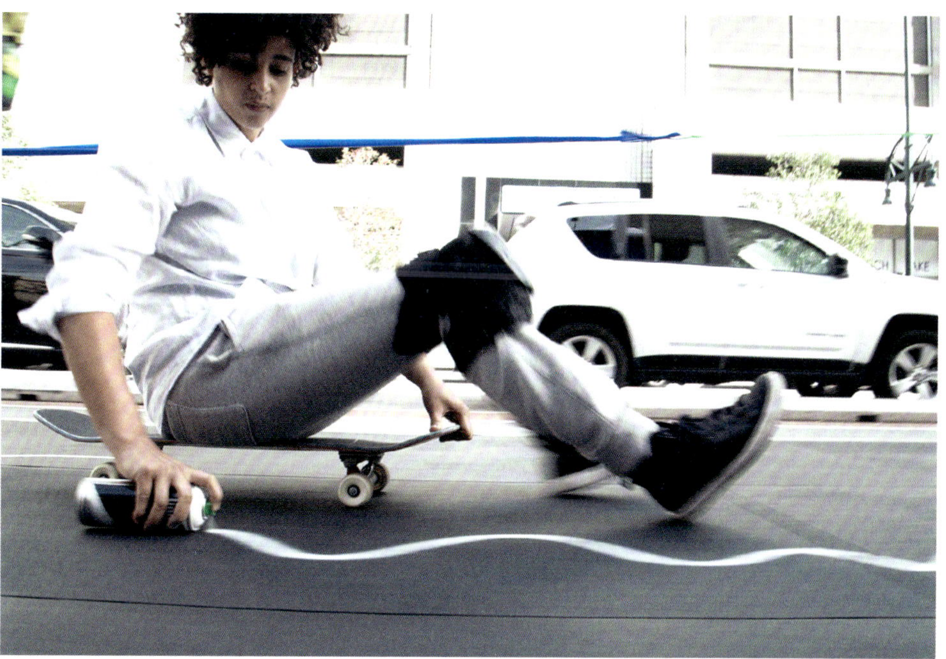

Right: Martin working on *Don't Hide* in October 2017.

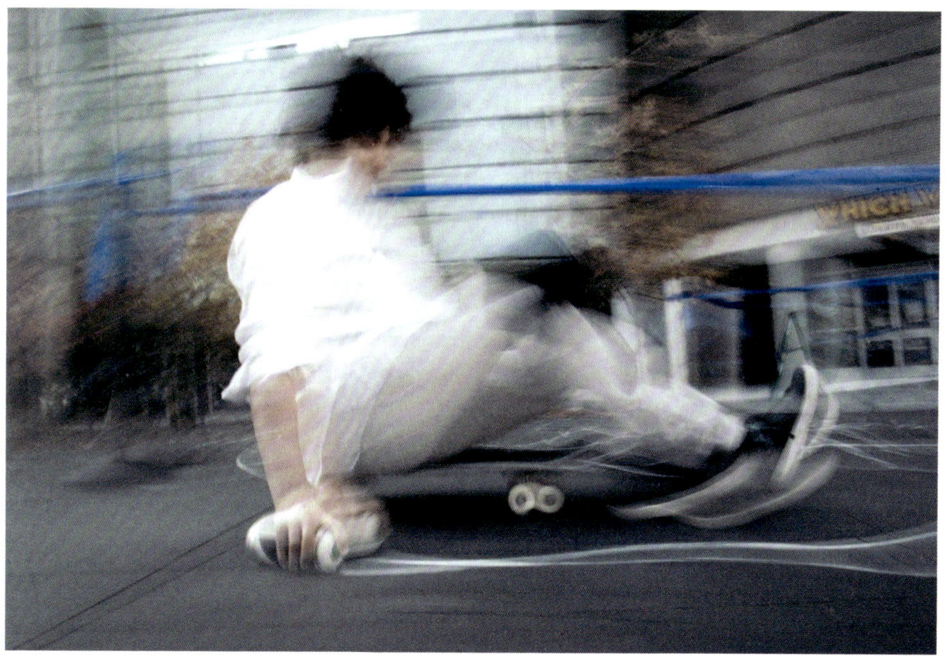

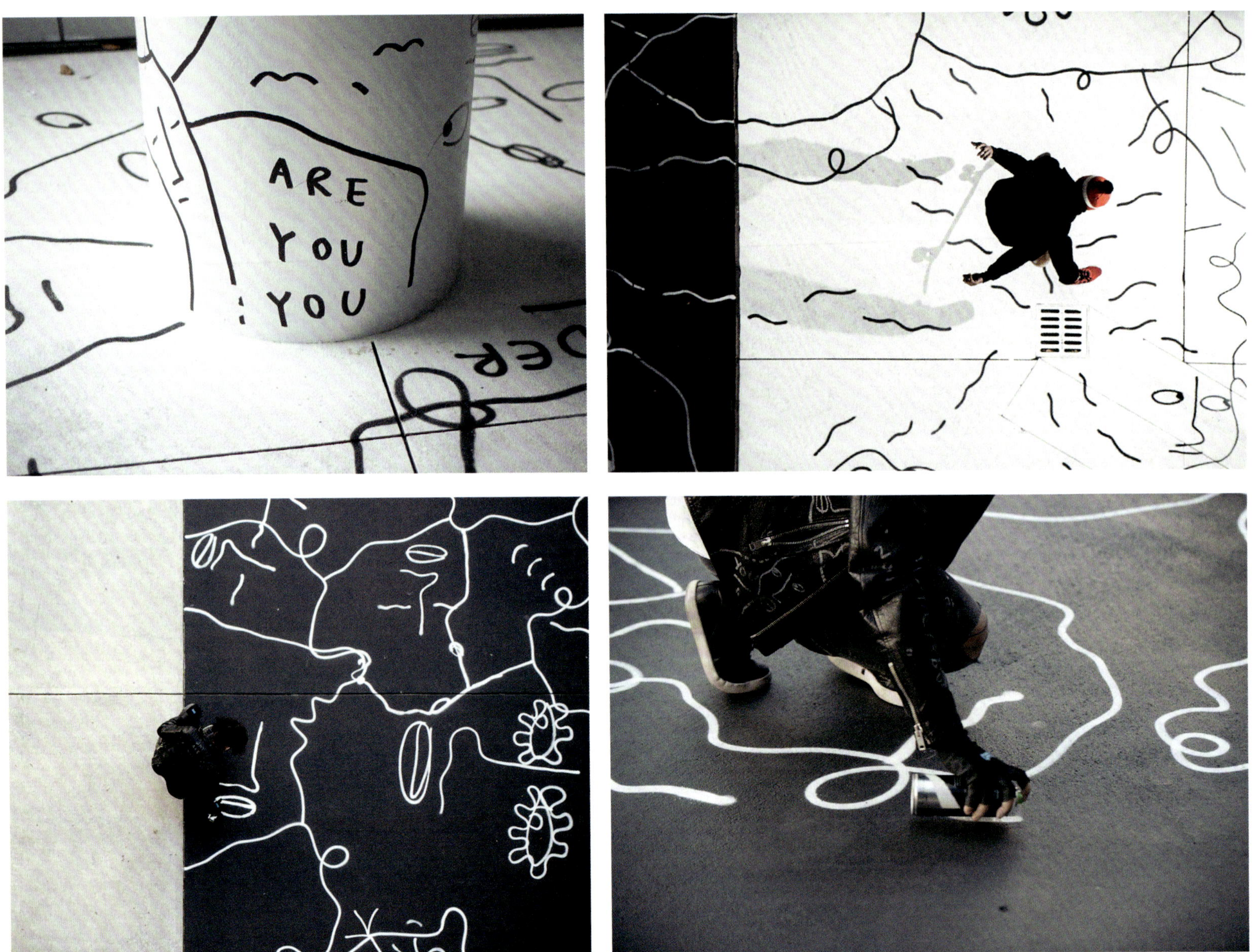

Above: Martin at work painting *Don't Hide* in Downtown Denver, October 2017.
Opposite: Detail of *Don't Hide* on columns outside the Colorado Convention Center.

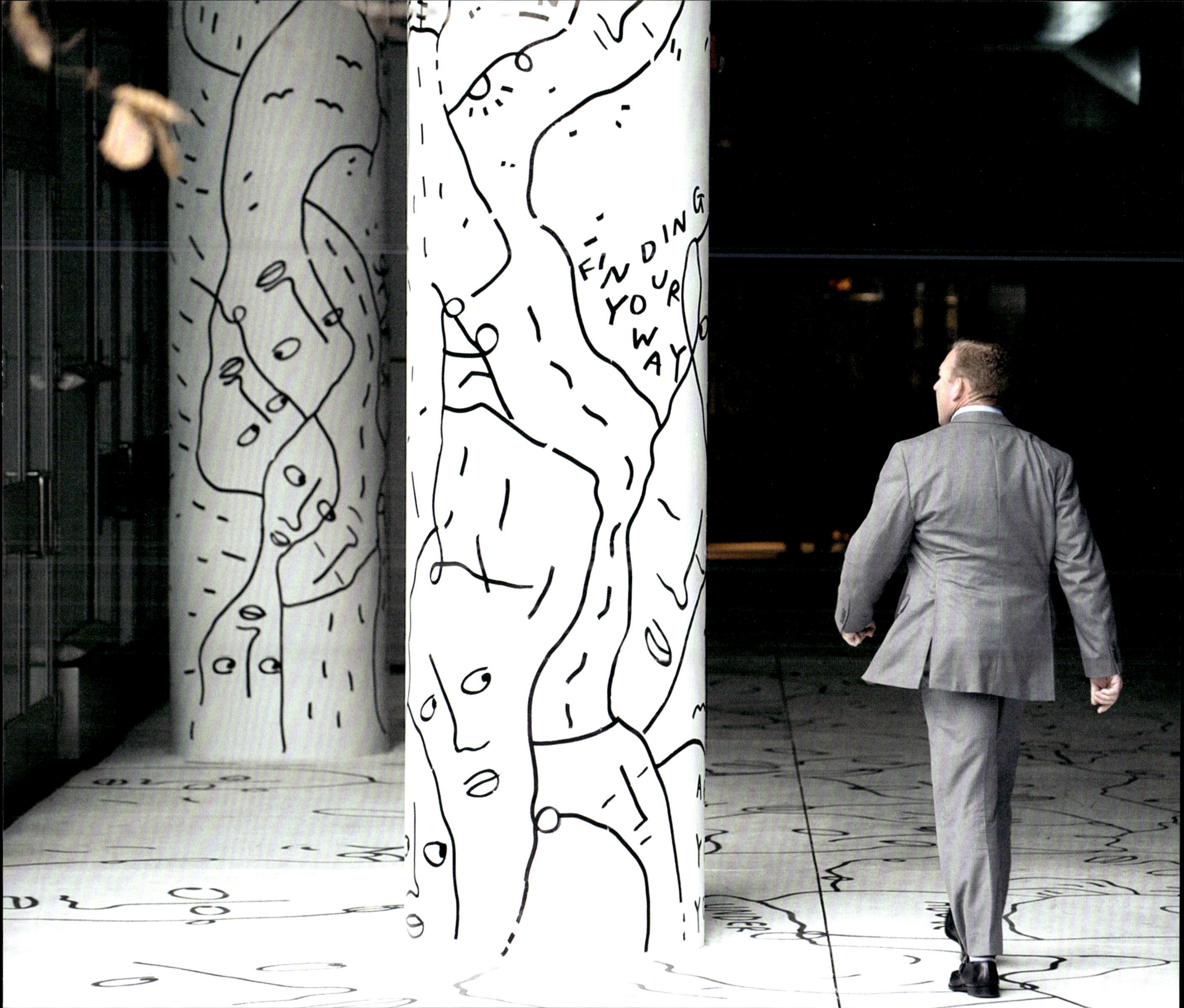

FINDING
YOUR
WAY

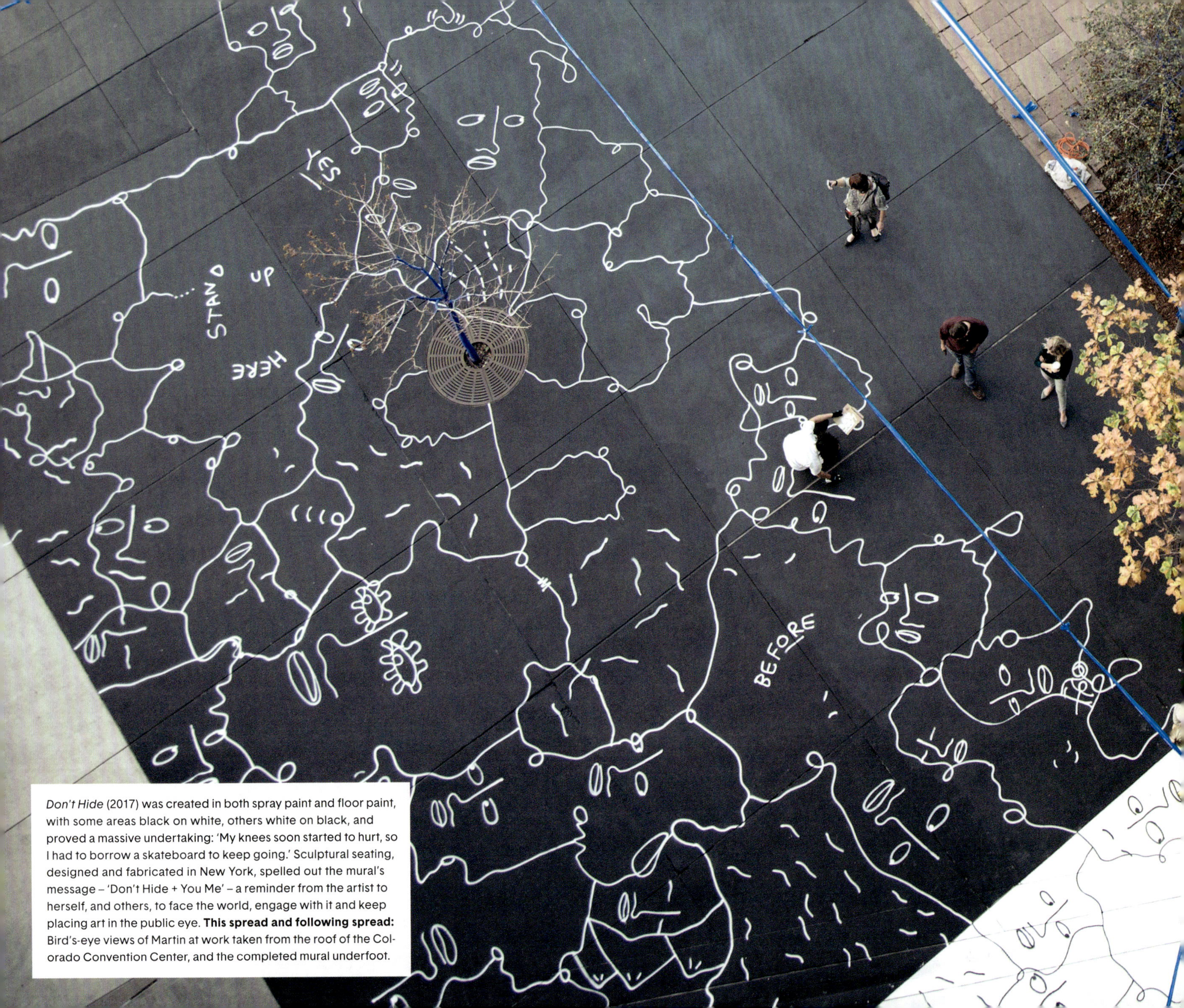

Don't Hide (2017) was created in both spray paint and floor paint, with some areas black on white, others white on black, and proved a massive undertaking: 'My knees soon started to hurt, so I had to borrow a skateboard to keep going.' Sculptural seating, designed and fabricated in New York, spelled out the mural's message – 'Don't Hide + You Me' – a reminder from the artist to herself, and others, to face the world, engage with it and keep placing art in the public eye. **This spread and following spread:** Bird's-eye views of Martin at work taken from the roof of the Colorado Convention Center, and the completed mural underfoot.

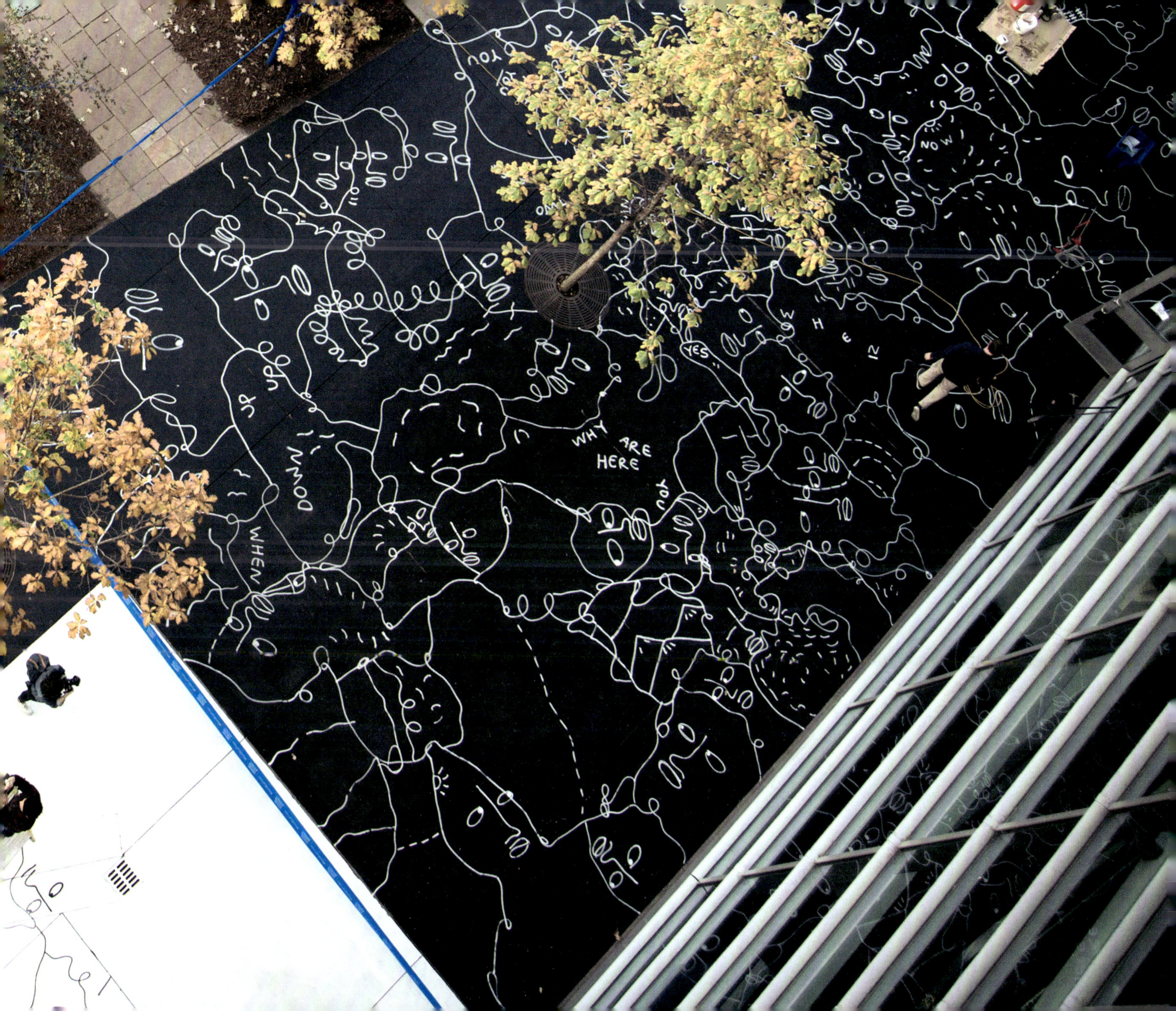

YOU
NOW
YES
WHEN
WHY
ARE
HERE
DOWN
WHEN
YOU

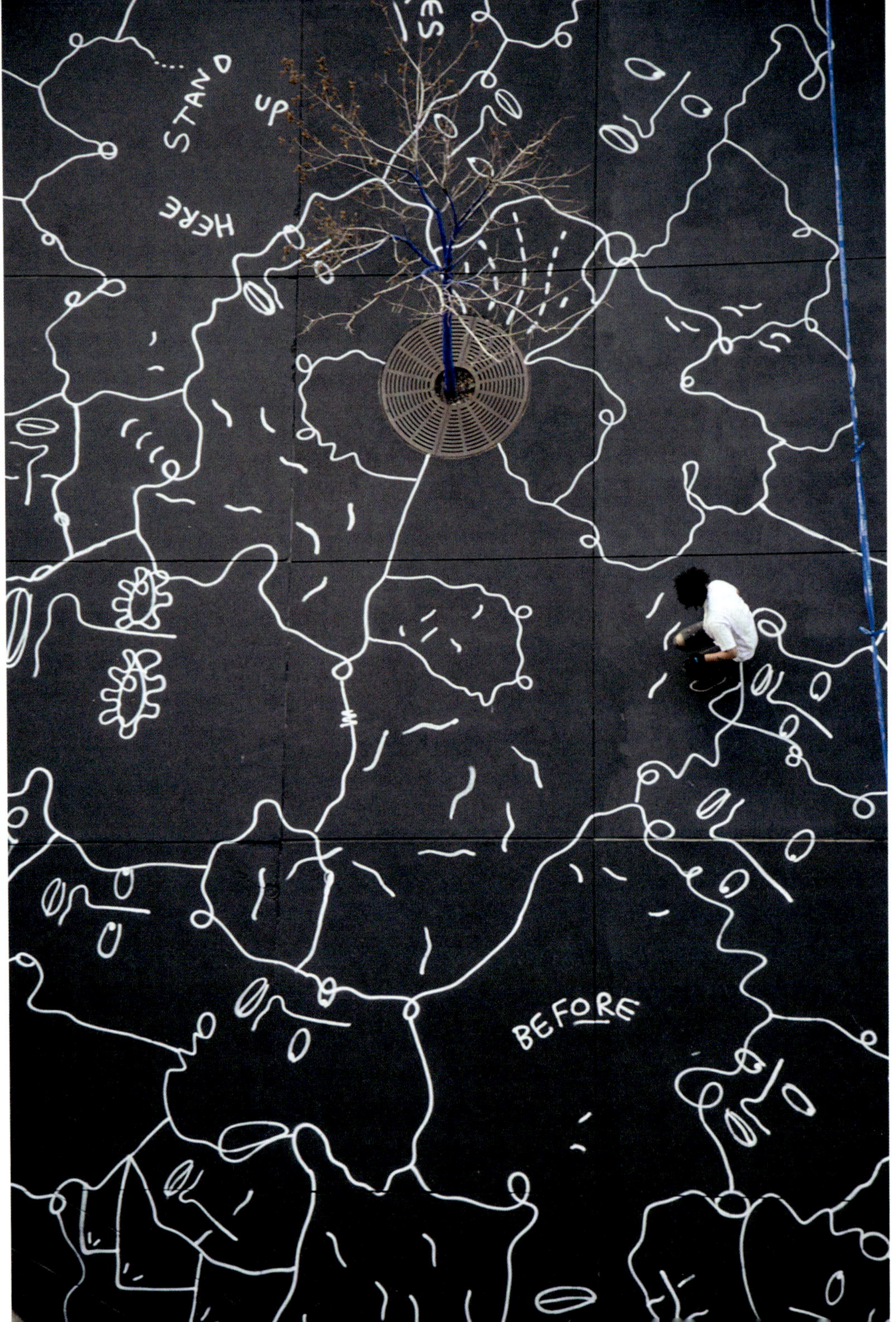

STAND UP
HERE
BEFORE

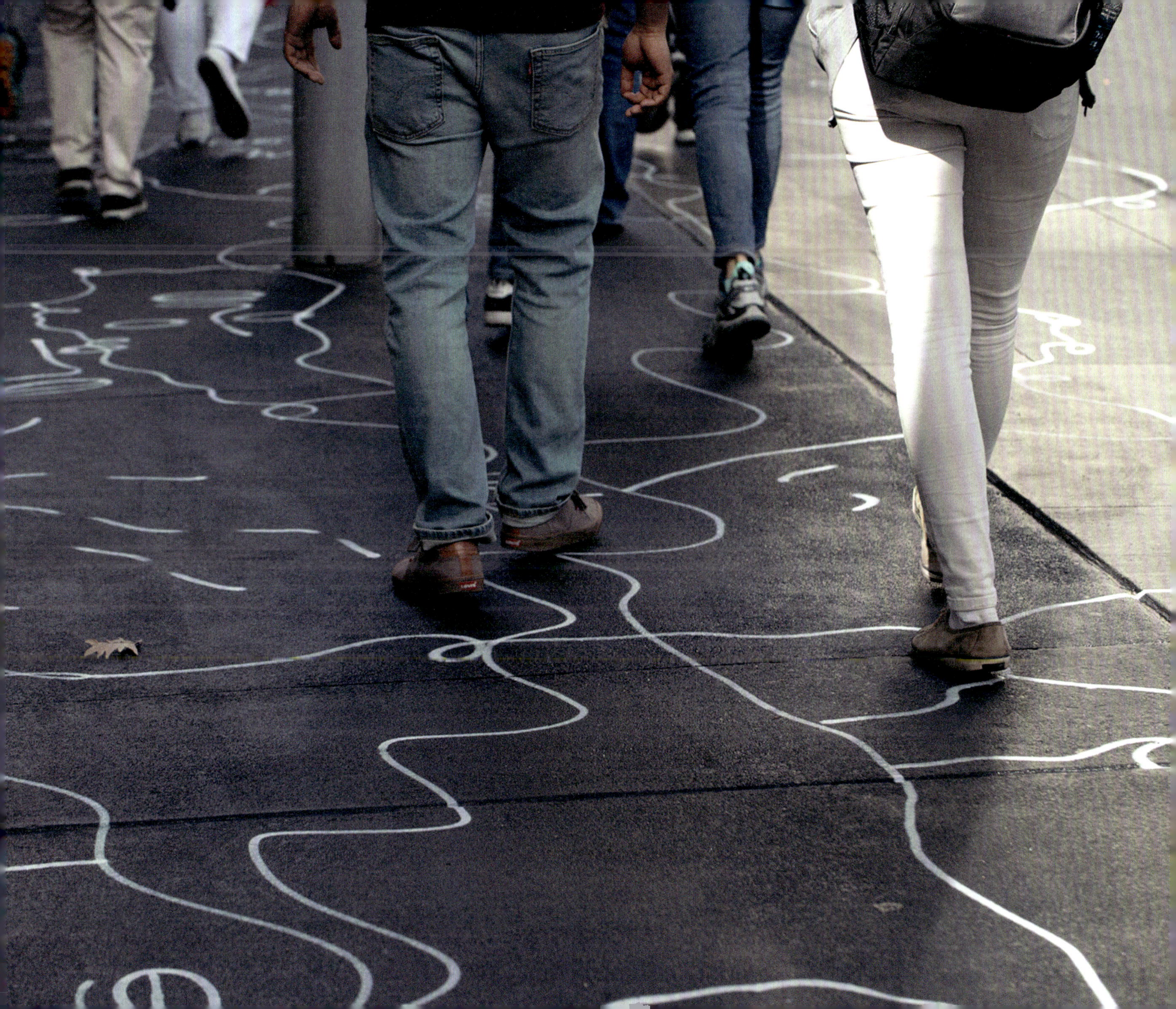

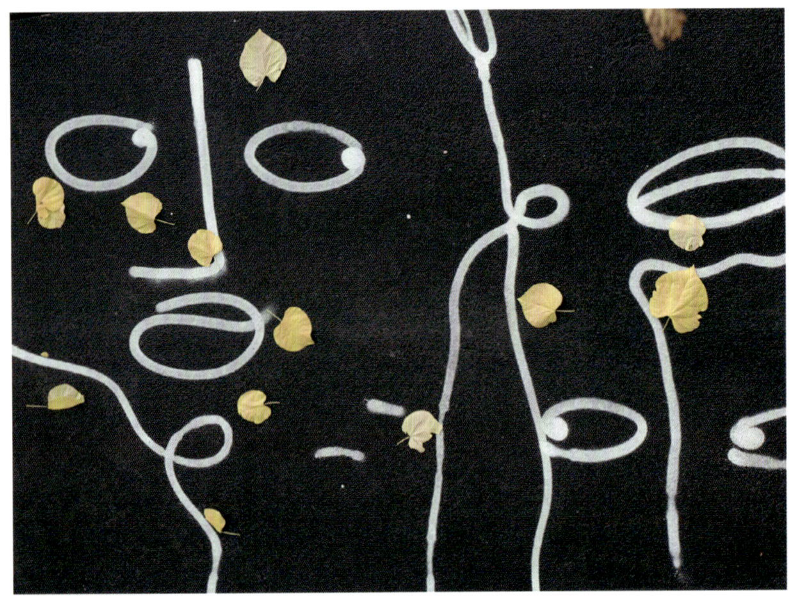
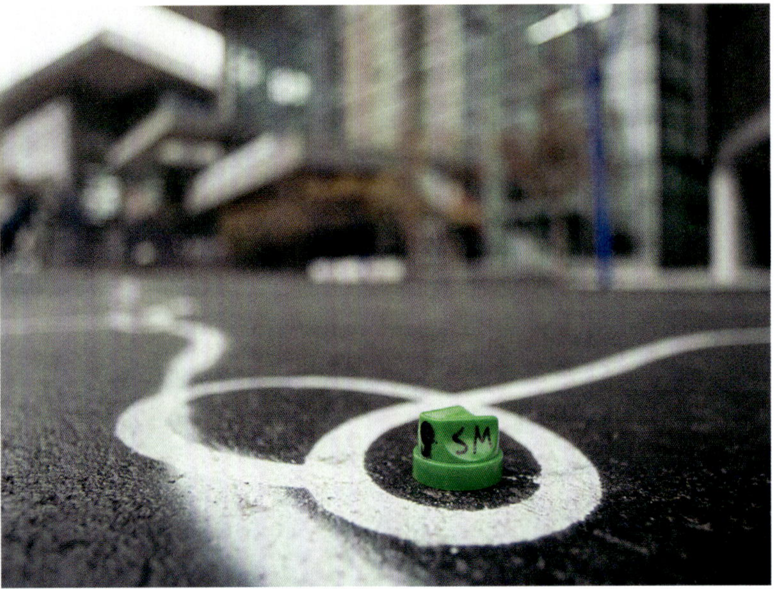
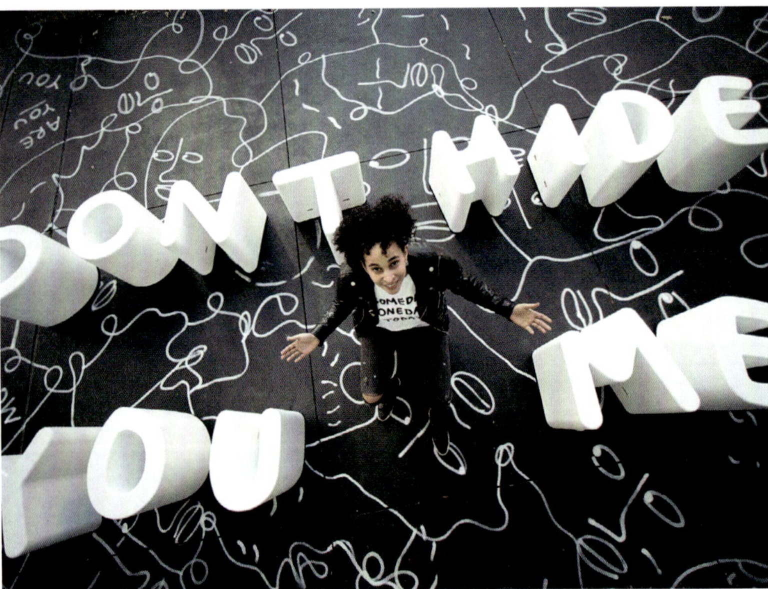

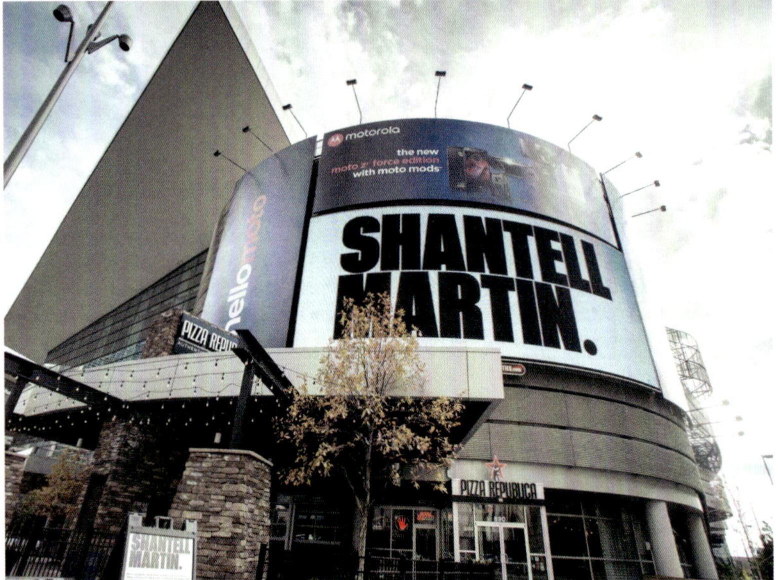

This spread: Details of *Don't Hide* (2017), including the seating installation; an LCD billboard, Colorado Convention Center, Denver; and Martin with a sticker from the 'Who Are You' series, October 2017.

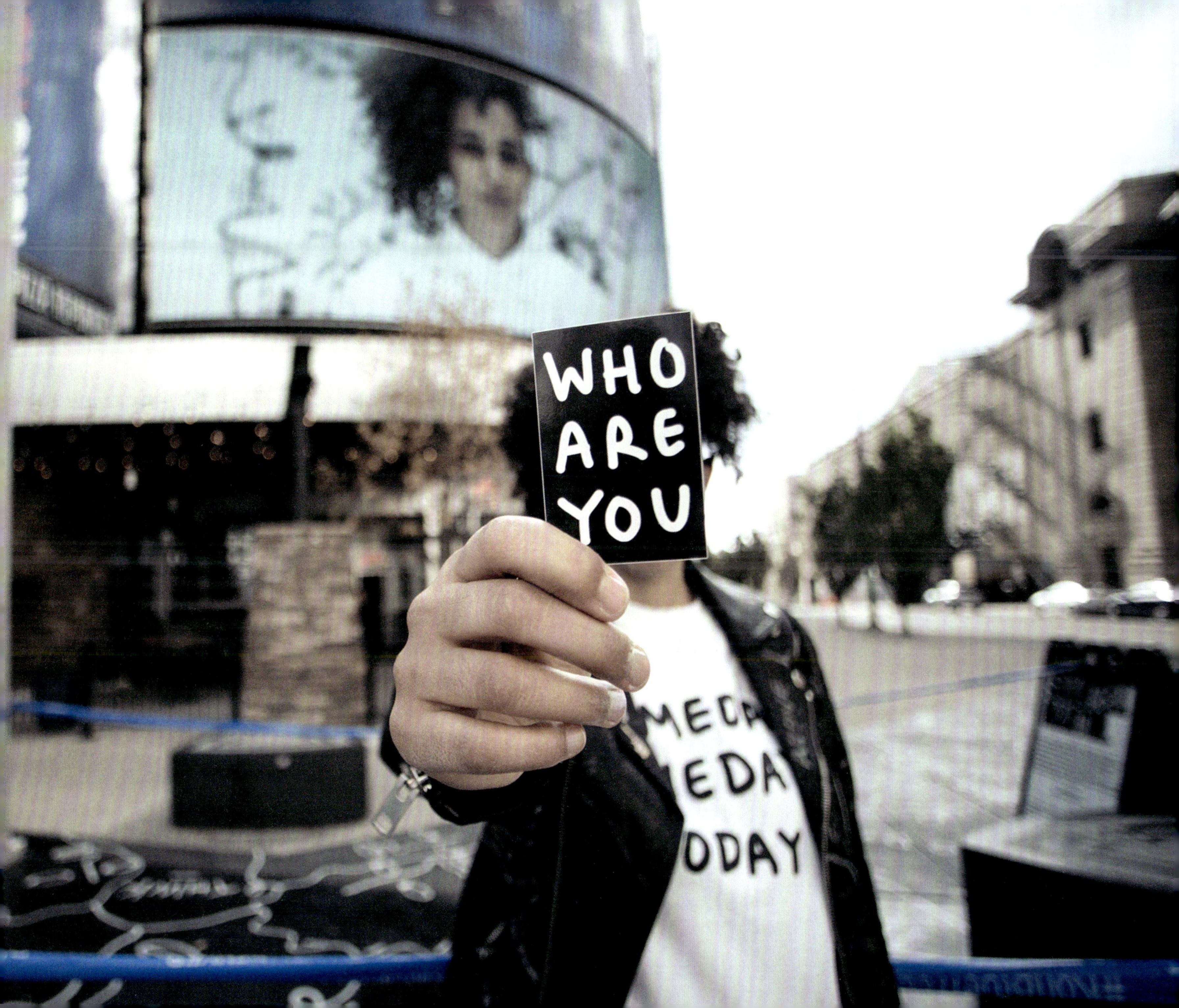

WHO
ARE
YOU

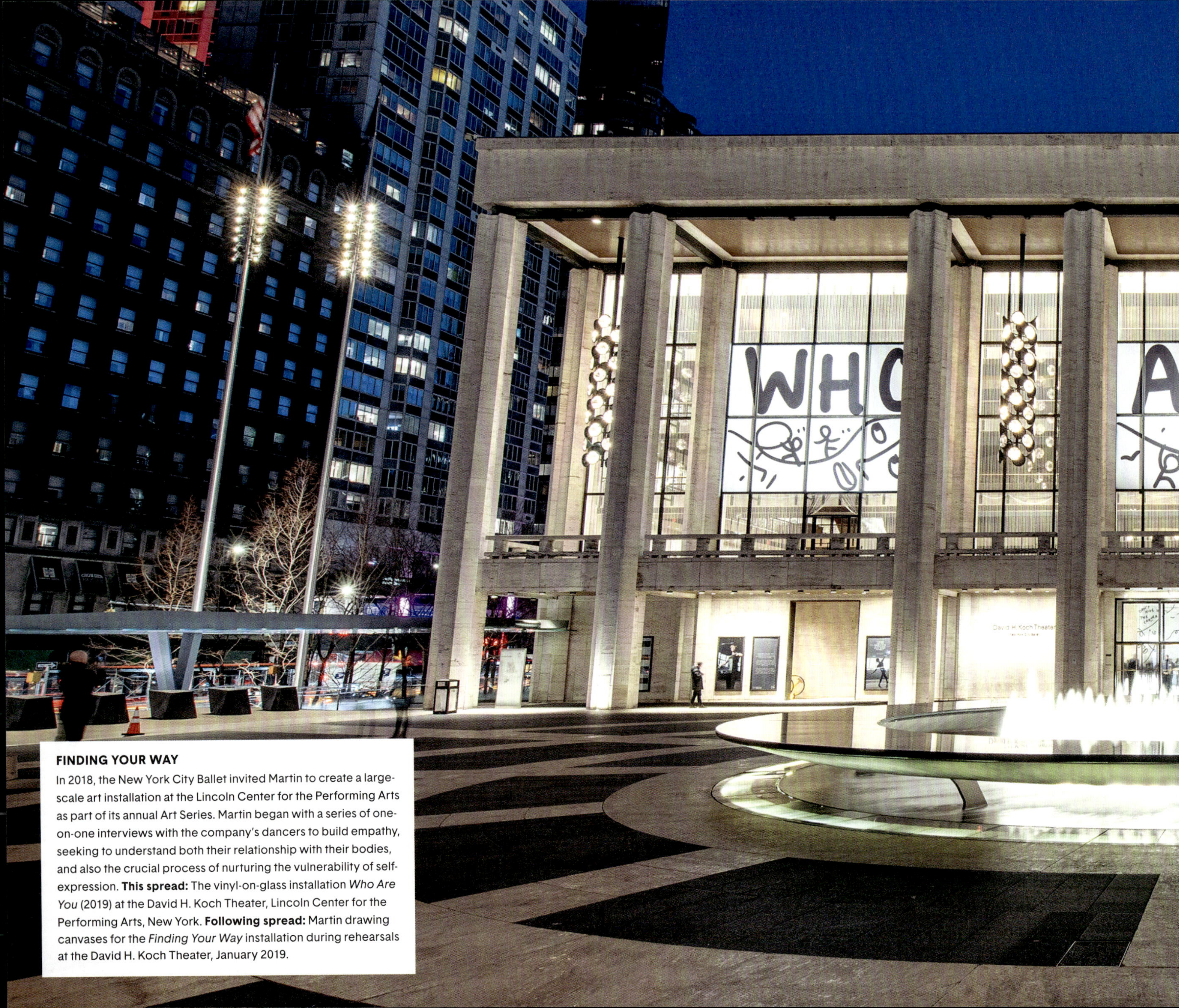

FINDING YOUR WAY

In 2018, the New York City Ballet invited Martin to create a large-scale art installation at the Lincoln Center for the Performing Arts as part of its annual Art Series. Martin began with a series of one-on-one interviews with the company's dancers to build empathy, seeking to understand both their relationship with their bodies, and also the crucial process of nurturing the vulnerability of self-expression. **This spread:** The vinyl-on-glass installation *Who Are You* (2019) at the David H. Koch Theater, Lincoln Center for the Performing Arts, New York. **Following spread:** Martin drawing canvases for the *Finding Your Way* installation during rehearsals at the David H. Koch Theater, January 2019.

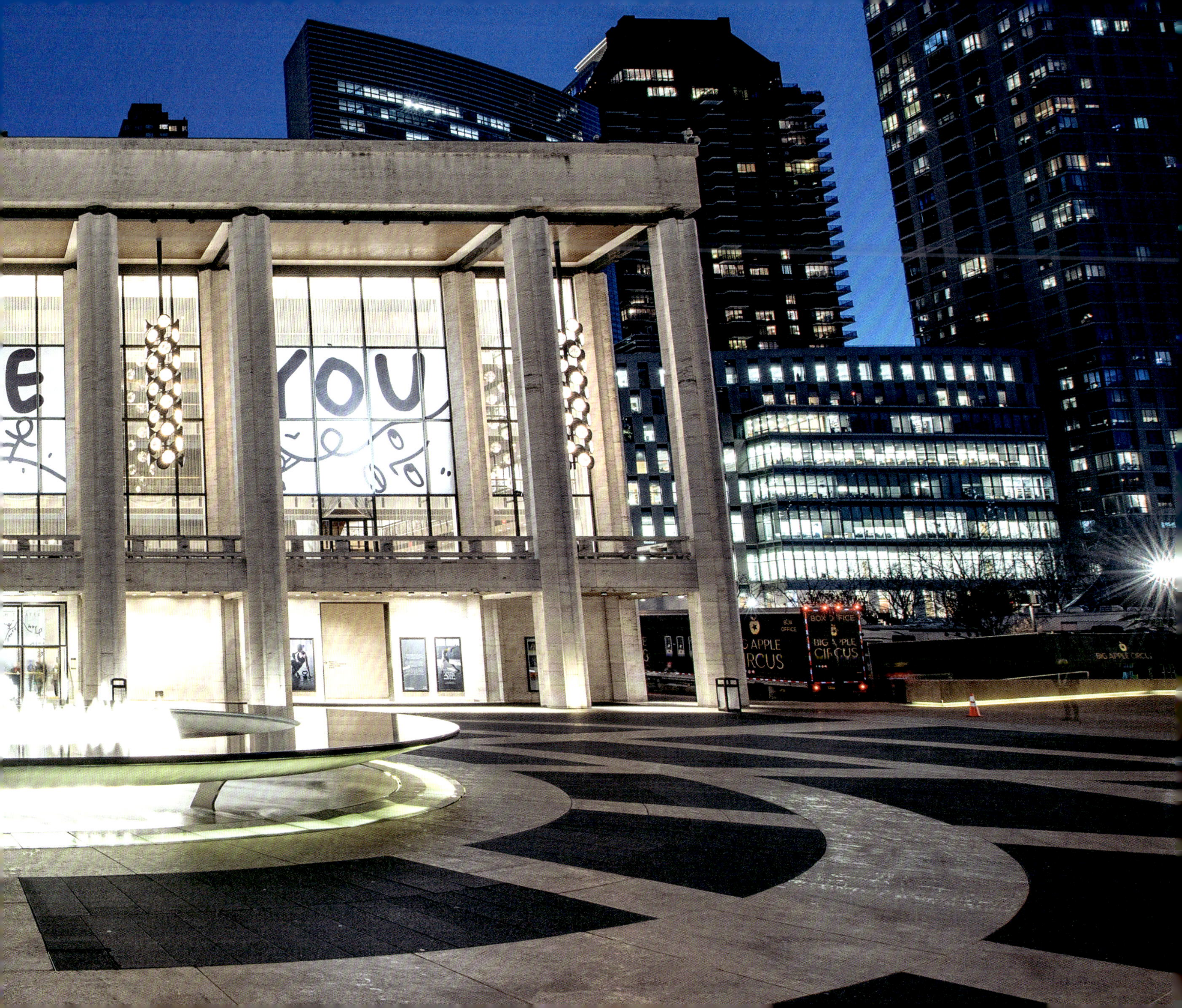

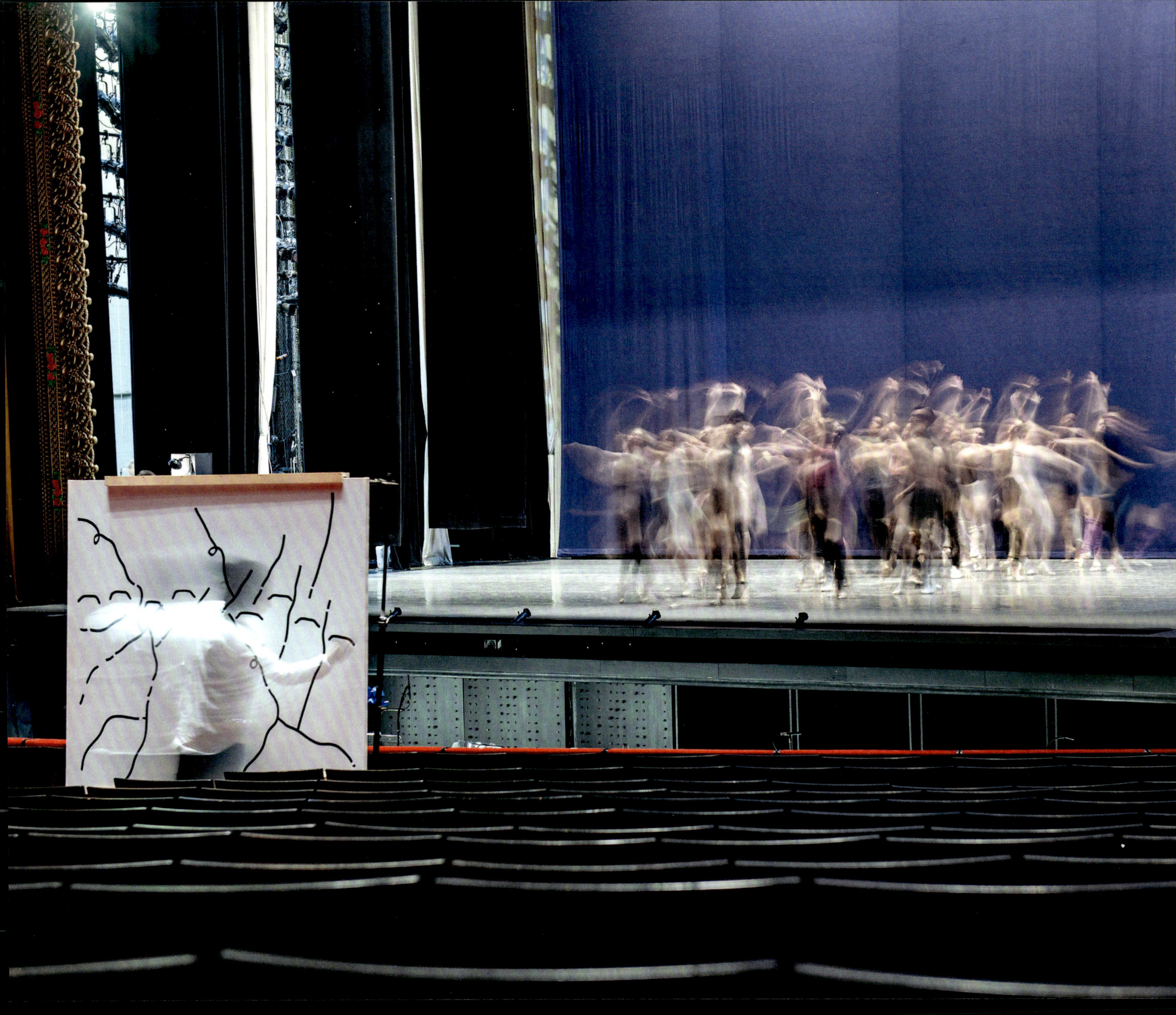

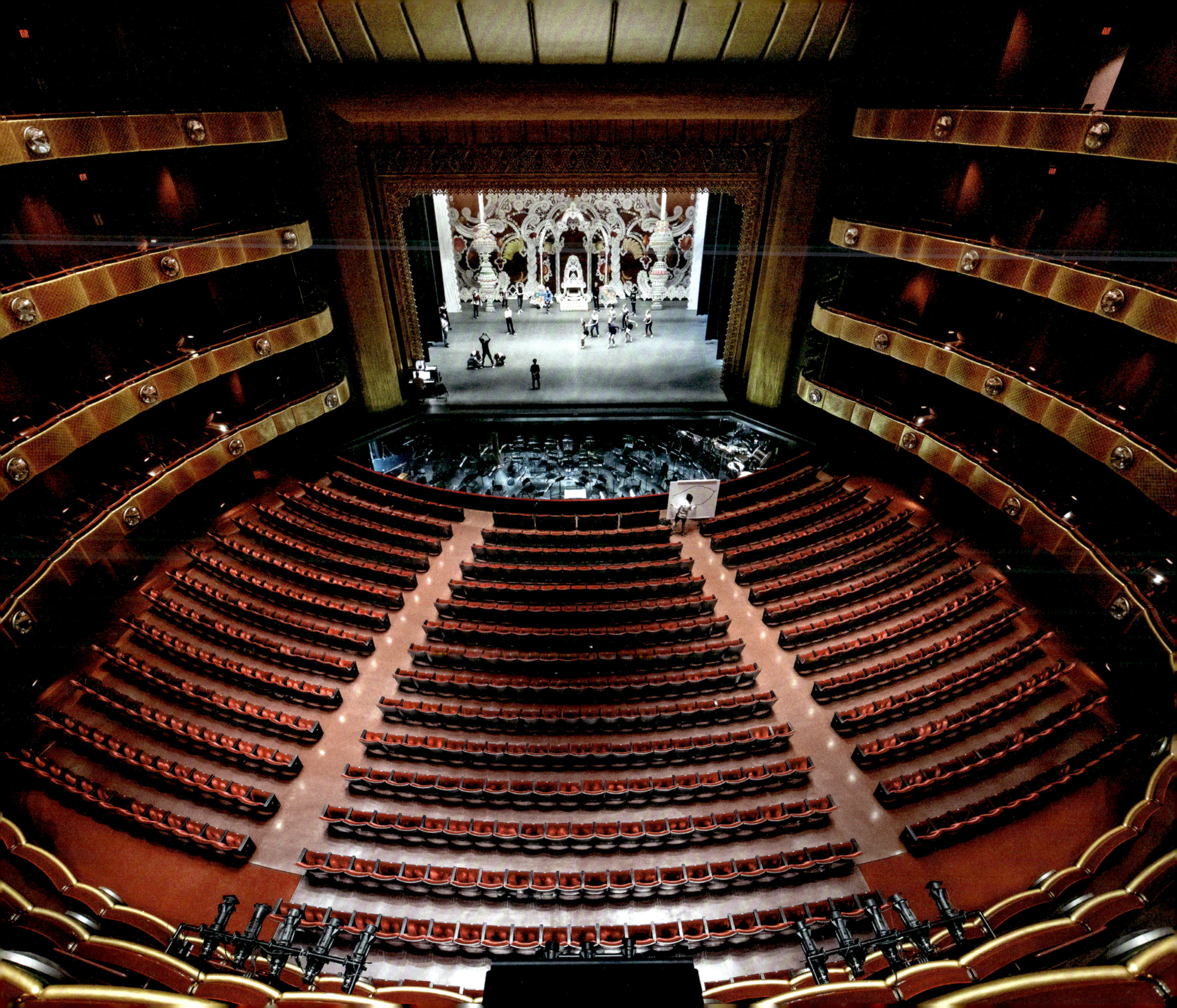

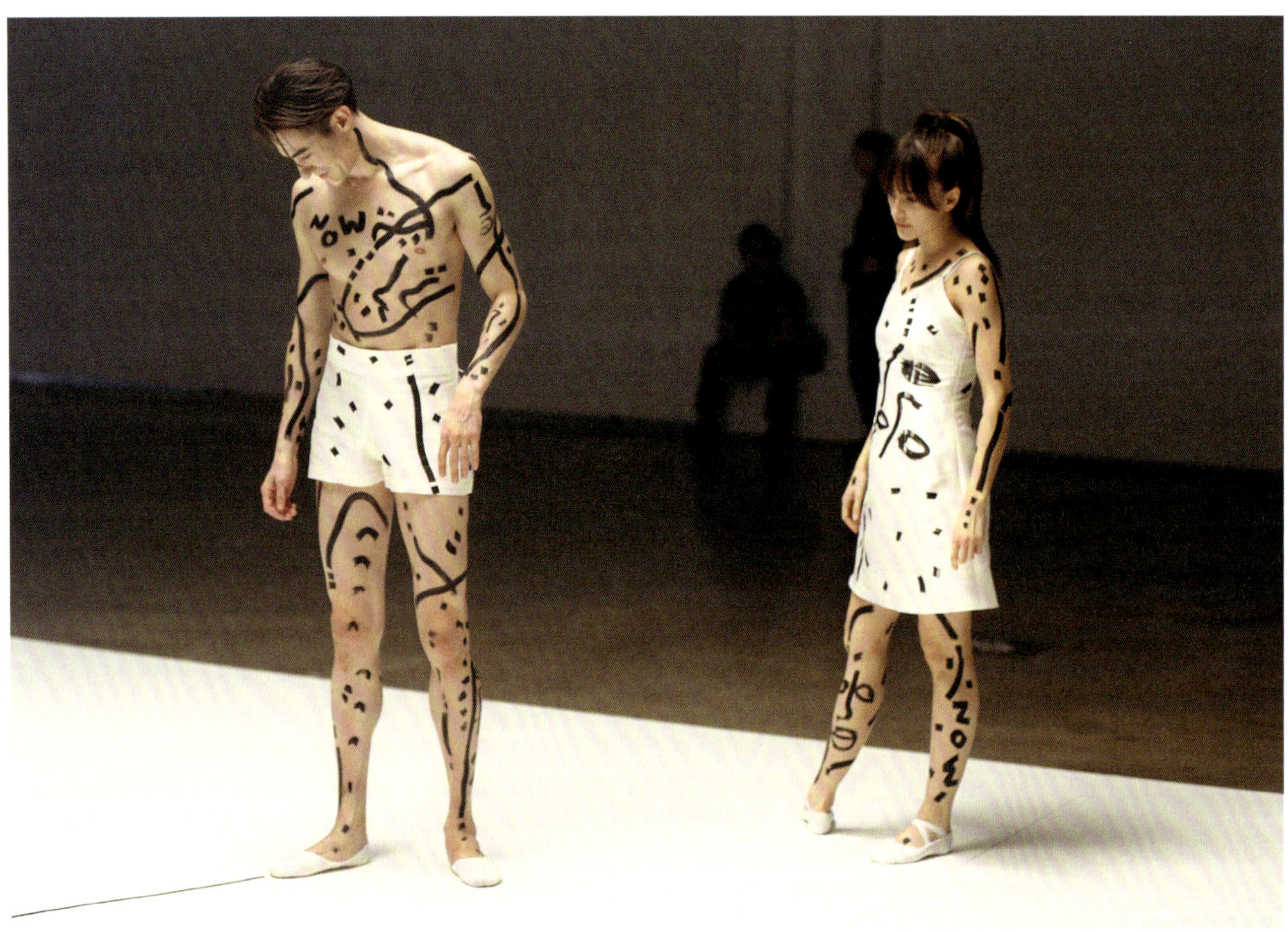

As an artist devoted to her own rules of engagement, Martin found relatability in the structure and traditions of dance, in the rules of choreography and in the parameters of a ballet company. While drawing the New York City Ballet's live rehearsals from December 2018 on, Martin carefully observed the dancers' movement across genres, from the more traditional sequences of *The Nutcracker* to contemporary pieces by resident choreographer Justin Peck. Her approach changed with the energy of each piece, until 'the dancers turned to lines and shapes, and faces began to disappear'. The unspoken conversation between the movement and flow of bodies and the repetitive piano cadences pushed Martin's work towards greater abstraction, which she later punctuated with words and phrases from her interviews. The project's outputs included a striking video of dancers Lauren Lovette and Daniel Applebaum performing with Martin's drawings inscribed on their skin. **This spread:** Applebaum and Lovette preparing for the *Shantell Martin x NYCB* video (2019) at Parlay Studios, Jersey City, and Martin drawing on the pair with washable ink, November 2018.

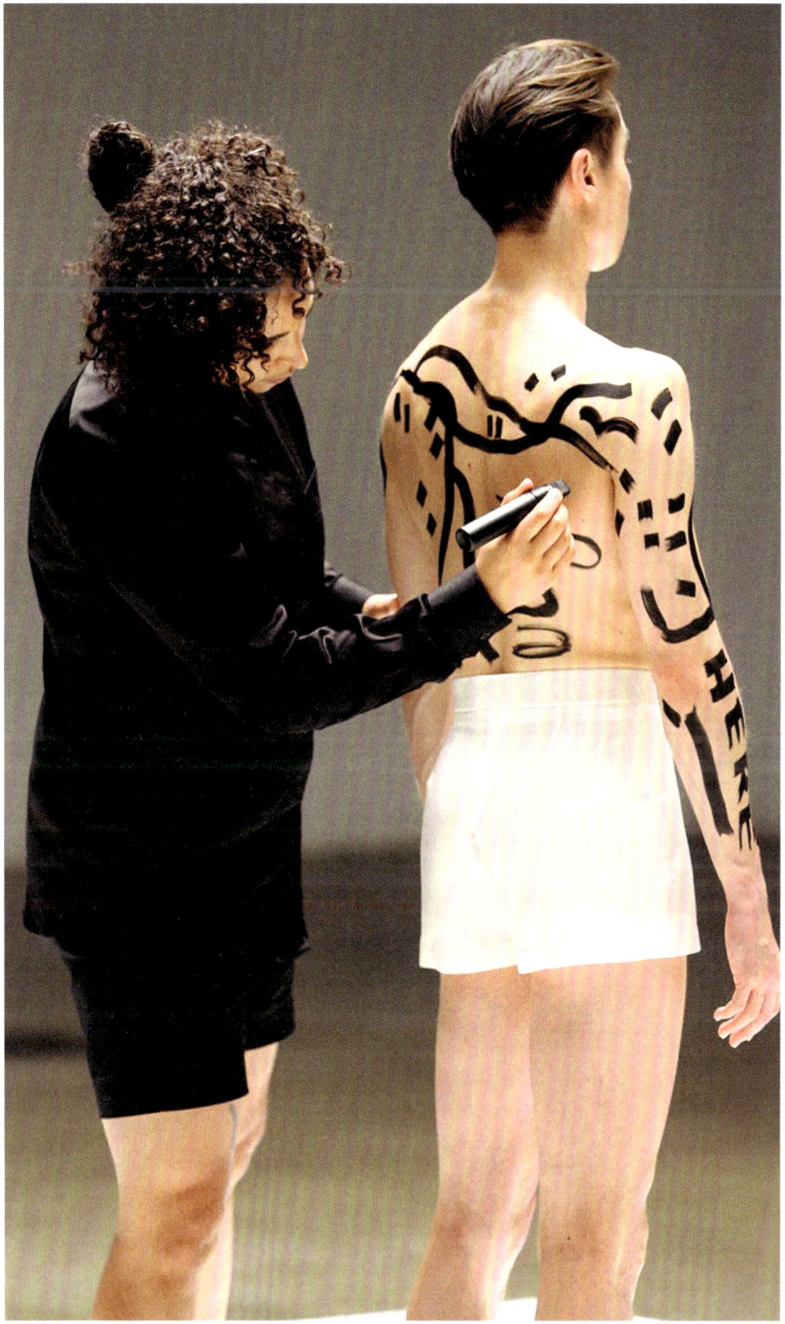

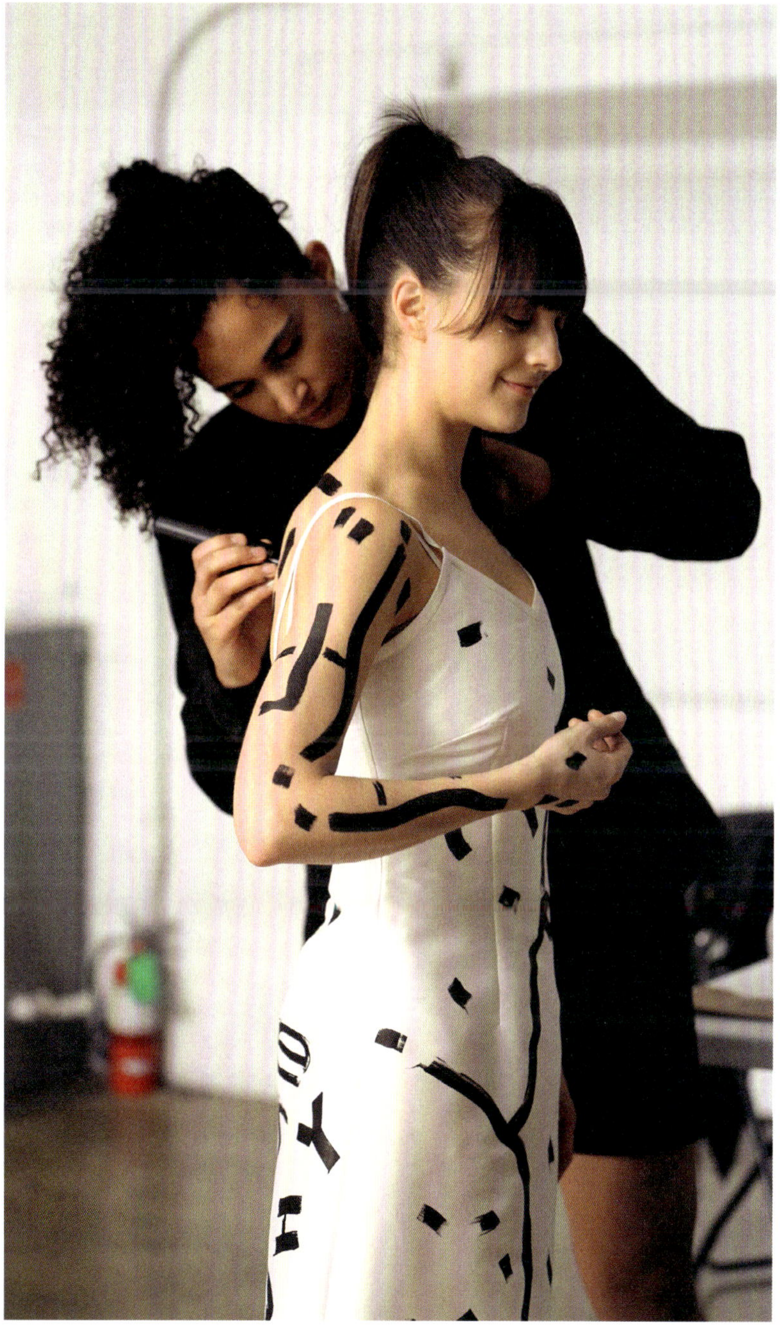

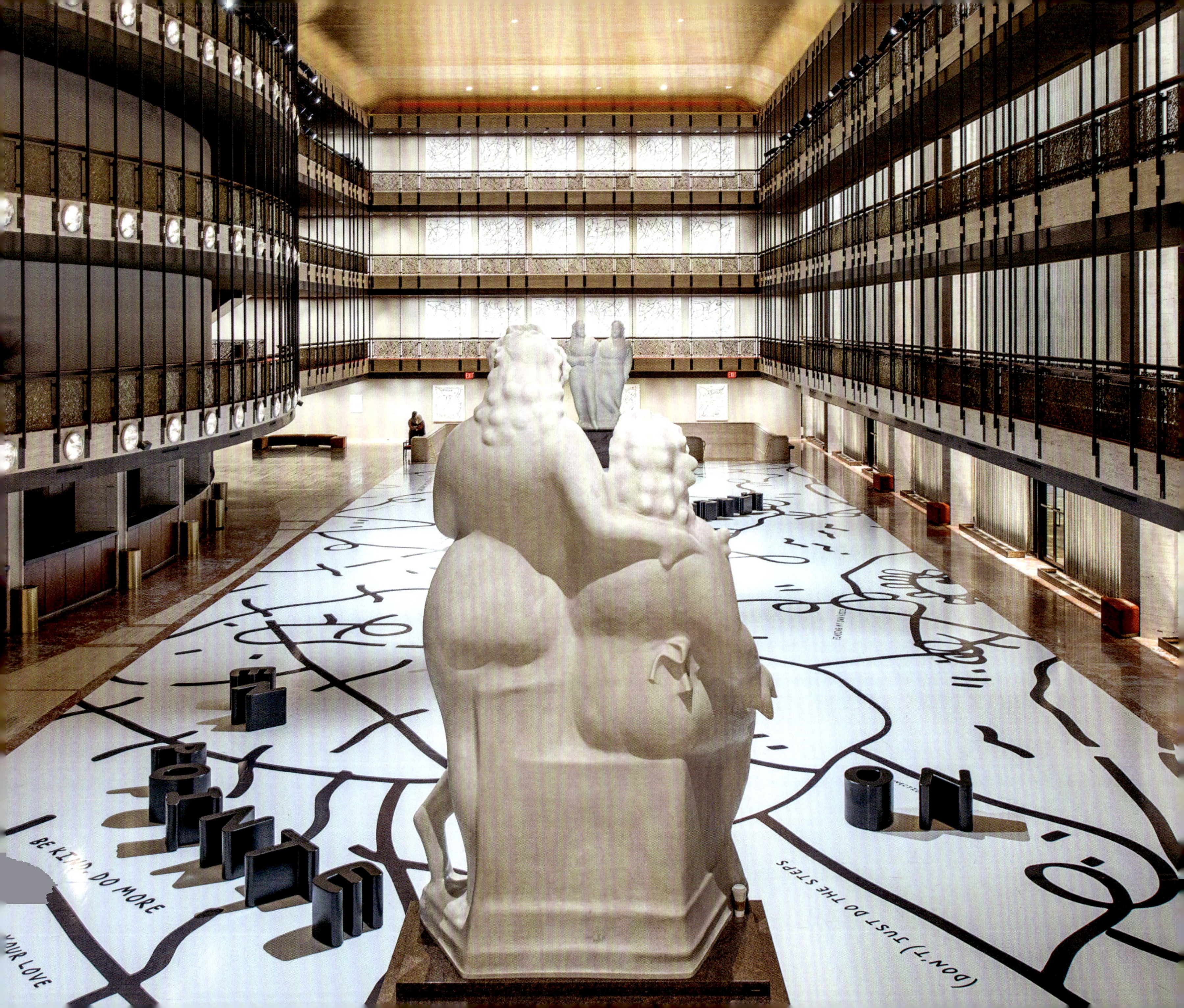
BE KIND, DO MORE
YOUR LOVE
(DON'T) JUST DO THE STEPS

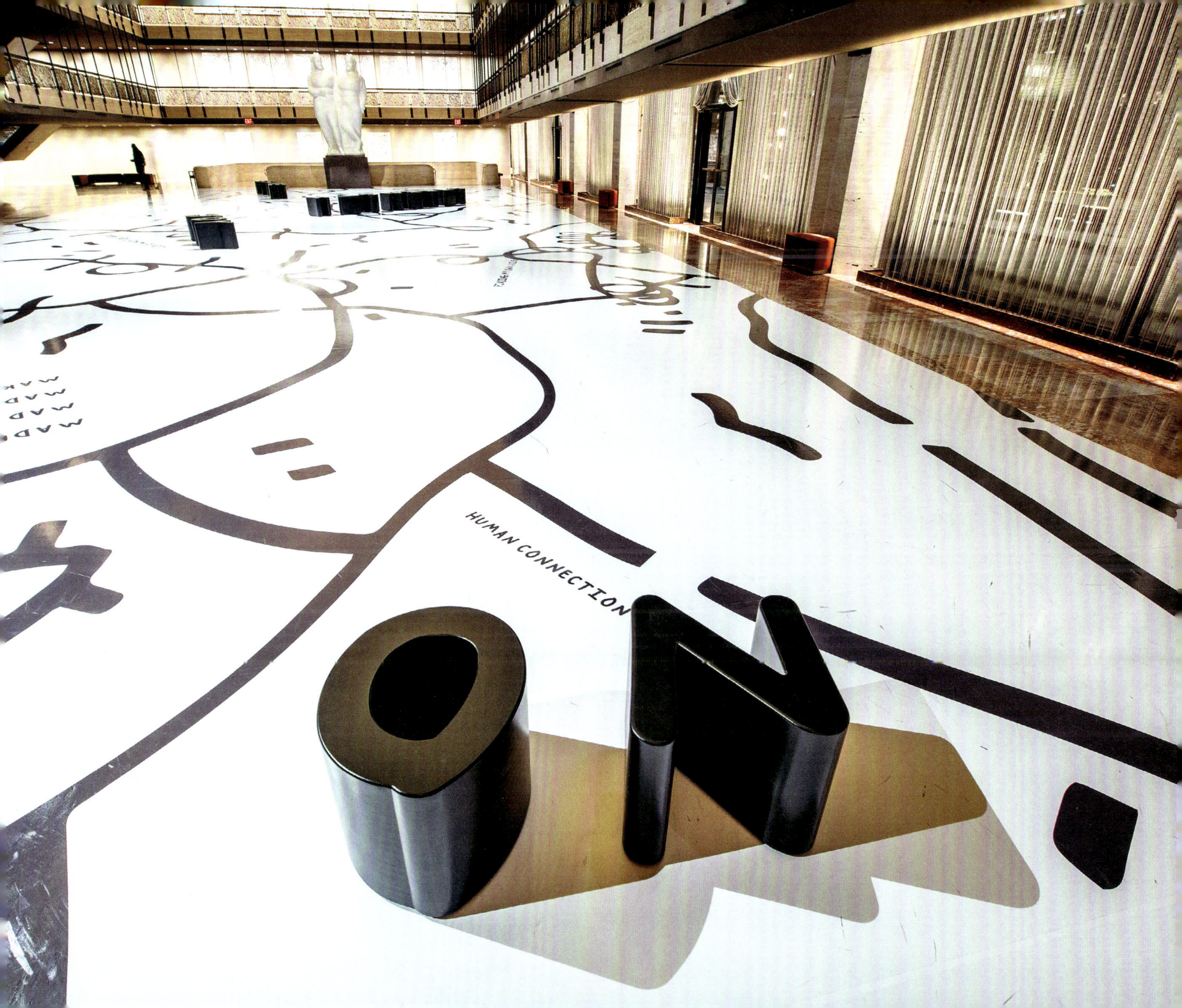

HUMAN CONNECTION

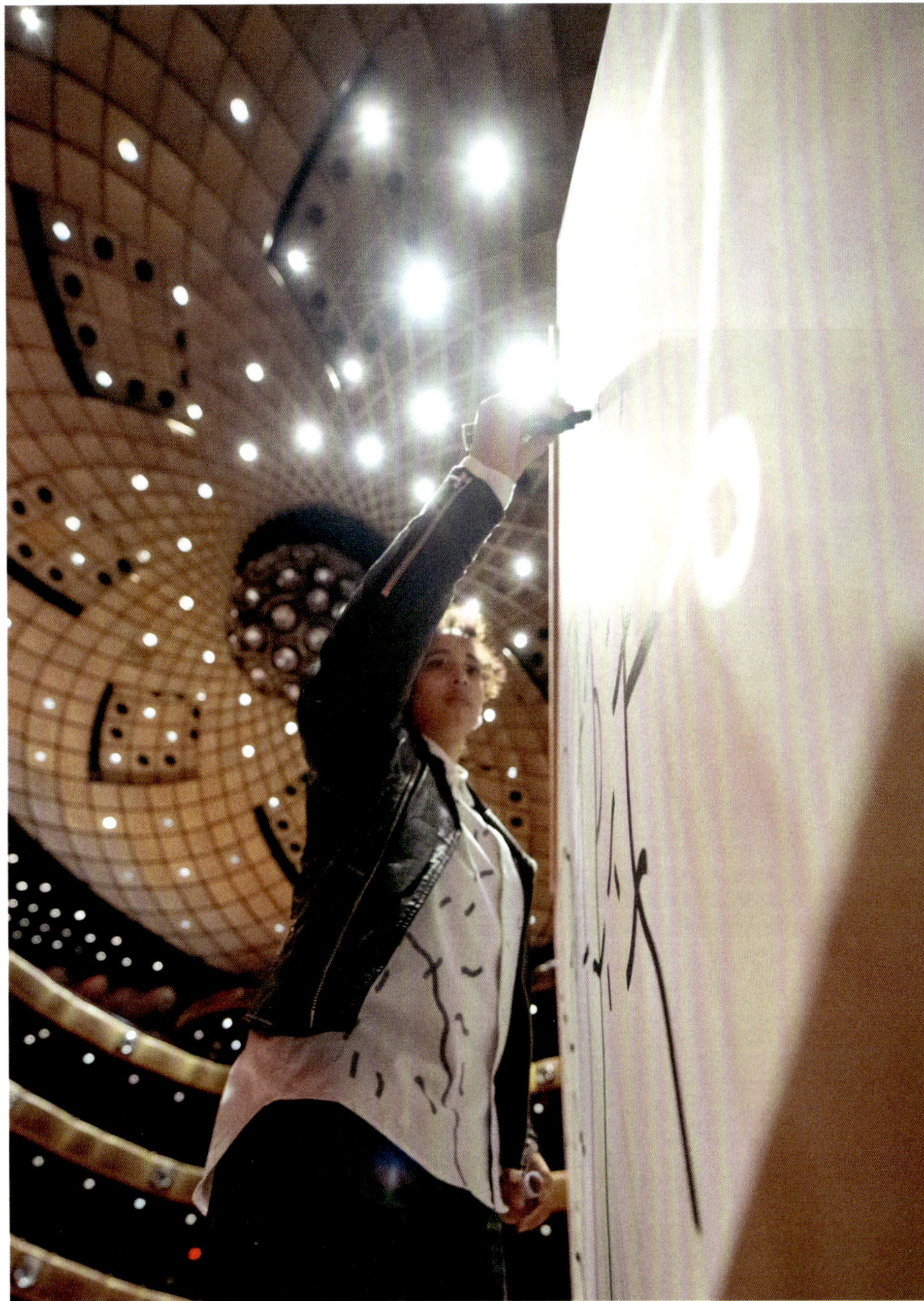

Martin's collaboration with the New York City Ballet culminated with the installation *Finding Your Way* (2019) in the tiered Promenade of the David H. Koch Theater at the Lincoln Center for the Performing Arts, New York. Ten large framed art pieces inspired by her interviews were displayed alongside thirty-six towering canvases created during rehearsals. A massive floor piece was also installed under the feet of guests, allowing them to experience Martin's pen dancing, before and after performances by her subjects – all the dancers she had shared time with, from soloists and principals to newcomers. Finally, over three nights in February and March 2019, Martin introduced productions by the New York City Ballet with her own presentations. These ranged from live drawing and storytelling to interviews and a collaboration with Peck and the principal dancers of his new ballet *Principia*, on each occasion in front of an audience of over 2,500 people. **Previous spread:** *Finding Your Way*, 2019. Ink on canvas, printed vinyl and fabricated letters. **Left:** Martin drawing on canvas during rehearsals in the David H. Koch Theater. **Opposite:** View of the final installation in the Promenade at the David H. Koch Theater.

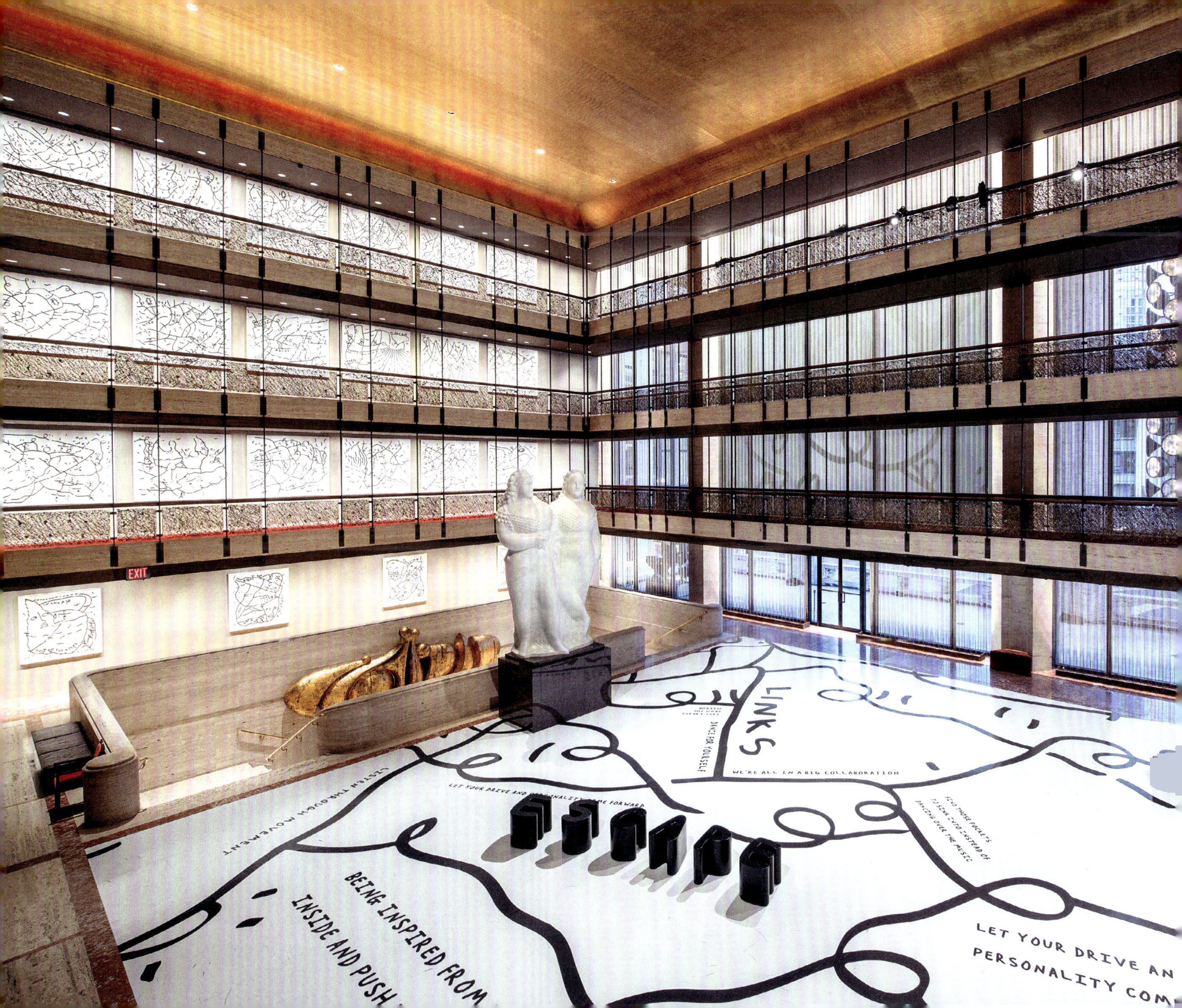
EXIT
LINKS
THINK FOR YOURSELF
WE'RE ALL IN A BIG COLLABORATION
LET YOUR DRIVE AND PERSONALITY COME FORWARD
LISTEN THROUGH MOVEMENT
BEING INSPIRED FROM INSIDE AND PUSH...
LET YOUR DRIVE AN
PERSONALITY COM

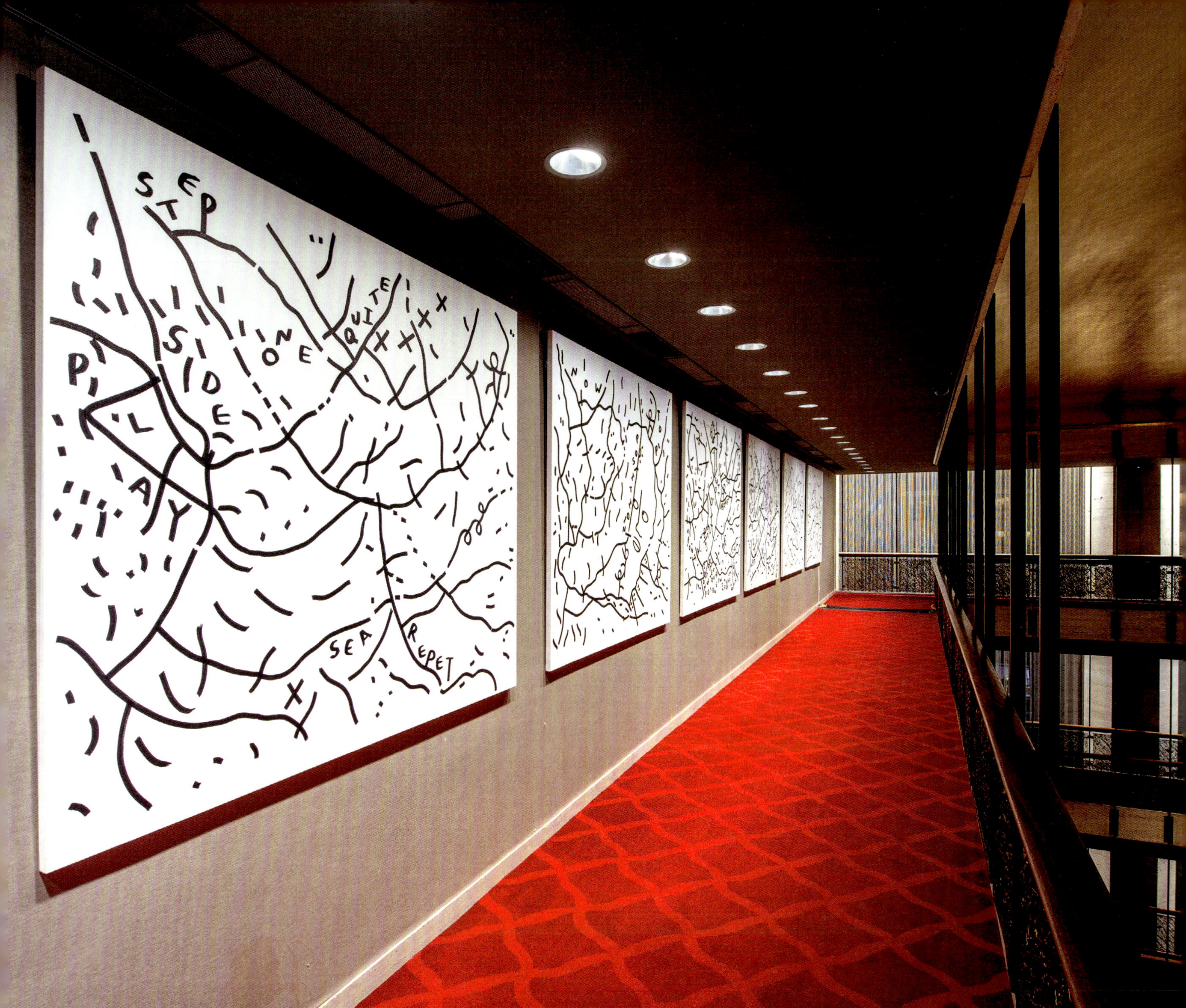
SEP
STP
SIDE
SIDE
LINE
QUITE
QUITE
PLAY
SEA
REPET

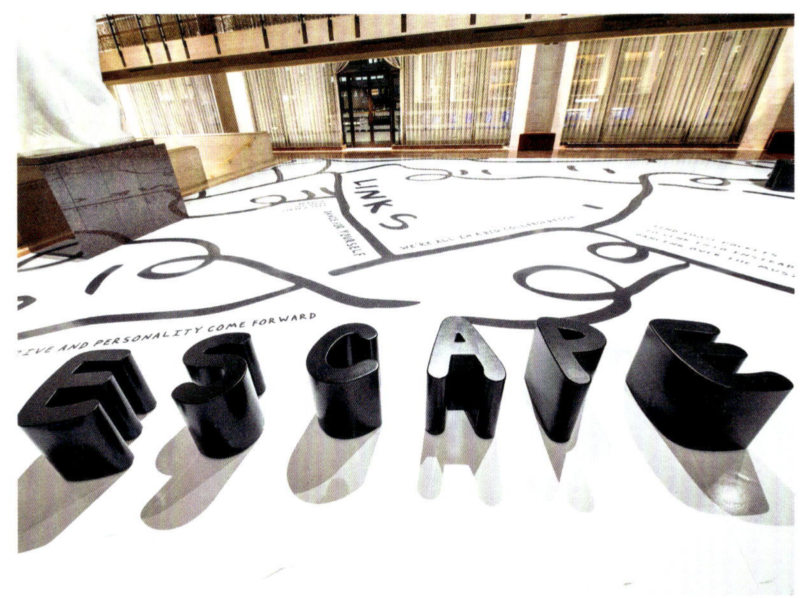

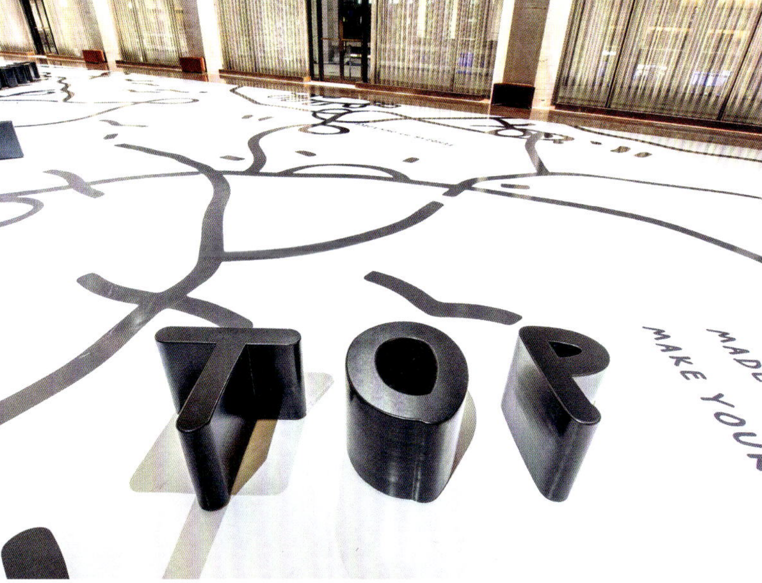

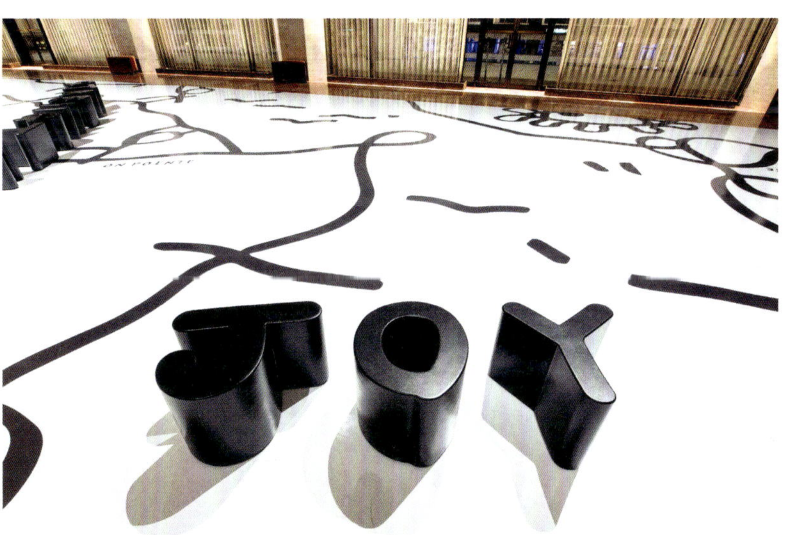

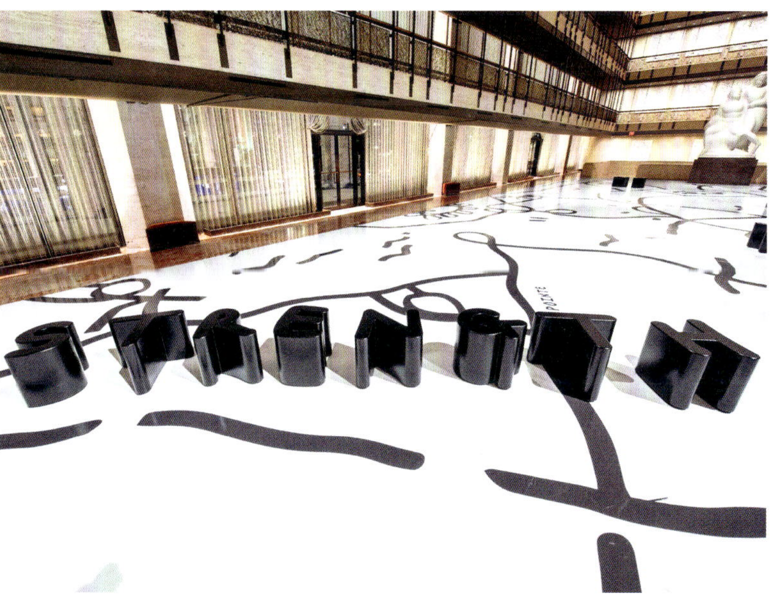

Opposite: Canvases from *Finding Your Way* (2019) on a balcony of the Promenade, David H. Koch Theater.
Above: Fabricated seating on the Promenade's floor – each word is taken from interviews with dancers.

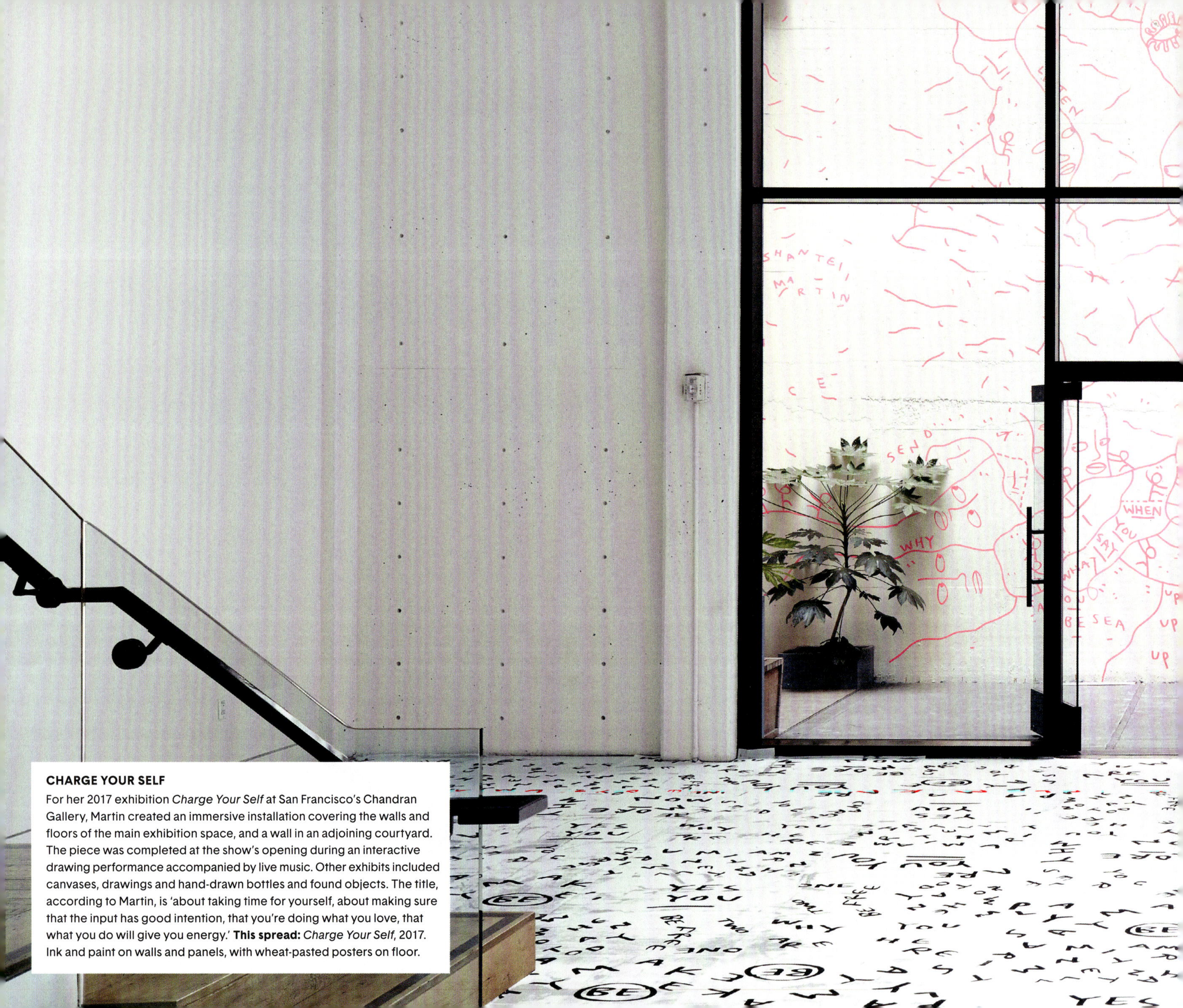

CHARGE YOUR SELF

For her 2017 exhibition *Charge Your Self* at San Francisco's Chandran Gallery, Martin created an immersive installation covering the walls and floors of the main exhibition space, and a wall in an adjoining courtyard. The piece was completed at the show's opening during an interactive drawing performance accompanied by live music. Other exhibits included canvases, drawings and hand-drawn bottles and found objects. The title, according to Martin, is 'about taking time for yourself, about making sure that the input has good intention, that you're doing what you love, that what you do will give you energy.' **This spread:** *Charge Your Self*, 2017. Ink and paint on walls and panels, with wheat-pasted posters on floor.

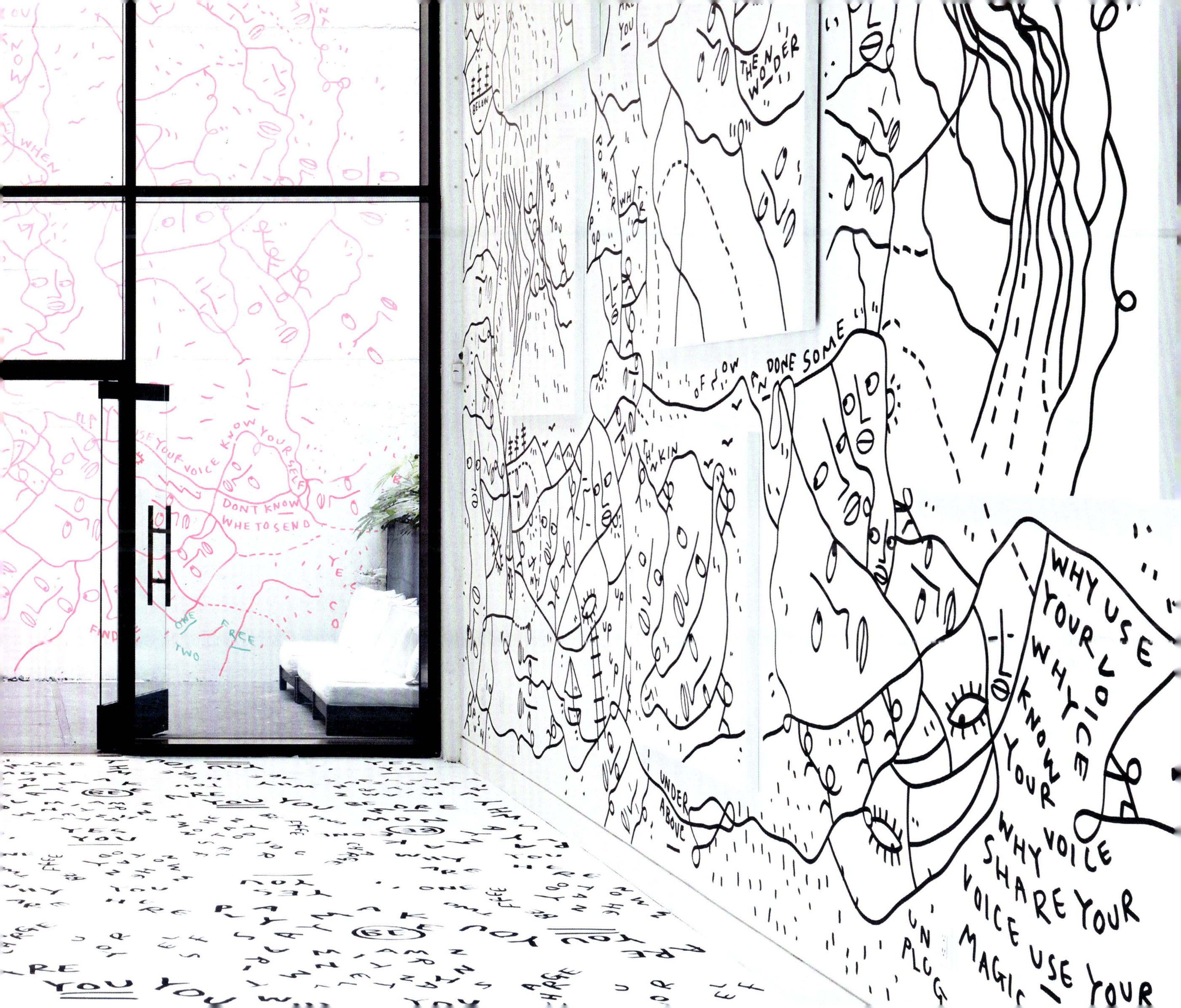
USE YOUR VOICE
KNOW YOURSELF
DON'T KNOW
WHE TO SEND
ONE
TWO
FREE
FIND
PLAY
WHEN
NOW
THE WONDER
BELOW
POWER WHY
DONE SOME
OF JOW
UNDER
ABOVE
WHY USE
YOUR VOICE
WHY
KNOW
YOUR
VOICE
WHY
SHARE YOUR
VOICE USE YOUR
MAGIC
UNPLUG
YOU
YOU WILL
ARE YOU

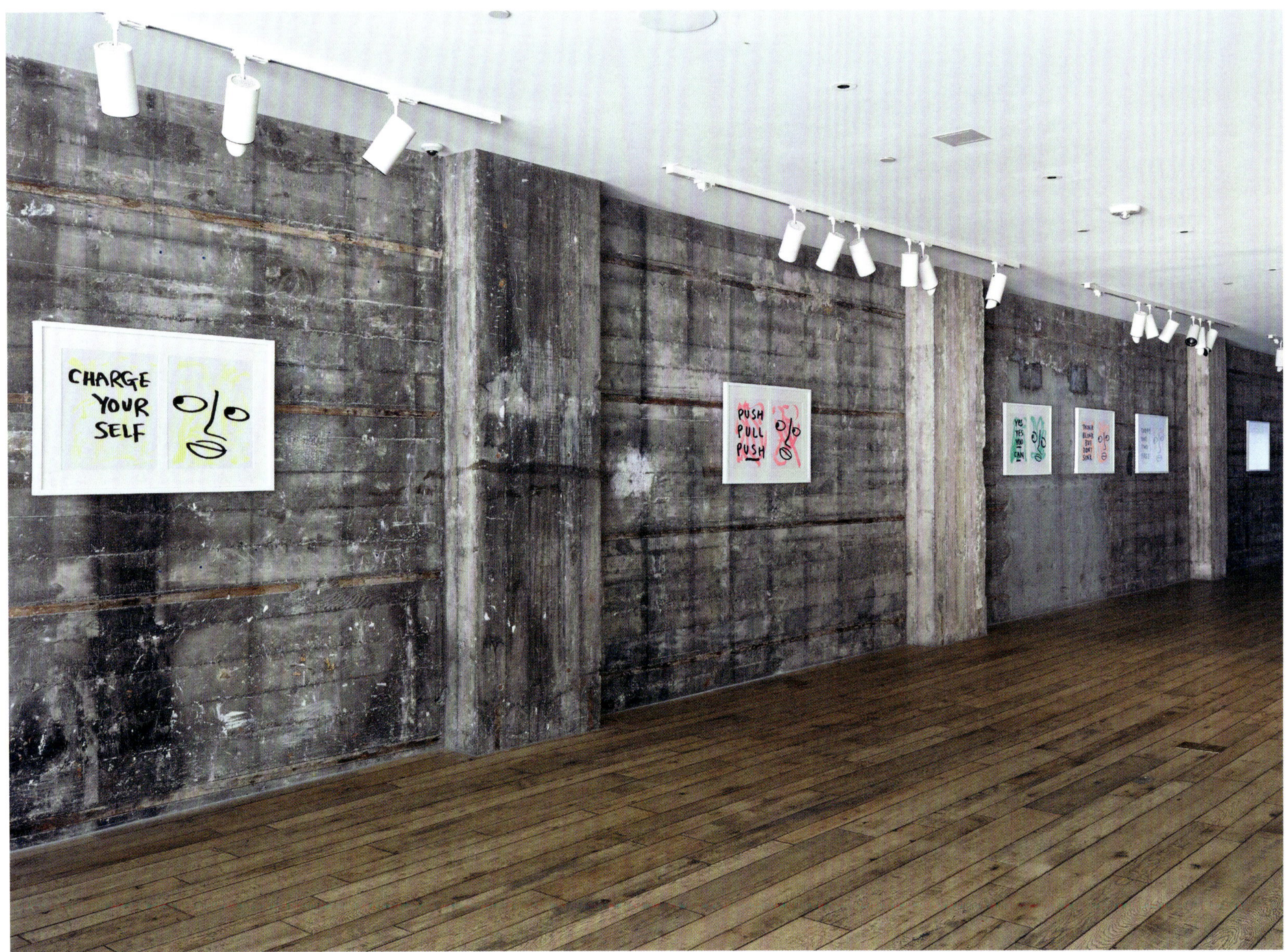

This spread: Installation views of *Charge Your Self*, Chandran Gallery, San Francisco, with ink drawings, hand-drawn bottles and found objects, in July 2017. **Following spread, left:** Details of the courtyard mural (left) and the ink-on-panel *In Between the Bay* (2017) (right). **Following spread, right:** *Think Blink But Don't Sink*, 2017; *Today One Two Free*, 2017. Ink on paper.

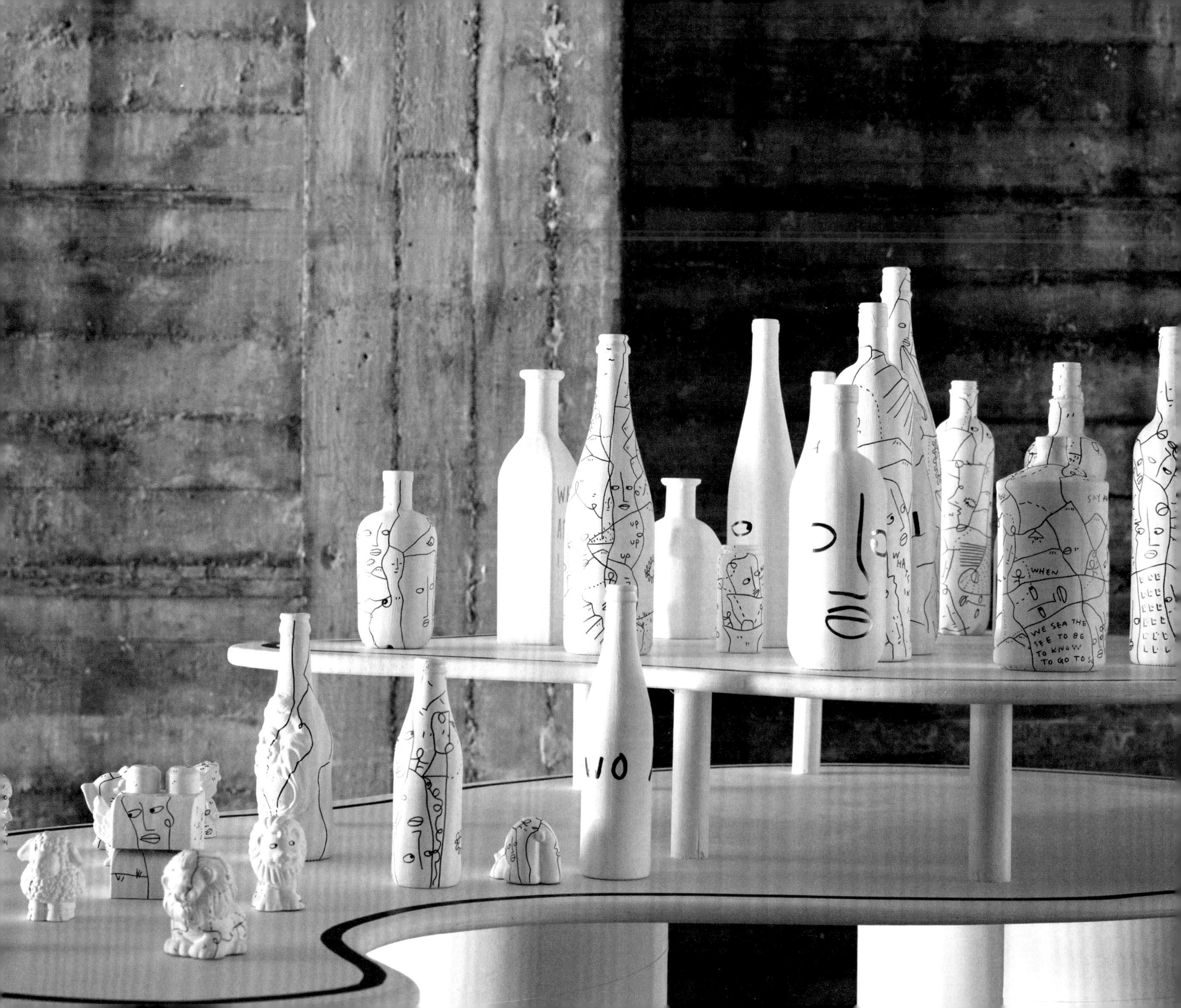

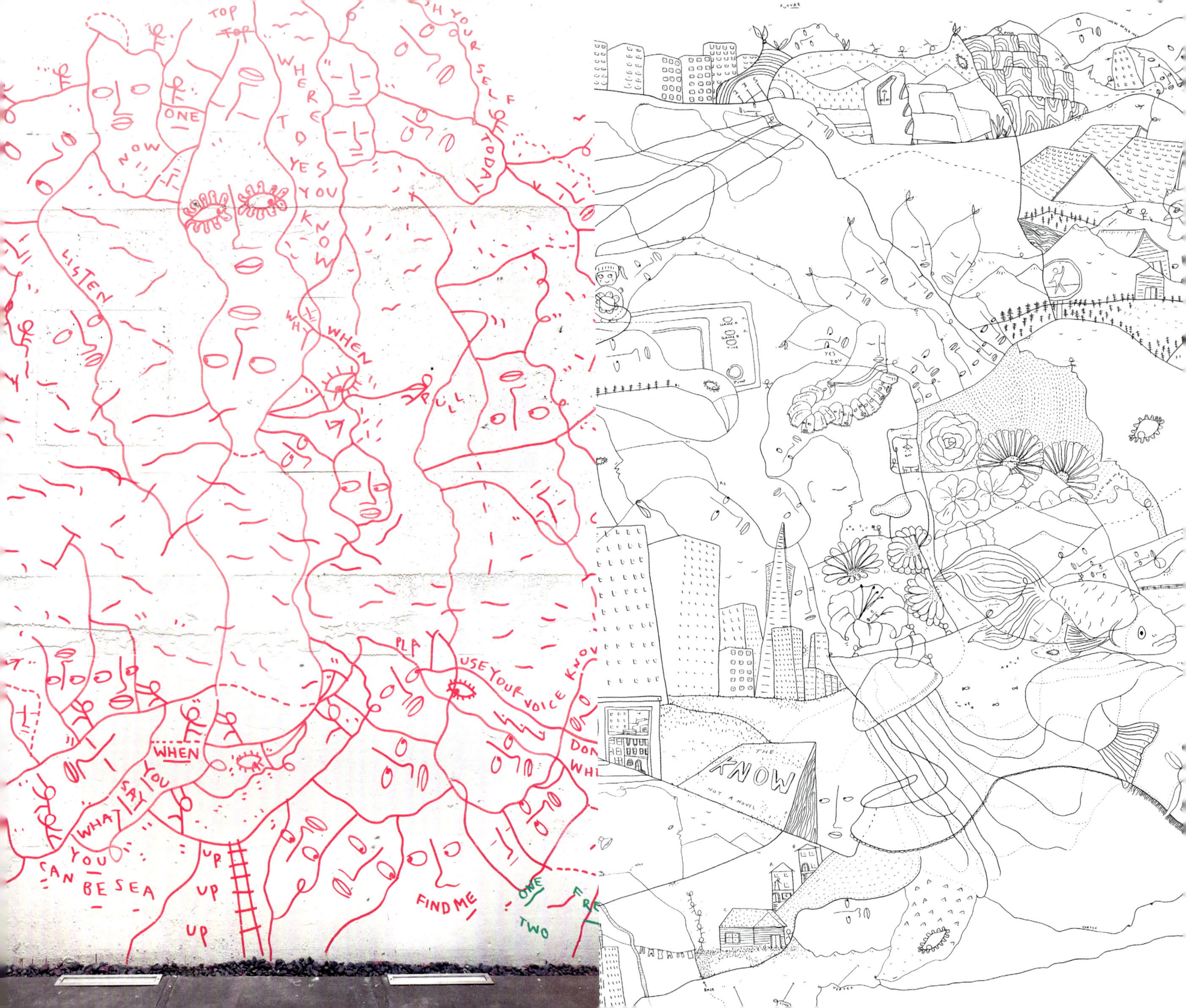
TOP
ONE
NOW
LISTEN
WHERE
TO
YES
YOU
KNOW
WHEN
PULL
WH
WHEN
WHAT
YOU
CAN BE SEA
UP
UP
UP
PLAY
USE YOUR VOICE KNOW
FIND ME
ONE
TWO
FREE
FUTURE
KNOW
NOT A NOVEL
YES
YOU

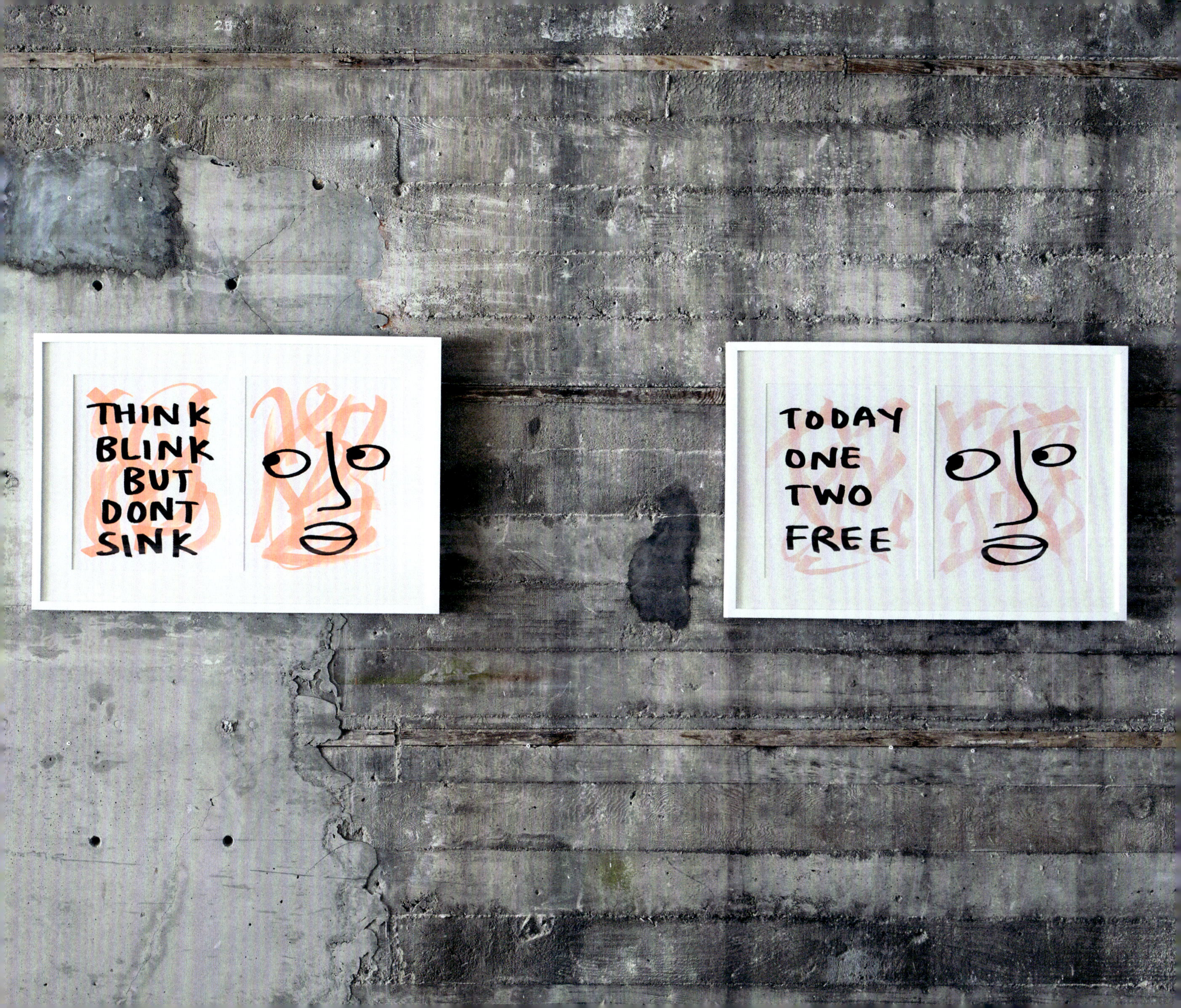
THINK
BLINK
BUT
DONT
SINK
TODAY
ONE
TWO
FREE

INTERVIEW

HANS ULRICH OBRIST & SHANTELL MARTIN

Let's begin with the beginning.

I'm from London. I grew up in a place called Thamesmead in south-east London. It was, and still is, an interesting place, in part because of the 1960s architecture, built as an effort to create new housing after the Second World War – it's a vast expanse of grey flats and maisonettes that go on for miles. It might actually be one of the biggest council estates in London, but they have started to knock it down. It's kind of like the Barbican [a major postwar housing estate and cultural centre in the City of London], but in south-east London and not as nice. Demographically, it was very white, very working-class. My mum's white. I don't know my real dad. My stepdads are both white. I'll show you a picture of me, my brothers and sisters when we were young. It shows me, brown, with an

afro, and my five blond-haired, blue-eyed siblings. Thamesmead wasn't the nicest place to grow up, not for me anyway. I'm sure some people had a great childhood there. I guess it depends a lot on what was going on in your own home. I used to write and draw a lot, which helped me get things out. I think I was a bit of an angry, quiet kid. When I look at my earlier drawings and writings, they feel so harsh, so lost.

Like social realism.

Yeah, completely. I didn't know at the time it was art.

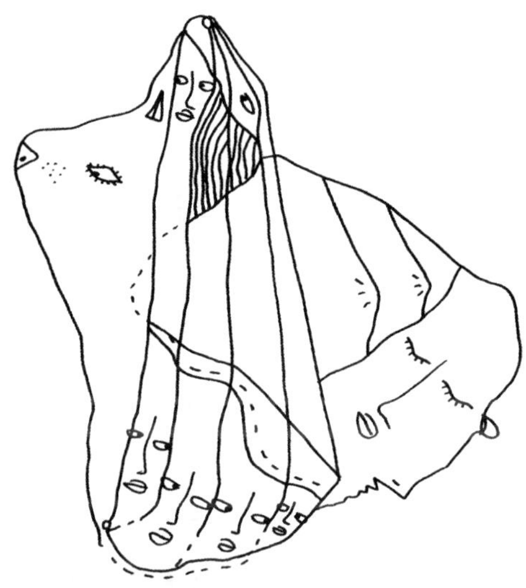

You grew up in a big family?

I'm the oldest of six. Initially, art came to me in the form of getting things out, in dealing with my environment, in feeling different, being different and expressing myself.

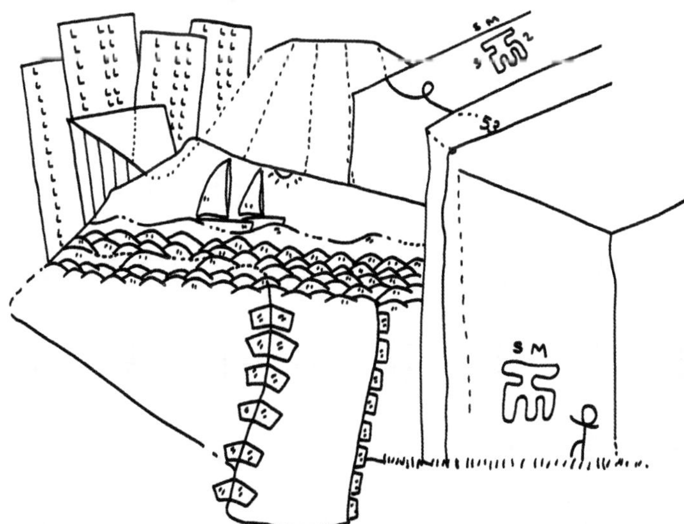

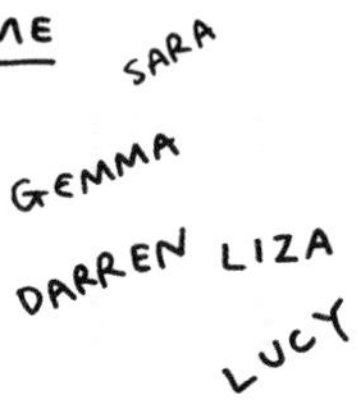

And who were your earliest heroes? What would you say were your influences then? Was it graffiti? I read that gaming was an influence? Alex Kidd and Sonic?

Yeah, I used to love playing Alex the Kidd back in the day. I don't think I really had any art influences when I was young. I didn't go to museums or galleries and there were no artists around me that I knew of. However, I did find graffiti later in life when I went to art school and moved in with my friend Daisuke Sakaguchi, who I met when doing my foundation at Camberwell College of Arts. Daisuke was into breakdancing and graffiti, and many nights walking home I would wait for him while he tagged something. I got bored of waiting so started doing it myself! My first real character was called Hangman.

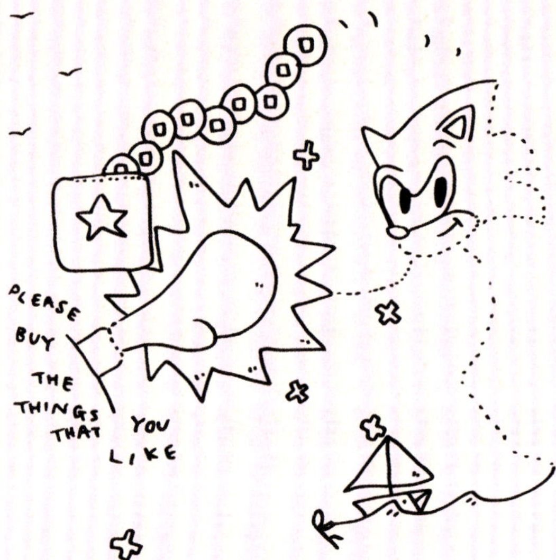

You never went to the centre of London?

Not really as a kid. I do remember my whole family once went to the Natural History Museum because one of my siblings won tickets. You can imagine, a single mum with six kids, it was a bit of a nightmare. It's quite a big trip to go to central London from Thamesmead.

So, there weren't really any influences from art, but you started to draw. Can you talk a little bit about that?

It's interesting, I think about this a lot. If art wasn't around me then, why did I do this thing obsessively? I have some faint memories of my mum drawing. I remember her drawing our dog sleeping in her bed and I was blown away by how you could take something from life and put it on paper. I also think I spent much of my childhood watching cartoons and Disney movies – I can still sing many of the songs.

What were your favourite cartoons?

ThunderCats, *The Smurfs*, *Gummi Bears*, *DuckTales*, *Transformers*. I loved cartoons and they are, in many ways, the closest thing to art that you have as a kid. And thinking about tools, pens and pencils are everywhere. You may not be surrounded by 'fine art', but you're definitely around pens, pencils and paper, so there is access, in a way.

You said that you don't really choose art as a career, it's the career that chooses you. It is a trajectory full of changes and hurdles, and even if you went to art school you are most likely not given the tools to be a self-sufficient and successful artist. Was there a revelation when suddenly you thought, 'I'm an artist'?

I went to Central Saint Martins [CSM] in London. It is, in many ways, a very well-known and highly regarded art school. I graduated from there with first-class honours, but it didn't mean anything, because it was, in a way, all about nepotism in London at the time. Perhaps this has changed now with social media; I've not lived in the UK for so long, so I'm unsure. When

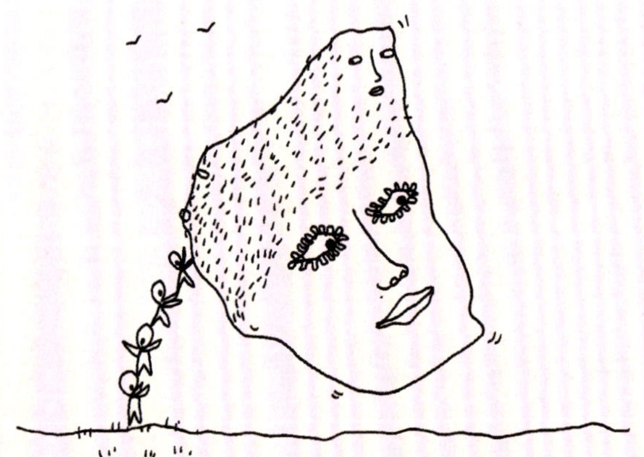

I left CSM, if you weren't coming from a certain privileged background – someone in your family being or knowing someone in the industry – then you'd never really have a career in England. I believe that if I had stayed in the UK, I would not have had the success that I have today. Recently, an old teacher of mine said that the art world in the UK has very subtle ways of blocking people out, and I agree.

The class system?

Absolutely, the class thing. It can be tough growing up in a classist society – but I guess that depends on where you fall. We all have these internal reflexes. When you're from a lower class and you go to university, learn a language or move abroad, you can be perceived as thinking that you are 'better than' wherever you are from. The upper class might use the phrase 'don't be common' as a joke, but without really thinking about what it means. Looking back, choosing to be an artist was a stupid career choice: why would I choose to be something that no one around me supported?

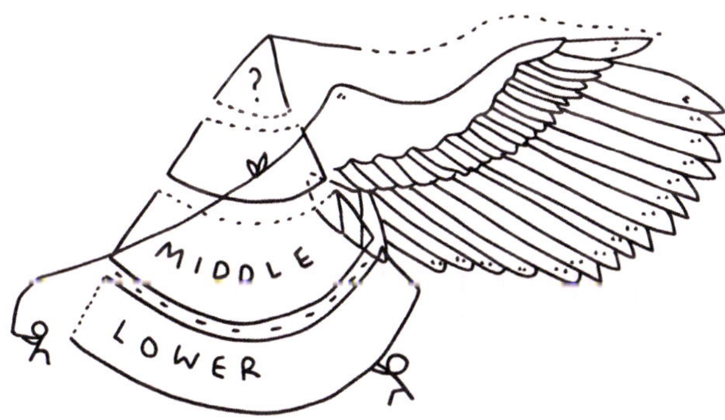

By the time you were at Central Saint Martins, you were obviously exposed to art, so who were your influences then?

At Saint Martins, my influences were the people around me: my friends, fellow students, exhibitions we visited and trips that we went on. I started there in 2000 and after the first week discovered I was totally dyslexic. It hadn't been diagnosed before but, being in a place where many people were dyslexic, a friend very quickly pointed it out. The internet still wasn't really a huge thing and I avoided the library apart from the

VHS section, where I discovered animators like Jan Švankmajer. I remember going to shows that had an impact on me, like the Turner Prize in 1999, where I saw Tracey Emin's work for the first time. I remember being slightly obsessed with a video piece by Yayoi Kusama that I saw at the Hayward Gallery. I also really enjoyed David Shrigley's work.

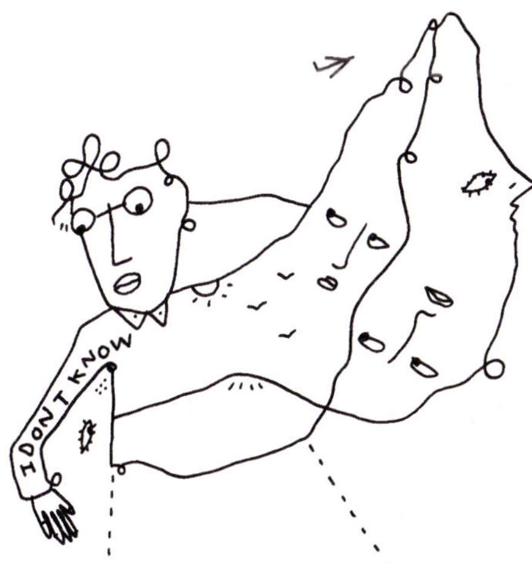

They have in common that they draw.

Exactly. It was affirming to see drawing out in the world; to see something that I also did, and recognise that people took it seriously.

And then of course there is your grandmother. She's the other artist in the family. I'm very interested to know more about your collaboration with your grandmother.

It's kind of funny, my grandmother never saw herself as an artist. I had to point out that she was making art. She would create these beautiful needlepoint tapestry pieces from pamphlets she would get in the mail with different designs, and then, using wool and a white grid with all the squares on, she would create a picture. Towards the end of art school, I asked her to sew two pieces for me. They both said, 'Half White 1980', but one was black on white and the other white on black. This was a commentary on having to denounce your otherness but not your 'whiteness'. This was around 2002. She sewed them for me and then asked, 'What else would you like?'

It became teamwork?

We just kept doing them! What was really great was that this was my white grandmother, in her eighties, from a completely different generation and race. We could have these conversations about race through the pieces we were making. One pair said 'British' and 'English' and, once they were completed, we had a conversation about what it means to be British and what it means to be English. I asked her, 'Do you realise that I don't call myself English because I'm brown? Being English in many ways is reserved for white people.' She didn't realise that. Another time, she sewed me a piece saying 'Go Home', and then she did one that said 'Come Home'. I didn't ask for the second piece, which made me laugh. She would interpret these things on her own. After the 'Go Home' piece, we had another conversation: 'Nan, do you realise people used to tell me to go home to my own country when I lived in London?' And she was like, 'Why would they tell you to go home? This is your home, you were born here!' And I said, 'It's because I don't look like you.' So we could have these conversations about race. It was a cross-racial and cross-generational collaboration. We didn't have to talk about the weather anymore!

You did a lot of work together?

We probably made close to a hundred works.

And they exist?

They all exist. We showed them at the Brooklyn Museum in a group show a few years back and now they are in my archive waiting to be shown again.

Before Brooklyn, there was Japan, where you started your career. There's an interesting attraction to Japan in your work. Can you remember what brought you there?

At Saint Martins, I became friends with many of the Japanese students and went to Japan a couple of times. I decided that my next step was to move there and so towards the end of my time at Saint Martins, everything became about how I would get there. Right after graduating I enrolled in a CELTA [Certificate in English Language Teaching to Adults] course and then moved. After some time, I started a career as a VJ doing live-drawn visuals in clubs.

In Japan?

Yes, in Tokyo. I remember the first time I drew live. There was a sketchbook under a camcorder, connected to a projector, and then the band started to play. You could see what I was drawing on a screen. I could bring my hands into view, magnifying glasses, Post-it notes, and create this whole new world in conjunction with the music that was being played. I believe this changed the course of my career. It put me in a position where I just drew and I didn't have time to overthink it, to plan, to hesitate, to be anyone else other than me, in that moment. When you're drawing live and you have an audience watching you, you just have to do it. I got really addicted to being in that situation and did it again and again. It evolved from analogue to digital and went from avant-garde venues to the mega-clubs of Tokyo.

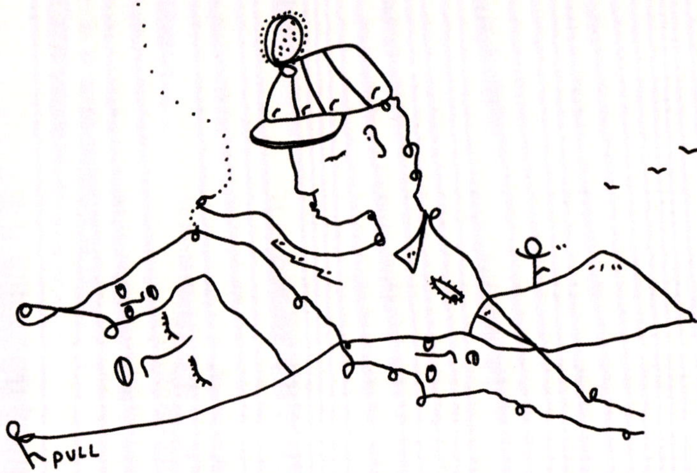

There was a big audience?

Sometimes thousands of people.

What type of music did you create visuals for?

Techno, minimal techno, house – lots of German and Japanese DJs.

Like who?

Tomcraft, Ko Kimura, D'Julz, Munoz, Rennie Foster, Hannah Holland.

How did you leave Japan? Did the VJ chapter come to a conclusion?

I would have liked to continue it. I visited New York for the first time in 2008 and loved it, just like a lot of people do when they first visit the city. Shortly after, I moved here and very quickly realised my mistake. The VJing scene and community that was in Tokyo didn't exist in New York, so I was forced to try new and different mediums or go back to the old. This made me move out of the clubs, because the New York clubs didn't have that same expectation or abundance of visuals that the Japanese ones did. So I thought to myself, 'I'm an artist, I should work with galleries, right?' I would meet with galleries and I'd show them the very small, detailed drawings I had been doing in Japan and they'd love them. They would ask 'Where have you shown?' and I hadn't, to which they would say 'Thank you, but no thank you.' It was a catch-22 situation. My world back in Japan did not exist in New York, so I was pushed to continue my work outside the gallery world and, ultimately, the art world. I had to strategise and use my resources, so I picked up pens again, drawing on whatever was around me. I decided to use everything as my canvas from then on, and that's when I started to draw on cars, walls, my shirts...

The last time we spoke you explained to me that you have this system, 'methodology' is maybe the word that you used, where you draw very fast – speed drawing – with a line that jumps ahead. Then there is a second layer, where you look at the shapes being created and fill them out. How did you come up with that system?

It came over time. The great thing about making art is that you have the time to reflect back on it. I've found that people who draw tend to inflict rules on themselves. Or perhaps those rules might simply be careful observations of our style. I've observed that I'm approaching my drawings in similar ways, with different places producing different stages for the work. I feel like London was about getting stuff out, Japan was about finding my voice and identity, and coming to New York has been about using, sharing and examining that voice. This may change in the future, but the process and experience are the work, as opposed to the final result.

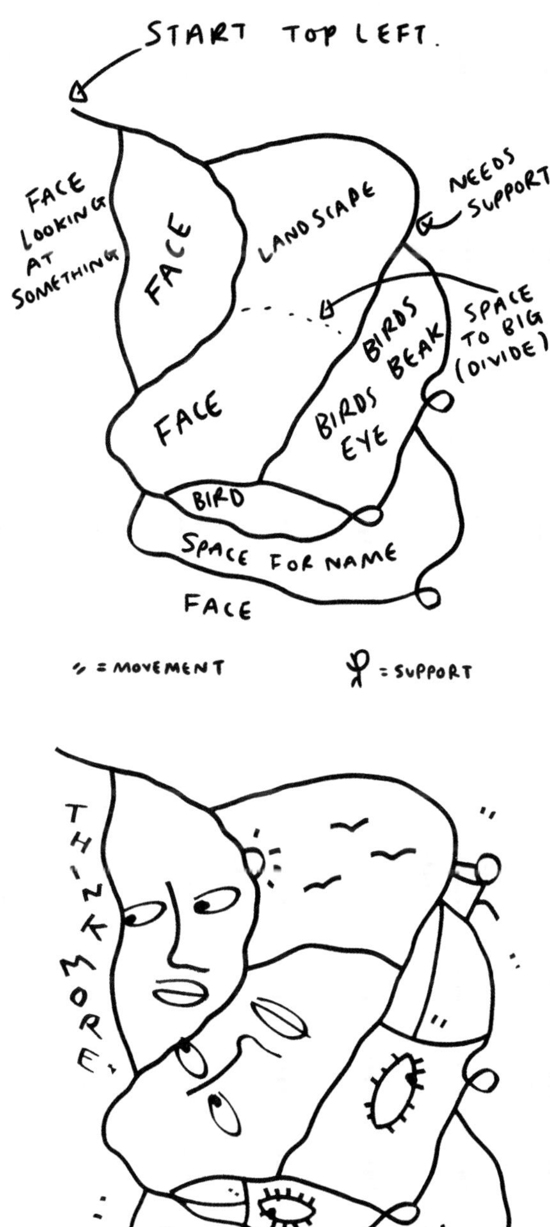

How does the algorithm enter? It seems that it's very manual.

It's very manual. The algorithm is an approach. The approach allows you to be very fast, to be spontaneous regardless of the size of the surface – it could be a canvas, it could be a shirt, it could be a 100-foot [30-metre] wall. With all my drawings, they typically start with an initial line, almost like a skeleton. I call this line the DNA of the drawing. Once you have the DNA in place, it becomes about the negative space, the pockets that are left. These spaces give me clues about what goes in them. The clues are the forms of the different types of lines in various positions on the surface, and the things that go in them are a mixture of faces, landscapes, words, stick figures and recurring characters.

In New York, the city became your canvas. There's this Vladimir Mayakovsky quote: 'The streets will be our brushes. The squares our palettes.'

That's nice! My mantra when I first moved here was 'Draw on everything', and I meant that physically and metaphorically. In Japan, I felt like I was moving ahead, there was technology everywhere, mega-clubs, amazing music, it was collaborative – and then coming to New York, it was almost like stripping everything back, going back to basics.

You're wearing a shirt that you've designed. Can you tell me about it?

I've been drawing on my clothes since I was a kid. It's actually something that I used to get into trouble for and now, as an adult, I get to do it as much as I like!

And when did the text pieces end? Because the last time we met there were these phrases 'Who Are You' and 'Are You You'. Then the text becomes kind of autonomous. How did that happen?

Sometimes, as an artist, when you create work, you think, 'Oh this is new, this is a new idea,' but then you look back at work you did over 20 years ago and it's there. Going back to Thamesmead, to growing up, to the beginnings of art school, there was always text present in my work, even more so than today, actually. I recently found old sketchbooks that are full of only writing. There is something about words and lines being the

same thing for me. There are lots of questions, like 'Why are you here?', 'What do you want to do with your life?', sometimes just the word 'Why', which I got tattooed on my arm a couple of years ago.

WHY

A lot of big questions.

A lot of big questions! The big questions that have always been here, they've always been a part of who I am and a part of the work. I believe they became clearer both for myself and for the wider world when I moved to New York. Now you can walk past the Lincoln Center and see one of these questions – 'WHO ARE YOU' – in enormous letters across its facade. It's amazing to see it so public and visible.

Different collaborations also started in New York. In Japan you mostly worked with VJs, but then in New York all kinds of collaborations kicked in: MIT Media Lab, Kendrick Lamar… Can you talk about some of these? What were the earliest ones?

Those early years in New York feel like a bit of a blur. Some of the earliest collaborations included doing visuals for an event for a pencil company called Blackwing; talking at a conference organised by media company PSFK; making site-specific work for the store of a denim brand called 3×1; and collaborating with Nigel Barker on a fashion shoot for *Asia Tatler*, for which I made live projections.

All outside the museum world?

Totally, I was outside all of that, I had been cut out. I couldn't do anything in a gallery or museum when I first got here. Although I did start working with the Museum of the Moving Image early on – I would do visuals at a couple of their events.

And collaborations with people?

I've always collaborated with friends, like Zach Lieberman, Amit Pitaru and Sougwen Chung. Zach and I have been collaborating for years now and we've made a variety of really interesting drawing experiments, including a documentary called *Clouds* and a commission for tech nonprofit AnitaB.org. Amit is an interaction designer, coder, musician and educator from Brooklyn and also a long-time collaborator of Zach's. He's worked on incredible projects over the years, from the *Sonic Wire Sculptor* to the *Hammond Flower*. We also like to play music together. And Sougwen and I have been drawing together since 2011. She's an artist; you may know her drawings with her robot D.O.U.G. and her beautiful projection-mapped projects and drawings using pen and pencil.

I am interested in artists' networks. Some artists have movements and groups around them, some artists have a circle of friends. Asked in an interview last year, you said Sougwen, Kristjana S. Williams and Niky Roehreke are your closest allies.

Niky is an illustrator and recently moved to Kōchi in Japan. She also went to Saint Martins and studied illustration, but we met in New York. Kristjana went to Saint Martins as well and makes beautiful collages. She's showing in museums and galleries and did a recent collaboration with Paul Smith. She has been a huge inspiration to me, as an artist who is creative, independent and has a great business.

And how about Kendrick? How did that come about? How did you connect? What did you do together?

I've found that if I make an approach, it never works. People always have to approach me, because that means they know me and my work, they get it, and more importantly they want to work with me. There's no convincing necessary. I was approached by Kendrick's team to collaborate for Art Basel Miami Beach in 2016. At first, I wasn't sure about it. I hadn't listened to his music before and was a bit cautious about doing something with a rapper. Little did I know, he's incredible!

And so are his politics.

Yeah! It was a really great experience. We flew out to Miami and got to sit down and chat about life. We interviewed each other, then Kendrick made some live beats and I drew to them, which then inspired new beats. We had this feedback loop going. His beats inspired my drawing and my drawing inspired his beats.

Like a rhythm.

Exactly. A rhythm of music and drawing, which ended with a concert at Faena Hotel Miami Beach. They had this big 360-degree projection dome. The projections doing their thing and Kendrick doing his. Sitting down artist to artist was really inspiring. It was a really positive, fun, inspiring collaboration. It would be good to see more projects created in this way.

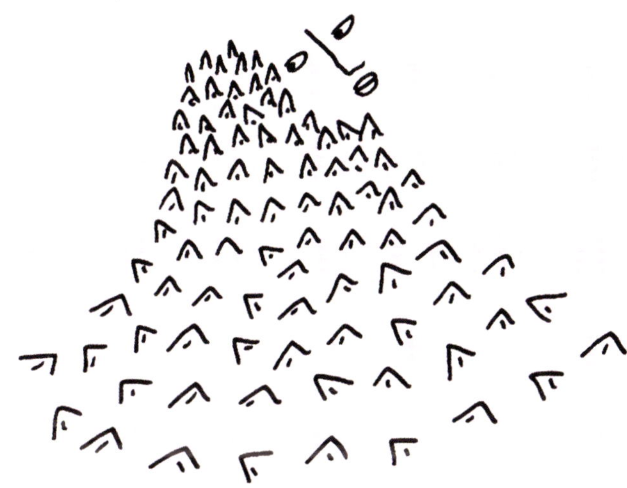

Any other collaborations that were as exciting?

The New York City Ballet has been pretty epic.

Tell us about the Ballet, because it's all over the press in New York. It's very visible in the city.

I think it's actually my biggest piece ever in New York. You get to take over the giant Promenade – the home of the Ballet. They've been doing this art series for seven years now; I'm the seventh artist. They've done it with Marcel Dzama, JR and Jihan Zencirli. I didn't want to go in there and create an installation that had nothing to do with the people that it's about, so I said I wanted to meet at least 15 of the dancers. I interviewed them and asked, 'Who are you?', as well as many other questions. I highlighted words and phrases from the answers, which became the backbone of the installation. Then I went to rehearsals for a couple of weeks and drew to works like *The Nutcracker*, *Liebeslieder Walzer* and Justin Peck's new ballet *Principia*, amongst others. It was an incredible experience. I had the whole theatre to myself.

Were there backdrops for the ballet dancers or did you create them?

There were no backdrops but there were three special art evenings where I was on stage. One was a solo live-drawing and talking performance; for another, I interviewed dancer Silas Farley live on stage; and for the final evening I collaborated with Justin Peck, taking a look at *Principia*. The Ballet also created a really beautiful video where I drew on dancers Lauren Lovette and Daniel Applebaum.

Like Keith Haring. Was he an influence?

I didn't know much about him until I moved to the US. I had seen his dog characters and people as a kid but didn't know who he was as an artist.

He drew everywhere, like you.

He drew on everything and very publicly. With the Ballet, it's been a really fun collaboration, because it is so public and because it is in an area where I wouldn't usually be involved. It ties in with the idea of working in any medium, in any industry, as long as it's meaningful.

Is there anything you've wanted to draw on that you haven't been able to yet? Any unrealised projects?

I'd love to draw on the facade of the Guggenheim! Imagine a show where you have your work inside and then you've drawn on the outside too. Maybe it can only be seen at night – glow in the dark. That would be pretty cool. I'd love to draw on a couple of aeroplanes too.

Alexander Calder did that.

Or a big soccer field or something like that.

Any other unrealised projects or collaborations?

I'd love to collaborate with more musicians. I'd also like to work in TV, hosting or playing myself in a show.

With whom?

Common, Queen Latifah, Lena Waithe, Ilana Glazer and Abbi Jacobson, Barry Jenkins, Kendrick again…

What are you doing with tech? In the 1960s, Billy Klüver did these experiments in art and technology with artists like Robert Rauschenberg, Frank Stella and Lillian Schwartz. Today, we have – need – new experiments in art and technology. Many artists are working with VR, augmented reality, AI, Tilt Brush. You did work at some point with MIT and you have worked with Google. What's your relationship with technology?

I've always loved technology, even as a kid. I was that kid who liked to take my NES [Nintendo Entertainment System] apart and put it back together. Japan was where I was really exposed to technology. It's funny – my collaborations here in New York, many of them have been technology-based. At MIT Media Lab we got to build a lot of programs, software and maps, and I made printed circuit boards with Jonathan Bobrow. At Google I worked on augmented-reality stuff. I love beta and alpha testing. I love picking something up before anyone else has and giving my feedback on it. I used to test a lot of programs and technology. A line doesn't just have to be pen on paper – a line is VR, it's augmented reality, circuit boards, maps, algorithms, code. A line is technology, a line is point A to point B. I think there's a natural connection there.

Where is your studio?

Currently it's in Jersey City at Mana Contemporary.

If I were in your studio today, what would I see?

On the walls there's a whole mixture of works on canvas. On the back wall are framed prints from live shows and projects by photographer Roy Rochlin. There is a stage that I had built to workshop my one-woman show and on it is a blank canvas, which is what I draw on during the shows. There is also a white, drawn-on mini grand piano, and in the middle of the room I have 30 seats that people sit on when they come and see the show.

And your day – what is your routine?

I don't really have a routine. I like to be in the studio Mondays and Fridays and then in between I'm meeting people or I'm doing interesting things. Like today, I have a meeting with Google.

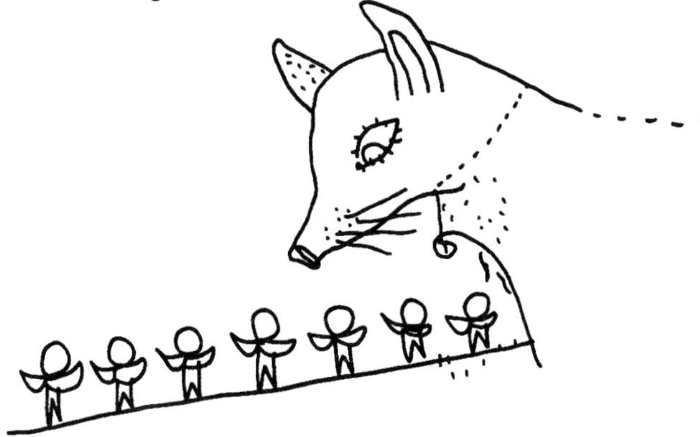

Where do colours enter, because most of the work is black and white. You draw lines and connect words. It's a lot about connections but there isn't much colour in your work. How come?

Even when I look back at my earliest work, it's all black and white. It's always been a preference, but that doesn't mean there is a lack of colour. Take a look at projects like the one with my grandmother, it's colourful; when I've drawn on people, it's colourful; when I VJed in Japan in the clubs, it was colourful. So, in a way, other people bring the colour. The collaborators bring the colour. If I'm VJing in a club, it's not just me and the program: there's an audience, they bring the colour, they invite it from me. When it's just me and a canvas, that's when the interaction is black and white. There's this sense of connection with myself, there's a sense of it being as personal as it can be. I feel you can hide with colour. You can throw a bunch of colour at something and it's pretty and you can hide in that.

It's the drawing. It's the 'brutal truth', as Elaine Sturtevant said.

And you can stare that brutal truth in the face. Also, there are no mistakes, or if there are, they stand out. They bite you. So you have to get good at it.

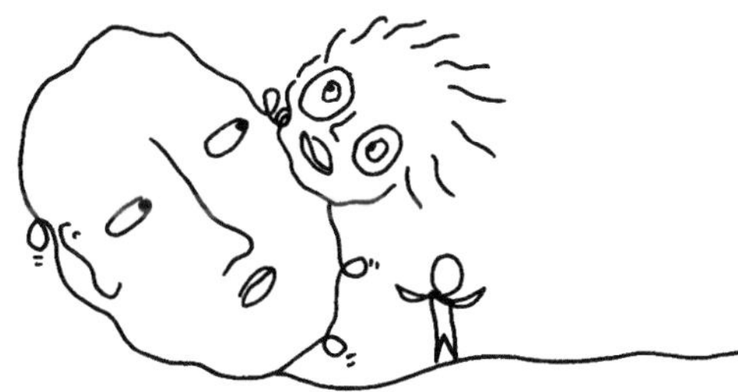

I spoke to Lena Henke the other day. She said, 'No rules'. What do you think?

I'm the opposite, I like rules. People ask me what happens if you make a mistake and I say, 'Everything's one big mistake, you just learn to enjoy the process.' The rules are all process. It's not about the result. The rules are when you put good intention behind what you are doing and the final output works. The rules are when you listen to yourself and you know when to stop. When something is black and white, you create this space for discovery and rediscovery. I love that you can keep coming back to a piece that is black and white, each time seeing something new. In a way you're not giving the whole picture away at once.

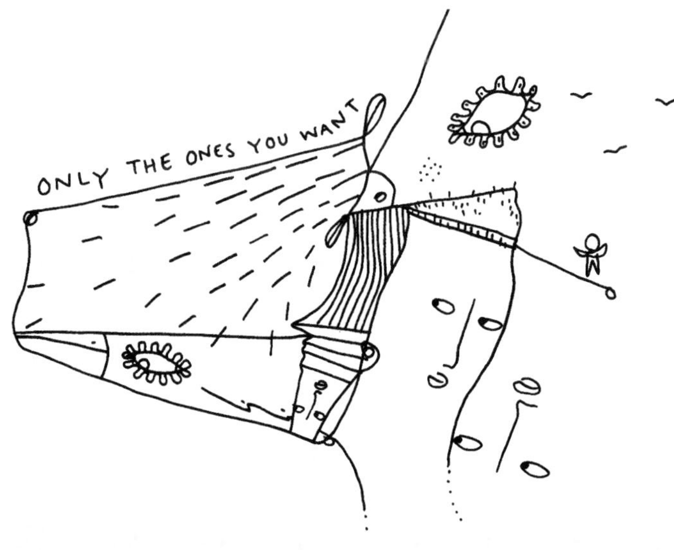

With your complex drawings you don't see everything. It's a bit like Alighiero Boetti and his works called *Tutto*. A Buddhist can find Buddha; someone who likes cars can find cars; somebody who loves the sky can find the sky.

With colour, your brain is programmed to know what colour to see first and so on, but with black and white those rules don't apply, and everyone can start in a different place.

You've been working for almost 20 years. What would be your advice to a young art student who is reading our interview?

You know 92nd Street Y? I was their first-ever artist in residence. I created a show, I did some talks and I gave a talk to 900 public-school kids. They bussed them all in. They had been learning about my work and then they got to meet me. When I walked out on stage, I felt like a rock star, because they all lost it – in a good way! Imagine being a kid, learning about an artist and then you get to meet them! Anyway, back to advice – if I was to give some advice, it would be to create your own opportunities and do it by using what you have access to.

That means not waiting for museums to knock at your door.

Don't play the 'if' game. What do you have? Start to use that to make and create.

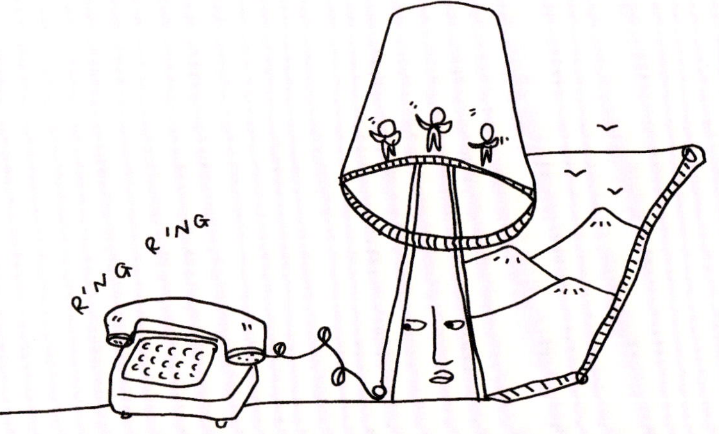

So just do it – it's a DIY project. And your work very much goes to the people. It is art for all. The other day in London, I had a taxi driver drop me in Kensington Gardens super early. He assumed that I worked there and said he had always wanted to talk to someone who works at the Serpentine. He told me a story about his daughter, how he came to the park with her one day and she ran into the pavilion – every year we build a pavilion with a different architect in the park, with no doors – and she had an epiphany to become an architect. He wanted to thank us. I asked him if he visited museums, to which he said he would never go to a museum. I asked why. He went silent and then he said, 'It's not for people like us.' We have to go to people outside. The artist Arthur Jafa made this point when we showed him at the Serpentine space – he always insists that his film *Love is the Message, the Message is Death* is shown in different neighbourhoods. You very much go to the people. Can you talk about accessibility?

Free doesn't mean welcome. If you walk into a museum here, they ask if you are a member. If you're not used to the system, that first interaction can be so intimidating. Some people see me as a successful artist – I have museum shows, I work with institutions, I have these big collaborations – but I typically will not walk into galleries by myself, because I feel intimidated. I totally relate to how the taxi driver felt, because there's so much BS and facade around the art world and in a way it's intentional. It's one thing to one group of people and something else to another. It's all built to cater to people who can spend a lot of money on art. It's a plus if these spaces feel exclusive and inaccessible because in a way that justifies the price tag of it all, but the downside is that you end up with the mass of people thinking that art isn't for them, which is crazy. We can do both. We can open up art to the masses and still make people feel important in the world. The more people we have seeing art, the more drawing and creating art there is, the happier we all are. There's a reason why we all draw as children, it's because we get to be personal with ourselves, we get to express things, we get to say things, we have an outlet. I'm not saying that everyone should be an artist, but that art should not be reserved only for artists.

So that's why you make it public?

Art was not accessible to me growing up. Why now, as an adult and an artist, would I want to create art that would not be seen by a younger version of myself? I can be an example, I can be visible. At the same time, I can still sell work, but the creation is quite public.

And what's the future? What are the next projects?

I'm working with an airline promoting a competition for female artists where the winners will have their artwork on a Boeing 757, and I'm also doing an installation on Governors Island, where I'm giving an abandoned church new life, creating drawings on the exterior and interior and turning it into a place for poetry and contemplation. Beyond that, at the end of 2019 I'm doing an installation at the Denver Art Museum, and I'm continuing to work on my one-woman show *Lines*, which is a mixture of storytelling about where I'm from, live drawing and live-composed music. I've been workshopping it in my studio.

Anywhere else you'd like to work?

I've never been to South Africa; I'd love to go there. I recently went to Mexico City and I'm actually thinking about taking a couple of weeks out and going there again.

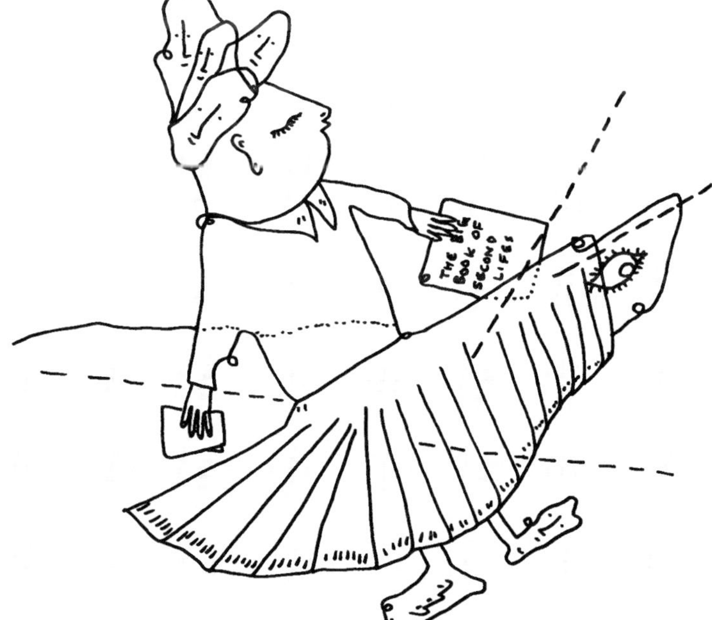

How many works have you created so far?

I have hundreds of drawings at home and in my archive. Most of it's been photographed and inventoried. I show and own a lot of my own art, but I'd rather it live in the world. I'm very curious to see what my future looks like. Do I work with galleries? I don't know. Will I work out how to sell my work myself? I don't know. What I do know is that I worked hard to get to where I am and be able to do what I do.

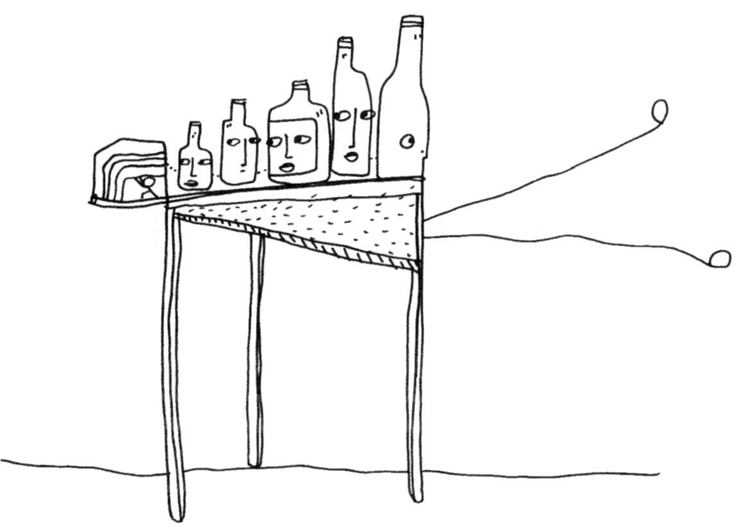

This conversation took place on 18 December 2018 at The Maritime Hotel, New York.

SELF   MIND   SELF   MIND   YOUR
MIND   SELF   MIND   YOU   YOU
YOUR   YOUR   YOU   YOU   MAKE
MIND   MIND   MAKE   YOU   YOU
MAKE   YOU   YOU   MIND   YOU
SHARE   YOU   SHARE   YOU
YOU   YOU   YOU   YOU   MAKE   MIND
YOU   YOU   YOU   YOU   MIND   MAKE
YOU   YOU   YOUR   WAKE   WAK
YOU   YOU   YOU   MIND   YOU

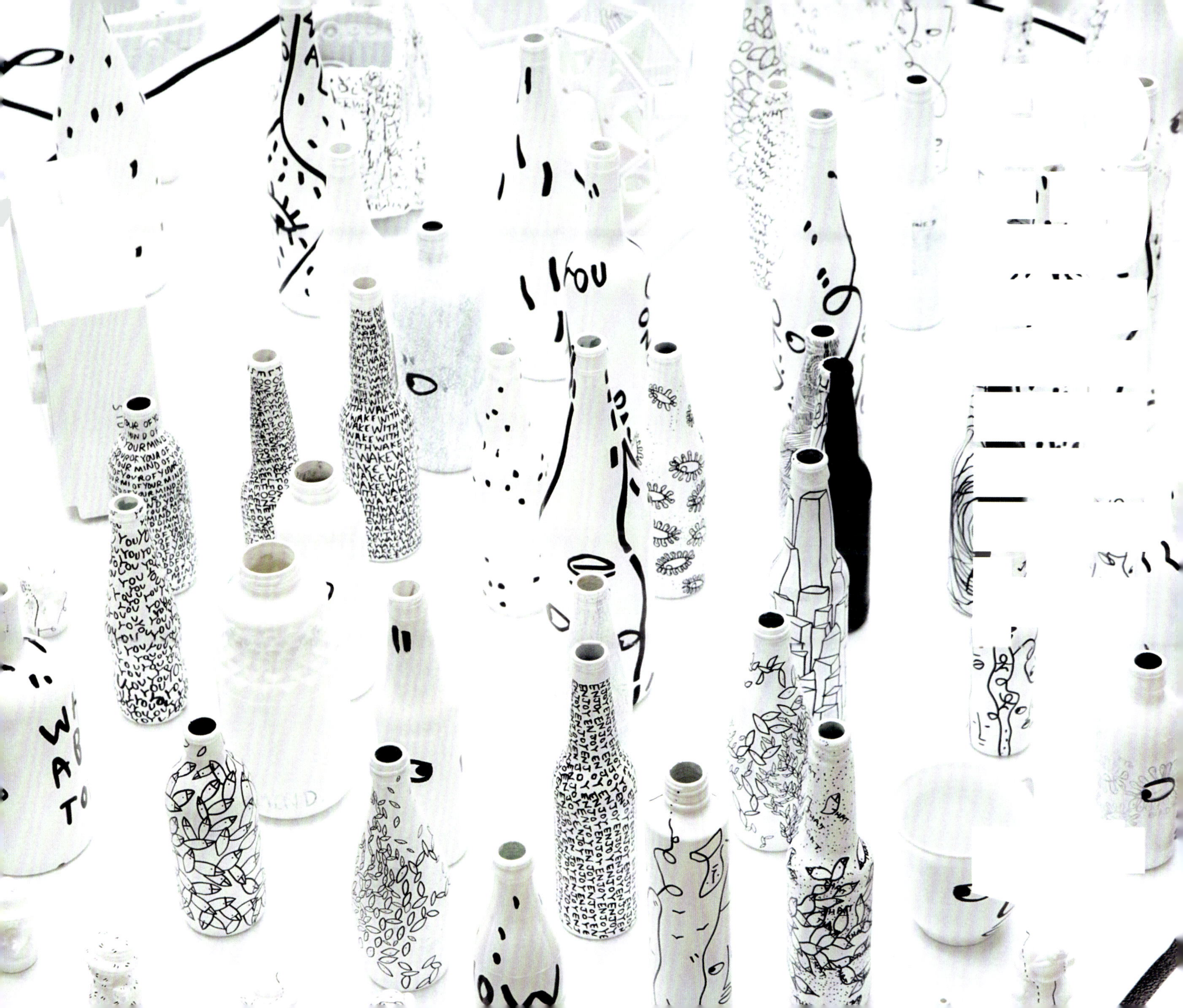

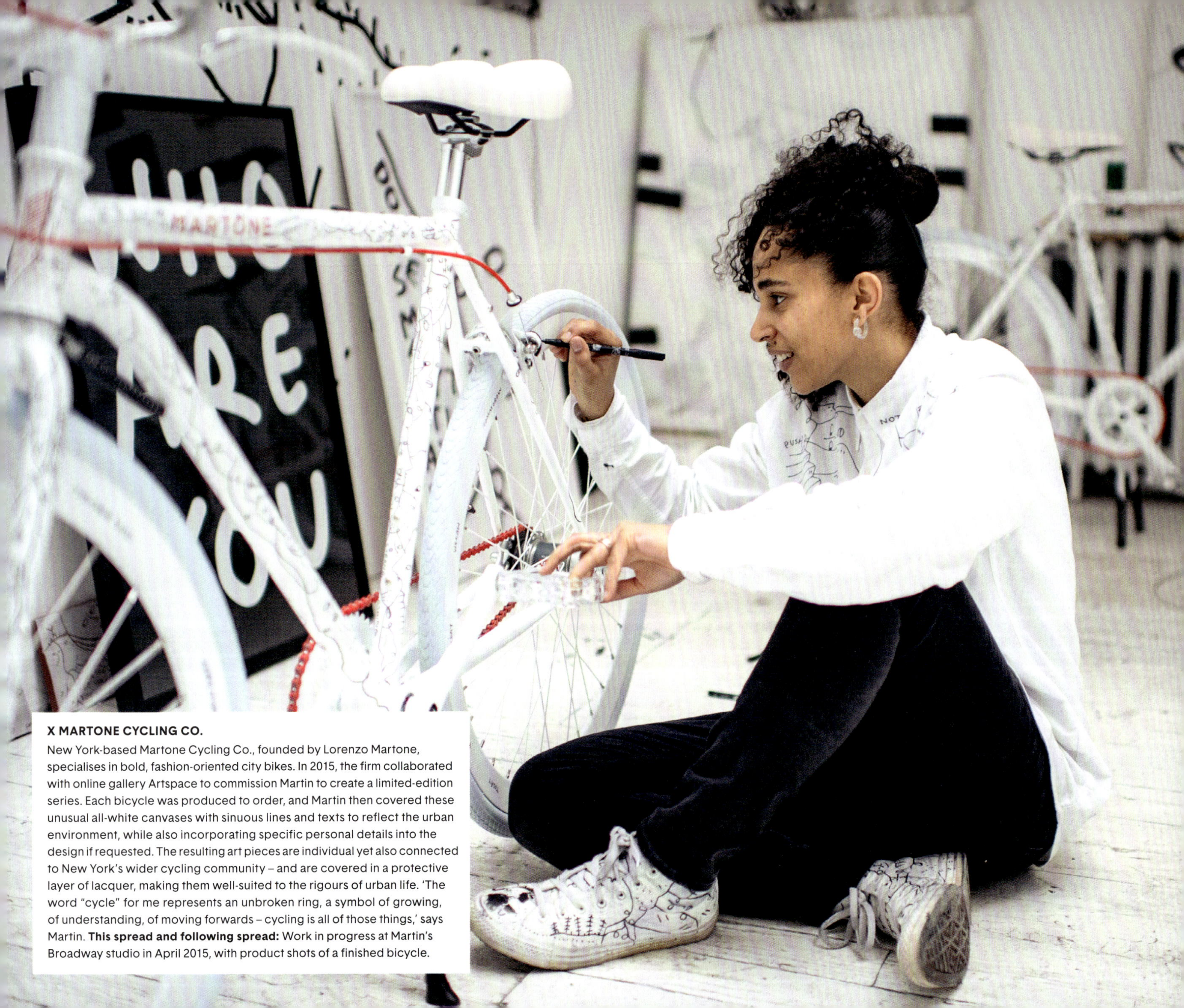

X MARTONE CYCLING CO.

New York-based Martone Cycling Co., founded by Lorenzo Martone, specialises in bold, fashion-oriented city bikes. In 2015, the firm collaborated with online gallery Artspace to commission Martin to create a limited-edition series. Each bicycle was produced to order, and Martin then covered these unusual all-white canvases with sinuous lines and texts to reflect the urban environment, while also incorporating specific personal details into the design if requested. The resulting art pieces are individual yet also connected to New York's wider cycling community – and are covered in a protective layer of lacquer, making them well-suited to the rigours of urban life. 'The word "cycle" for me represents an unbroken ring, a symbol of growing, of understanding, of moving forwards – cycling is all of those things,' says Martin. **This spread and following spread:** Work in progress at Martin's Broadway studio in April 2015, with product shots of a finished bicycle.

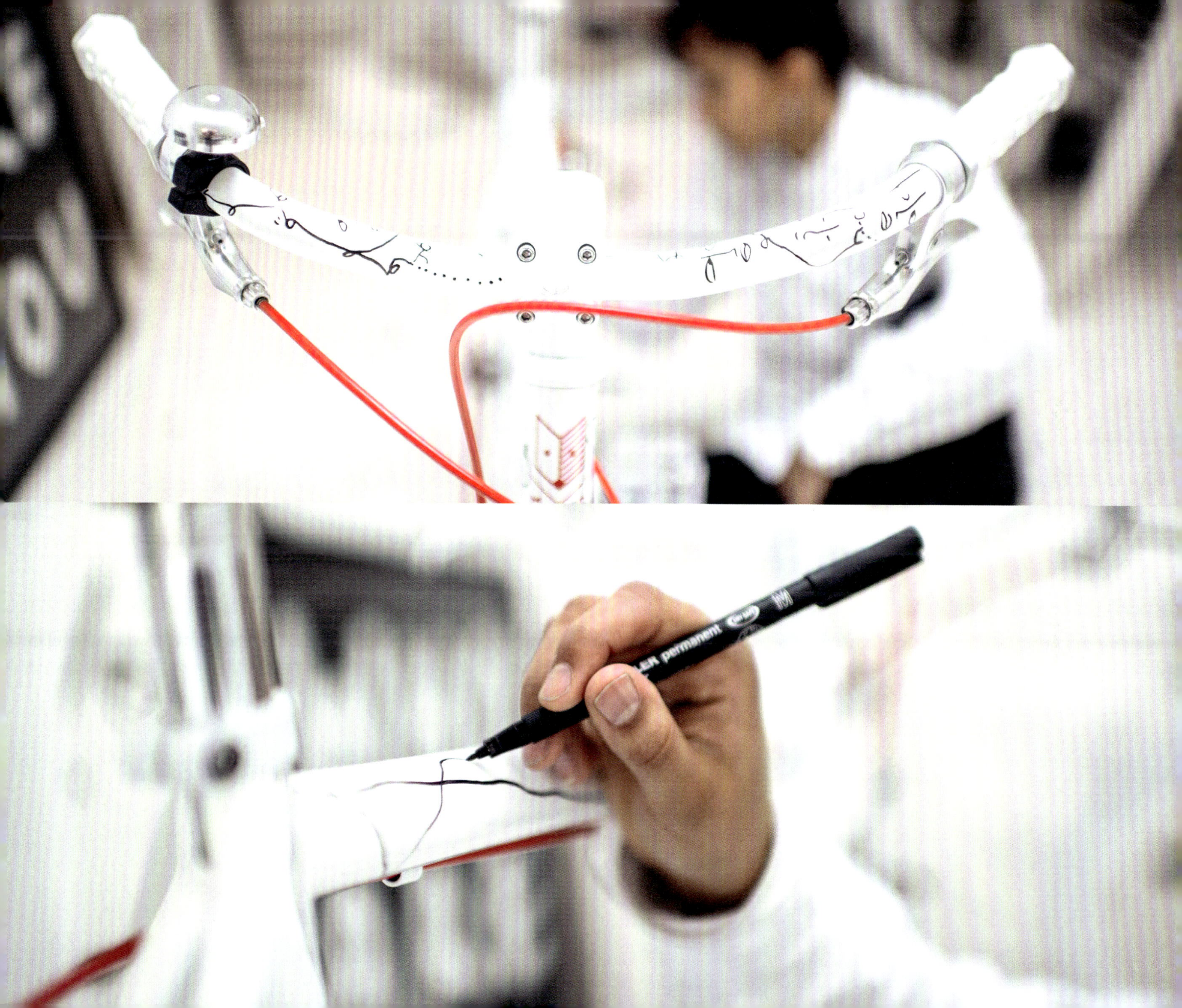

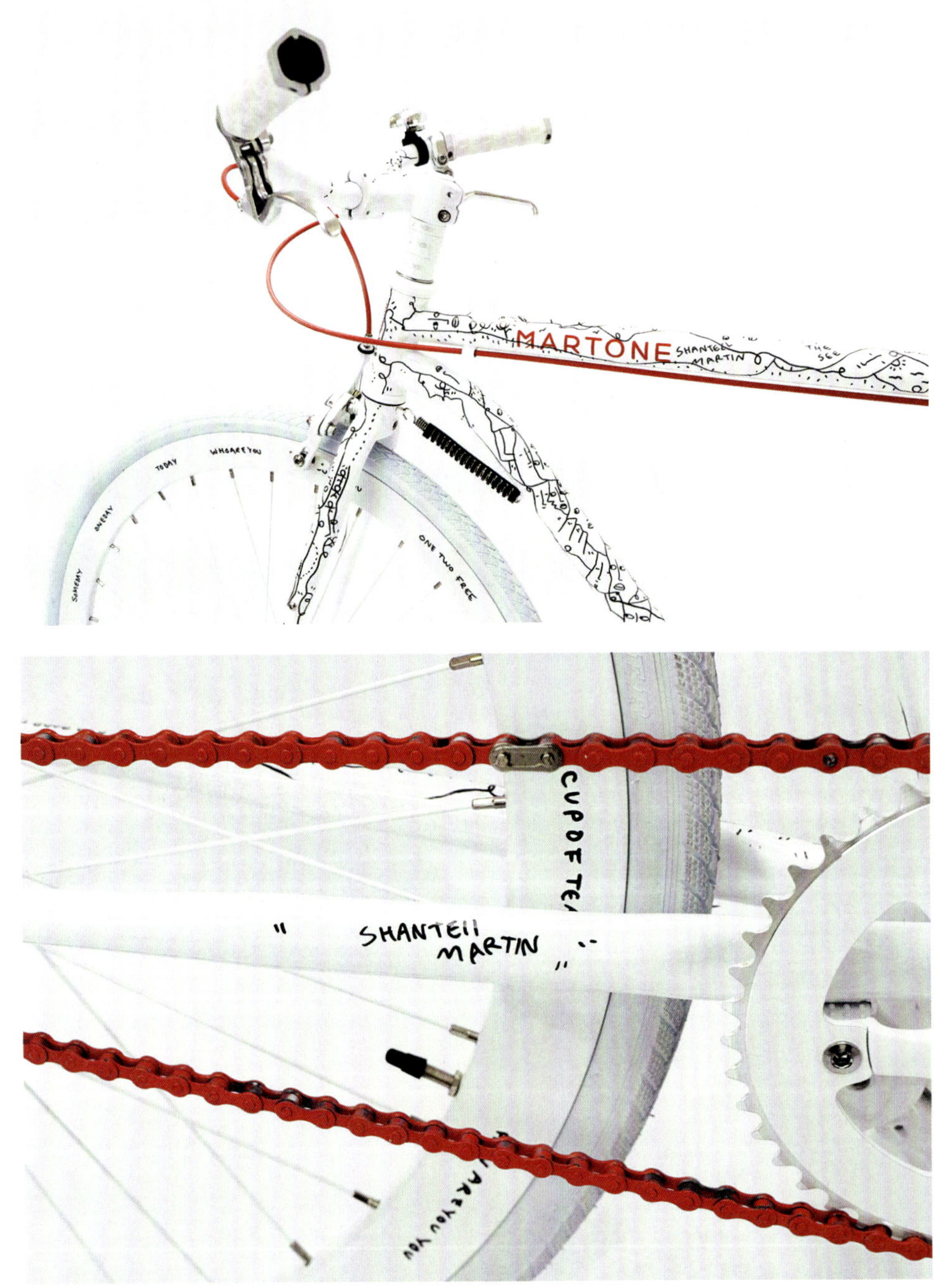
MARTONE
SHANTELL
MARTIN
THE
SEE
WHOAREYOU
TODAY
SOREADY
SOREADY
ONE TWO FREE
CUPDFTE
" SHANTELL
MARTIN "
ARE YOU YOU

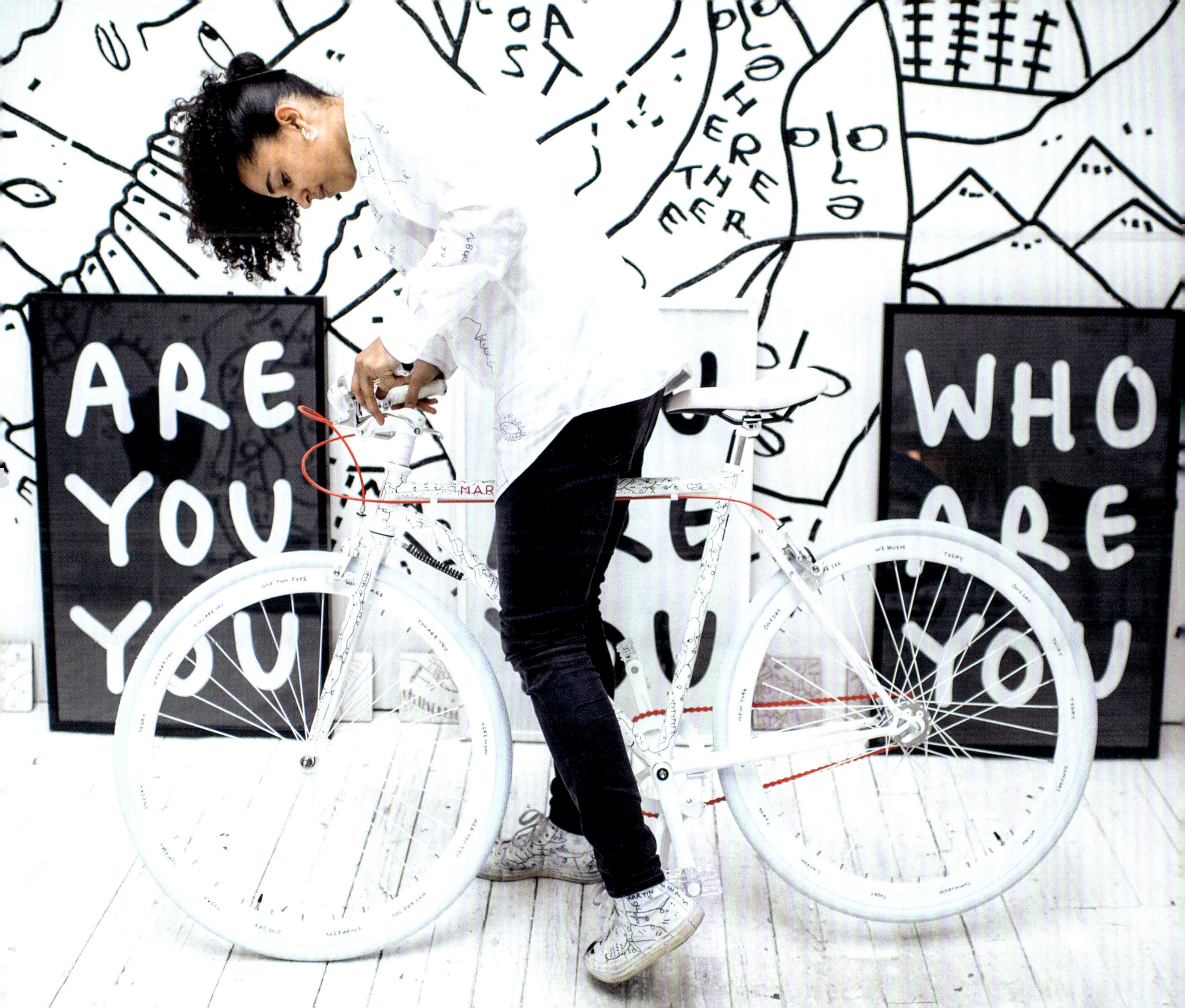

ARE
YOU
YOU
WHO
ARE
YOU
MAR

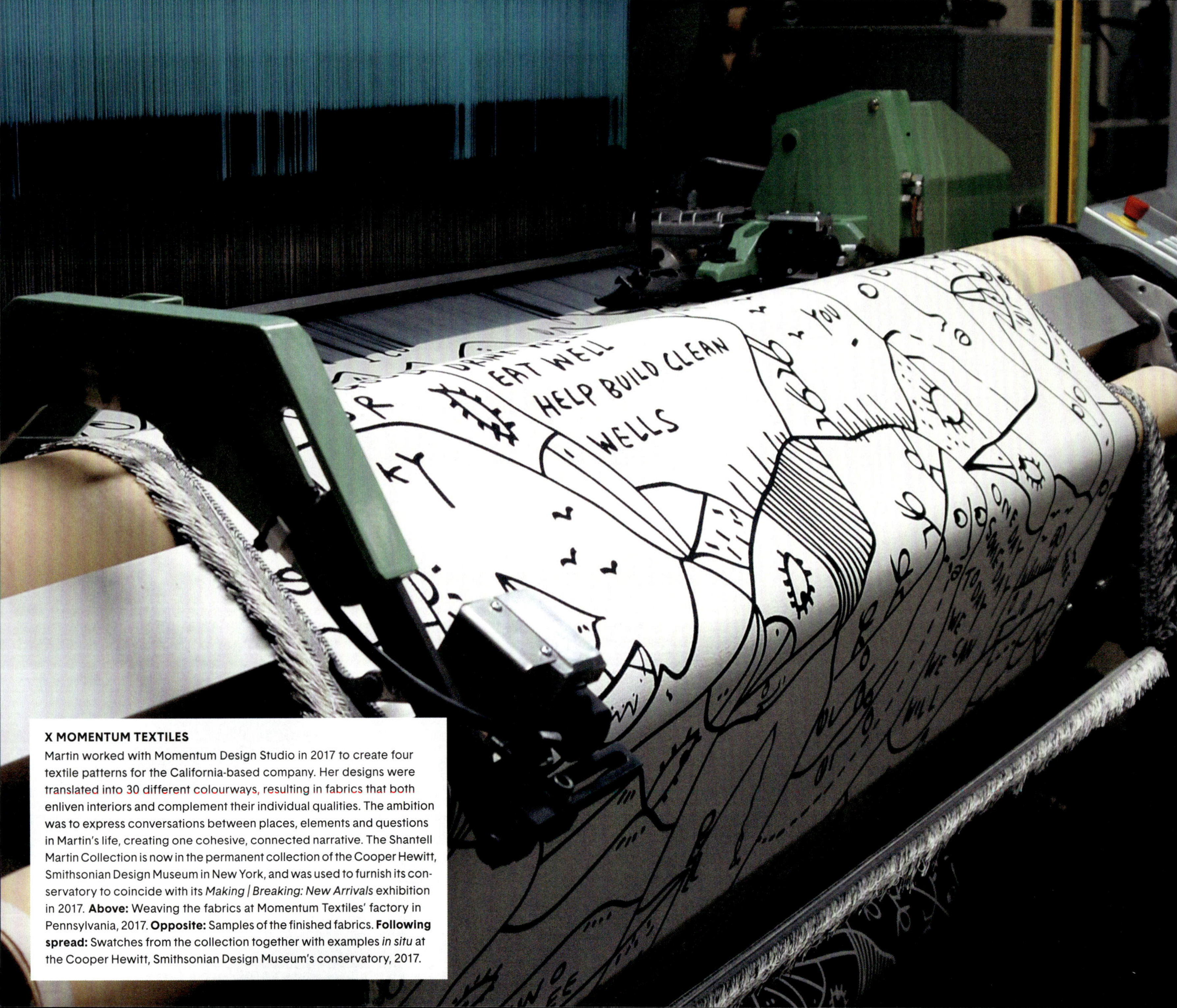

X MOMENTUM TEXTILES

Martin worked with Momentum Design Studio in 2017 to create four textile patterns for the California-based company. Her designs were translated into 30 different colourways, resulting in fabrics that both enliven interiors and complement their individual qualities. The ambition was to express conversations between places, elements and questions in Martin's life, creating one cohesive, connected narrative. The Shantell Martin Collection is now in the permanent collection of the Cooper Hewitt, Smithsonian Design Museum in New York, and was used to furnish its conservatory to coincide with its *Making | Breaking: New Arrivals* exhibition in 2017. **Above:** Weaving the fabrics at Momentum Textiles' factory in Pennsylvania, 2017. **Opposite:** Samples of the finished fabrics. **Following spread:** Swatches from the collection together with examples *in situ* at the Cooper Hewitt, Smithsonian Design Museum's conservatory, 2017.

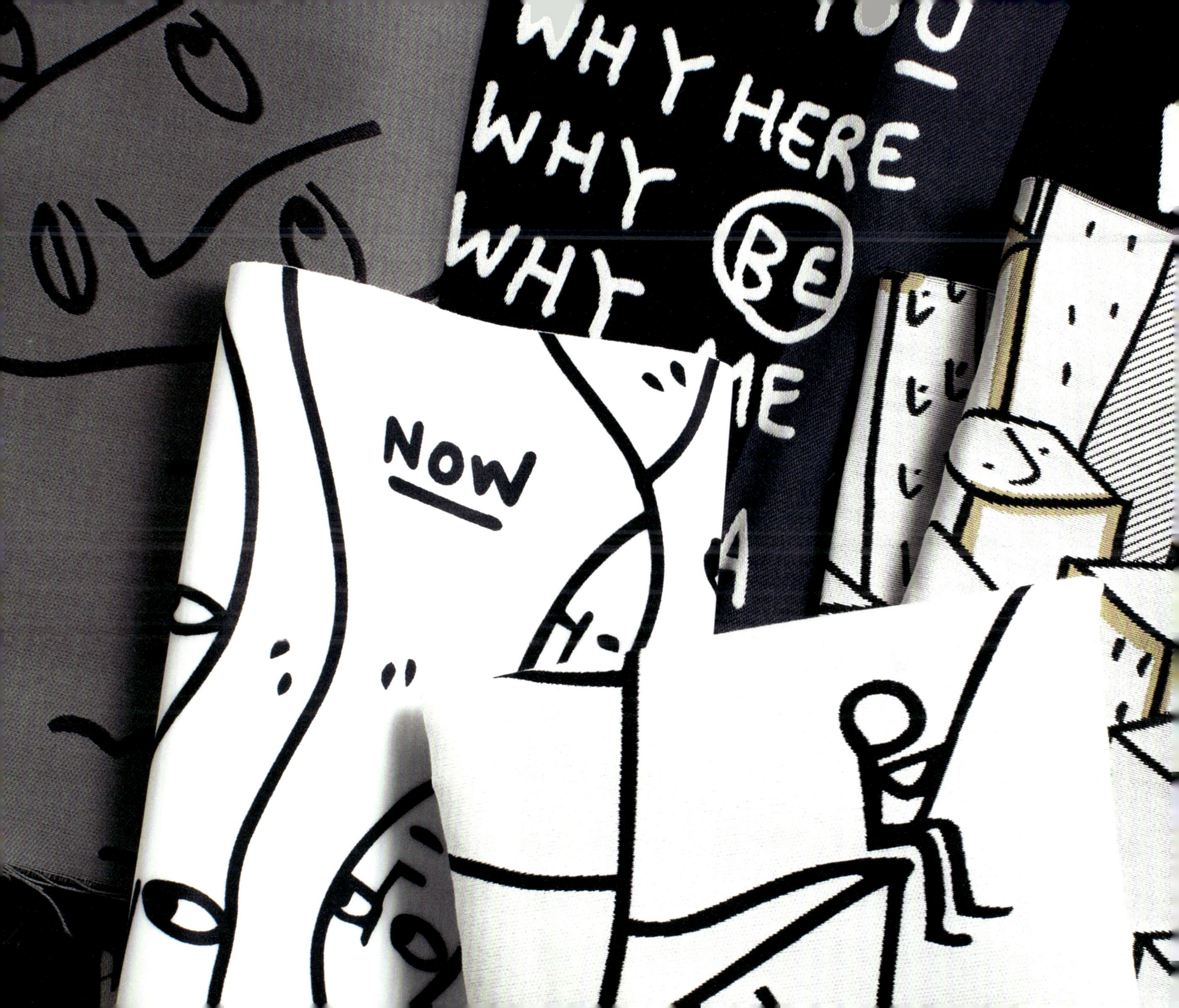

WHY
WHY HERE
WHY
WHY
BE
NOW

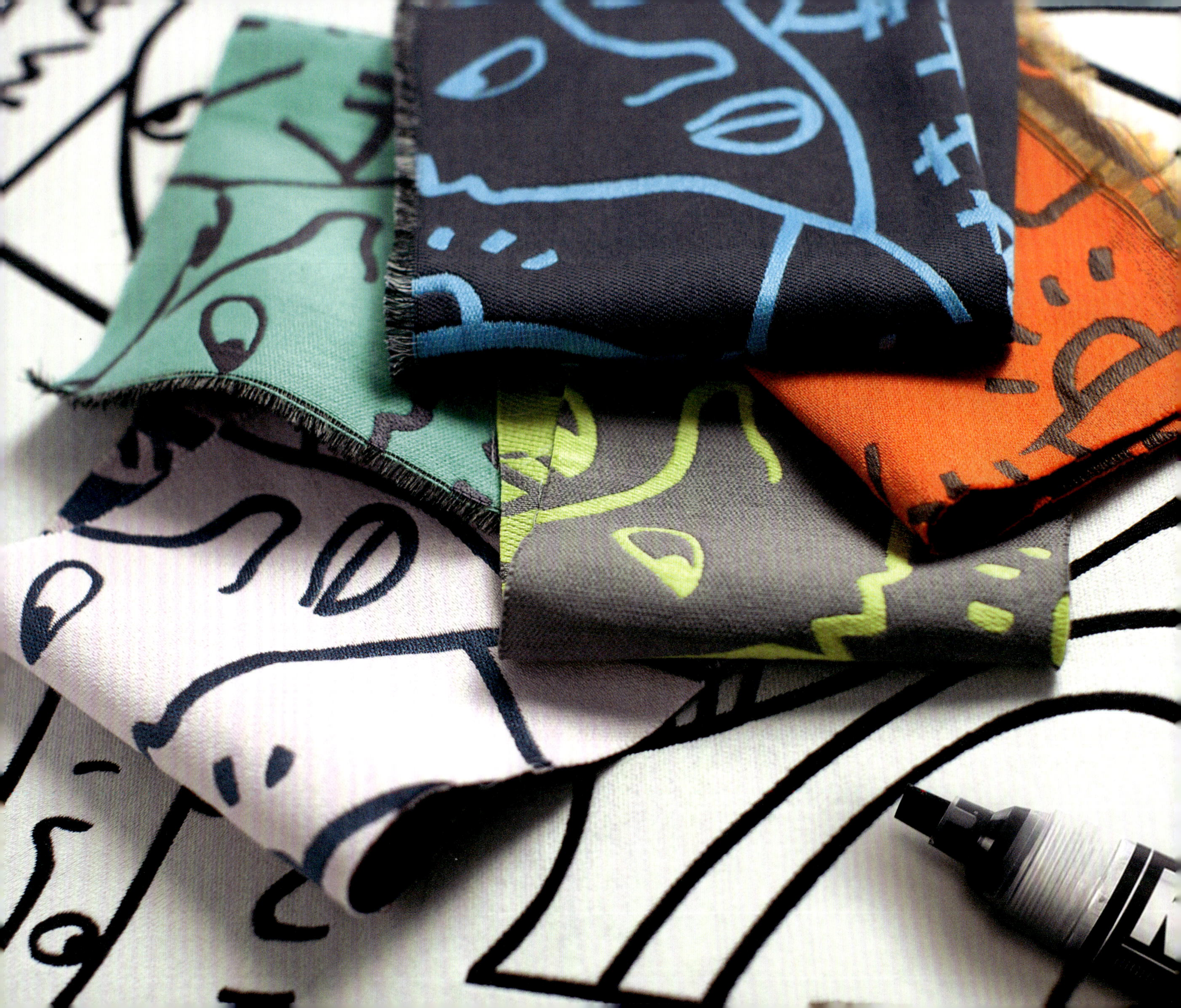

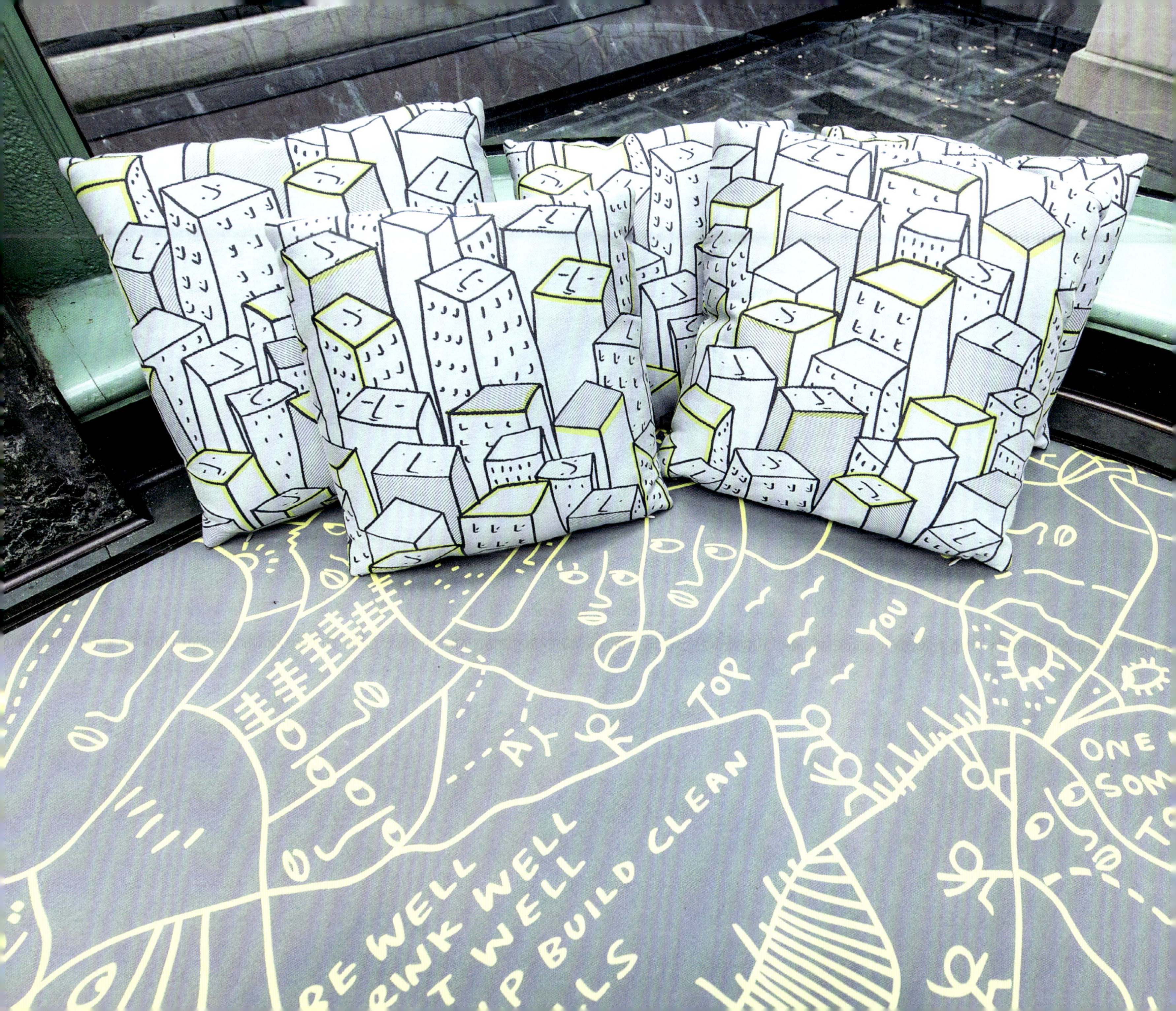
BE WELL
RINK WELL
T WELL
P BUILD CLEAN
LS
AT
TOP
YOU
ONE
SOM
T

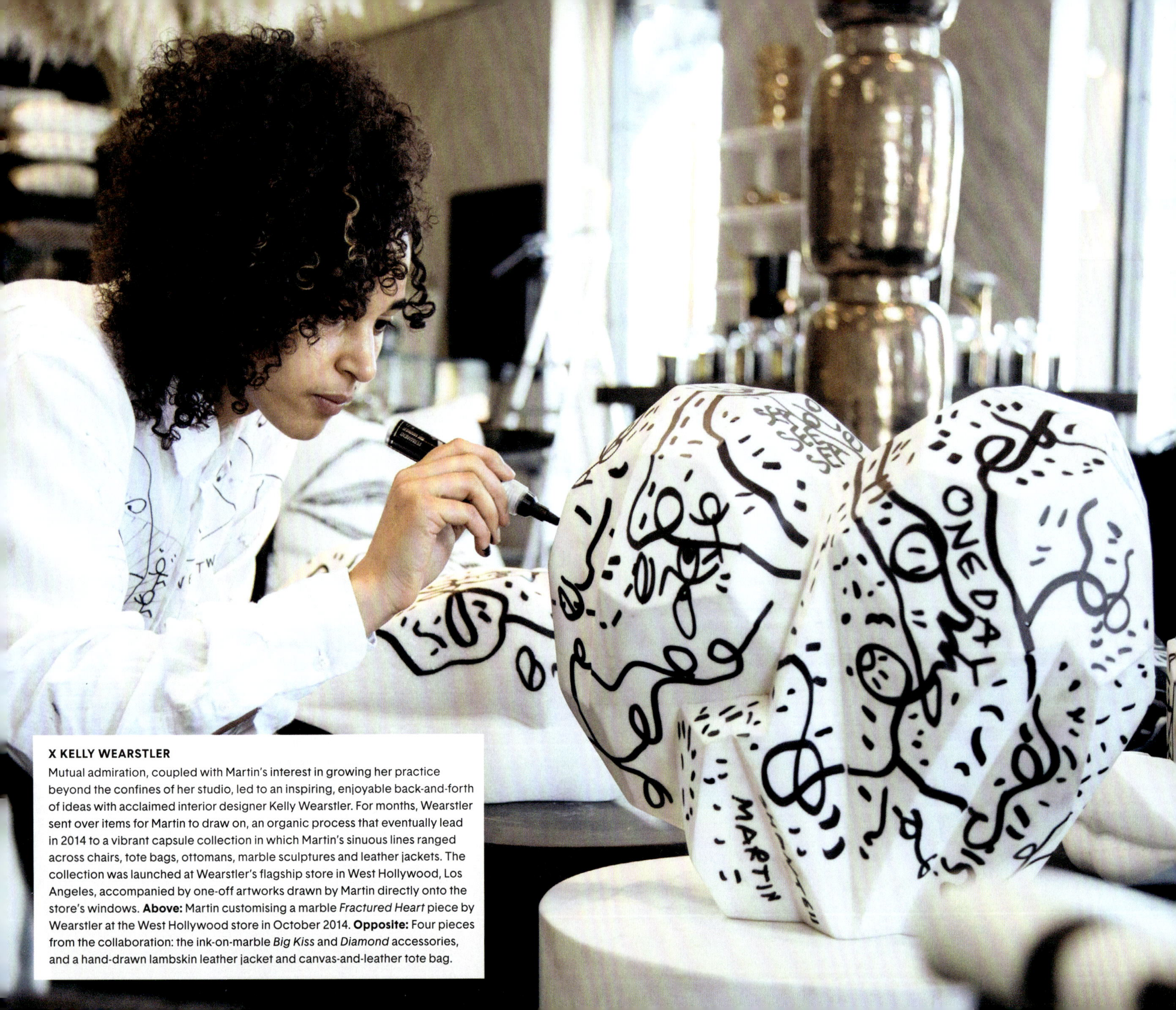

X KELLY WEARSTLER

Mutual admiration, coupled with Martin's interest in growing her practice beyond the confines of her studio, led to an inspiring, enjoyable back-and-forth of ideas with acclaimed interior designer Kelly Wearstler. For months, Wearstler sent over items for Martin to draw on, an organic process that eventually lead in 2014 to a vibrant capsule collection in which Martin's sinuous lines ranged across chairs, tote bags, ottomans, marble sculptures and leather jackets. The collection was launched at Wearstler's flagship store in West Hollywood, Los Angeles, accompanied by one-off artworks drawn by Martin directly onto the store's windows. **Above:** Martin customising a marble *Fractured Heart* piece by Wearstler at the West Hollywood store in October 2014. **Opposite:** Four pieces from the collaboration: the ink-on-marble *Big Kiss* and *Diamond* accessories, and a hand-drawn lambskin leather jacket and canvas-and-leather tote bag.

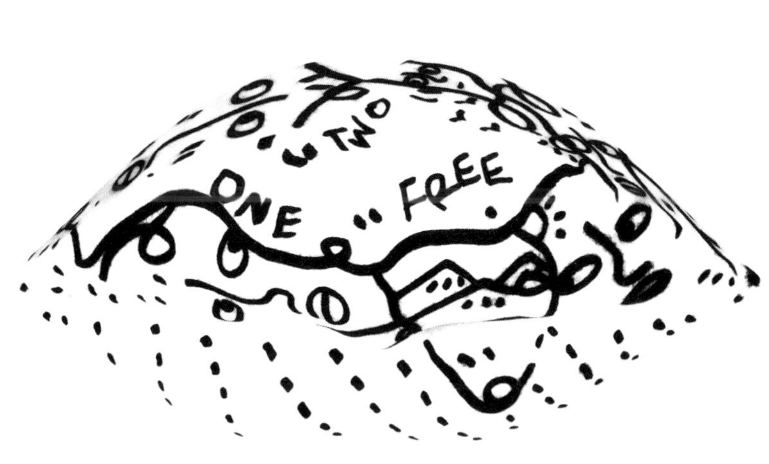
ONE TWO
ONE FREE

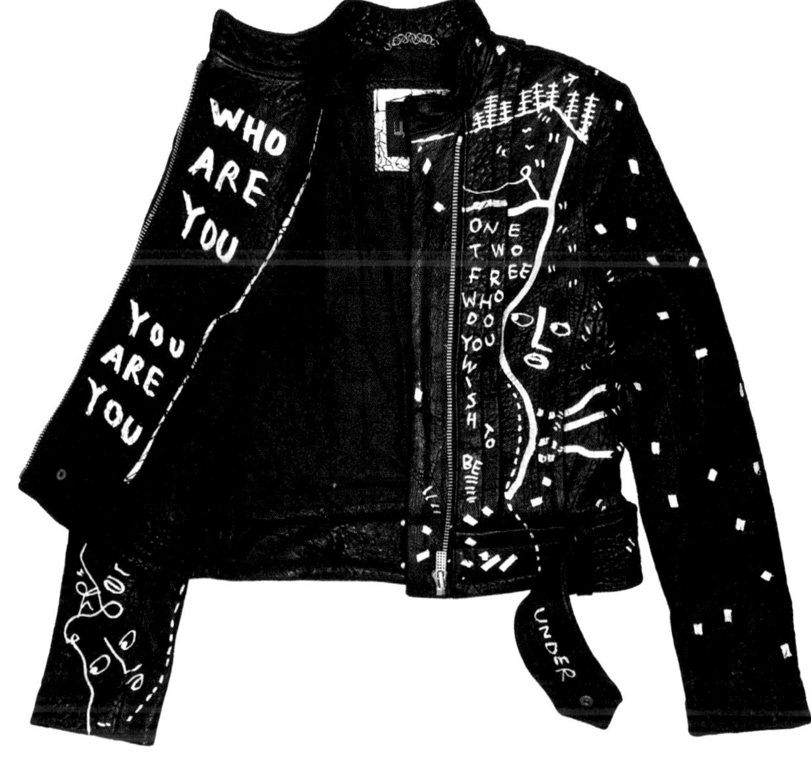
WHO
ARE
YOU
YOU
ARE
YOU
ONE
TWO
FREE
WHO
DO
YOU
WISH
TO
BE
UNDER

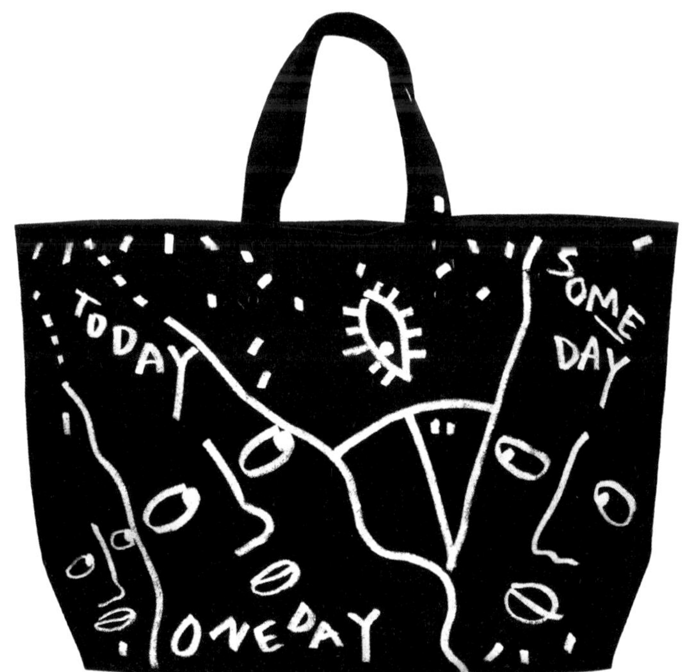
SOME
DAY
TODAY
ONE DAY

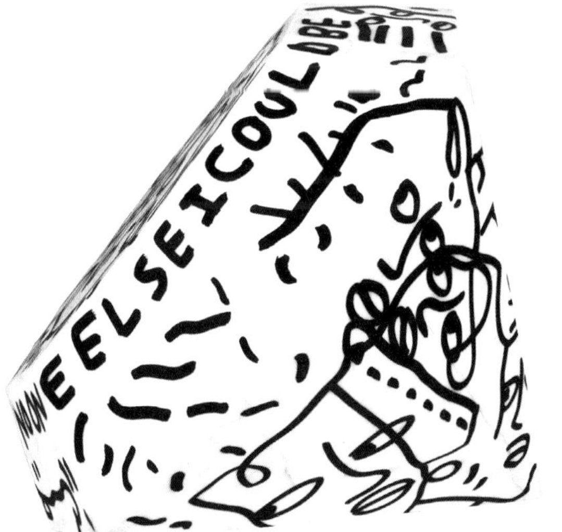
WHO ELSE I COULD BE

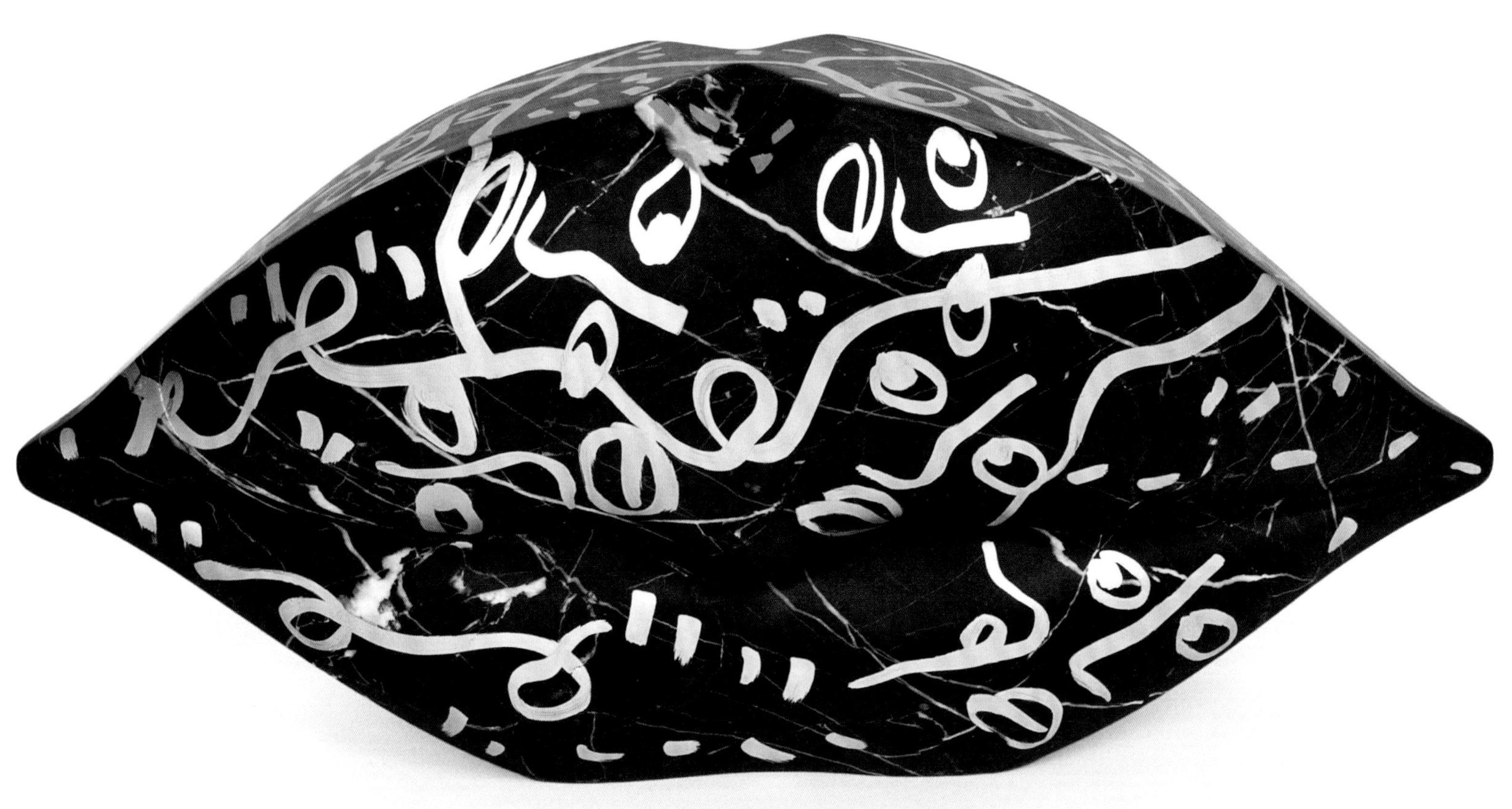

Above: *Classic Big Kiss*, 2014. Ink on marble.
Collaboration with Kelly Wearstler. **Opposite:**
Martin with a window display at Wearstler's West
Hollywood store in October 2014, and the finished
ink-on-marble *Fractured Heart* sculpture.

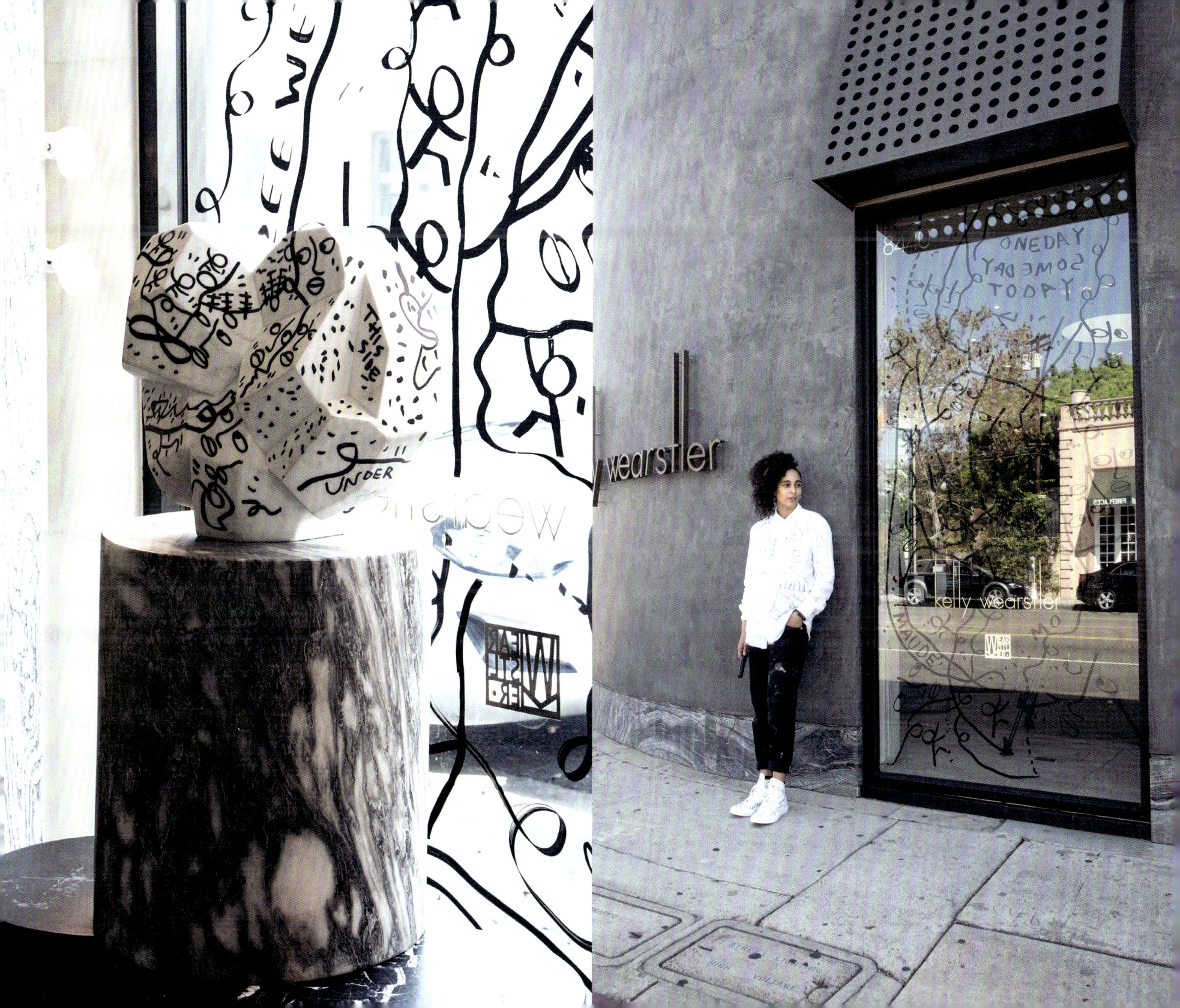
wearstler
kelly wearstler
THIS SIDE
UNDER
ONE DAY
SOME DAY
TODAY

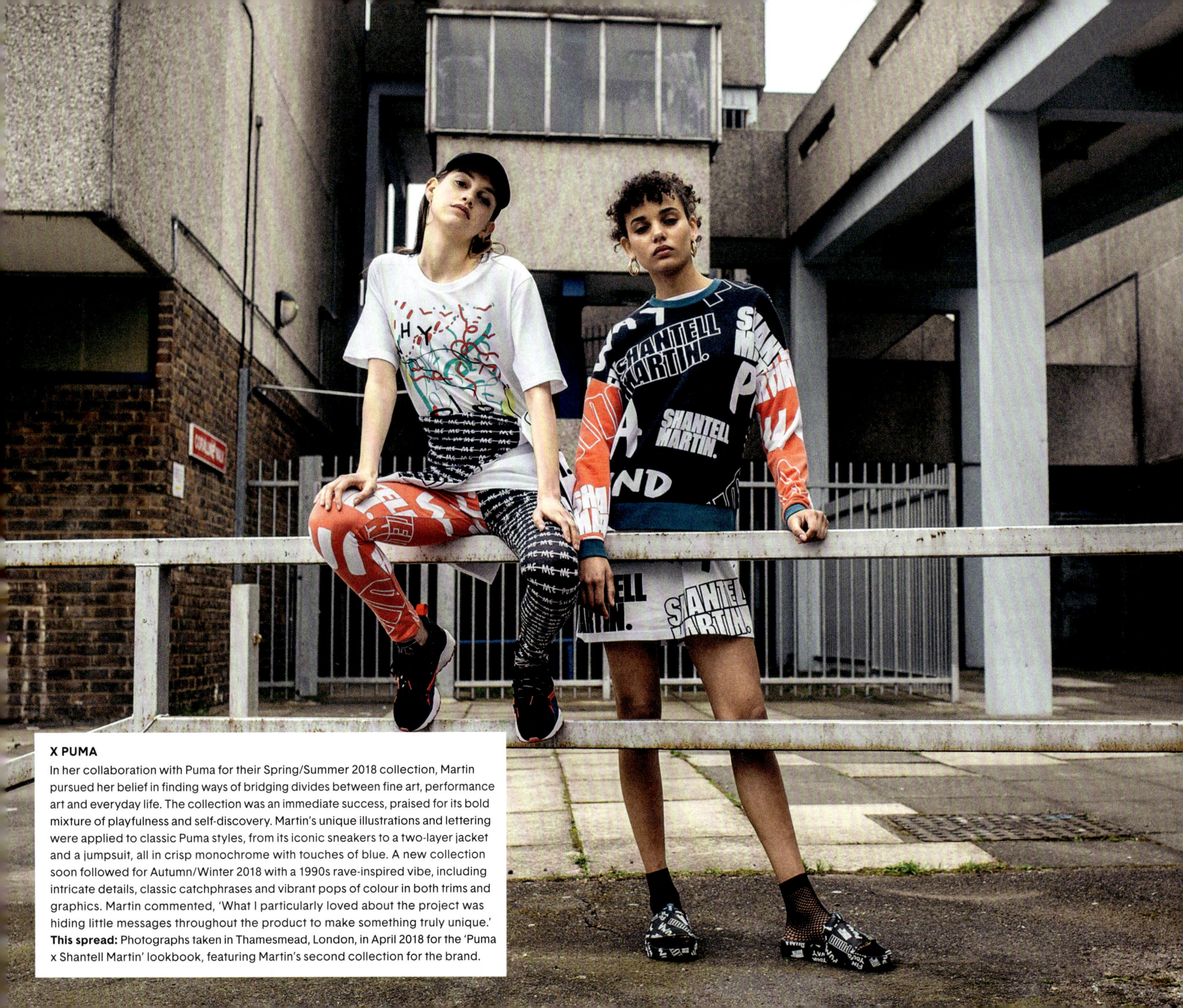

X PUMA

In her collaboration with Puma for their Spring/Summer 2018 collection, Martin pursued her belief in finding ways of bridging divides between fine art, performance art and everyday life. The collection was an immediate success, praised for its bold mixture of playfulness and self-discovery. Martin's unique illustrations and lettering were applied to classic Puma styles, from its iconic sneakers to a two-layer jacket and a jumpsuit, all in crisp monochrome with touches of blue. A new collection soon followed for Autumn/Winter 2018 with a 1990s rave-inspired vibe, including intricate details, classic catchphrases and vibrant pops of colour in both trims and graphics. Martin commented, 'What I particularly loved about the project was hiding little messages throughout the product to make something truly unique.'
This spread: Photographs taken in Thamesmead, London, in April 2018 for the 'Puma x Shantell Martin' lookbook, featuring Martin's second collection for the brand.

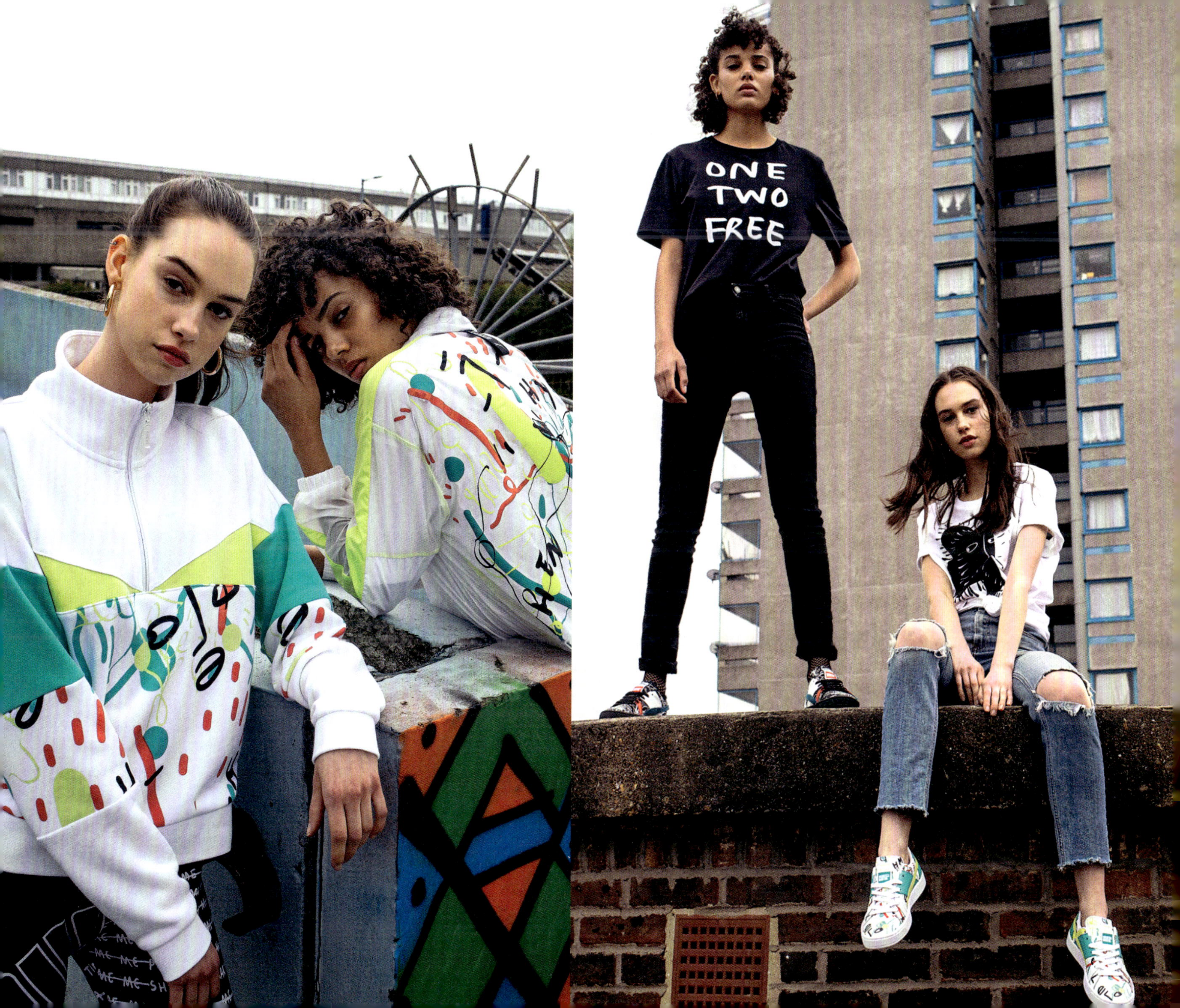
ONE
TWO
FREE

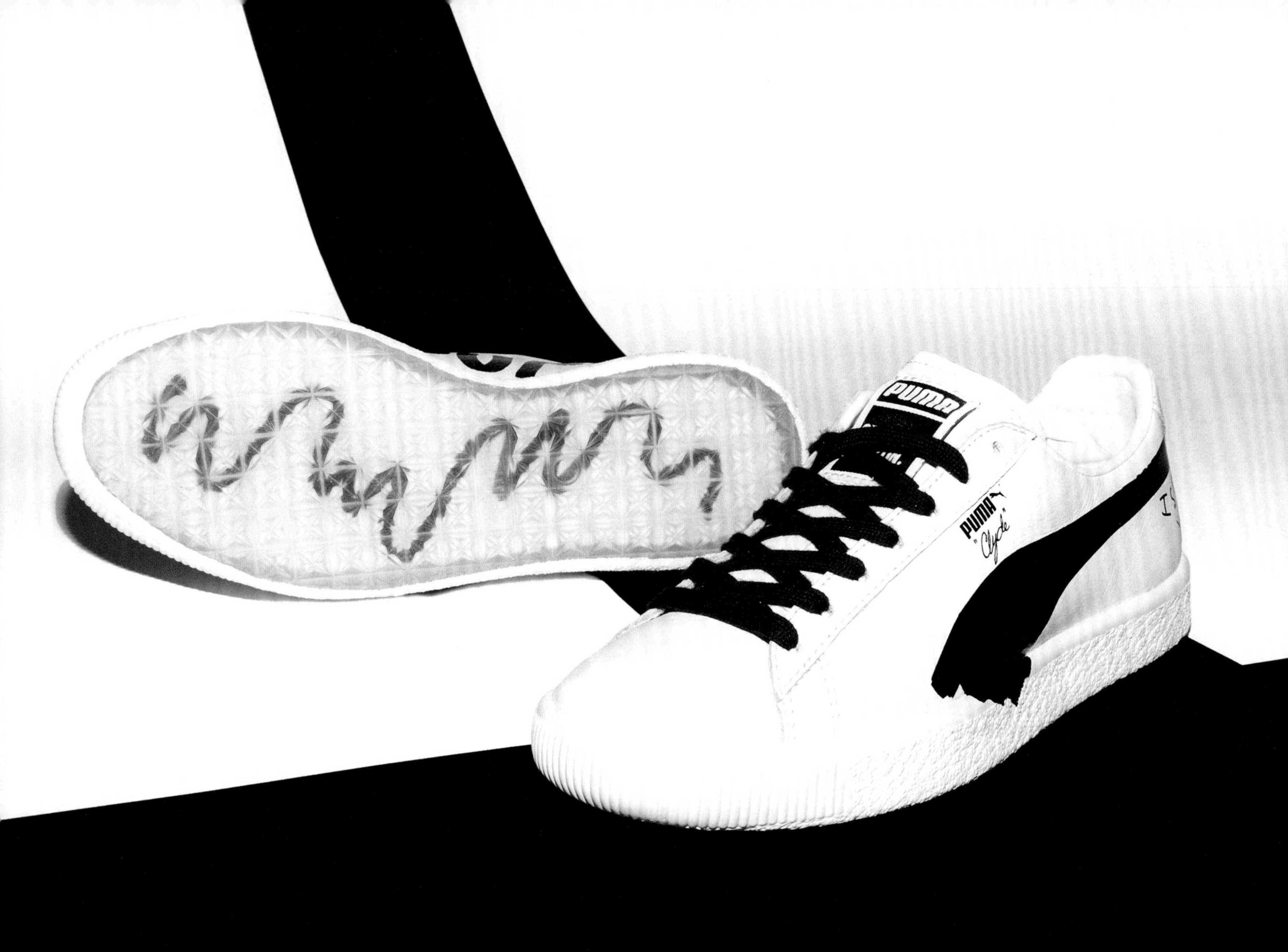

This spread: Customised Clyde and Platform Strap sneakers, pants and two-layer jacket from 'Puma x Shantell Martin' Spring/Summer 2018 collection

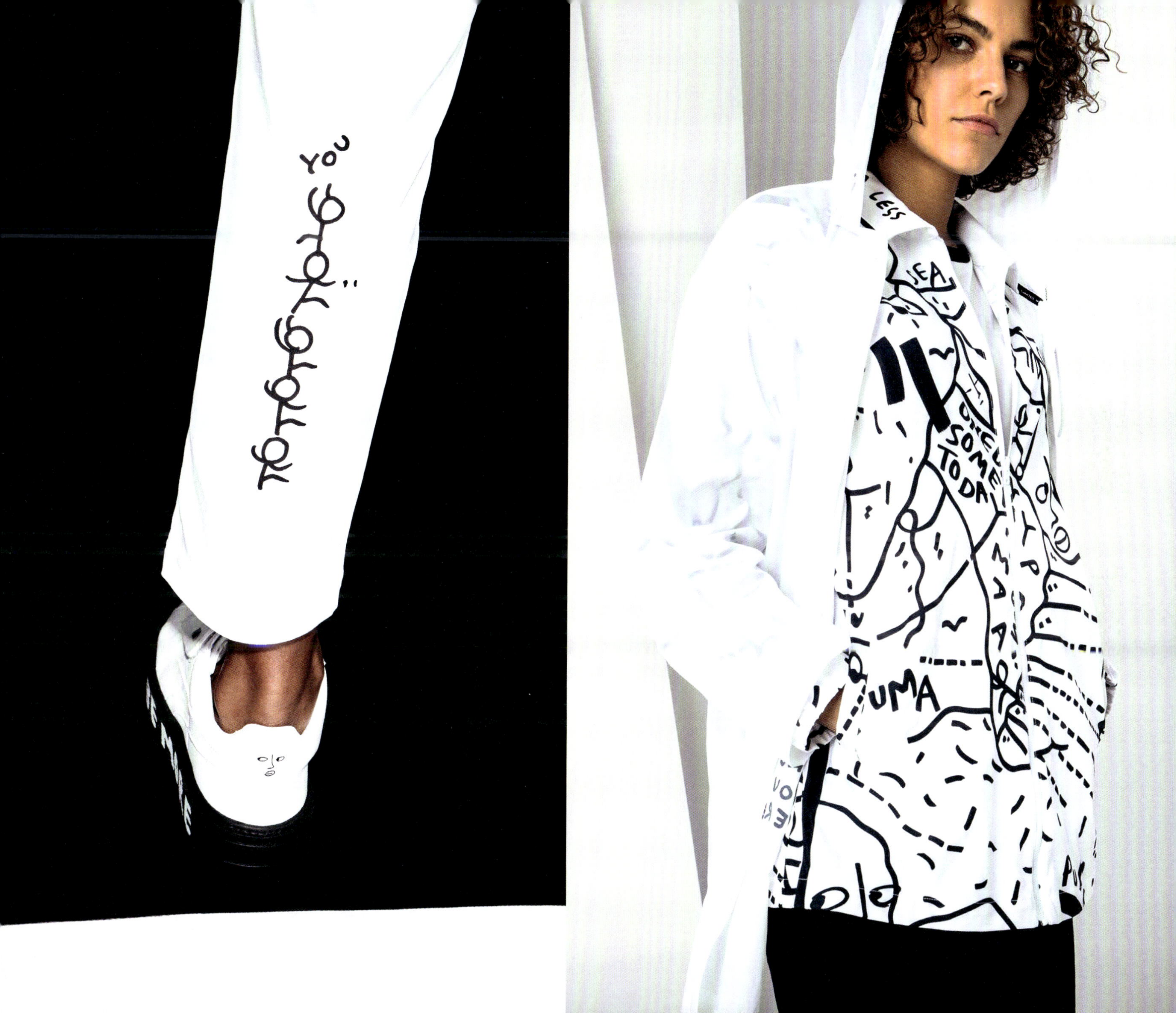
YOU
LESS
SOME
TODAY
PUMA

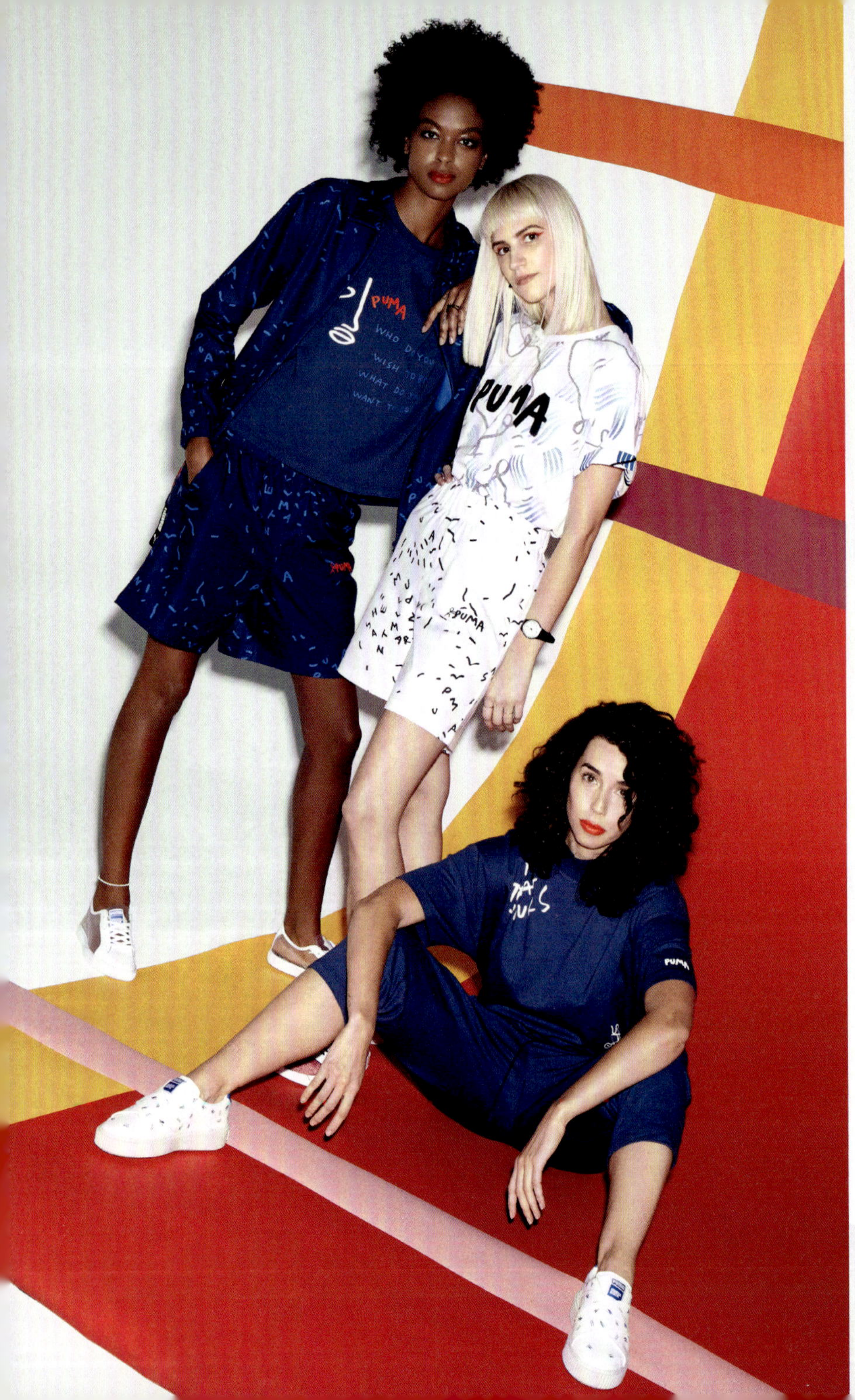

PUMA
PUMA
PUMA

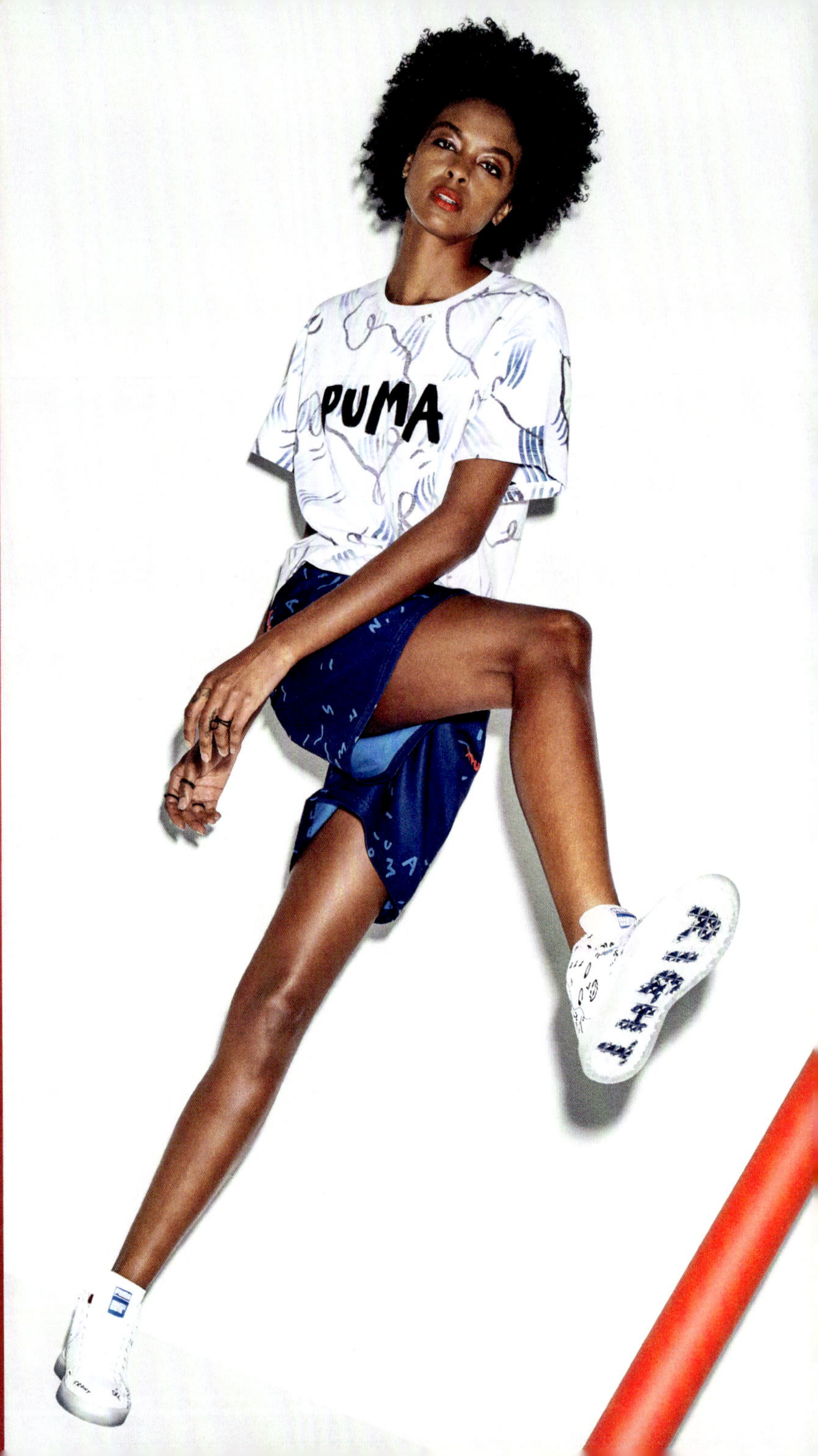

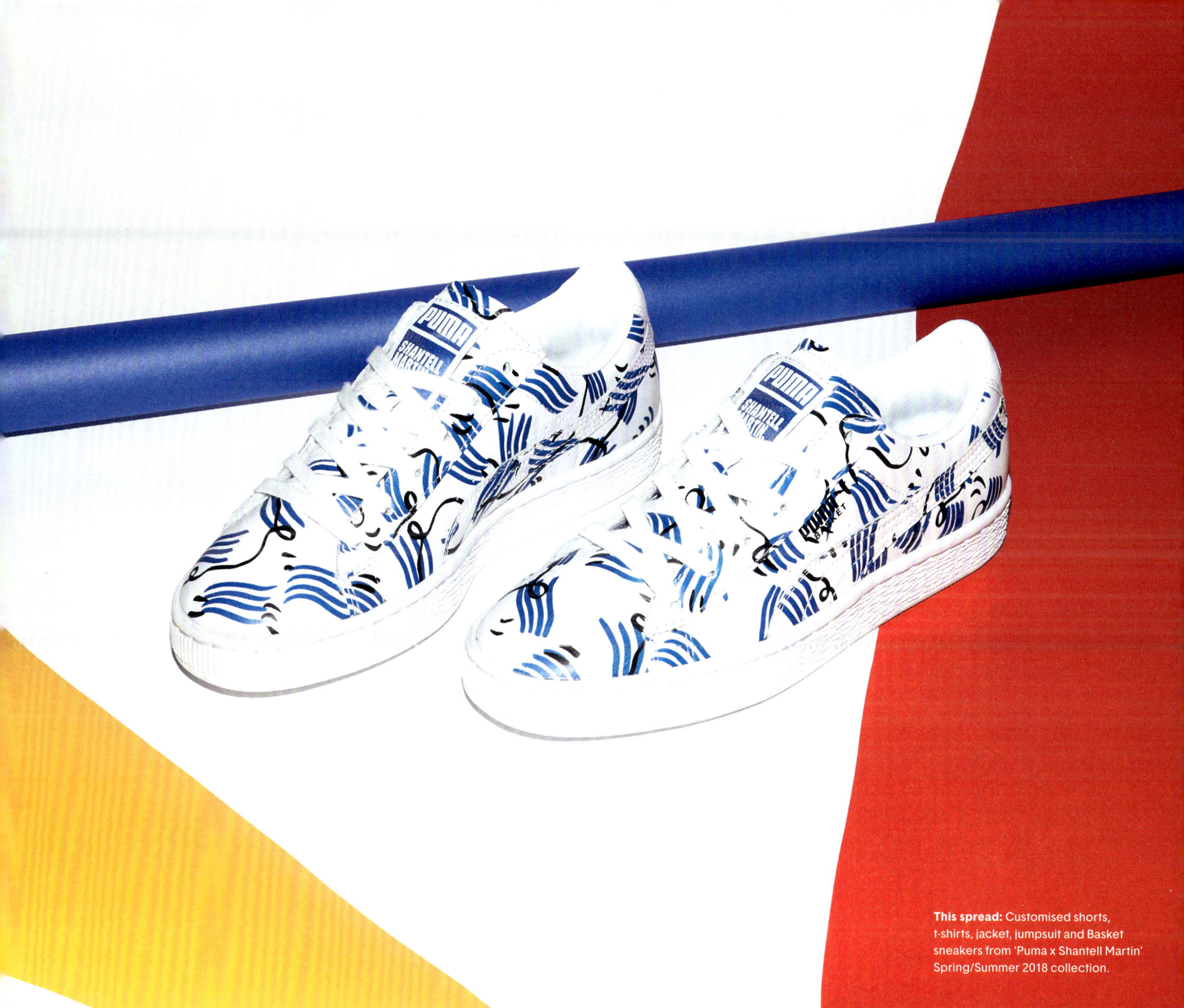

This spread: Customised shorts, t-shirts, jacket, jumpsuit and Basket sneakers from 'Puma x Shantell Martin' Spring/Summer 2018 collection.

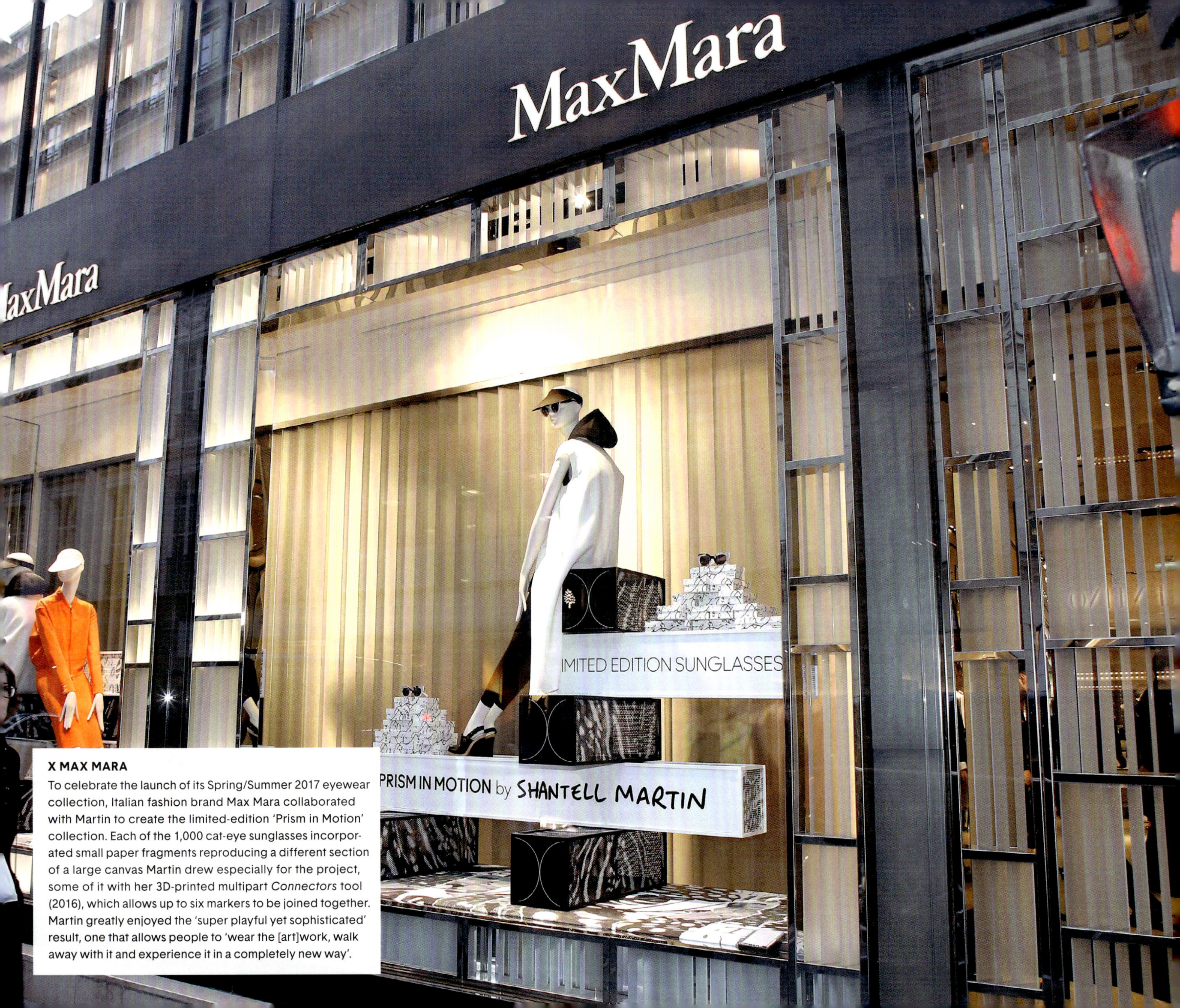

X MAX MARA

To celebrate the launch of its Spring/Summer 2017 eyewear collection, Italian fashion brand Max Mara collaborated with Martin to create the limited-edition 'Prism in Motion' collection. Each of the 1,000 cat-eye sunglasses incorporated small paper fragments reproducing a different section of a large canvas Martin drew especially for the project, some of it with her 3D-printed multipart *Connectors* tool (2016), which allows up to six markers to be joined together. Martin greatly enjoyed the 'super playful yet sophisticated' result, one that allows people to 'wear the [art]work, walk away with it and experience it in a completely new way'.

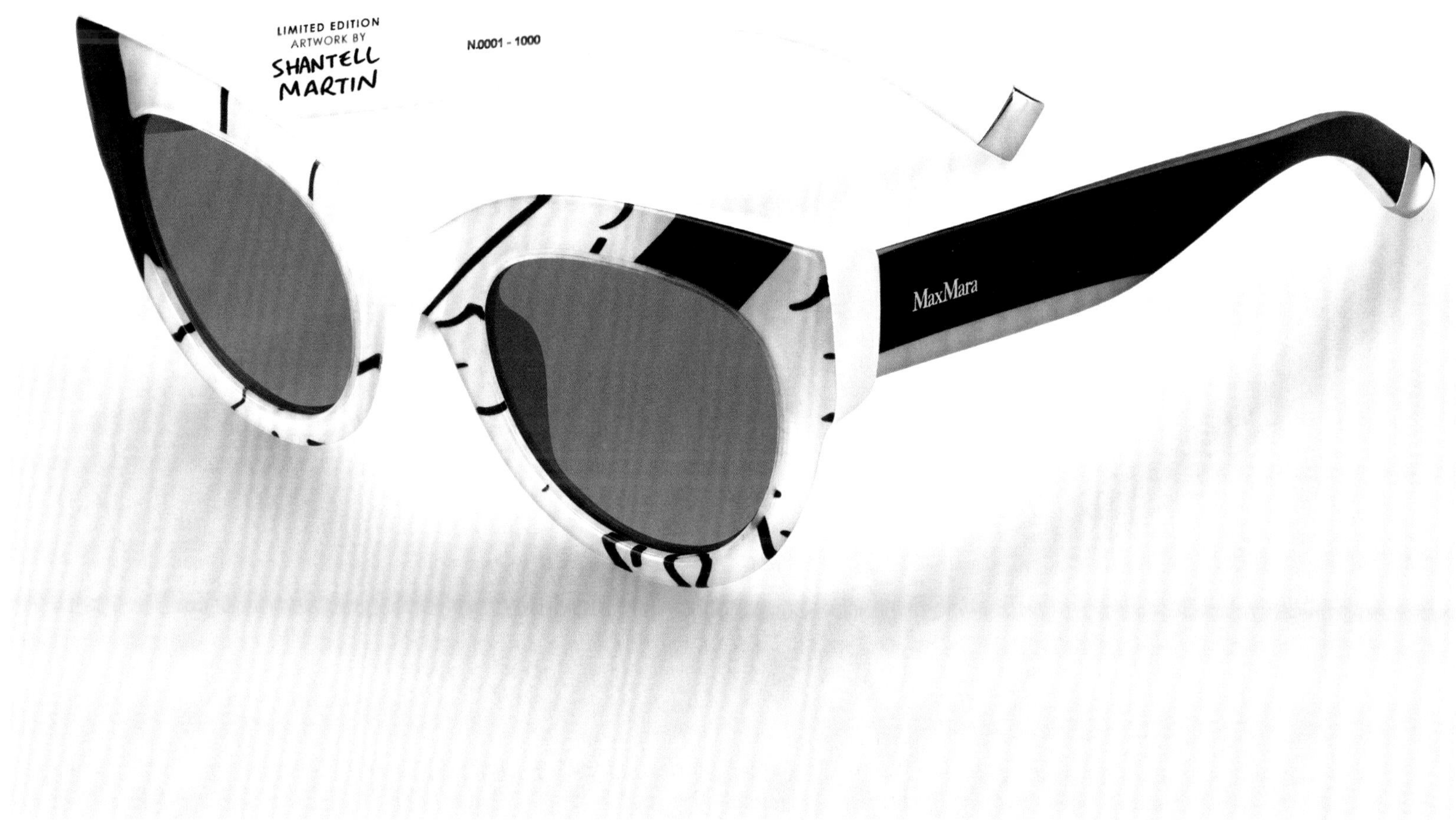

Above: Limited-edition sunglasses from the 'Prism in Motion' collection, 2017. **Opposite:** Window display at Max Mara's store on rue Saint-Honoré, Paris, for the collection's launch, March 2017.

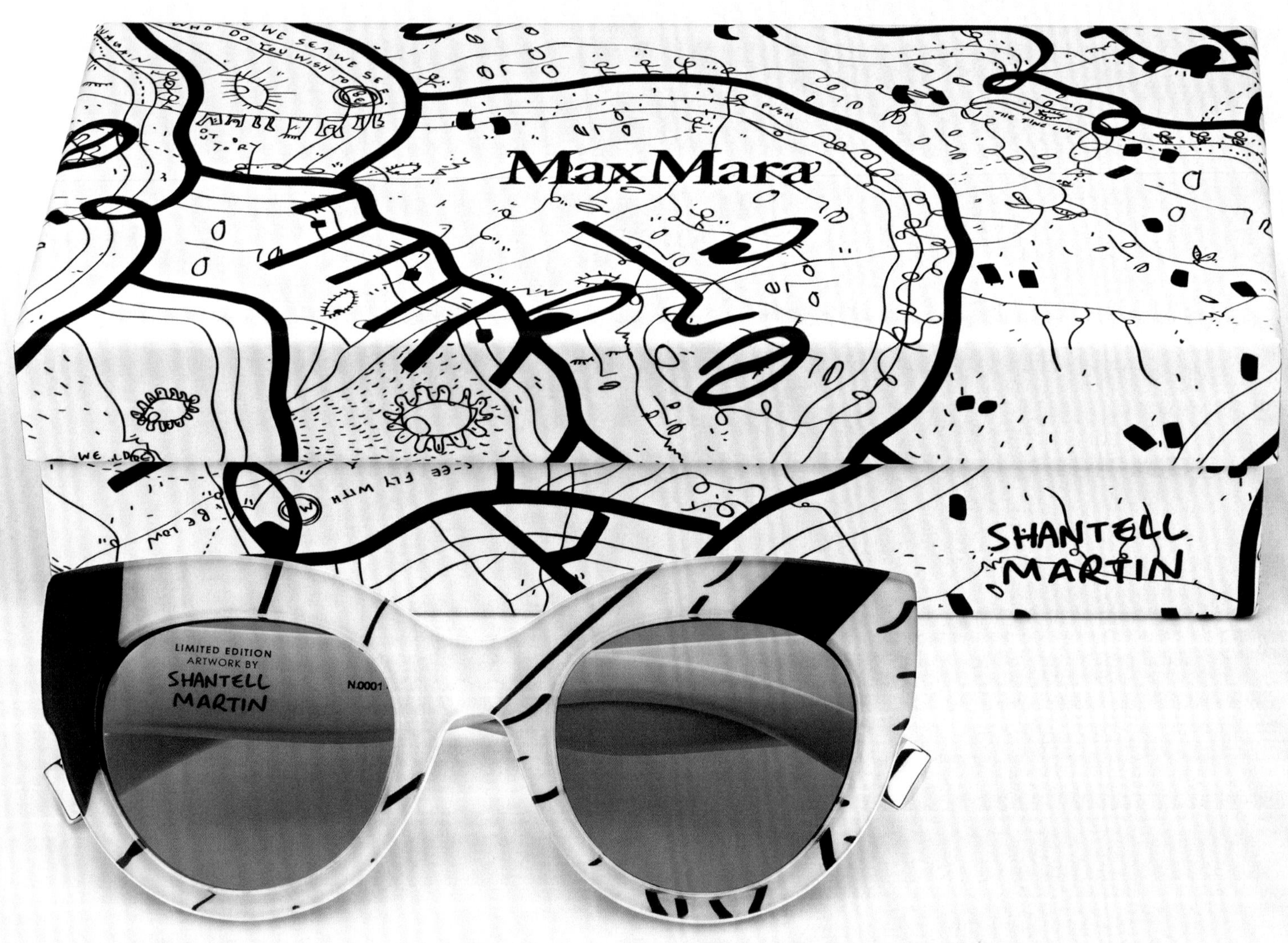

Above: Sunglasses and case from the 'Prism in Motion' collection, 2017. **Opposite:** Martin at work in November 2016 on the canvas *Prism in Motion (Max Mara)*, details of which were later reproduced on the 'Prism in Motion' sunglasses.

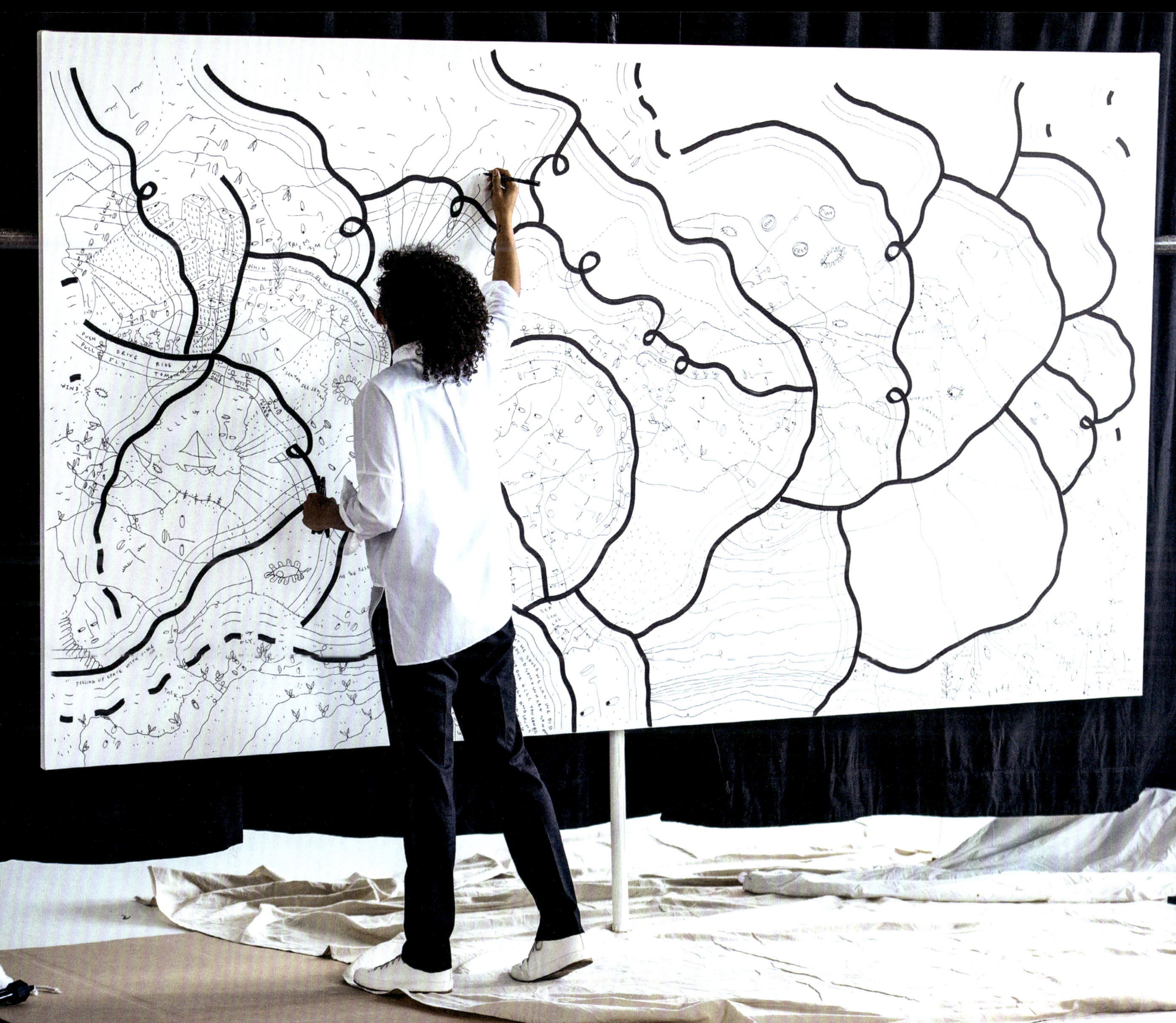

INTERACT
KNOW THE FACTS
INTERACT
KNOW THE-----

INTERACT.

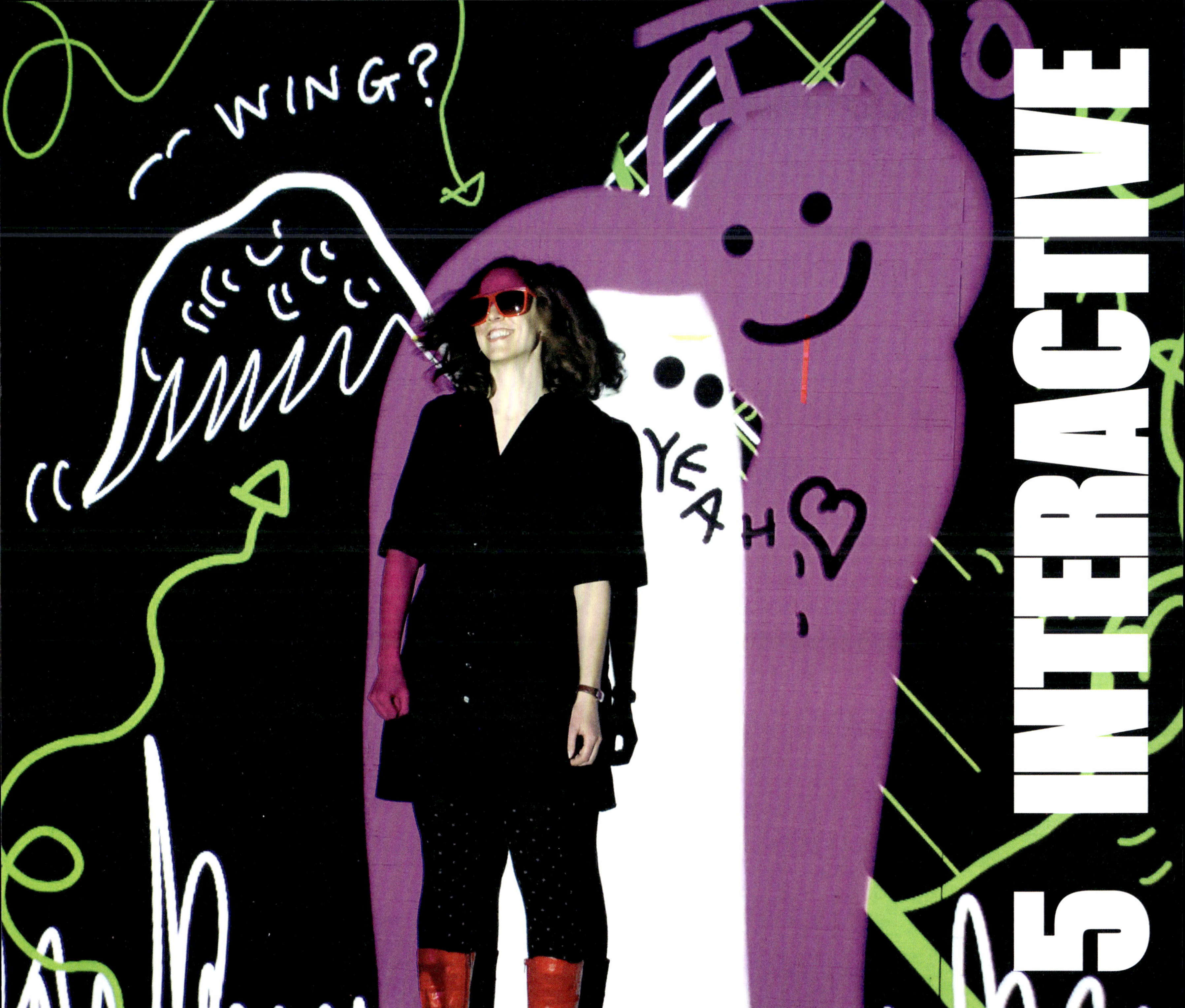
WING?
YEAH
5 INTERACTIVE

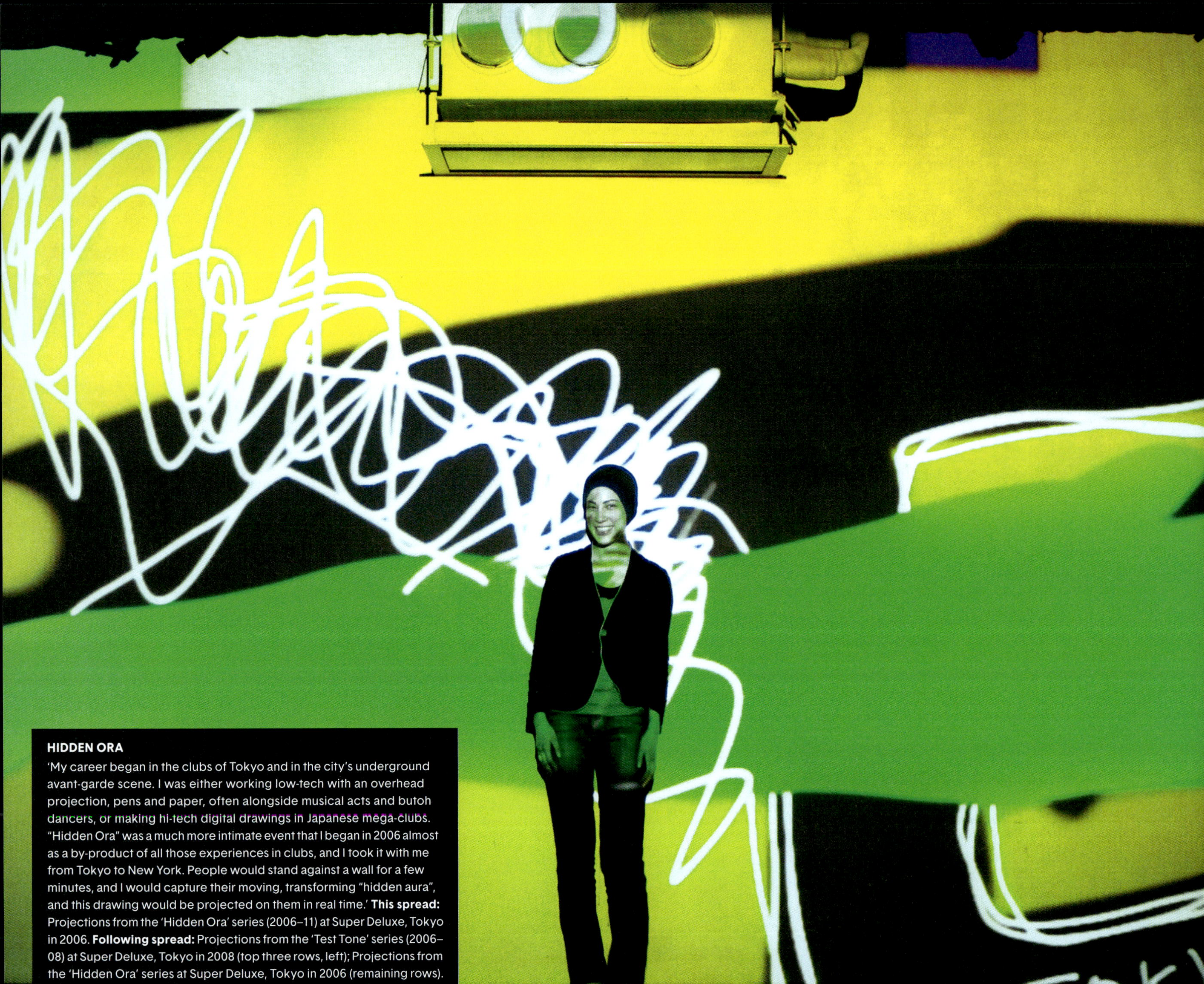

HIDDEN ORA

'My career began in the clubs of Tokyo and in the city's underground avant-garde scene. I was either working low-tech with an overhead projection, pens and paper, often alongside musical acts and butoh dancers, or making hi-tech digital drawings in Japanese mega-clubs. "Hidden Ora" was a much more intimate event that I began in 2006 almost as a by-product of all those experiences in clubs, and I took it with me from Tokyo to New York. People would stand against a wall for a few minutes, and I would capture their moving, transforming "hidden aura", and this drawing would be projected on them in real time.' **This spread:** Projections from the 'Hidden Ora' series (2006–11) at Super Deluxe, Tokyo in 2006. **Following spread:** Projections from the 'Test Tone' series (2006–08) at Super Deluxe, Tokyo in 2008 (top three rows, left); Projections from the 'Hidden Ora' series at Super Deluxe, Tokyo in 2006 (remaining rows).

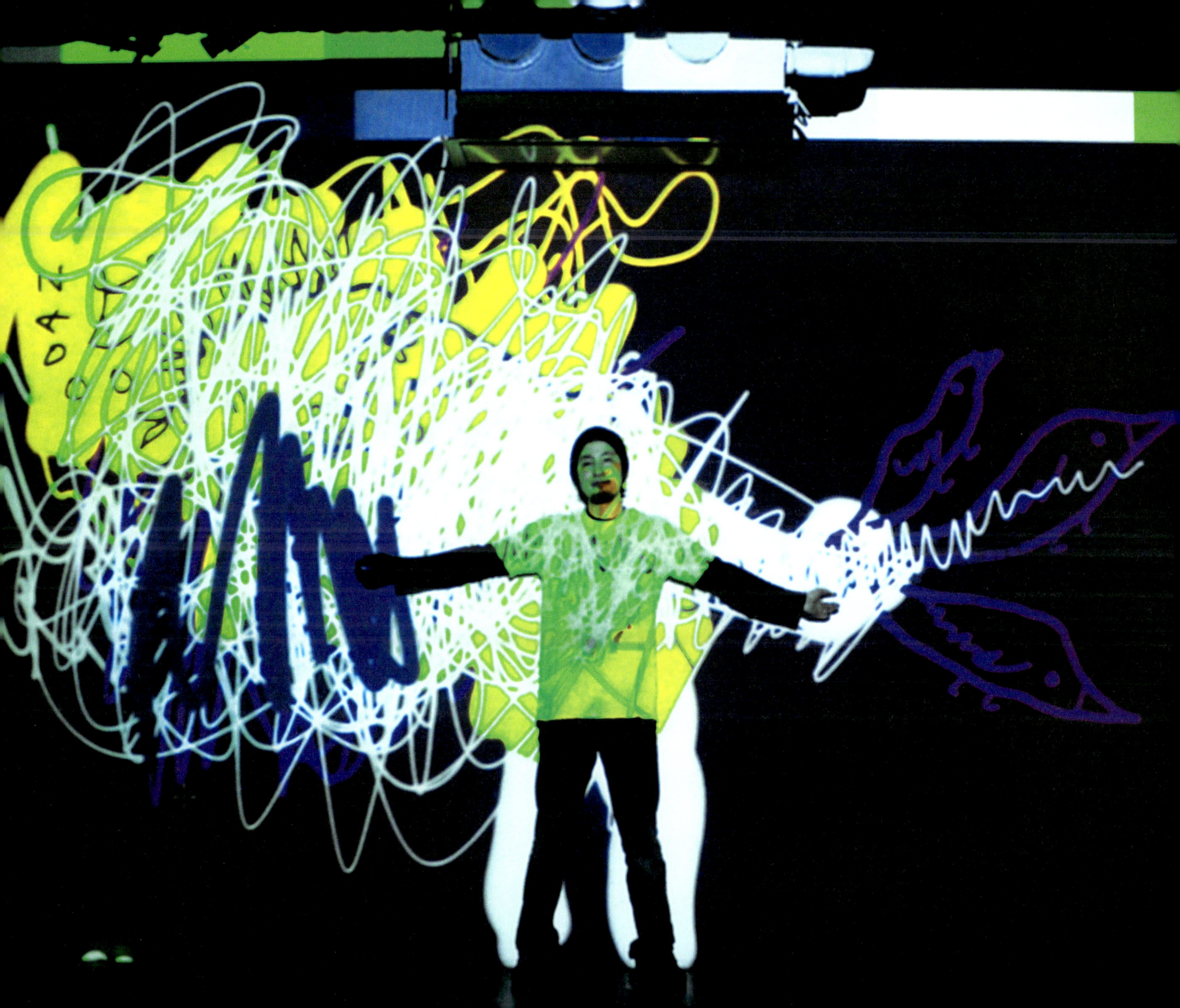

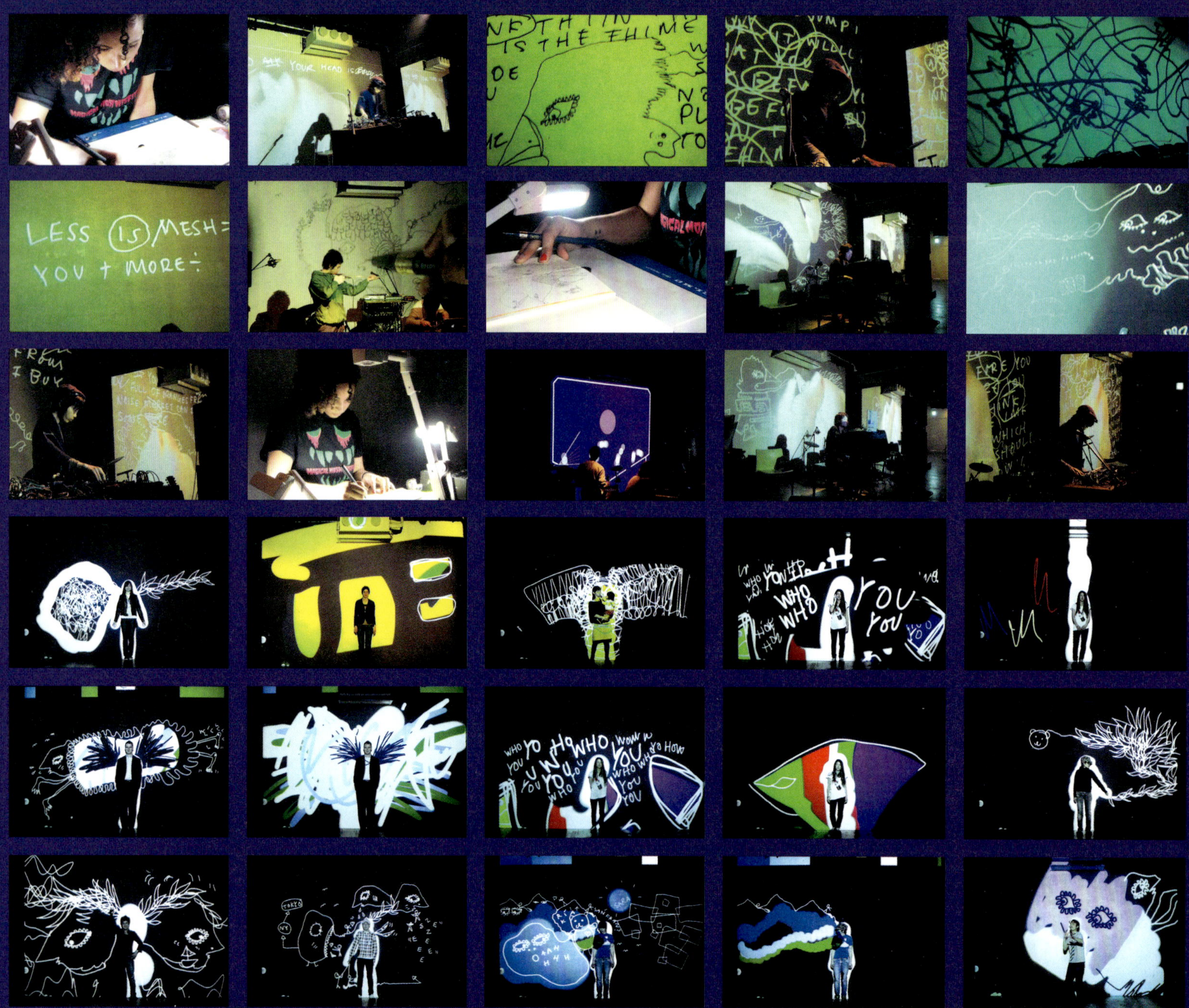

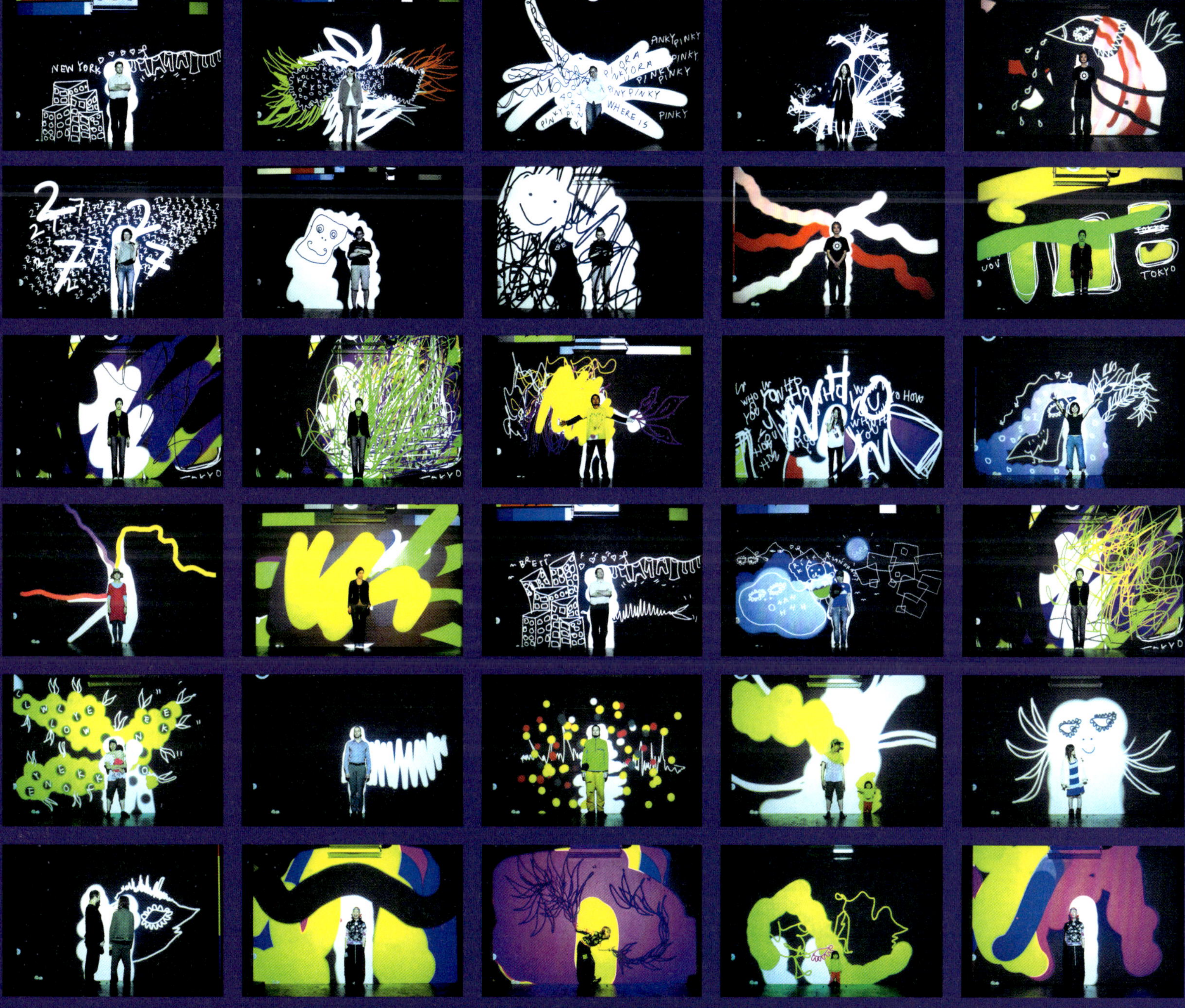

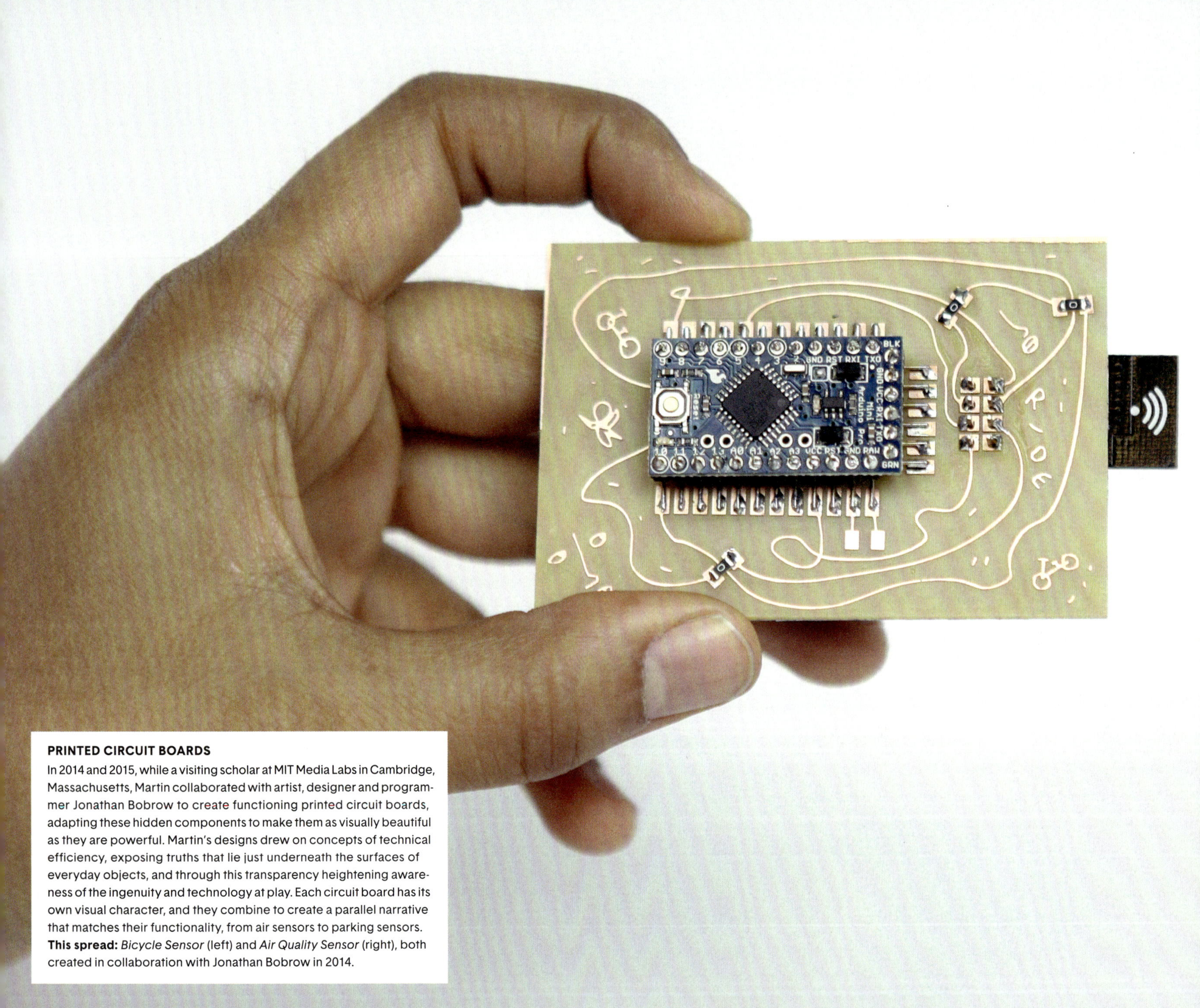

PRINTED CIRCUIT BOARDS

In 2014 and 2015, while a visiting scholar at MIT Media Labs in Cambridge, Massachusetts, Martin collaborated with artist, designer and programmer Jonathan Bobrow to create functioning printed circuit boards, adapting these hidden components to make them as visually beautiful as they are powerful. Martin's designs drew on concepts of technical efficiency, exposing truths that lie just underneath the surfaces of everyday objects, and through this transparency heightening awareness of the ingenuity and technology at play. Each circuit board has its own visual character, and they combine to create a parallel narrative that matches their functionality, from air sensors to parking sensors.
This spread: *Bicycle Sensor* (left) and *Air Quality Sensor* (right), both created in collaboration with Jonathan Bobrow in 2014.

PLAY
BE
NICO
PUS
SAVAGES
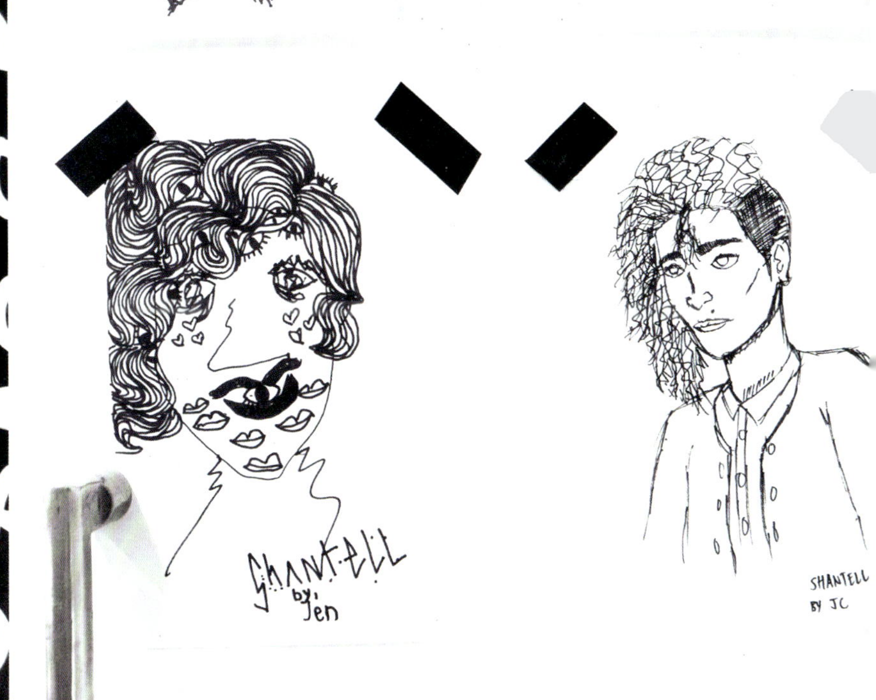
SHANTELL
by Jen
SHANTELL
BY JC
YOU ARE
YOU
YOU
YOU ARE
YOU
YOU ARE
YOU
YOU
WHO
ARE
YOU
ARE
1. TAKE A POSTCARD
2. SCAN BARCODE
3. STAND HERE
4. ANSWER QUESTION
(TALK NICE + LOUD)

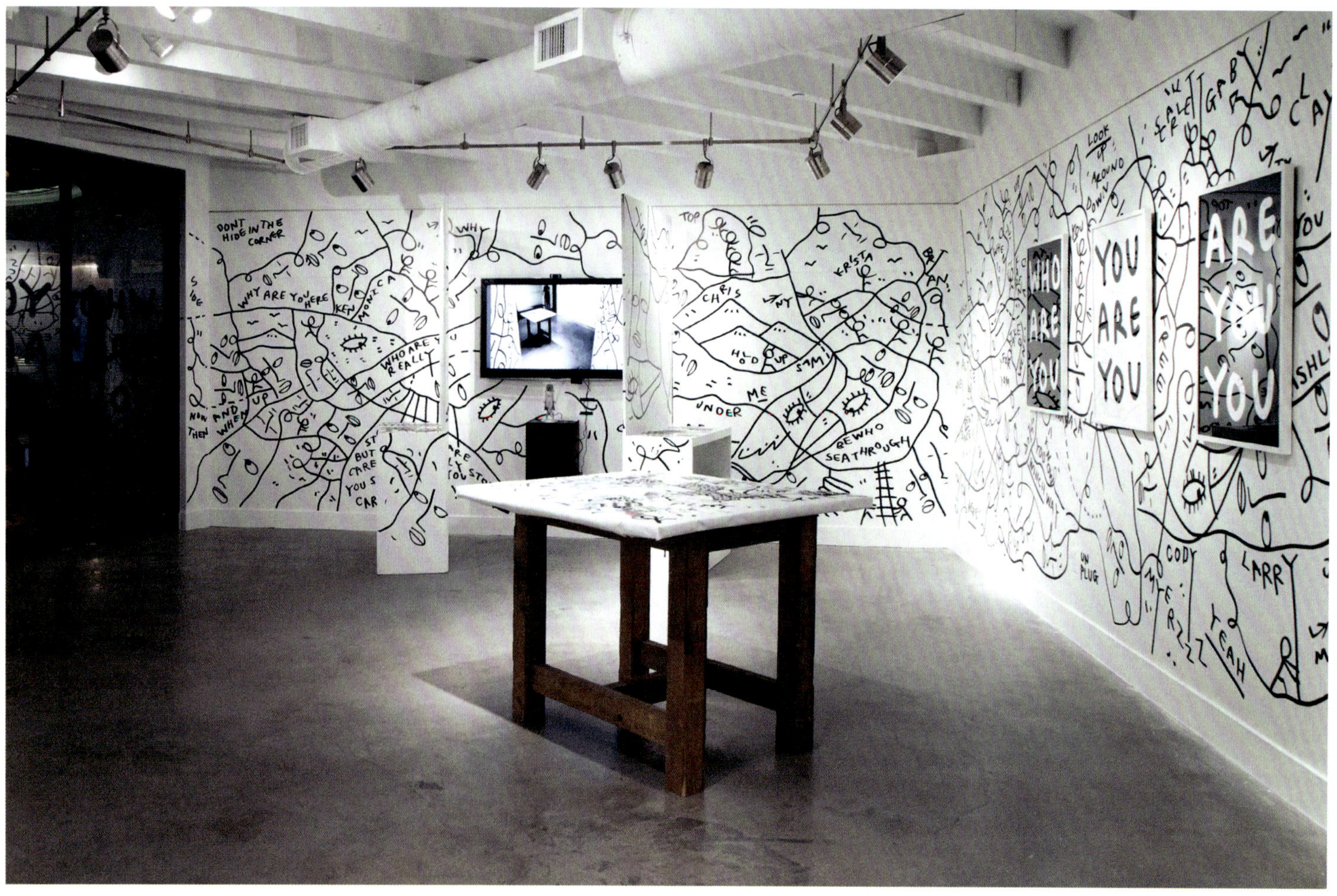

In a further space of her *Record + Play* installation at P3 Studio, the Cosmopolitan, Las Vegas, Martin asked participants to draw her as she drew them, suggesting that they surrender arbitrary constraints around concepts of 'artistic ability'. She then invited them to 'Leave It Behind', relinquishing anything they wished, whether a MetroCard, a dog collar or a letter to a friend, creating a cathartic moment of vulnerability and intimacy. Her ambition was hinged on the concern that 'when faced with questions of our core, we all struggle', and a recognition that being with oneself, especially in safe environments, can be a powerful tool towards attaining some form of fulfilment – it is one of the most important experiences art can offer. **Above:** The completed *Record + Play* installation in 2015. **Opposite:** Polaroids of visitors. **Following spread, left:** Details of the installation, including 'You Are You' postcards with barcodes, portraits of Martin by visitors, instructions on the floor and the interactive video. **Following spread, right:** The 'Leave It Behind' section, including portraits by Martin of visitors (right), and visitors' portraits of her (left).

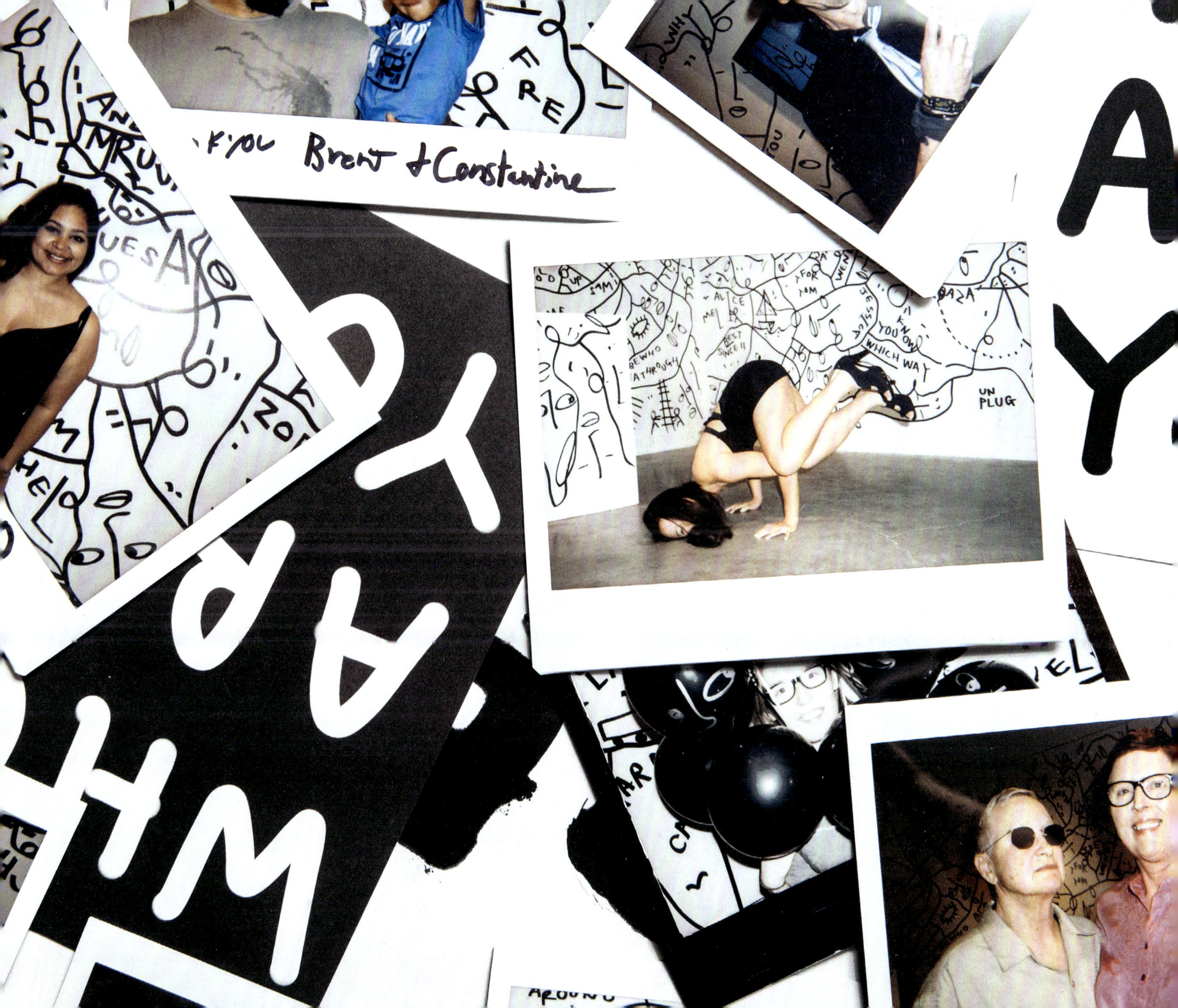
Brent & Constantine

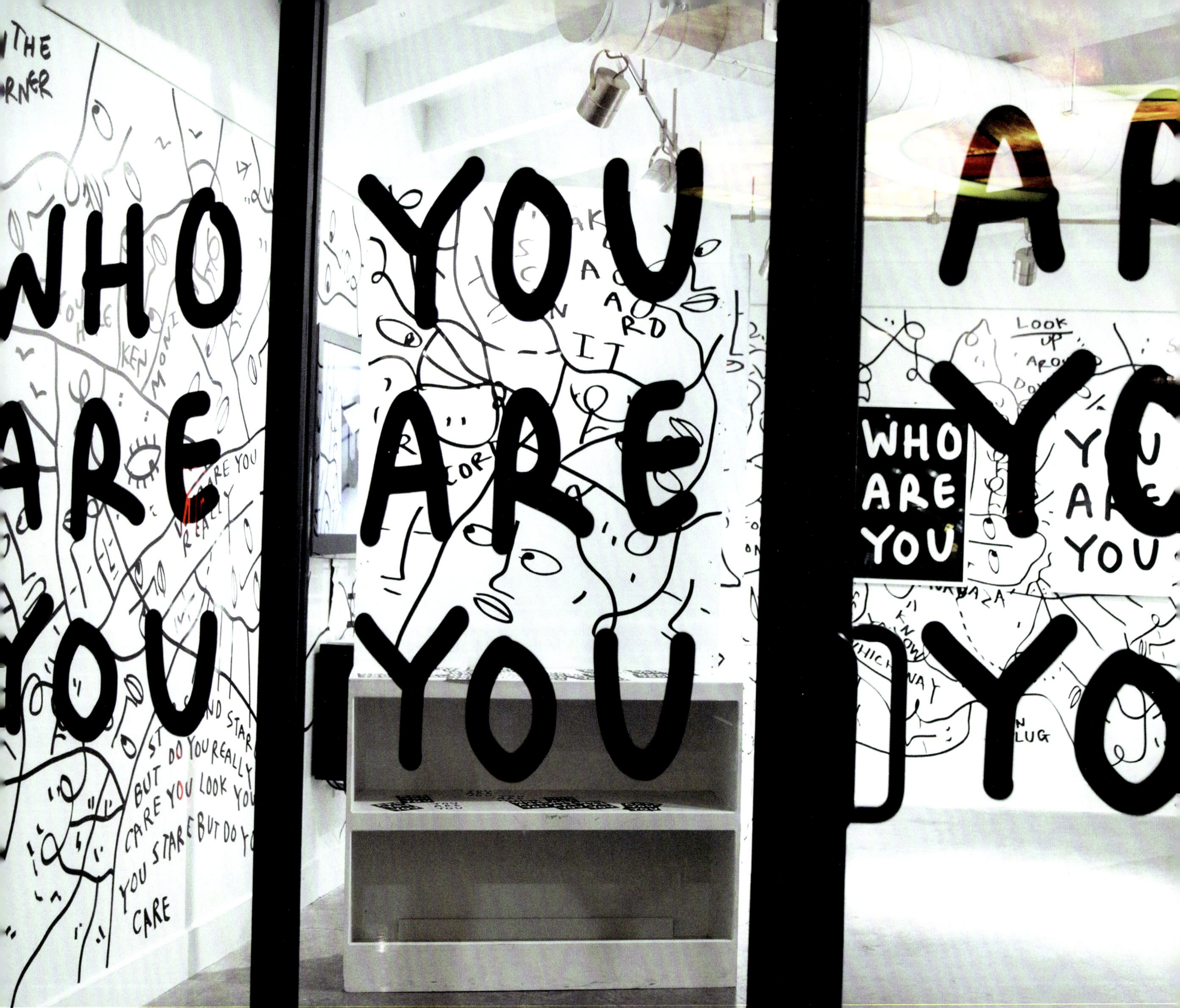

WHO
ARE
YOU
YOU
ARE
YOU
WHO
ARE
YOU

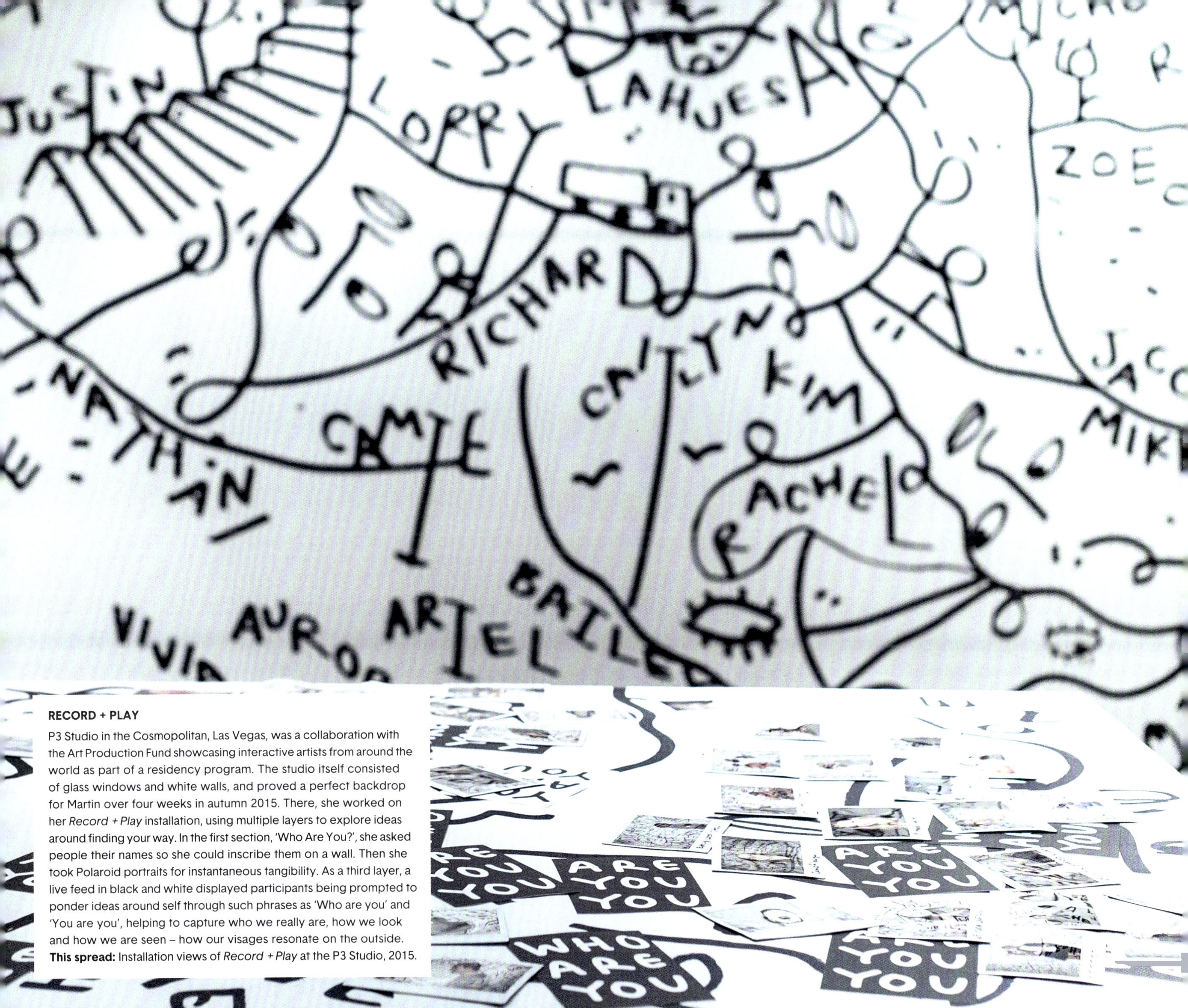

RECORD + PLAY

P3 Studio in the Cosmopolitan, Las Vegas, was a collaboration with the Art Production Fund showcasing interactive artists from around the world as part of a residency program. The studio itself consisted of glass windows and white walls, and proved a perfect backdrop for Martin over four weeks in autumn 2015. There, she worked on her *Record + Play* installation, using multiple layers to explore ideas around finding your way. In the first section, 'Who Are You?', she asked people their names so she could inscribe them on a wall. Then she took Polaroid portraits for instantaneous tangibility. As a third layer, a live feed in black and white displayed participants being prompted to ponder ideas around self through such phrases as 'Who are you' and 'You are you', helping to capture who we really are, how we look and how we are seen – how our visages resonate on the outside.

This spread: Installation views of *Record + Play* at the P3 Studio, 2015.

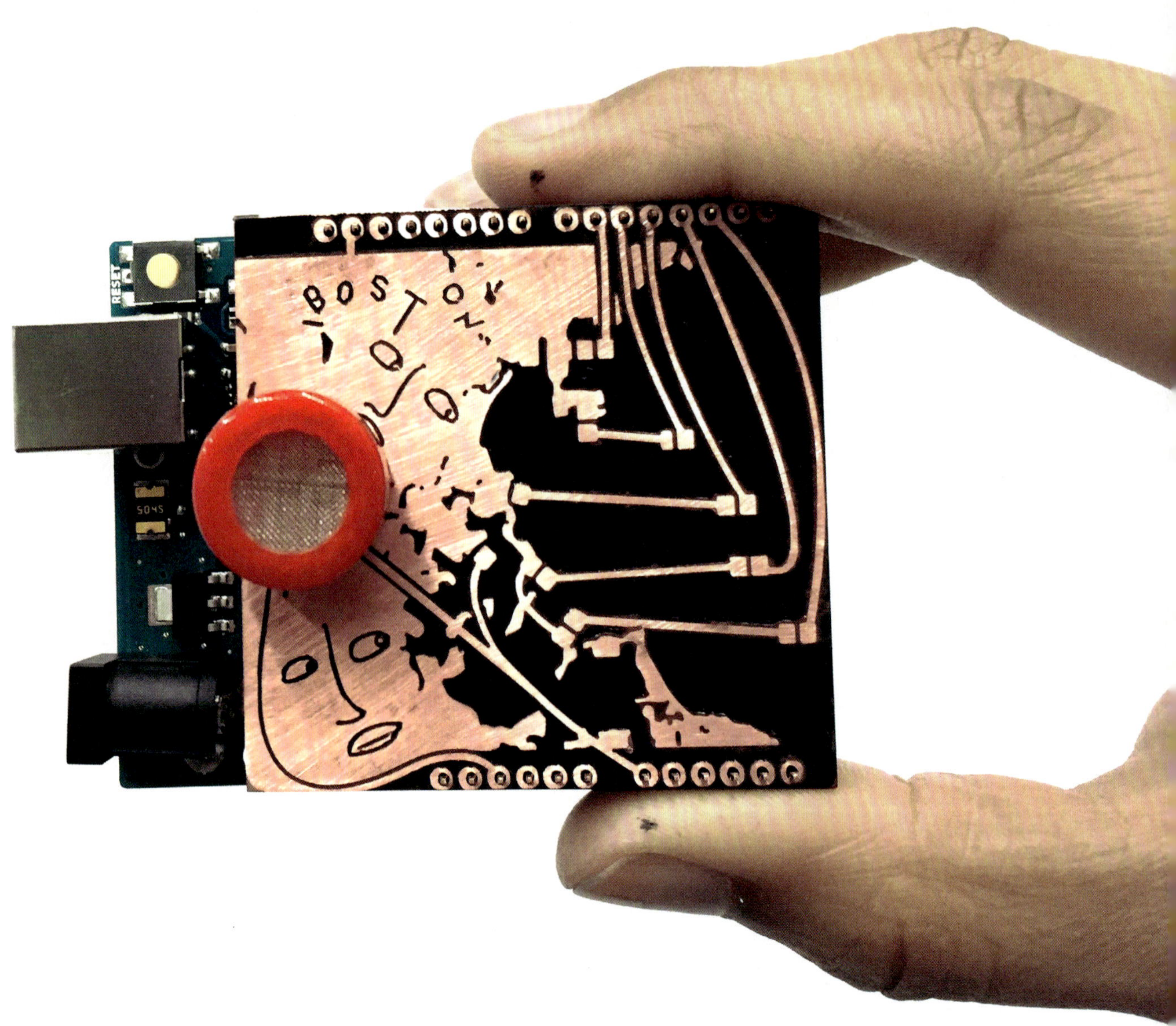

Above: *Boston Air Quality Sensor* (2014), a milled printed circuit board created in collaboration with Jonathan Bobrow at MIT Media Lab, Cambridge, MA. **Opposite:** Work in progress on the circuit boards, October 2014.

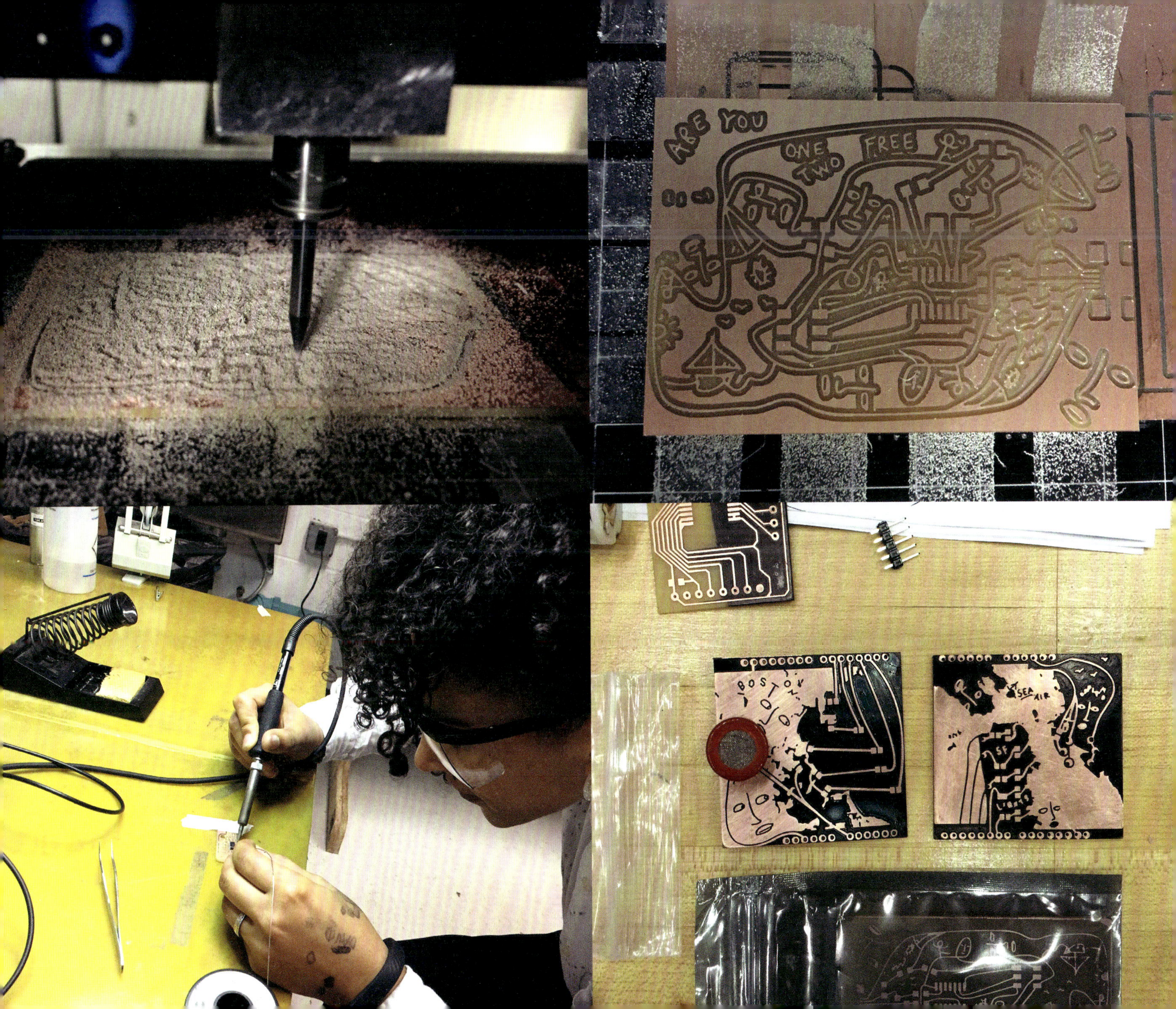

ARE YOU
ONE
TWO
FREE
BOSTON
SEA
AIR
SF

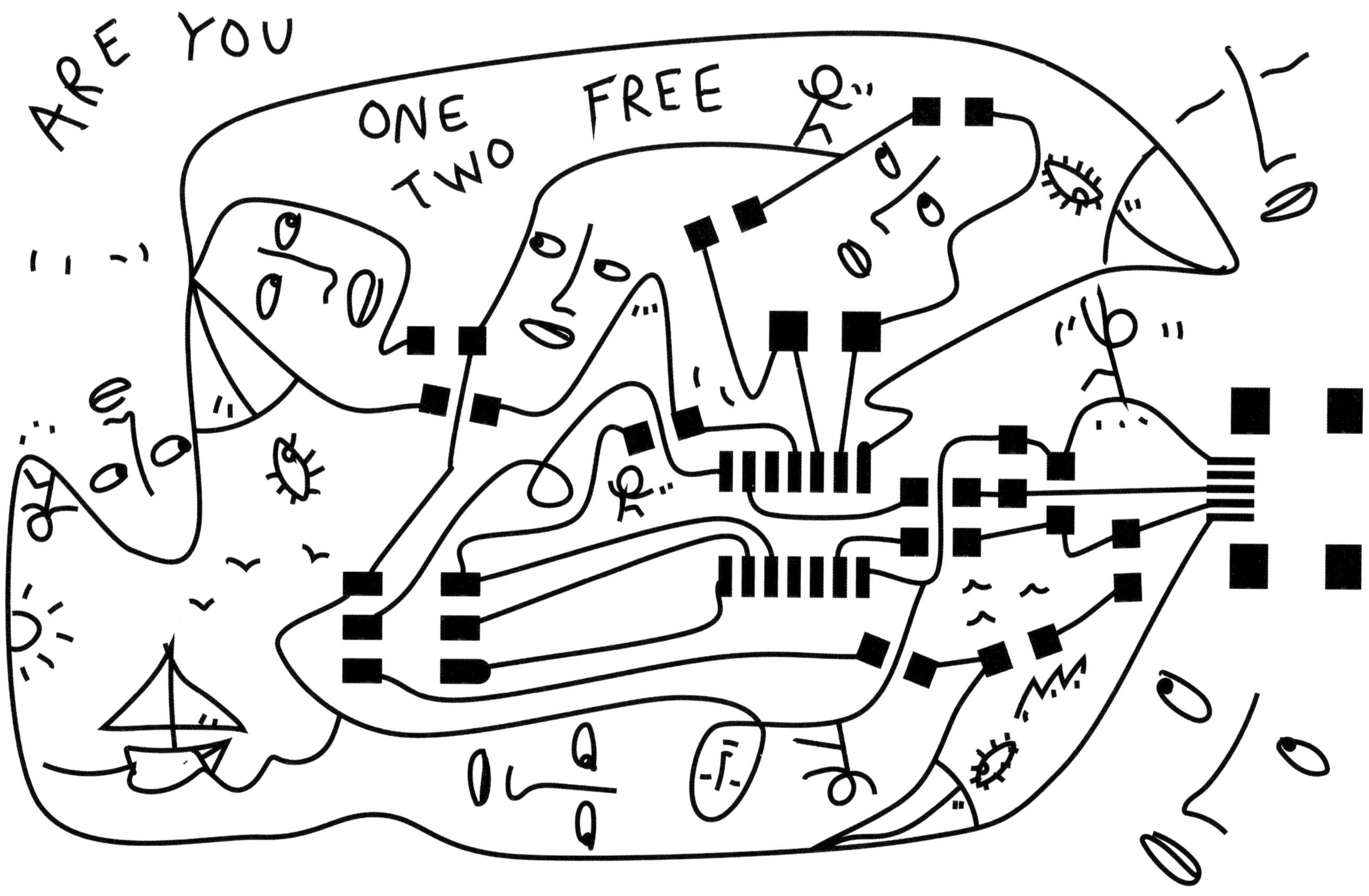

Final artwork for test
circuit board, 2014.

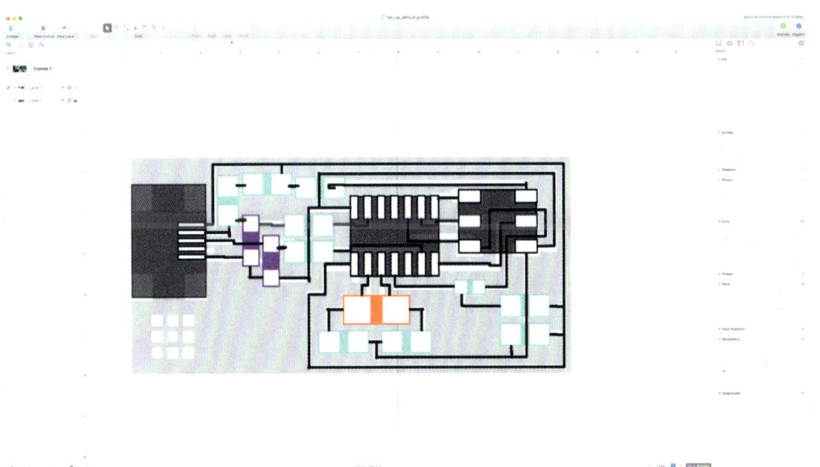

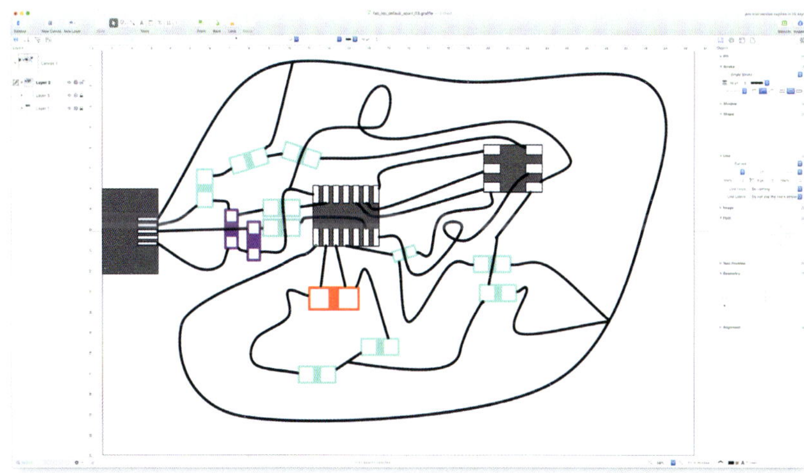

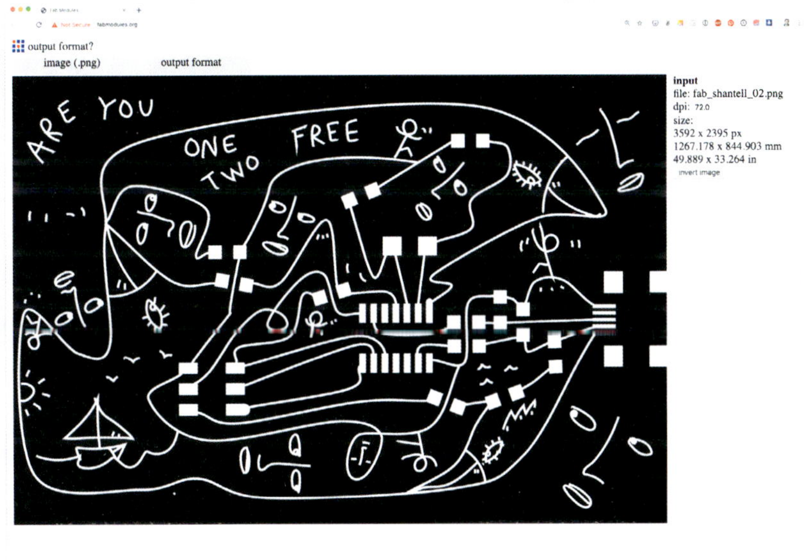

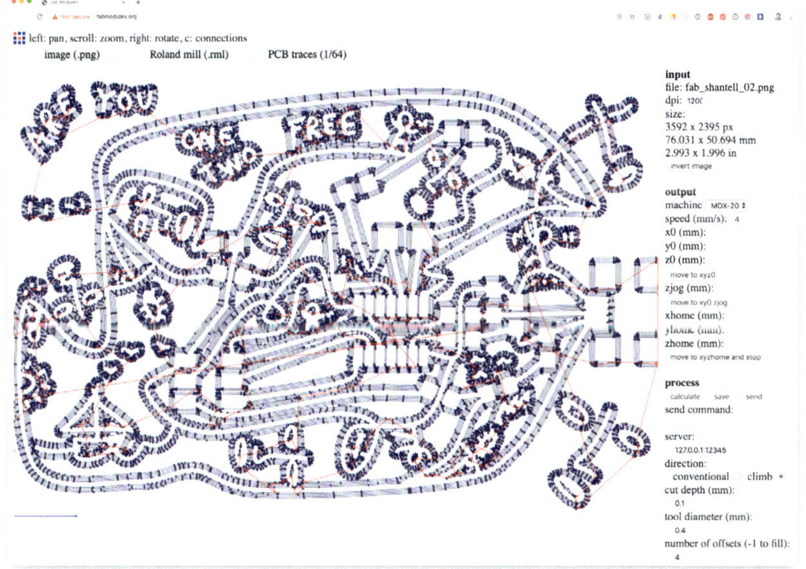

Screenshots of work in progress on printed circuit boards and traces created with Jonathan Bobrow at MIT Media Lab, Cambridge, MA, 2014.

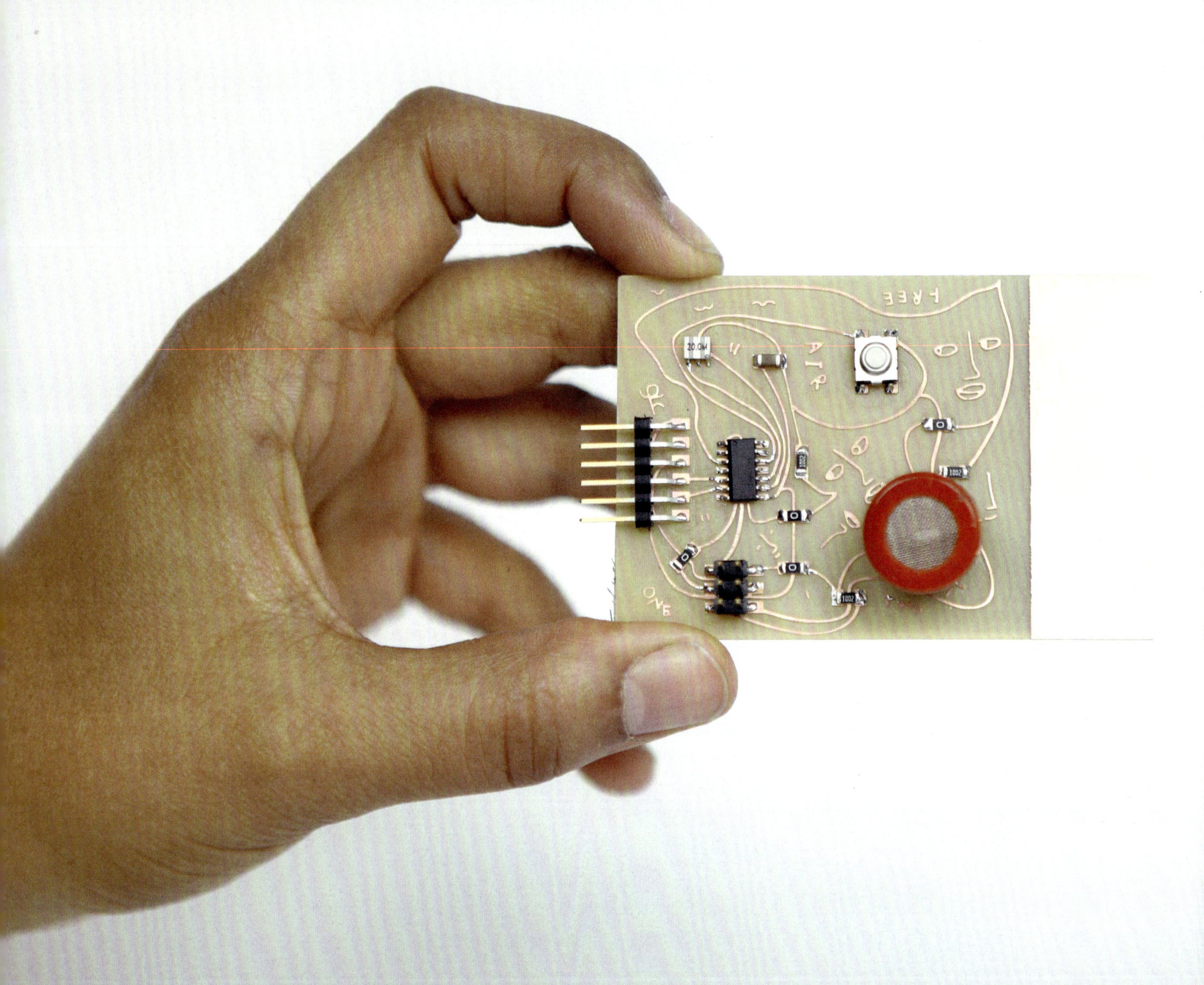

FREE
AIR
ONE
20.0M
1002
1002
1002

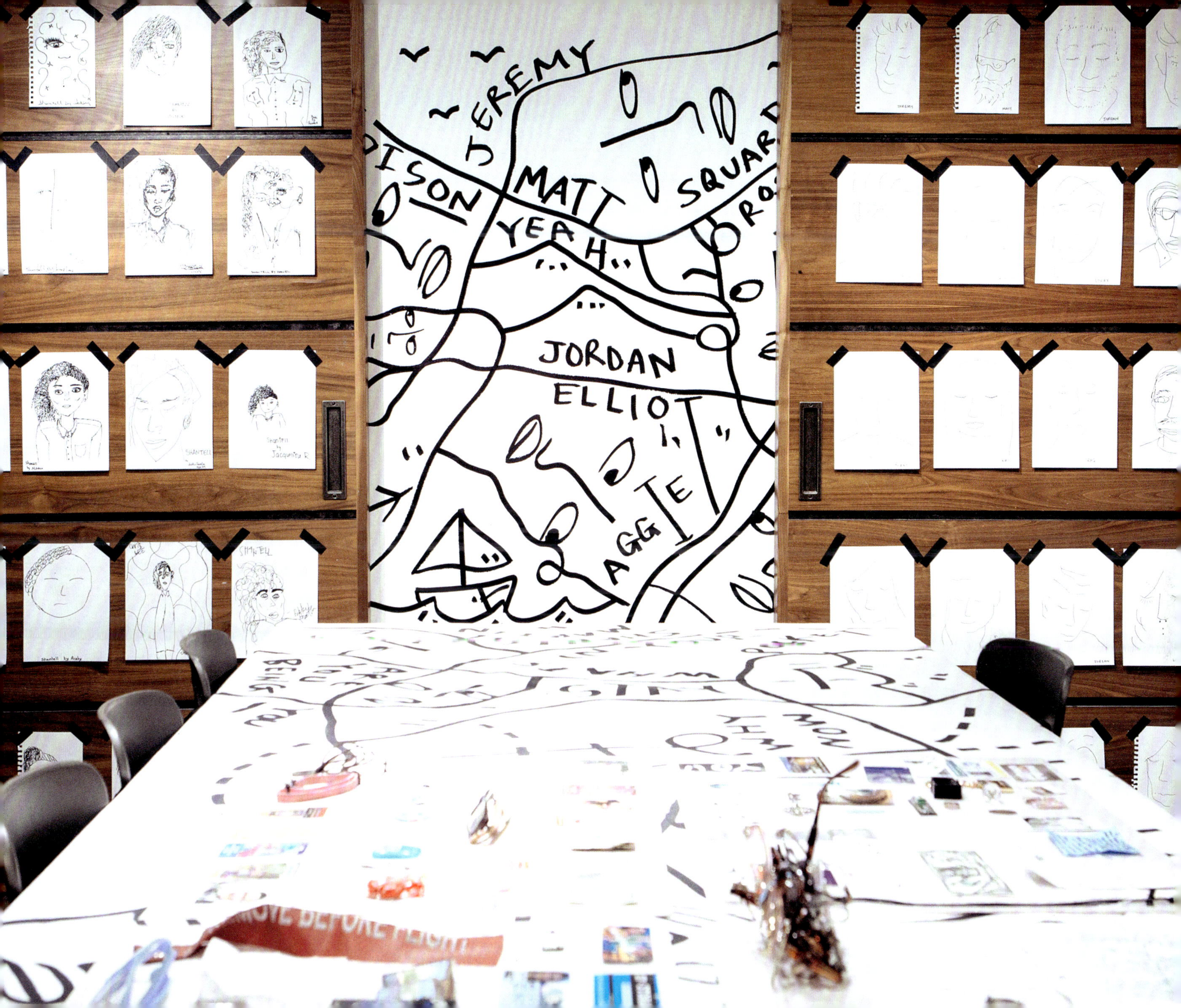

JEREMY
MADISON
MATT
SQUARE
YEAH
JORDAN
ELLIOT
AGGIE
BEING
GIRL
NOW
REMOVE BEFORE FLIGHT

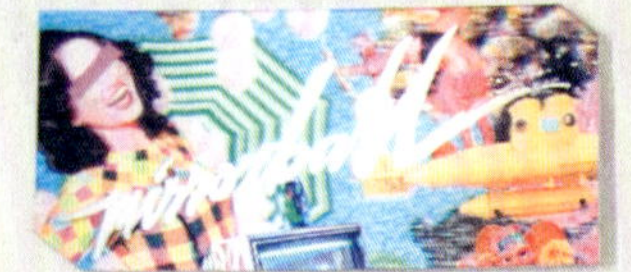
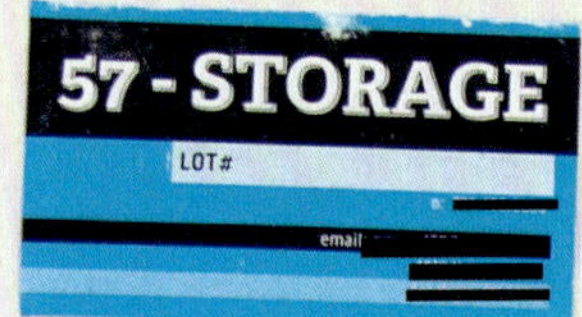

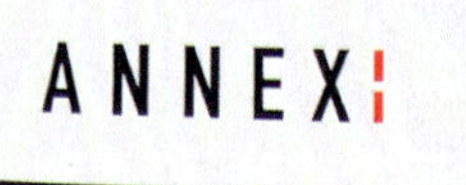

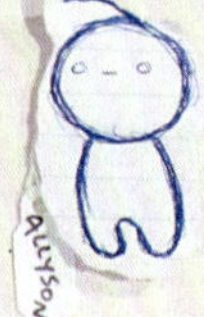
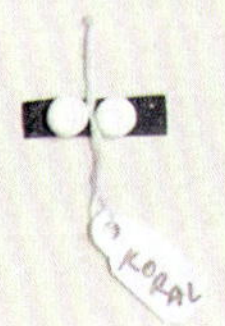
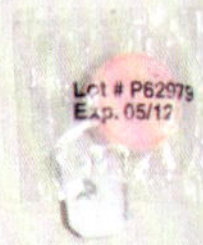
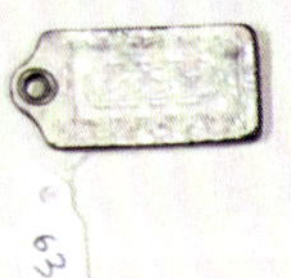
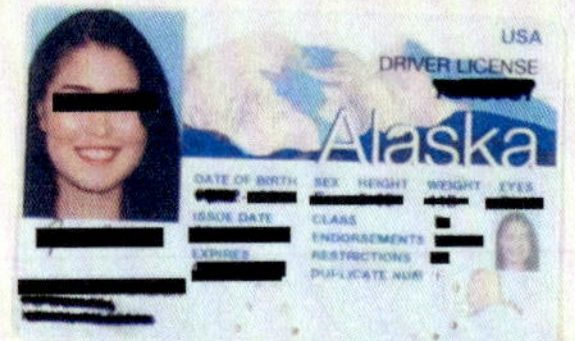

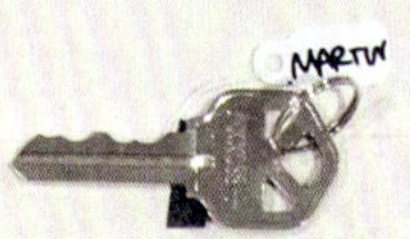
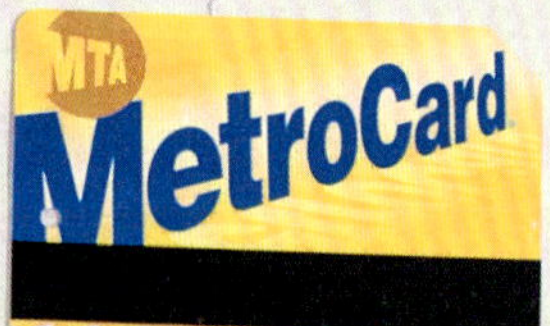

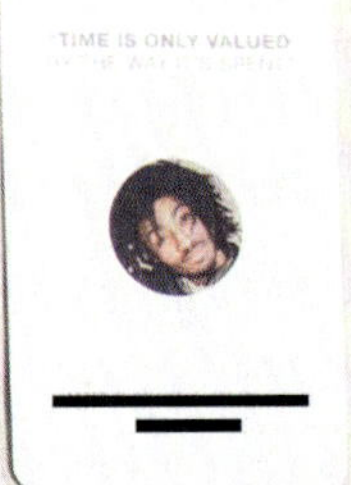

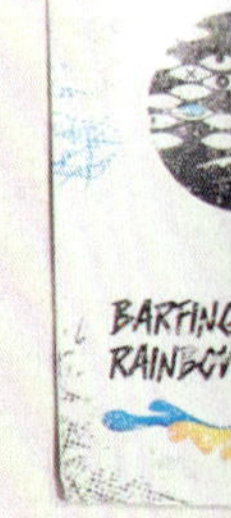

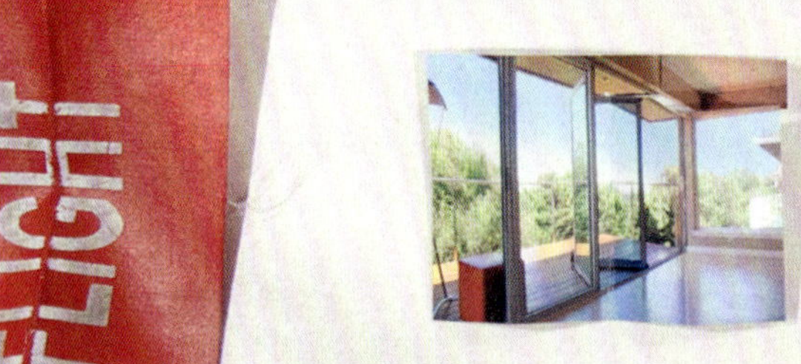
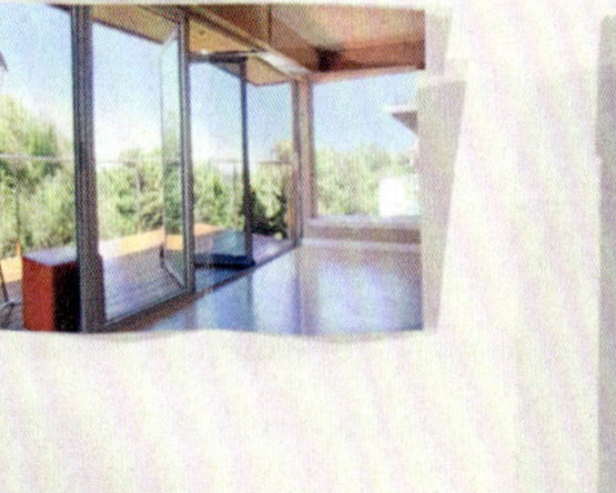

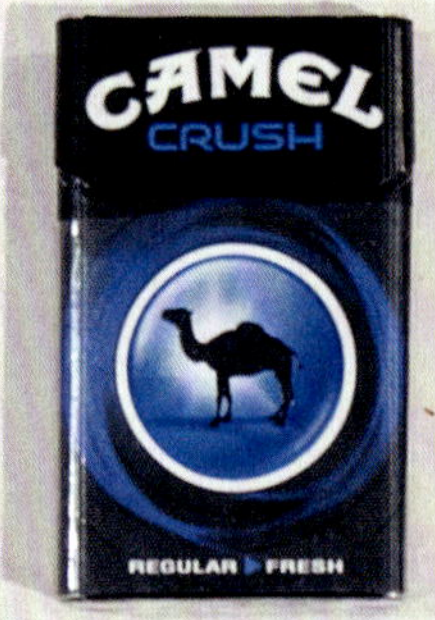
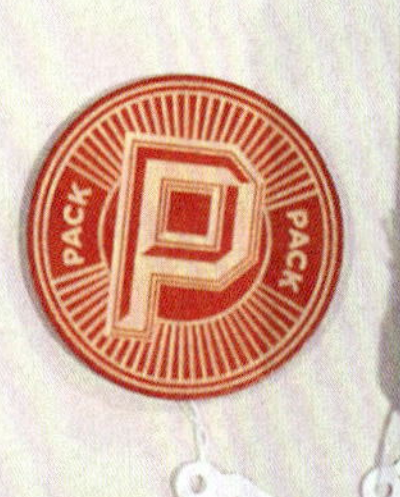

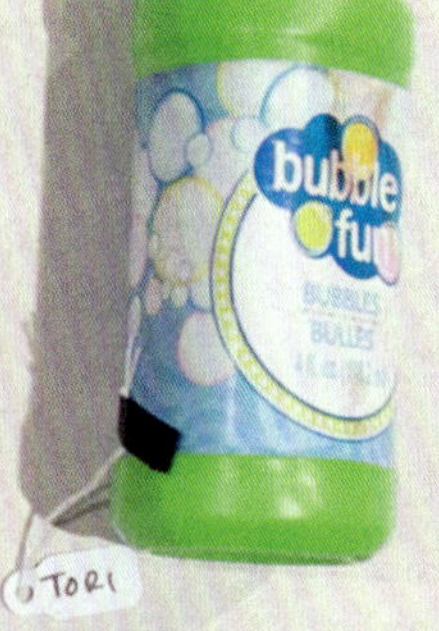

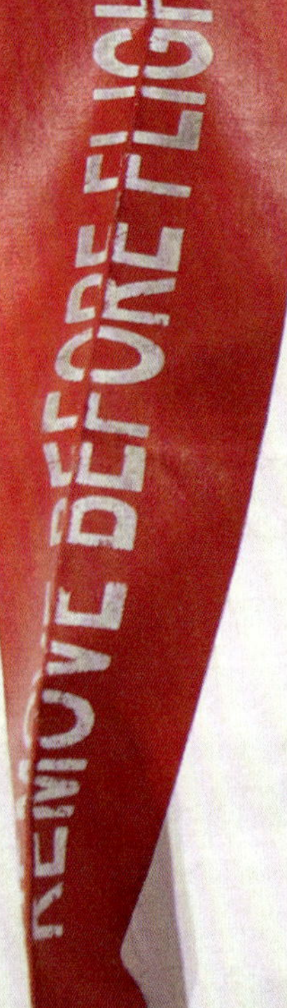

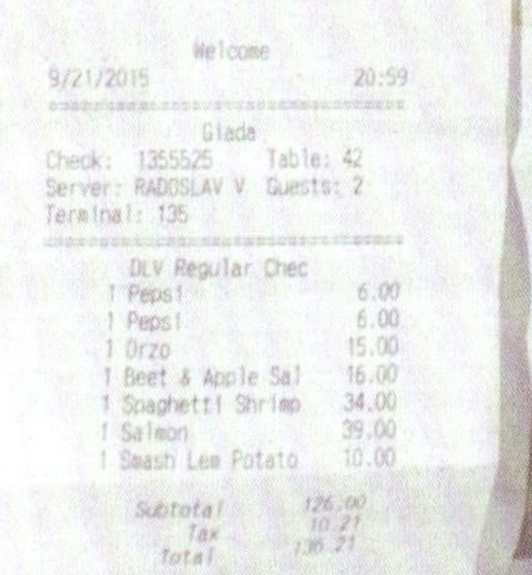

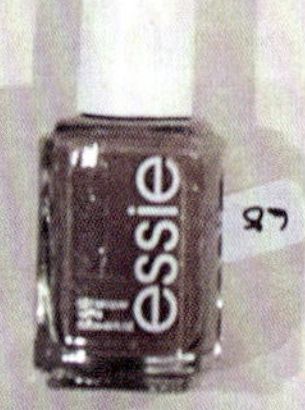

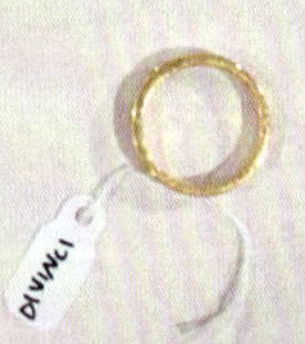
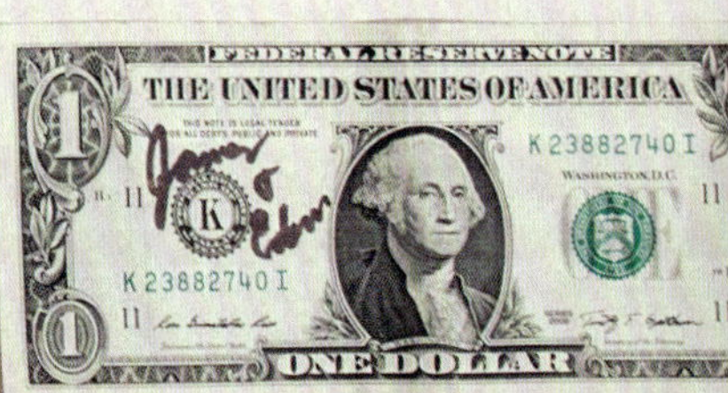

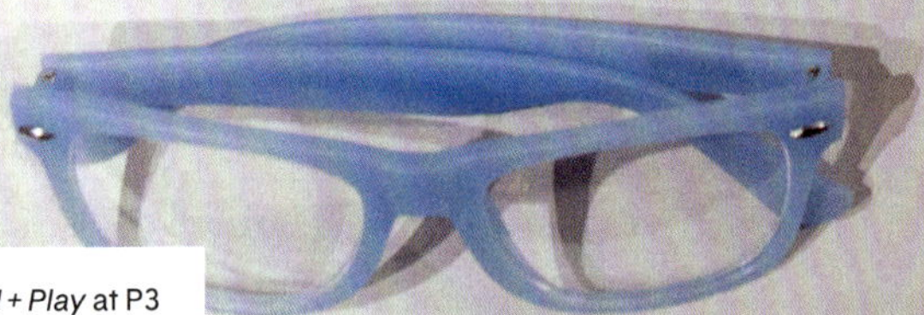
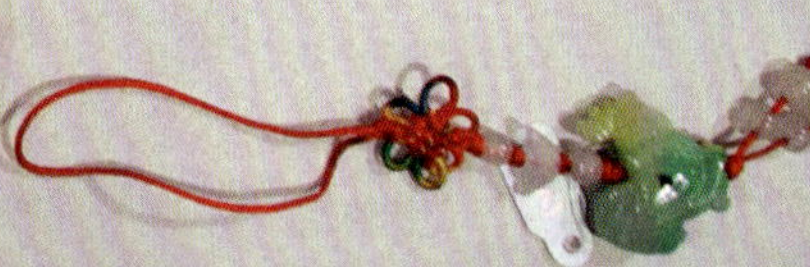

Items left by visitors to *Record + Play* at P3 Studio, the Cosmopolitan, Las Vegas, 2015.

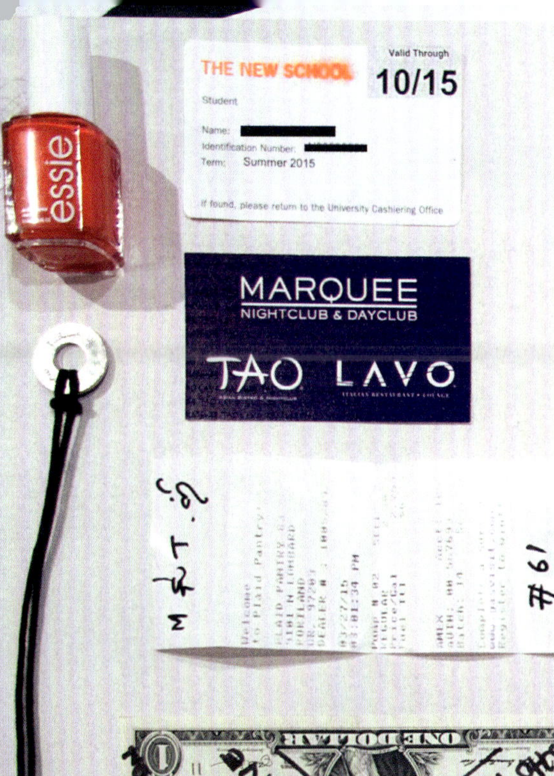

essie
THE NEW SCHOOL
Valid Through
10/15
Student
Name:
Identification Number:
Term: Summer 2015
If found, please return to the University Cashiering Office
MARQUEE
NIGHTCLUB & DAYCLUB
TAO LAVO

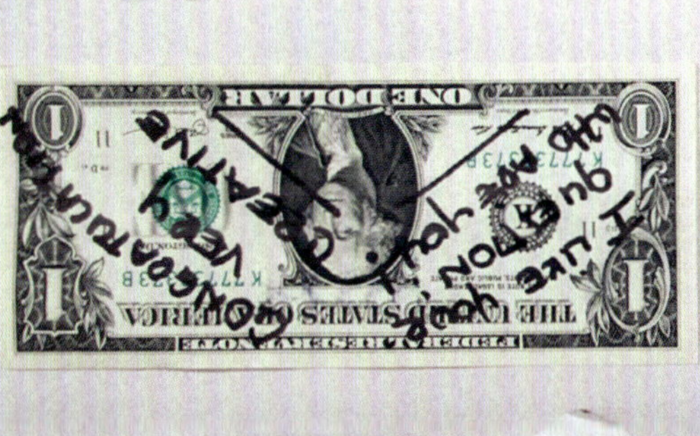

I LIVE IN A VERY LOUD AND
QUESTION, YOU + CREATING
THE UNITED STATES OF AMERICA
ONE DOLLAR

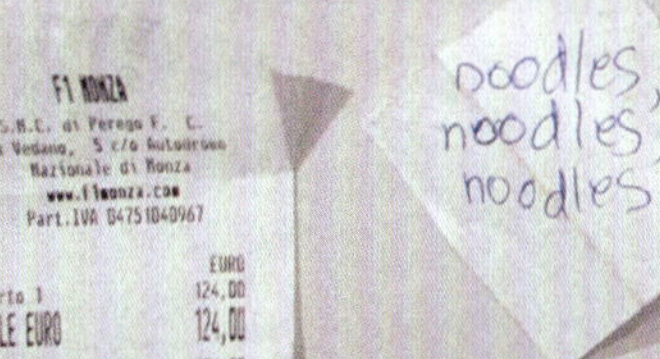

noodles,
noodles,
noodles!

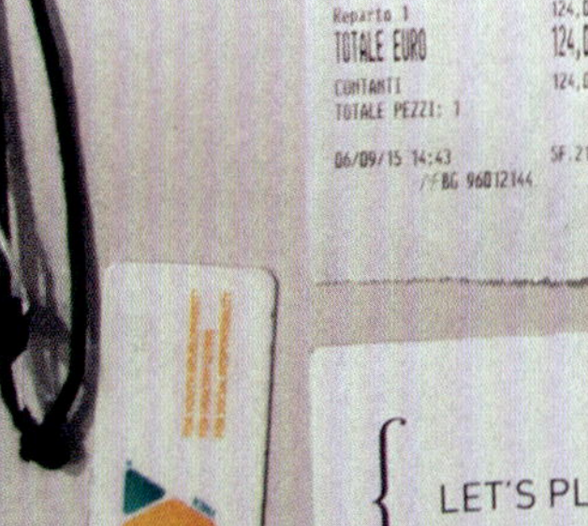

F1 MONZA
TOTALE EURO   124,00

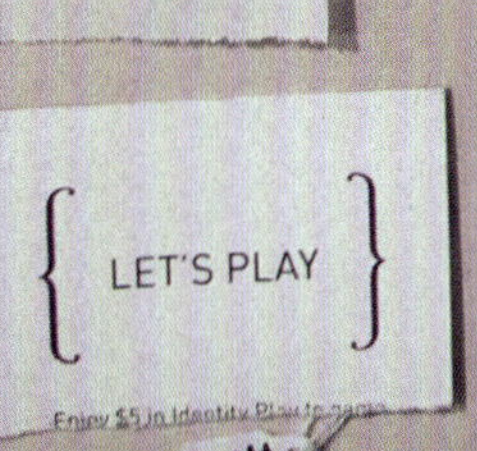

{ LET'S PLAY }

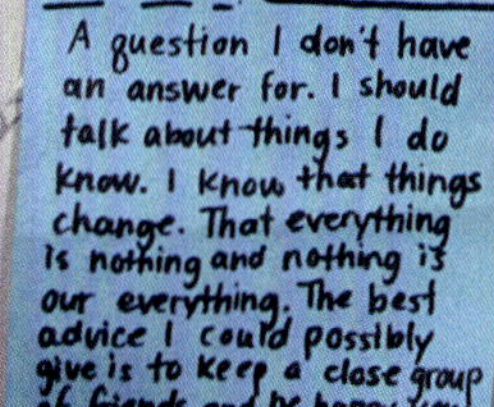

WHO AM I? | G+E 10/2/15
A question I don't have an answer for. I should talk about things I do know. I know that things change. That everything is nothing and nothing is our everything. The best advice I could possibly give is to keep a close group of friends and be happy you are capable of love. —g

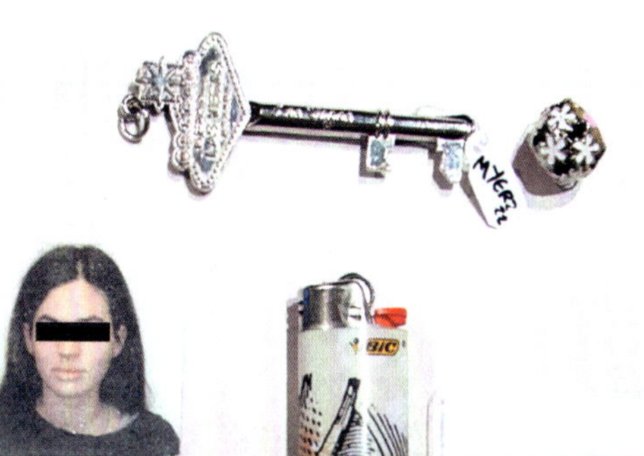

Zumanity
At New York New York
Zumanity Has Been Created For Guests
18 Years Of Age Or Older
Friday, September 25, 2015 7:00PM
Photography and/or Recordings Strictly Prohibited
101   D   18

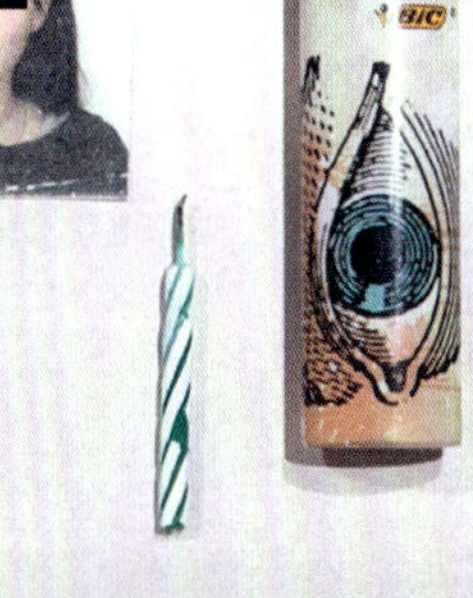
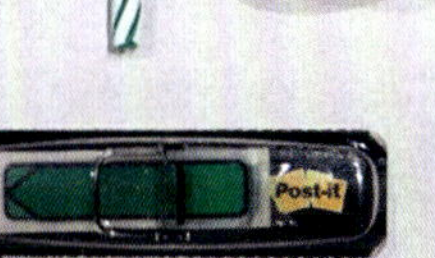

BIC
Post-it

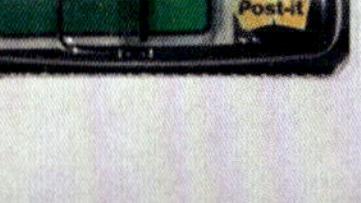
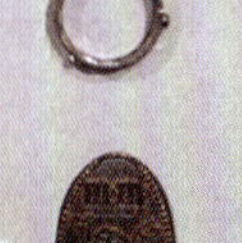
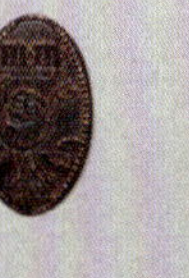
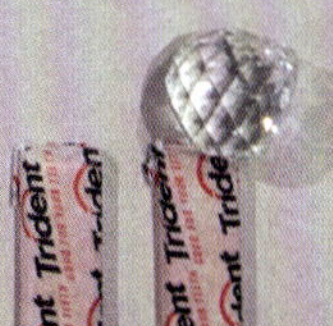

LAS VEGAS

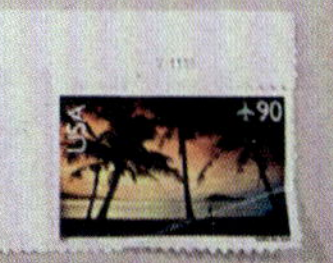

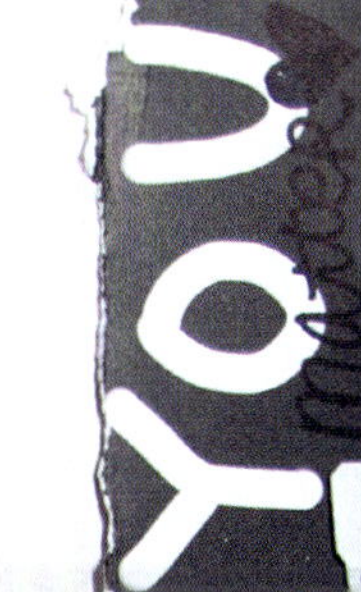

7
7
Rendr Design
YOU

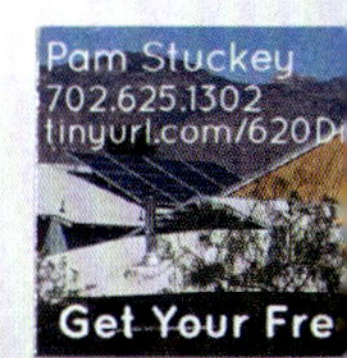

MetroCard
SingleRide
Pam Stuckey
702.625.1302
tinyurl.com/620D
Get Your Fre

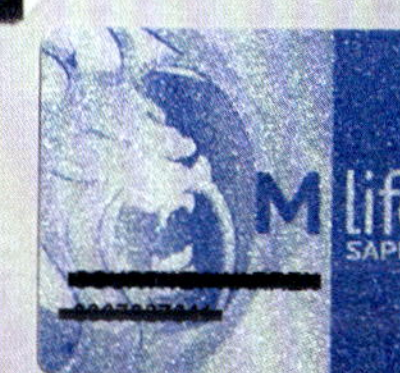

Mlife

A Card for my
blos CBx
A SYMPHONY OF BOOKS, MOVIES, T
www.nuts4r2.blogsp

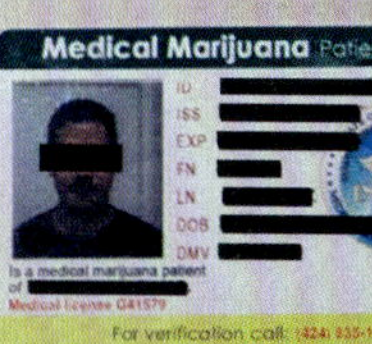

Medical Marijuana Patient

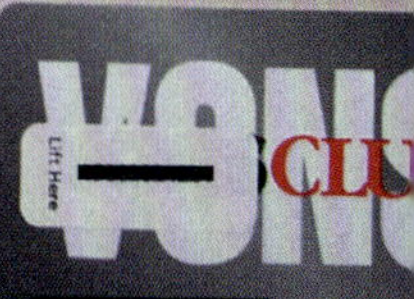

Trident
VONS
CLUB

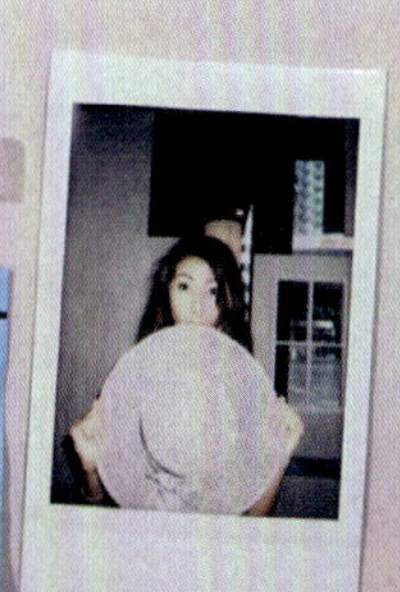
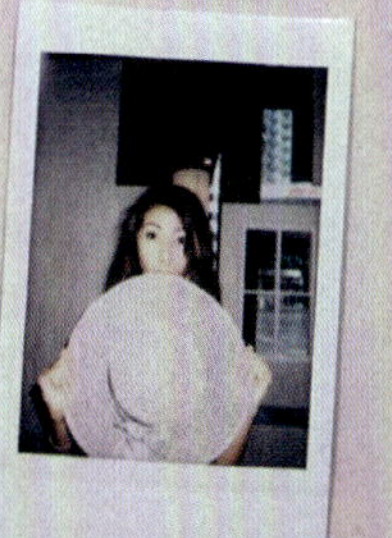
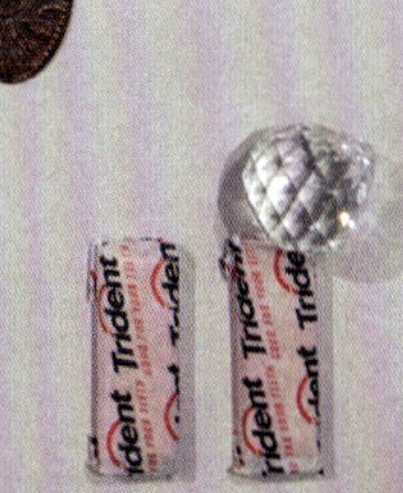
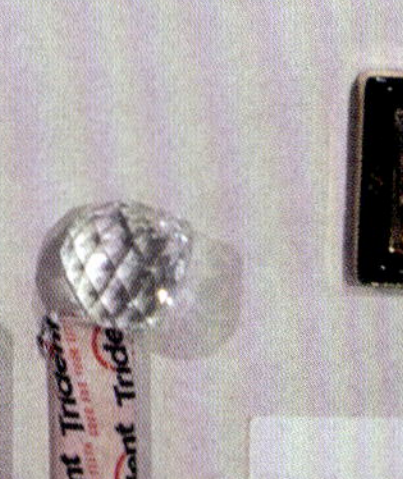

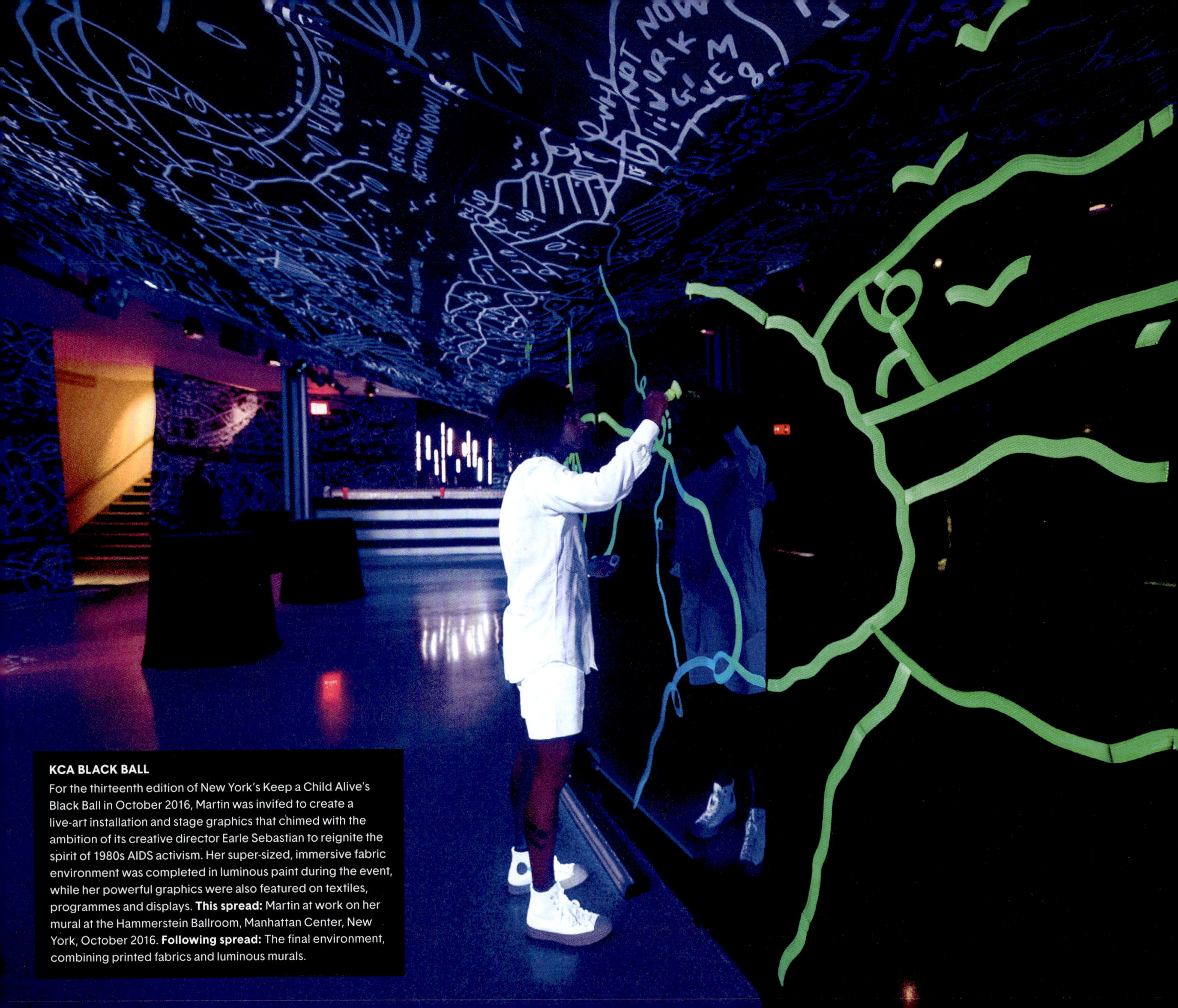

KCA BLACK BALL

For the thirteenth edition of New York's Keep a Child Alive's Black Ball in October 2016, Martin was invited to create a live-art installation and stage graphics that chimed with the ambition of its creative director Earle Sebastian to reignite the spirit of 1980s AIDS activism. Her super-sized, immersive fabric environment was completed in luminous paint during the event, while her powerful graphics were also featured on textiles, programmes and displays. **This spread:** Martin at work on her mural at the Hammerstein Ballroom, Manhattan Center, New York, October 2016. **Following spread:** The final environment, combining printed fabrics and luminous murals.

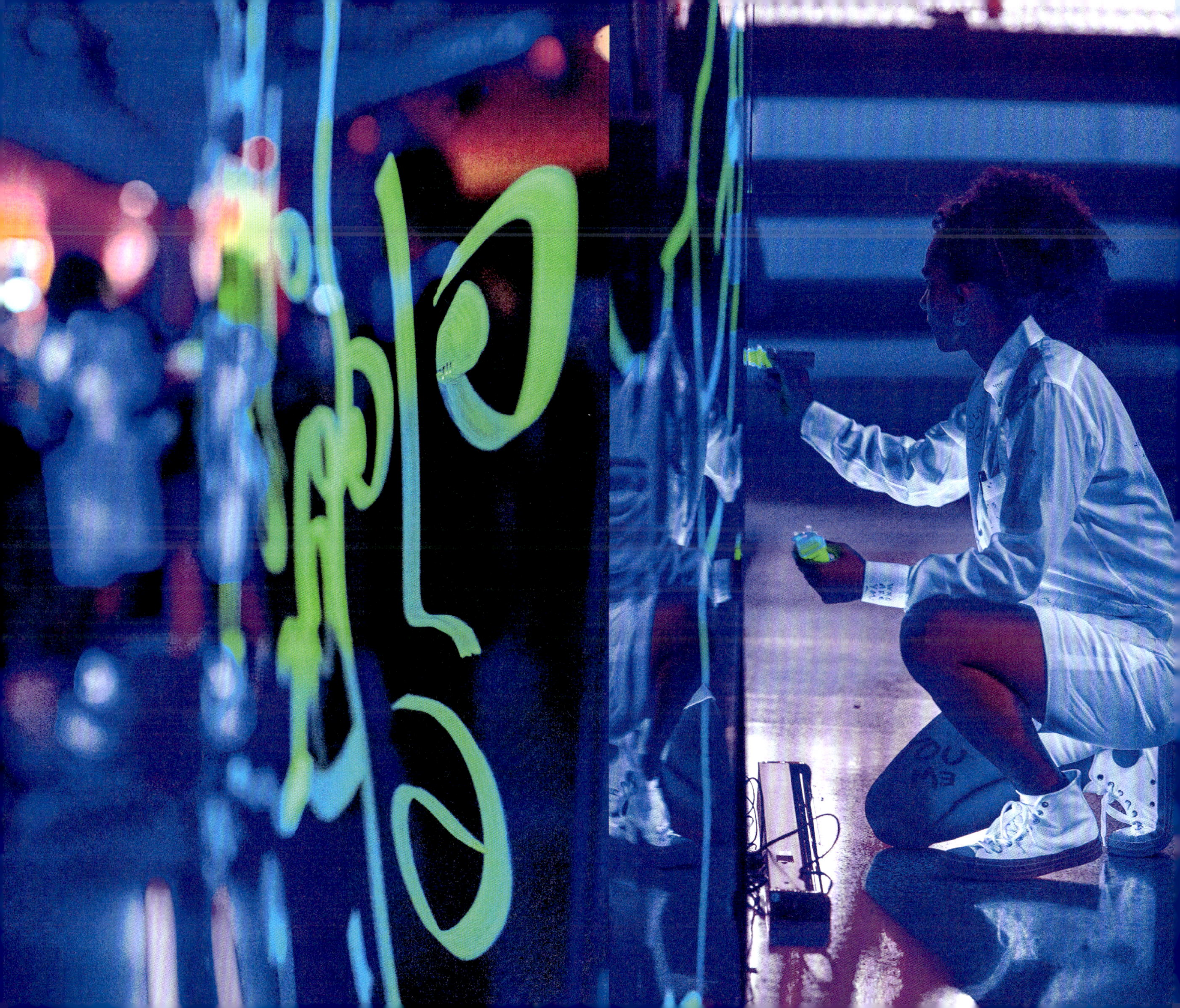

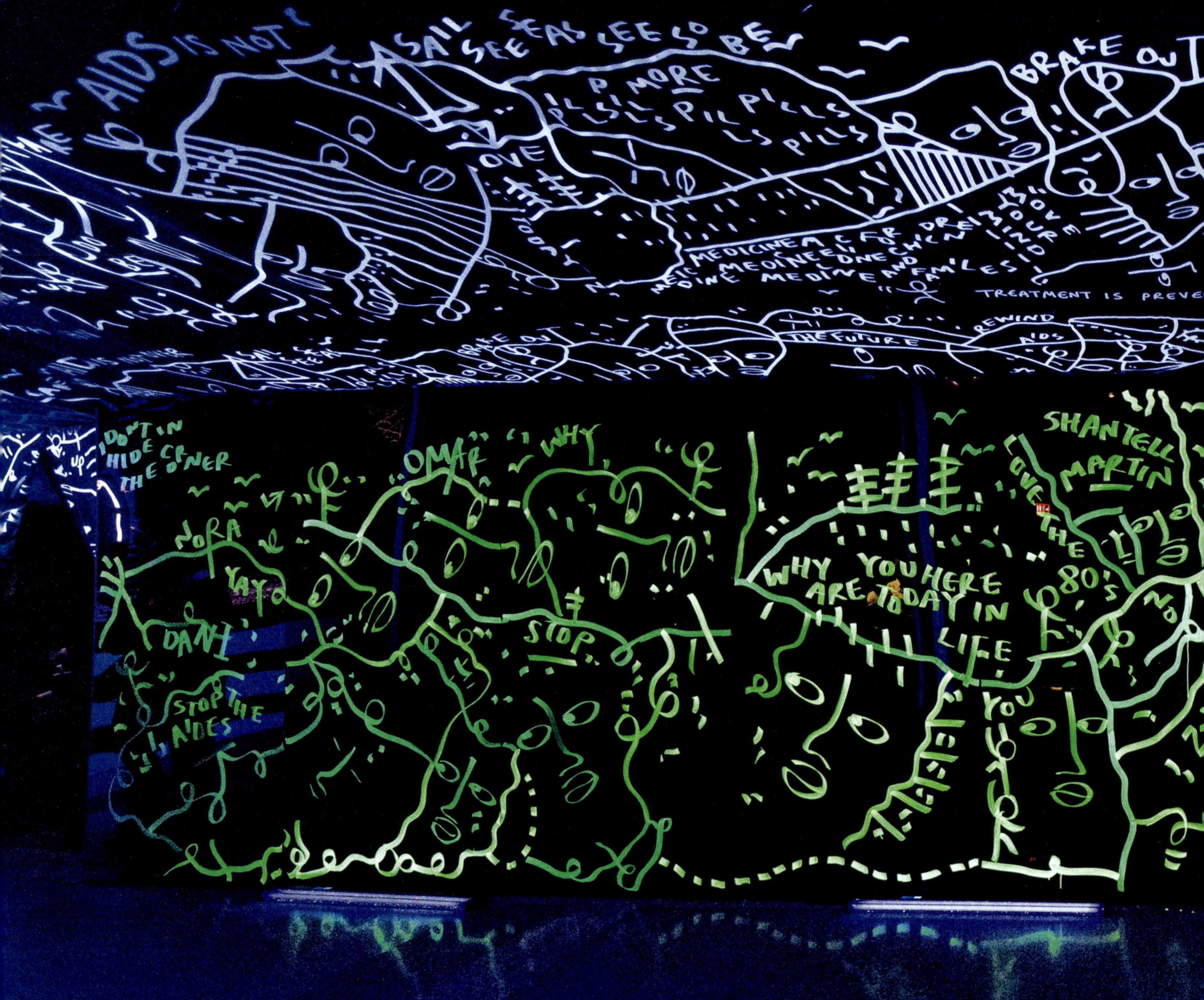

AIDS IS NOT
SAIL SEE AS SEE SO BE
BRAKE OUT
P MORE
PILLS PILLS PILLS PILLS
MEDICINE
TREATMENT IS PREVE
THE FUTURE
REWIND
AIDS
DON'T
HIDE IN
THE CORNER
OMAR
WHY
SHANTELL
MARTIN
NORA
WHY YOU HERE
ARE TODAY IN
LIFE
80'S
DAN
STOP
STOP THE
AIDS

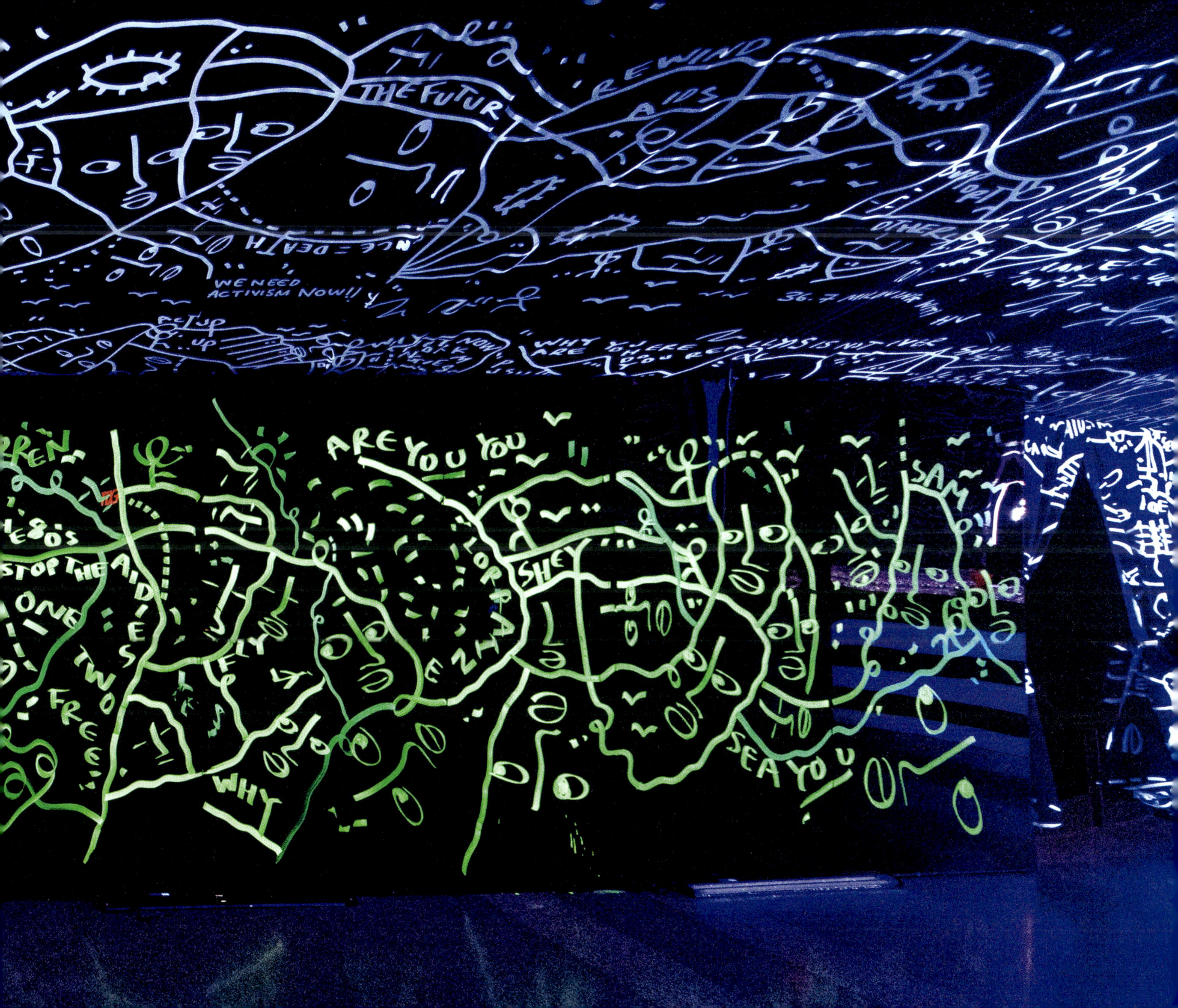
THE FUTUR
REWIND
WE NEED
ACTIVISM NOW!!
WHY DO YOU
ARE YOU YOU
SHEY
STOP THE AIDS
ONE
TWO
FREE
WHY
SEA YOU
SAM

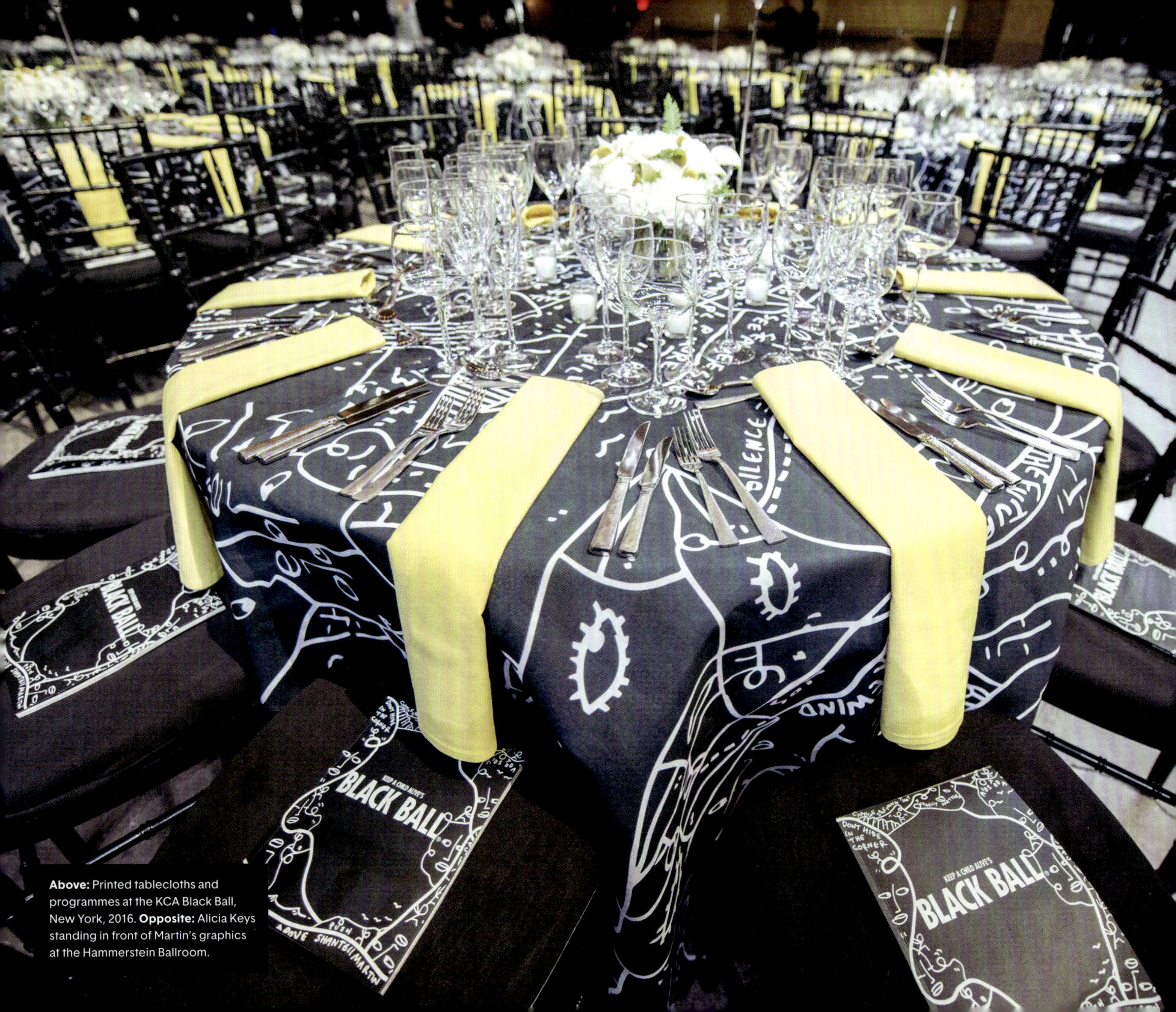

Above: Printed tablecloths and programmes at the KCA Black Ball, New York, 2016. **Opposite:** Alicia Keys standing in front of Martin's graphics at the Hammerstein Ballroom.

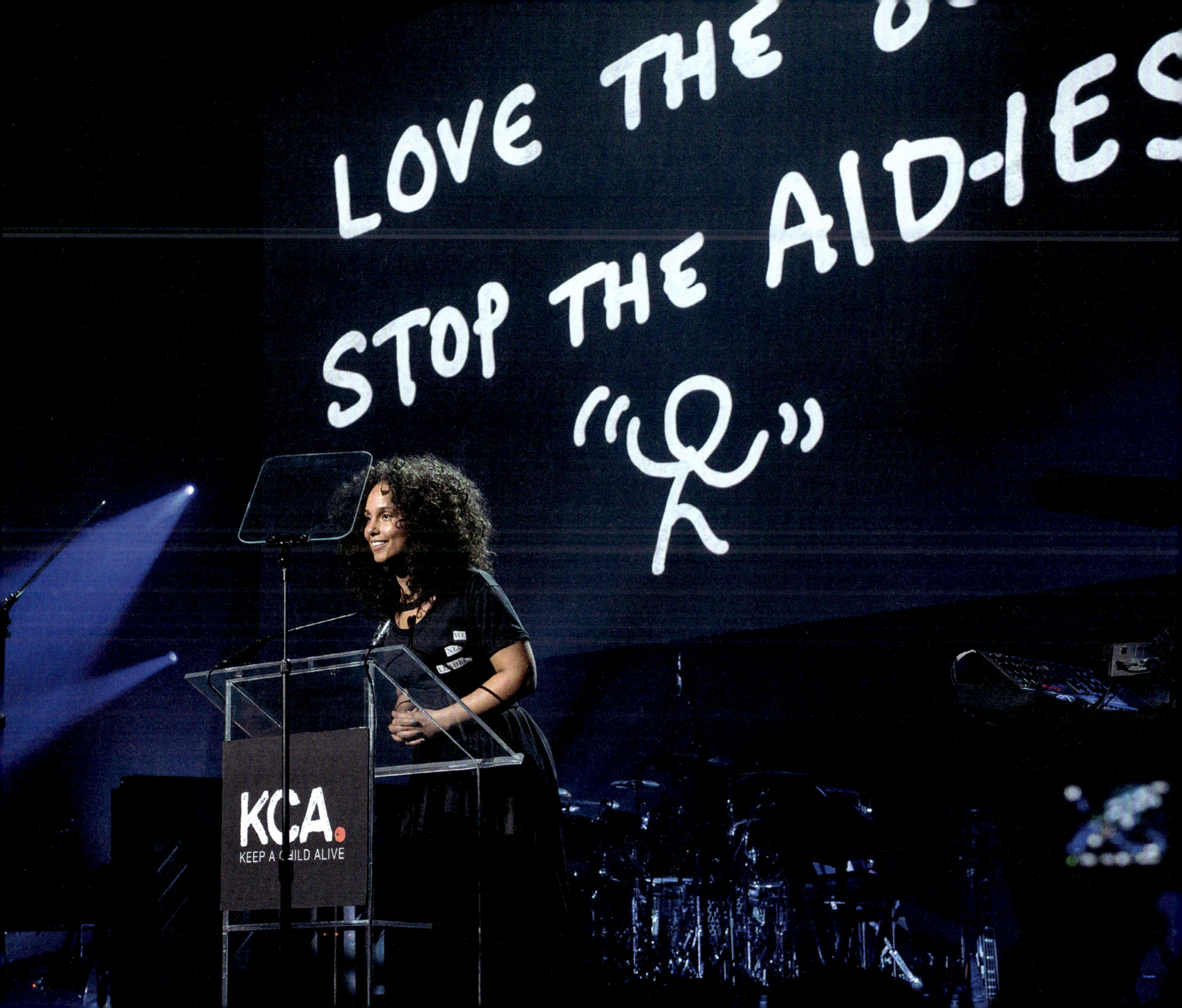

LOVE THE
STOP THE AID-IES
"Ω"
KCA.
KEEP A CHILD ALIVE

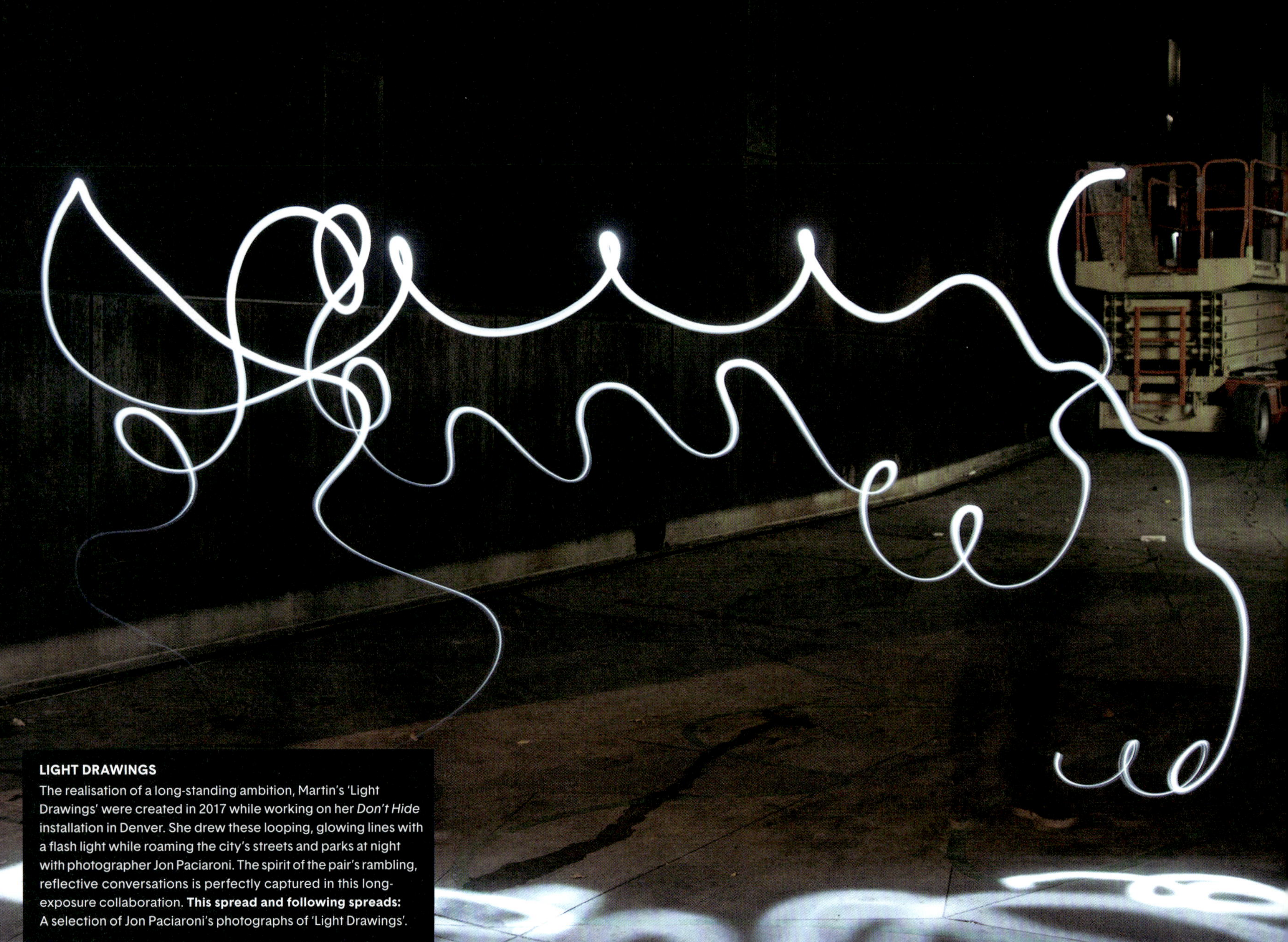

LIGHT DRAWINGS
The realisation of a long-standing ambition, Martin's 'Light Drawings' were created in 2017 while working on her *Don't Hide* installation in Denver. She drew these looping, glowing lines with a flash light while roaming the city's streets and parks at night with photographer Jon Paciaroni. The spirit of the pair's rambling, reflective conversations is perfectly captured in this long-exposure collaboration. **This spread and following spreads:** A selection of Jon Paciaroni's photographs of 'Light Drawings'.

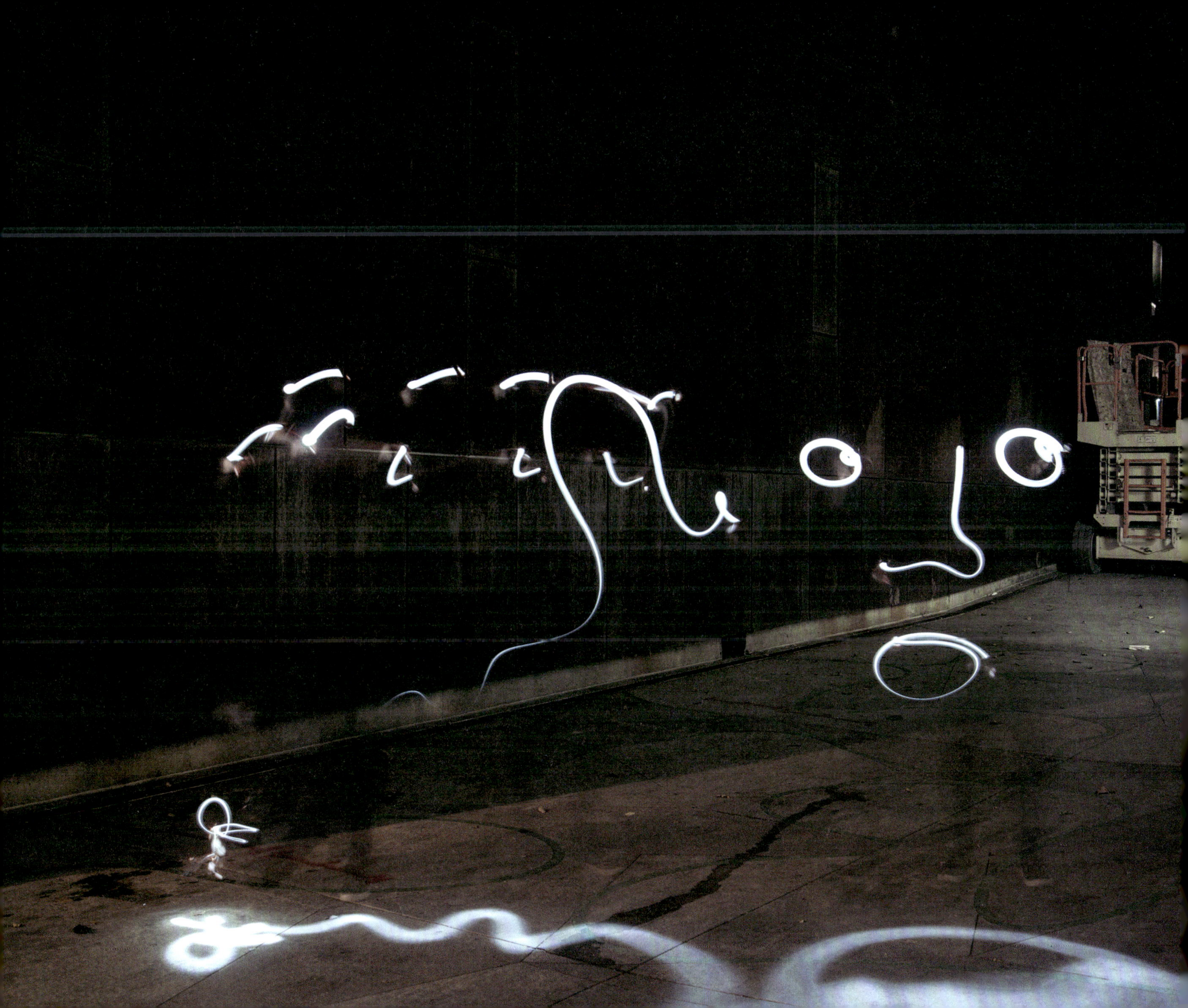

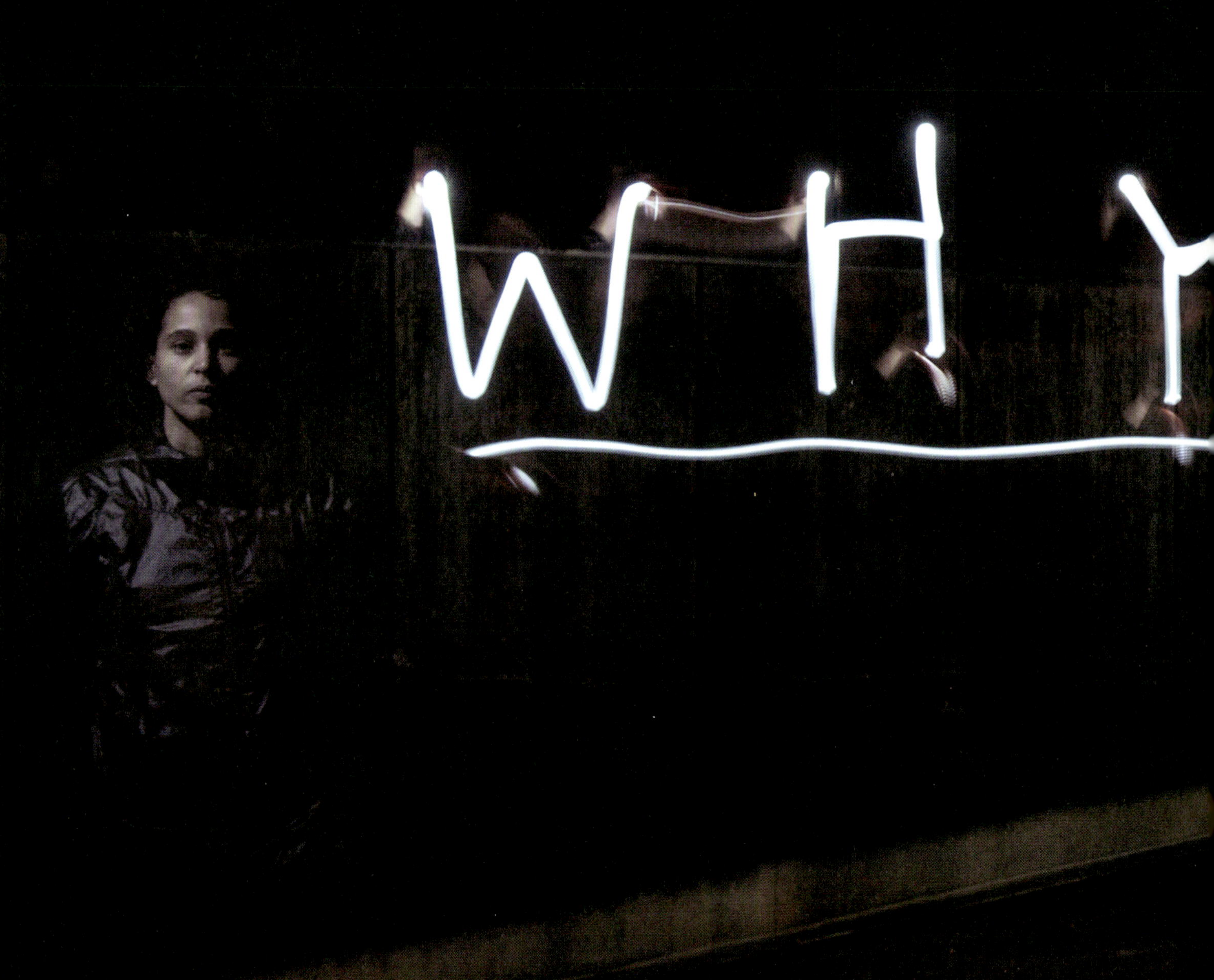

WHY

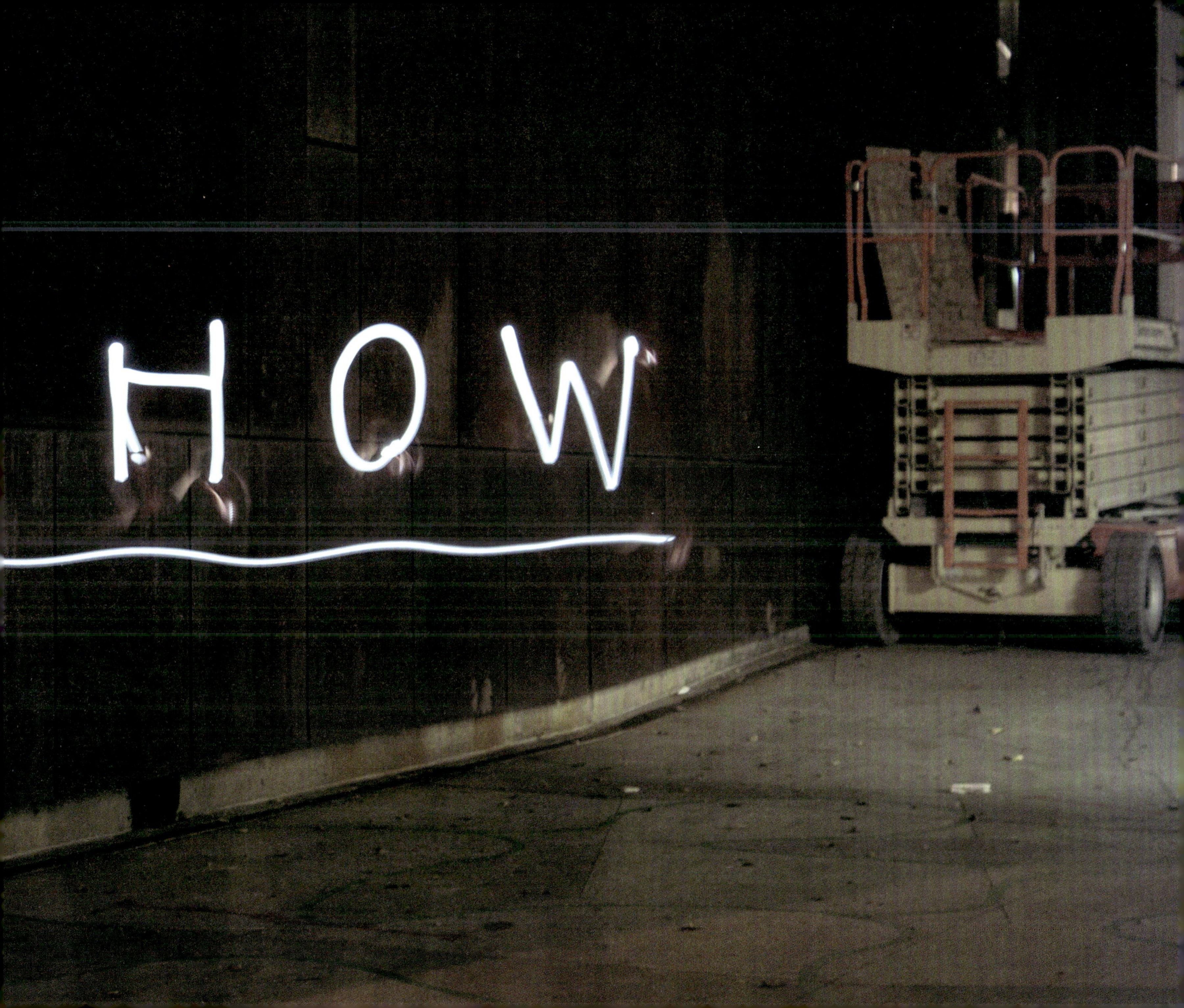
HOW

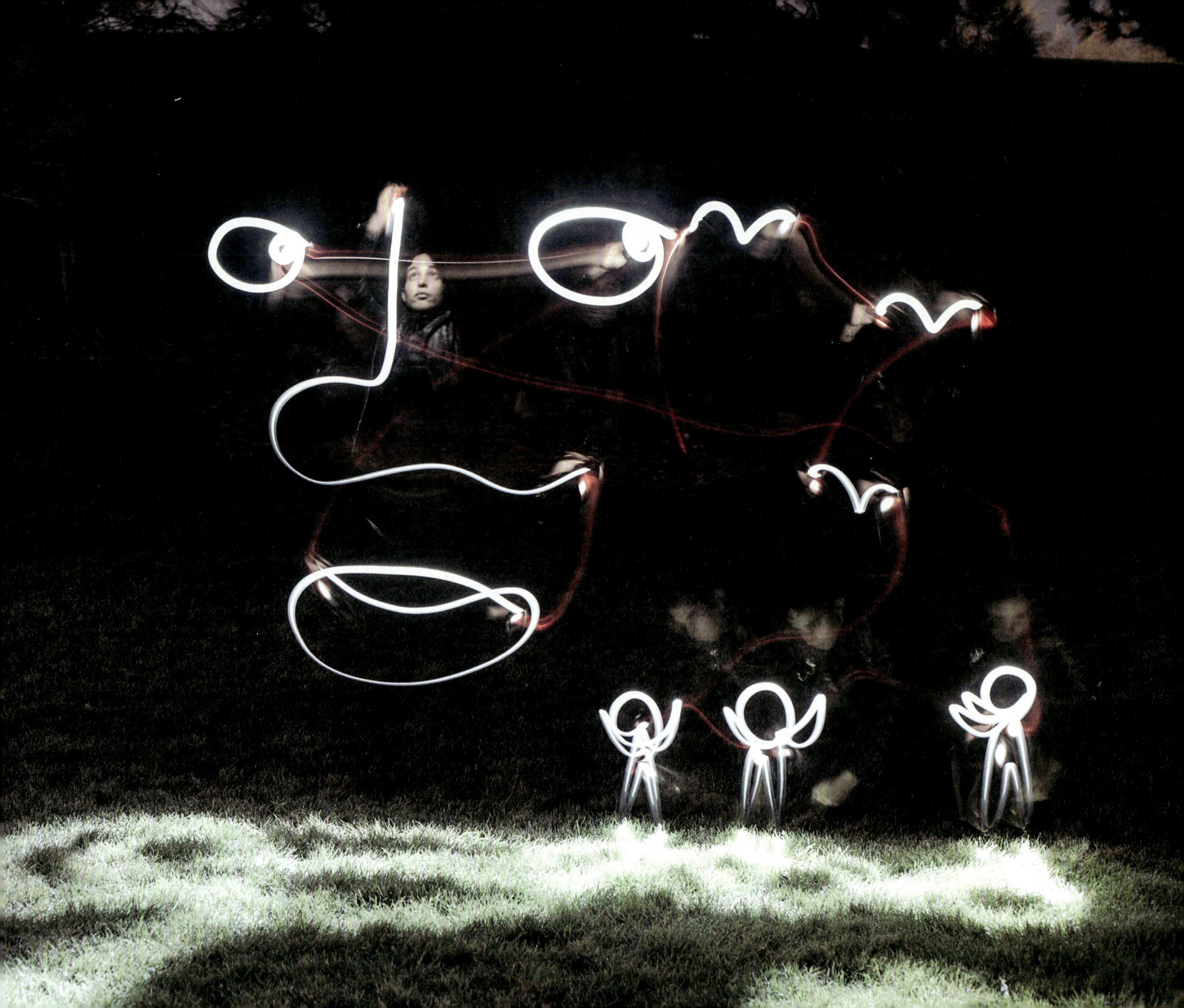

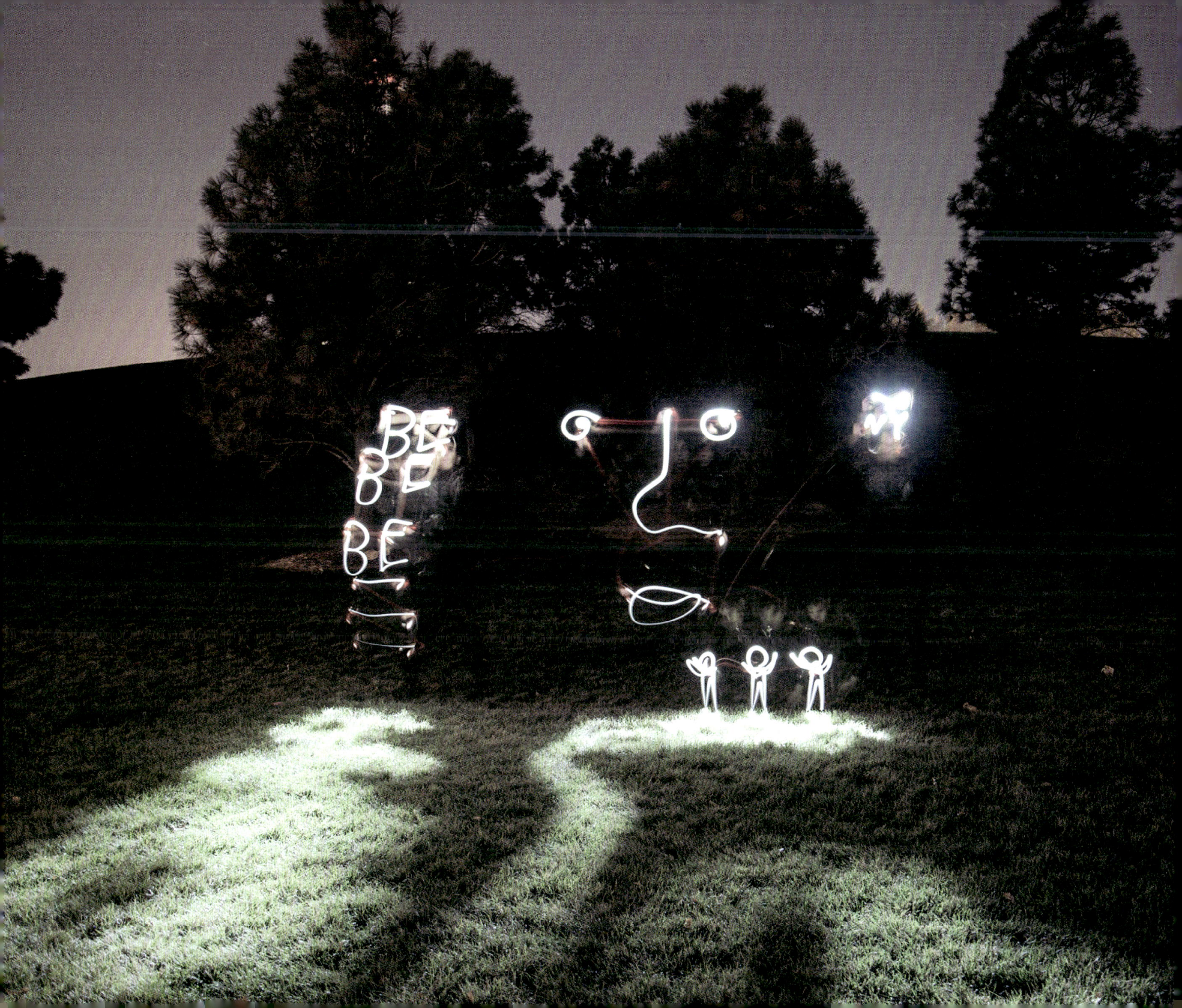
BE
BE
BE

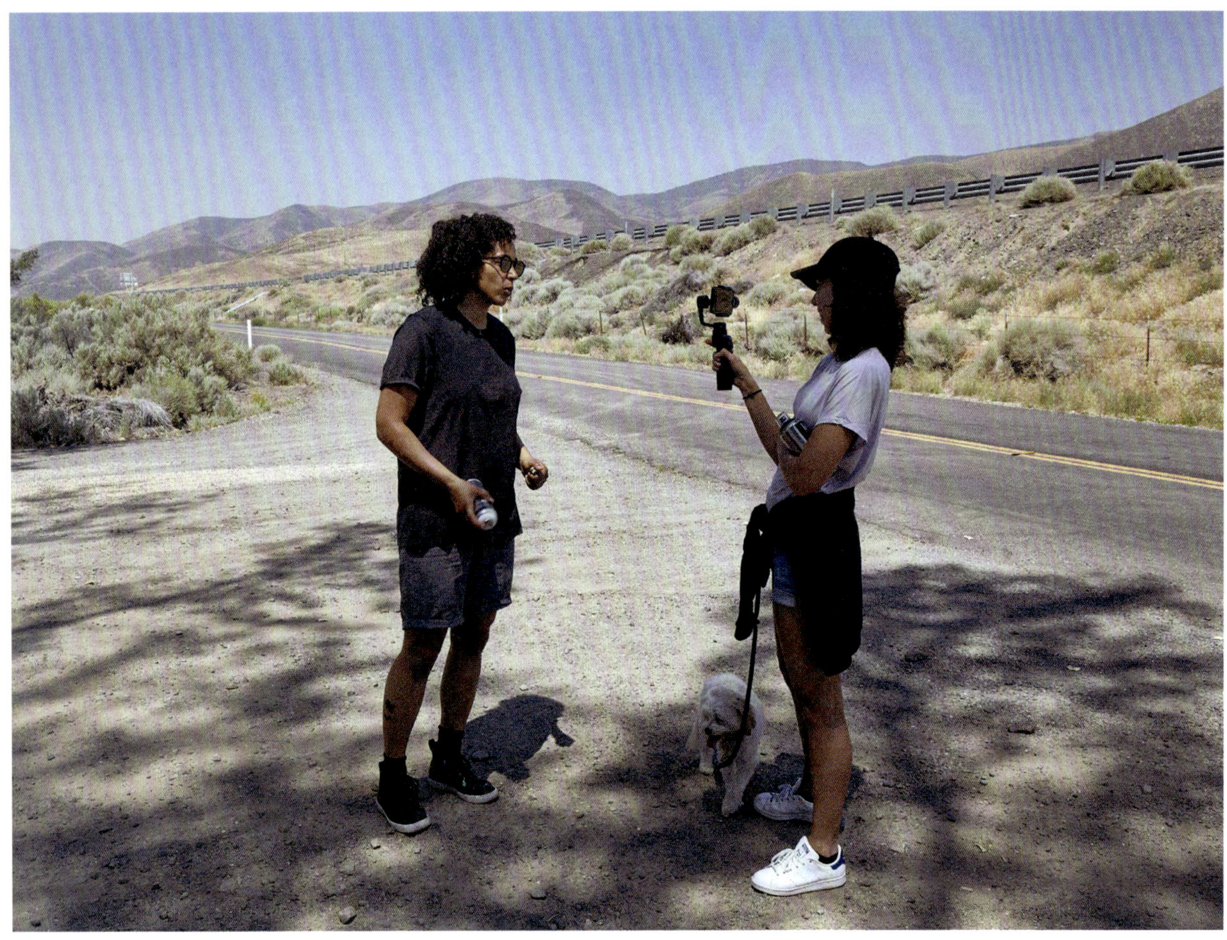

#SHANTELLONTHEROAD

In summer 2017, Martin embarked on a quintessential American cross-country road trip, travelling from Los Angeles back to her studio in Jersey City. Along the way, she appropriated the open road as a canvas, creating temporary, site-specific drawings in continuous lines of water-soluble spray paint. The result was a series of mesmeric, map-like drawings – autobiographical meditations on line and the language of dreams – created against immense landscapes such as Utah's Bonneville Salt Flats and the shores of Lake Michigan. The trip was captured on large-format film by Theo Coulombe and exhibited in December 2018 as part of the show *We'll Get There* at Standard Space, Sharon, Connecticut, with drawings made during the trip and a video by Laksmi Hedemark. **Above:** Martin with Hedemark in Nevada, July 2017. **Opposite:** Martin at work in Wyoming, July 2017. **Following spread:** Martin at the Bonneville Salt Flats, July 2017. **Page 232:** Martin enjoying the sun, Wyoming, July 2017.

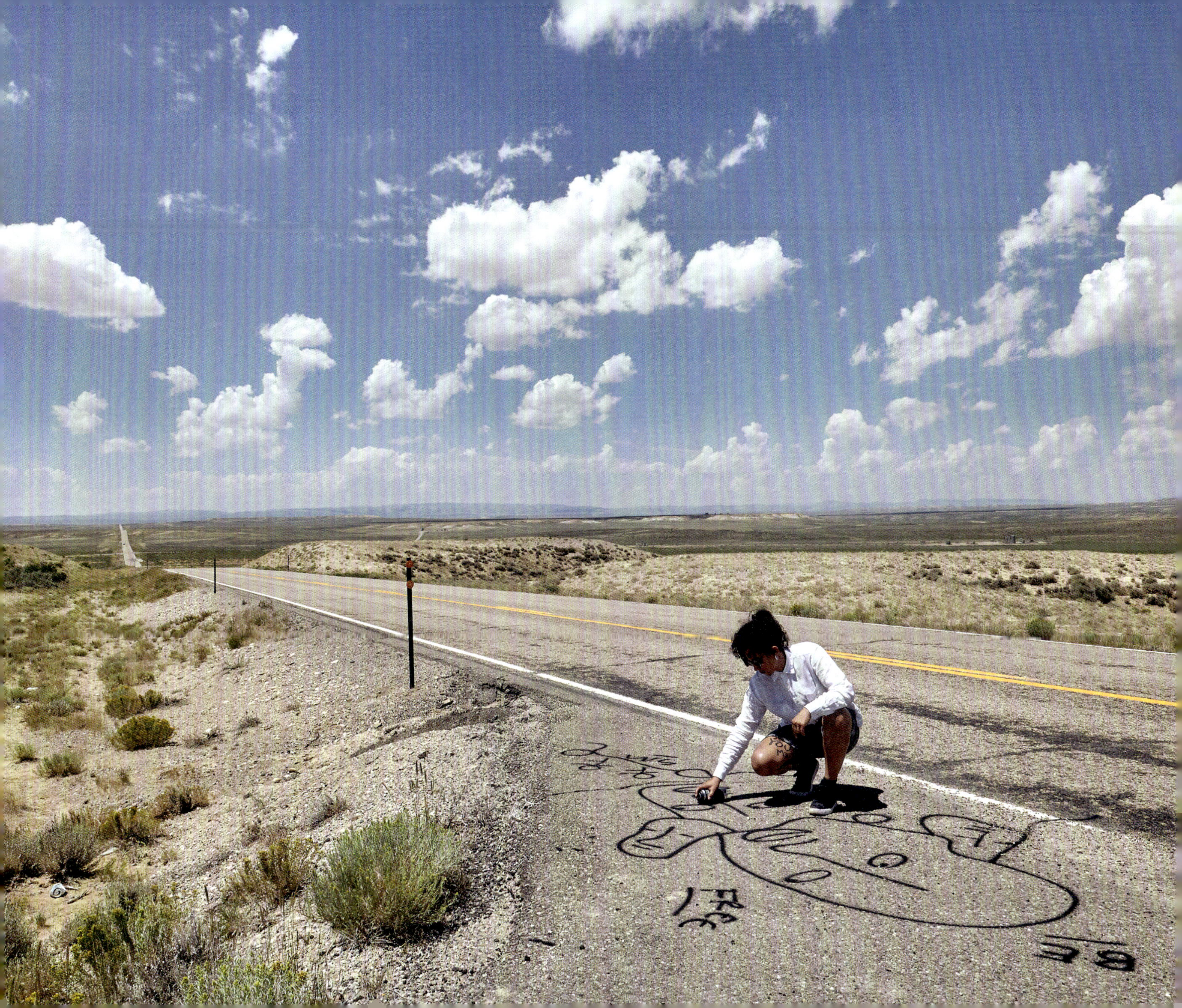

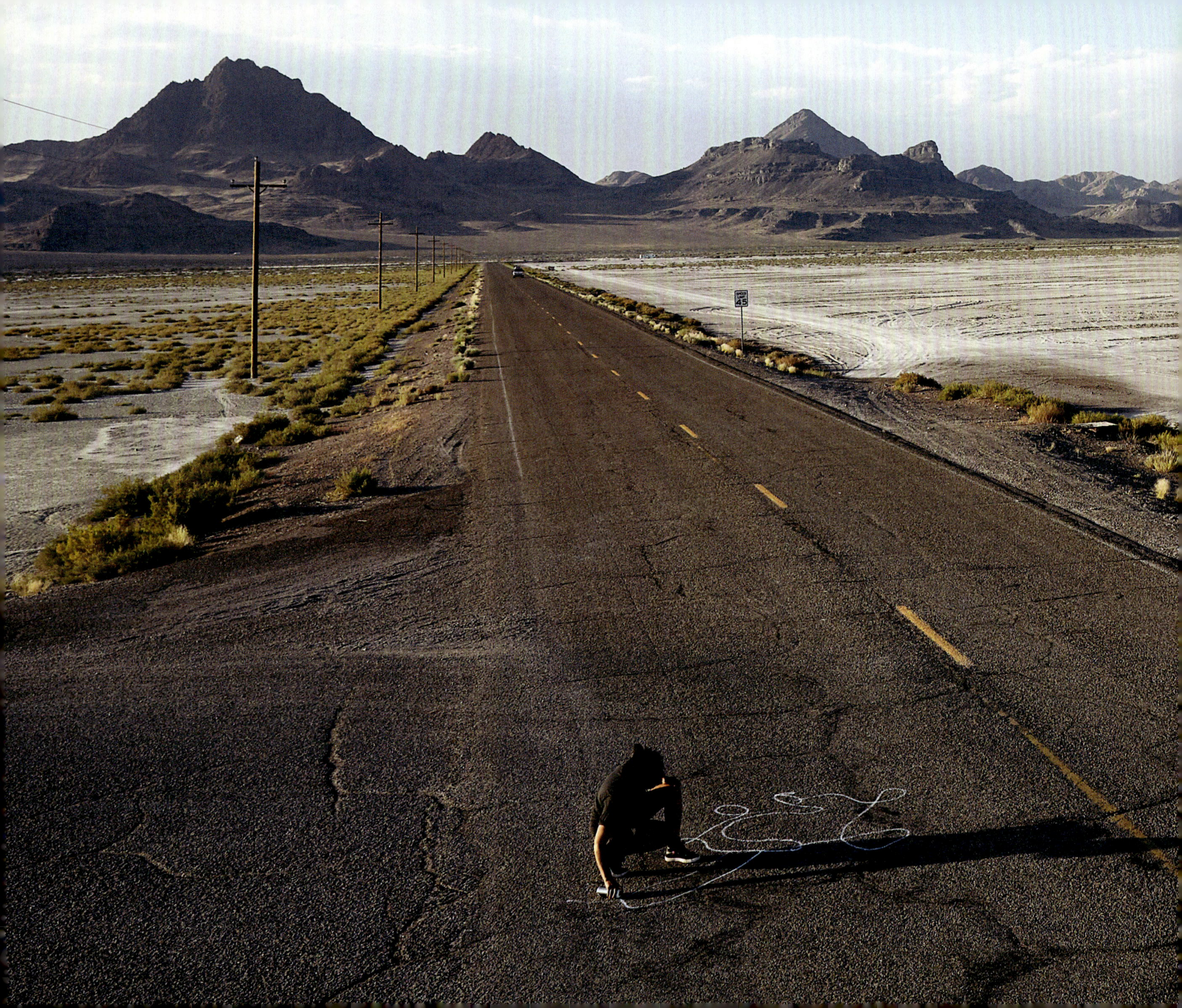

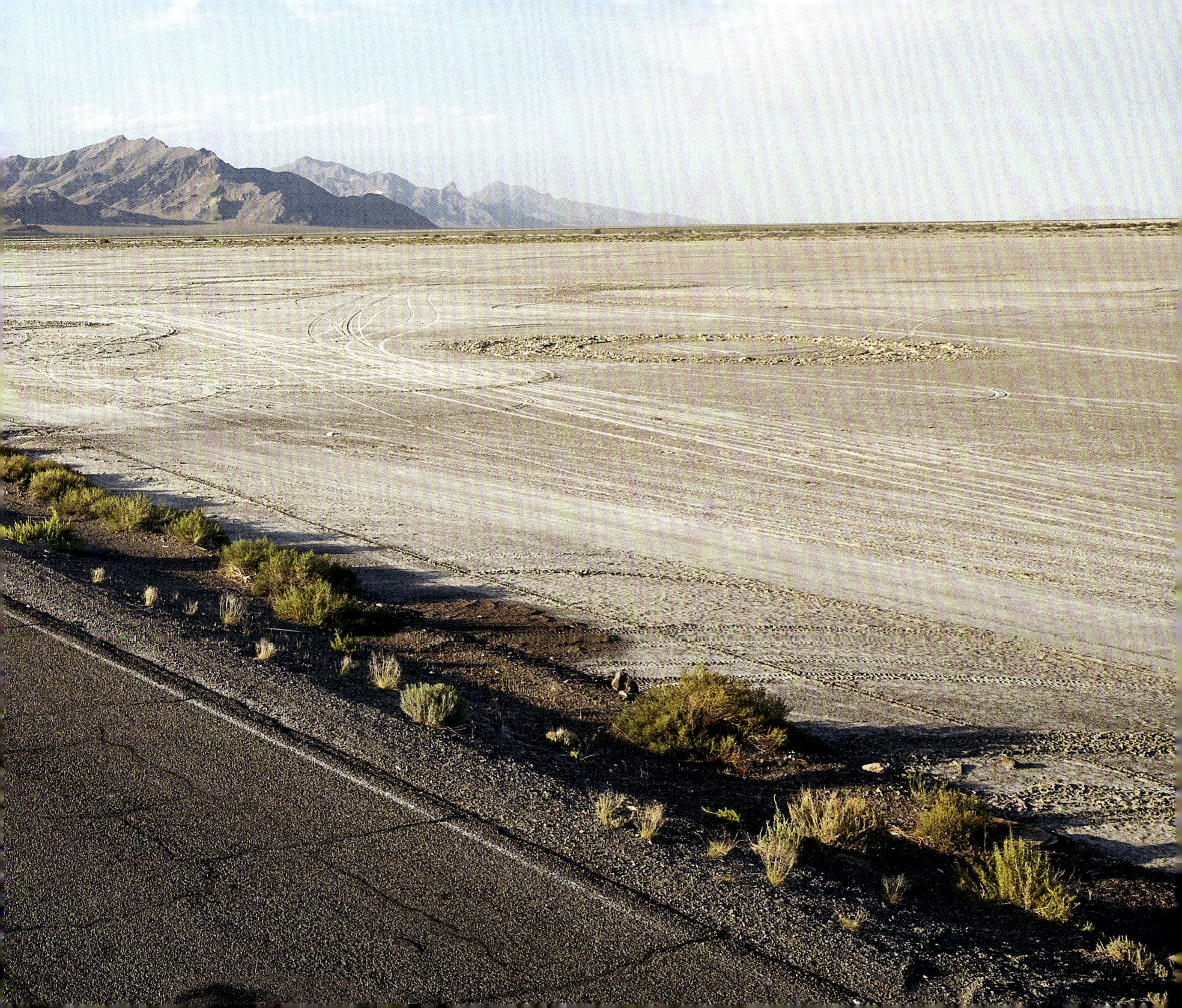

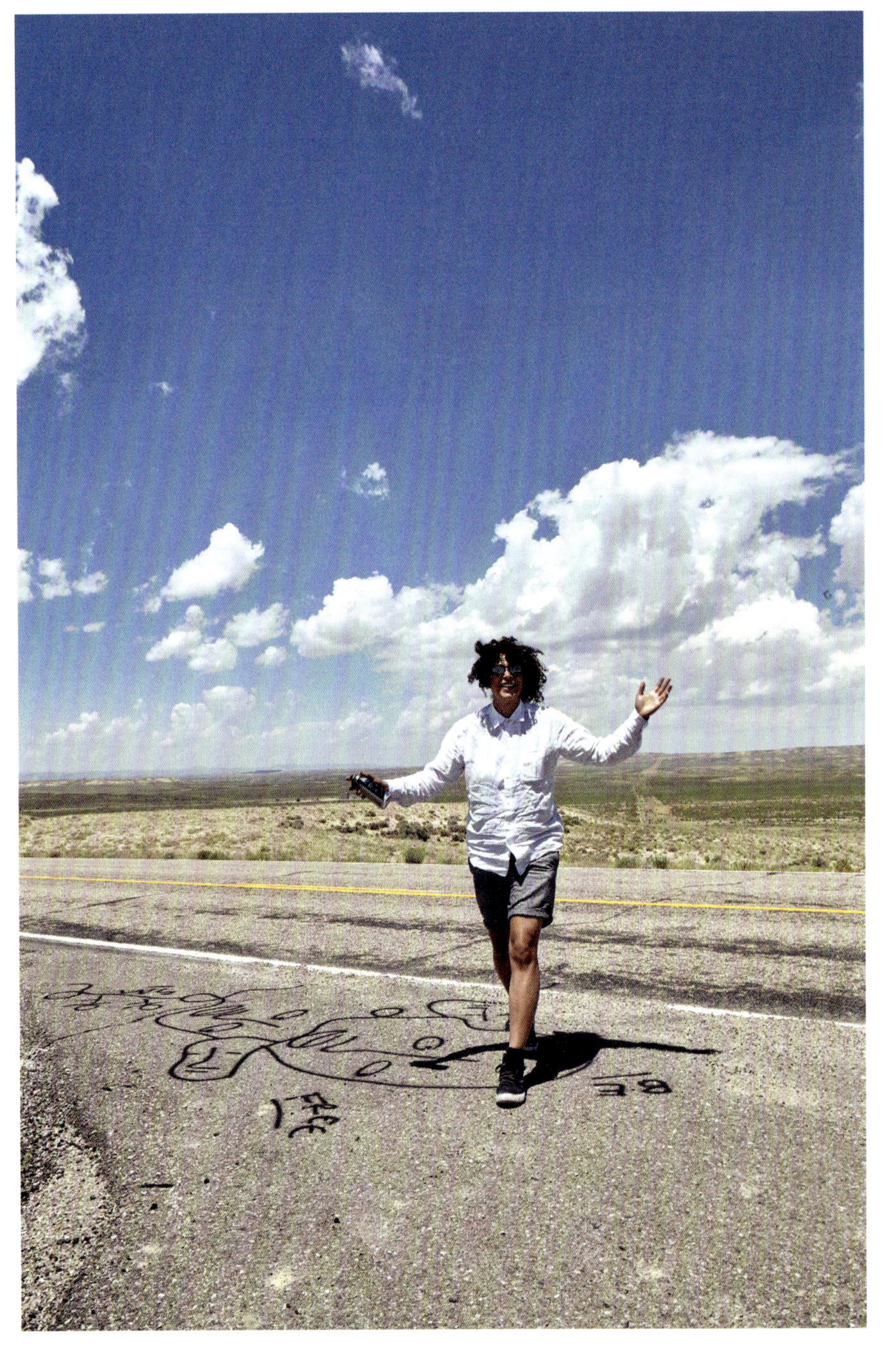

BIOGRAPHIES

Shantell Martin was born in 1980 in Greenwich, London, and grew up in Thamesmead, London. From 1999 to 2000 she studied at Camberwell College of Arts, London (Foundation Course) and from 2000 to 2003 at Central Saint Martins, London (BA Graphic Design/Illustration). She lives and works in Jersey City, New Jersey.

Katharine Stout is Director of Focal Point Gallery, Southend-on-Sea. She is also the co-founder and Associate Director of Drawing Room, London.

Hans Ulrich Obrist is Artistic Director of the Serpentine Galleries, London.

EXHIBITIONS – SOLO

2019 *Underlined*, David B. Smith Gallery, Denver
2019 *Words and Lines*, Denver Art Museum, Denver
2019 *Church* and *The May Room*, Governors Island, New York
2019 *Finding Your Way*, Lincoln Center, New York
2018 *We'll Get There*, Standard Space Gallery, Sharon, Connecticut
2018 *Why Now*, Weill Art Gallery, 92Y, New York
2017 *Charge Your Self*, Chandran Gallery, San Francisco
2017 *Someday We Can*, Albright-Knox Art Gallery, Buffalo, New York
2016 *Gone*, 3 Howard Street, New York
2016 *Connecting*, Open Gallery, Boston
2016 *Drawing Toronto*, Coldstream Fine Art, Toronto
2014 *Are You You*, Museum of Contemporary African Diasporan Arts, Brooklyn, New York
2012 *3×1 + Shantell Martin*, 3×1, New York
2012 *Continuous Line*, Black & White Gallery, Williamsburg, New York
2011 *Message on a Bottle*, World Six Gallery, Rosemary Beach, Florida
2010 *Project InsideOut Outsideln*, Collette Blanchard Gallery, New York
2010 *Shantell Martin*, Studio B, Alys Beach, Florida

EXHIBITIONS – GROUP

2015 *New/Idols*, Studio 301 NYC, Brooklyn, New York

2015 *The Rise of Sneaker Culture*, Brooklyn Museum, Brooklyn, New York
2015 *De Con Struct*, Noosphere Arts, New York
2014 *Crossing Brooklyn*, Brooklyn Museum, Brooklyn, New York

AWARDS

2019 Best in Art Award, The Shorty Awards
2017 Artist Advocacy Award, Museum of Contemporary African Diasporan Arts
2016 Women Who Spark Award for Women in Technology, Intel Corp. in partnership with Time Inc.

RESIDENCIES / FELLOWSHIPS / ADVISORY ROLES

2016 Artist in Residence, Autodesk, Pier 9, San Francisco
2015 Artist in Residence, P3 Studio, Las Vegas
2014–18 Advisory Council Member, The Climate Museum, New York
2014–16 Artist in Residence New Frontier Lab, Sundance Institute (online)
2014–16 Visiting Scholar, MIT Media Lab, Cambridge, Massachusetts
2014–15 Artist in Residence, ITP, New York University Tisch School of the Arts, New York
2014 Fellow, Brown Institute of Media Innovation, Columbia University, New York
2013–present Adjunct Professor, ITP, New York University Tisch School of the Arts, New York
2013 Artist in Residence, Clark College, Vancouver

SELECTED LIVE PERFORMANCES

2018 In conversation with Ilana Glazer, 92Y, New York
2017 Samsung Creators Unpacked, David Geffen Hall, Lincoln Center, New York
2016 *Kendrick Lamar x Shantell Martin*, Faena Art Dome, Art Basel Miami Beach
2016 Keep a Child Alive's Black Ball, Hammerstein Ballroom, Manhattan Center, New York
2011 Digital Graffiti, Alys Beach, Florida
2011 Mapping Festival, Geneva

2011 Museum of the Moving Image, New York
2010 Yota Space, St Petersburg
2010 Onedotzero Adventures in Motion Festival, British Film Institute, London
2010 Museum of Modern Art, New York
2009 Motion Graphics Festival, Washington, D.C.

SELECTED COLLABORATIONS

2019 United Airlines
2018 Tiffany & Co.
2018 + 2014 Flos
2018 Puma Select
2018 Jose Cuervo 1800
2017 Max Mara
2016 Art Basel Miami Beach and American Express (with Kendrick Lamar)
2016 Interview Magazine
2016 (RED)
2016 United Arrows & Sons
2016 Warby Parker
2016 Keep a Child Alive's Black Ball
2015 + 2014 Vitra
2015 Martone Cycling Co.
2015 WME-IMG / New York Fashion Week
2015 Saks Fifth Avenue Canada
2015 AMFAR, The Foundation for AIDS Research
2014 Kelly Wearstler
2014 American Express

FURTHER RESOURCES

https://shantellmartin.art

'The New Wave: Shantell Martin', *Elle Canada*, 2 February 2016 *http://www.ellecanada.com/culture/celebrity/article/the-new-wave-shantell-martin#.Vsf5HfJ96Um*

'Shantell Martin', *Interview*, 22 November 2016 *https://www.interviewmagazine.com/art/shantell-martin-decjan*

Khadija Abuyousif, 'Shantell Martin: This is What an Artist Looks Like', *Topic*, February 2018 *https://www.topic.com/shantell-martin-this-is-what-an-artist-looks-like*

Liz Arnold, 'A Very Fine Line', *New York Times*, 23 May 2012 *http://www.nytimes.com/2012/05/24/garden/a-brooklyn-artist-free-associates-on-her-walls.html?_r=0*

Ann Binlot, 'Art in Motion: Shantell Martin Puts her Stamp on Martone Cycling Co's Designs', *Wallpaper*, 2 June 2015 *http://www.wallpaper.com/lifestyle/art-in-motion-shantell-martin-puts-her-stamp-on-martone-cycling-cos-designs*

Michael Cooper, 'When These Lines Are Drawn, Artist and Dancers Connect', *New York Times*, 24 January 2019 *https://www.nytimes.com/2019/01/24/arts/dance/new-york-city-ballet-shantell-martin-artist.html*

Charles Curkin, '60 Seconds With... Shantell Martin', *Elle Decor*, 11 December 2018 *https://www.elledecor.com/design-decorate/interior-designers/a25396460/shantell-martin-interview*

Sky Dylan-Robbins, 'Follow the Pen', *New Yorker*, 23 October 2013 *http://www.newyorker.com/culture/culture-desk/video-follow-the-pen*

Sarah Lawson, 'Business Models for a Modern Artist', *Fast Company*, 14 October 2015 *https://www.fastcompany.com/3052055/how-i-get-it-done/business-models-for-a-modern-artist*

Debbie Millman, 'Shantell Martin', *Design Matters Podcast*, 20 May 2019 *https://soundcloud.com/designmatters/shantell-martin*

Antwaun Sargent, 'A Studio Visit with Artist Shantell Martin', *Vogue*, 24 July 2014 *http://www.vogue.com/946865/shantell-martin-illustrator-mocada-exhibition*

ACKNOWLEDGEMENTS

The questions that are asked and explored in my art are questions that were perhaps planted in me as a young child growing up in Thamesmead, London. I don't know if I could have been formed, as I am now, had I grown up anywhere else. Because of this, I must express immense gratitude to the place and people of my childhood.

I owe a debt of gratitude to my family, to my mother, sisters and brother, who have always let me be myself, even if they didn't understand who that person was. This acceptance enabled me to grow and to step into other environments around the globe with courage and curiosity and trust.

To my friends and fellow artists from Central Saint Martins, who provided me with considerable support throughout the years and whose own work has influenced and inspired me to work hard and share more, thank you.

To my friends, fellow artists, collaborators, teachers, students, the strangers who I've not yet met but who have supported my journey as a working artist for all these years – you have shaped me with your kindness, with your support, with your truth and I hope to continue being a witness and participant in your lives and a source of support for your own work and in this way continue to grow alongside you.

I'm also indebted to the following people who gave their time and energy in the creation of this book: Joe Hage, Hans Ulrich Obrist, Katharine Stout, the team at HENI Publishing, and the countless photographers and collaborators whose work is also featured in this book.

To my partner and our dog Blanche, your loving support and patience does not go unnoticed and strengthens me in ways that I cannot express.

ARTWORK DIMENSIONS

All dimensions are given with height before width, followed by depth where applicable.

pp. 8–9 *Open Your Door*, 2018, 4.9 x 9.1 m (16 x 30 ft)

p. 32 *Half White 1980*, 2007, 14 x 18.4 cm (5 ½ x 7 ¼ in); *Half White 1980*, 2007, 14 x 18.4 cm (5 ½ x 7 ¼ in); *Tower*, 2008, 24.1 x 17.8 cm (9 ½ x 7 in); *Let's Be Friends*, 2009, 12.7 x 24.1 cm (5 x 9 ½ in); *Love*, 2008, 27.9 x 33.7 cm (11 x 13 ¼ in); *Lucky in Life*, 2009, 14 x 21 cm (5 ½ x 8 ¼ in).

p. 37 *English*, 2010, 15.2 x 31.8 cm (6 x 12 ½ in); *British*, 2010, 14.6 x 29.8 cm (5 ¾ x 11 ¾ in); *Go Home*, 2009, 14 x 24.1 cm (5 ½ x 9 ½ in); *Come Home*, 2009, 14 x 24.1 cm (5 ½ x 9 ½ in).

p. 38 *Who You Are*, 2010, 8.3 x 16.5 (3 ¼ x 6 ½ in); *I Wake*, 2010, 36.2 x 33.7 cm (14 ¼ x 13 ¼ in); *Shantell Martin*, 2007, 18.4 x 26.7 cm (7 ¼ x 10 ½ in); *Me*, 2010, 9.5 x 12.7 cm (3 ¾ x 5 in); *You*, 2010, 9.5 x 12.7 cm (3 ¾ x 5 in).

p. 54 *Scrunched*, 2013, 102 x 89 x 63.5 cm (40 x 35 x 25 in).

p. 55 *Garden Faces*, 2012, 45.7 x 61 cm (18 x 24 in).

p. 56 *Eat Apple Pie*, 2013, 91.4 x 61 cm (36 x 24 in); *One Day Once*, 2012, 61 x 45.7 cm (24 x 18 in).

p. 57 *Who You Knew*, 2013, 208 x 153.7 cm (82 x 60 ½ in); *Gone Alone*, 2013, 160 x 152.5 cm (63 x 60 in).

p. 58 *We Once When Push*, 2013, 35.6 x 43.2 cm (14 x 17 in).

p. 61 *Four Faces*, 2013, 35.6 x 43.2 cm (14 x 17 in).

p. 62 *Six Faces*, 2014, 45.7 x 61 cm (18 x 24 in).

p. 63 *Scrunched*, 2013, 51 x 102 x 51 cm (20 x 40 x 20 in).

p. 64 *Marble Head*, 2013, 20.3 x 5 x 3.8 cm (8 x 2 x 1 ½ in); *Marble Head: Someday Remember Me*, 2013, 12.7 x 11.5 x 3.8 cm (5 x 4 ½ x 1 ½ in).

p. 65 *Keep Cover*, 2013, 61 x 91.4 cm (24 x 36 in).

p. 66 *Pull and Hold*, 2014, 45.7 x 61 cm (18 x 24 in).

p. 68 *Marble Head*, 2013, 20.3 x 17.8 x 3.8 cm (8 x 7 x 1 ½ in); *Marble Head*, 2013, 20.3 x 17.8 x 3.8 cm (8 x 7 x 1 ½ in).

p. 69 *Leave It All Behind*, 2013, 61 x 91.4 cm (24 x 36 in).

p. 70 *Hold On Up*, 2014, 45.7 x 61 cm (18 x 24 in).

p. 72 *Marble Head: Open Eyes*, 2013, 33 x 19 x 5 cm (13 x 7 ½ x 2 in); *Marble Head: Who Are You*, 2013, 17.8 x 6.4 x 5 cm (7 x 2 ½ x 2 in).

p. 73 *Meat the Meet*, 2013, 91.4 x 61 cm (36 x 24 in); *Always Playing*, 2014, 91.4 x 61 cm (36 x 24 in).

p. 74 *Play Sign Dance*, 2013, 61 x 91.4 cm (24 x 36 in).

p. 77 *I Love You*, 2014, 45.7 x 61 cm (18 x 24 in).

p. 78 *Tall*, 2013, 61 x 91.4 cm (24 x 36 in).

p. 79 *Marble Head: One Day Someday Could Be Today*, 2013, 17.8 x 16.5 x 3.8 cm (7 x 6 ½ x 1 ½ in); *Marble Head: Closed Eyes*, 2013, 17.8 x 12.7 x 3.8 cm (7 x 5 x 1 ½ in).

p. 81 *Why Now*, 2013, 121.9 x 73.7 cm (48 x 29 in); *One Day to the Next*, 2014, 91.4 x 61 cm (36 x 24 in).

p. 82 *Walk Run Jump*, 2014, 45.7 x 61 cm (18 x 24 in).

p. 85 *Six Faces*, 2012, 45.7 x 61 cm (18 x 24 in).

p. 86 *All You*, 2013, 43 x 60 cm (17 x 23 ½ in).

pp. 112–15 *Dance Everyday*, 2017, 7.5 x 60 m (25 x 200 ft).

pp. 116–19 *Someday We Can*, 2017, mural 5.5 x 12.5 m (18 x 41 ft).

pp. 142–3 *Who Are You*, 2019, each window 4.65 x 8.74 m (15 ft 3 in x 28 ft 8 in).

pp. 144–53 *Finding Your Way*, 2019, rehearsal canvases 165 x 193 cm (65 x 76 in); interview canvases 140 x 124.5 cm (55 x 49 in).

p. 156 *In Between the Bay* (detail), 2017, 152.5 x 152.5 cm (60 x 60 in).

p. 159 *Think Blink But Don't Sink*, 2017, 61 x 91.4 cm (24 x 36 in); *Today One Two Free*, 2017, 61 x 91.4 cm (24 x 36 in).

p. 185 *Fractured Heart*, 2014, 38.1 x 47 x 20.3 cm (15 x 18 ½ x 8 in).

p. 195 *Prism in Motion (Max Mara)*, 2016, 177.8 x 327.7 cm (70 x 129 in).

p. 240 *Future Higher Self, Two Faces*, 2014, 91.4 x 61 cm (36 x 24 in).

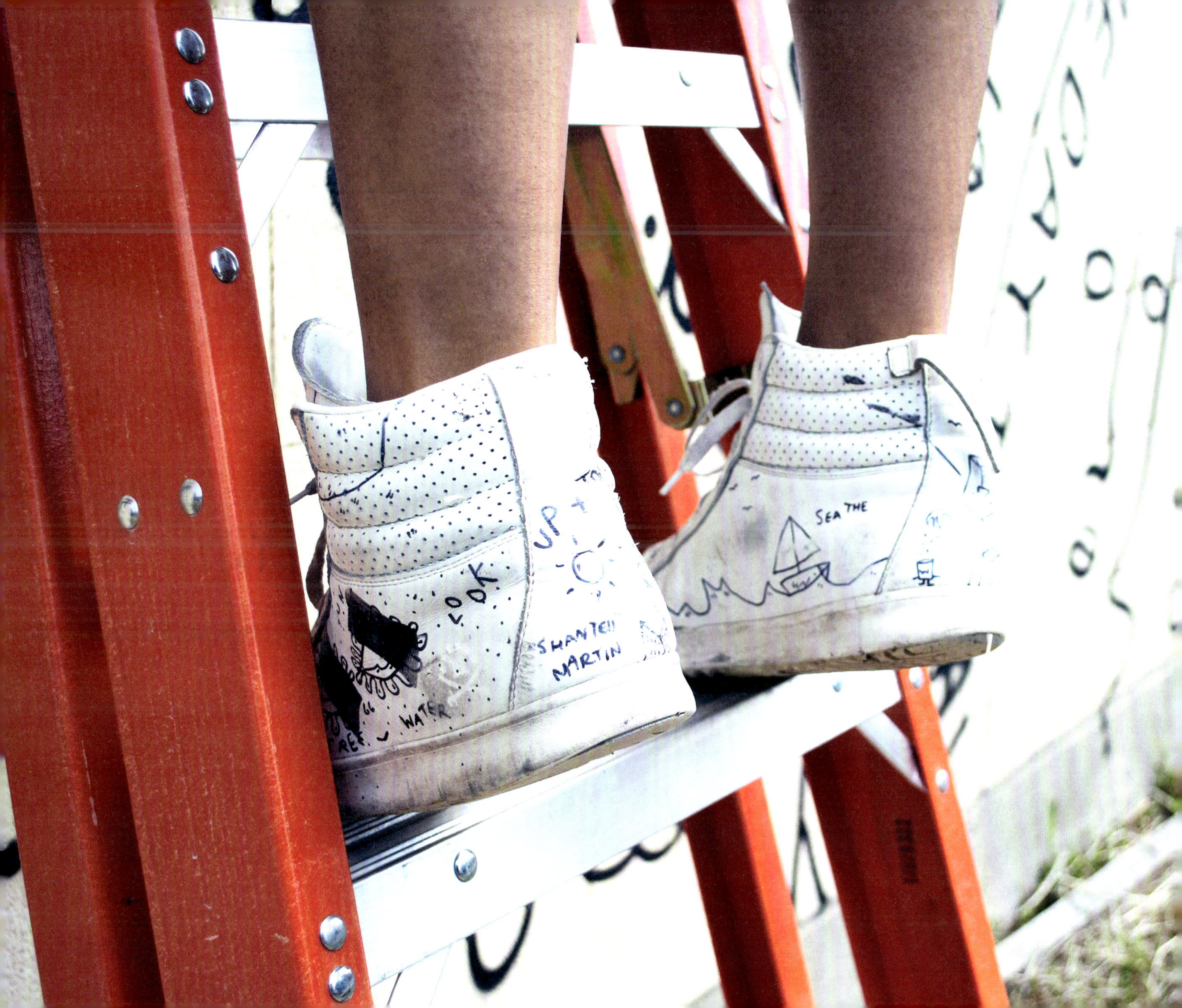

LOOK
UP +
SHANTELL
MARTIN
WATER
SEA THE

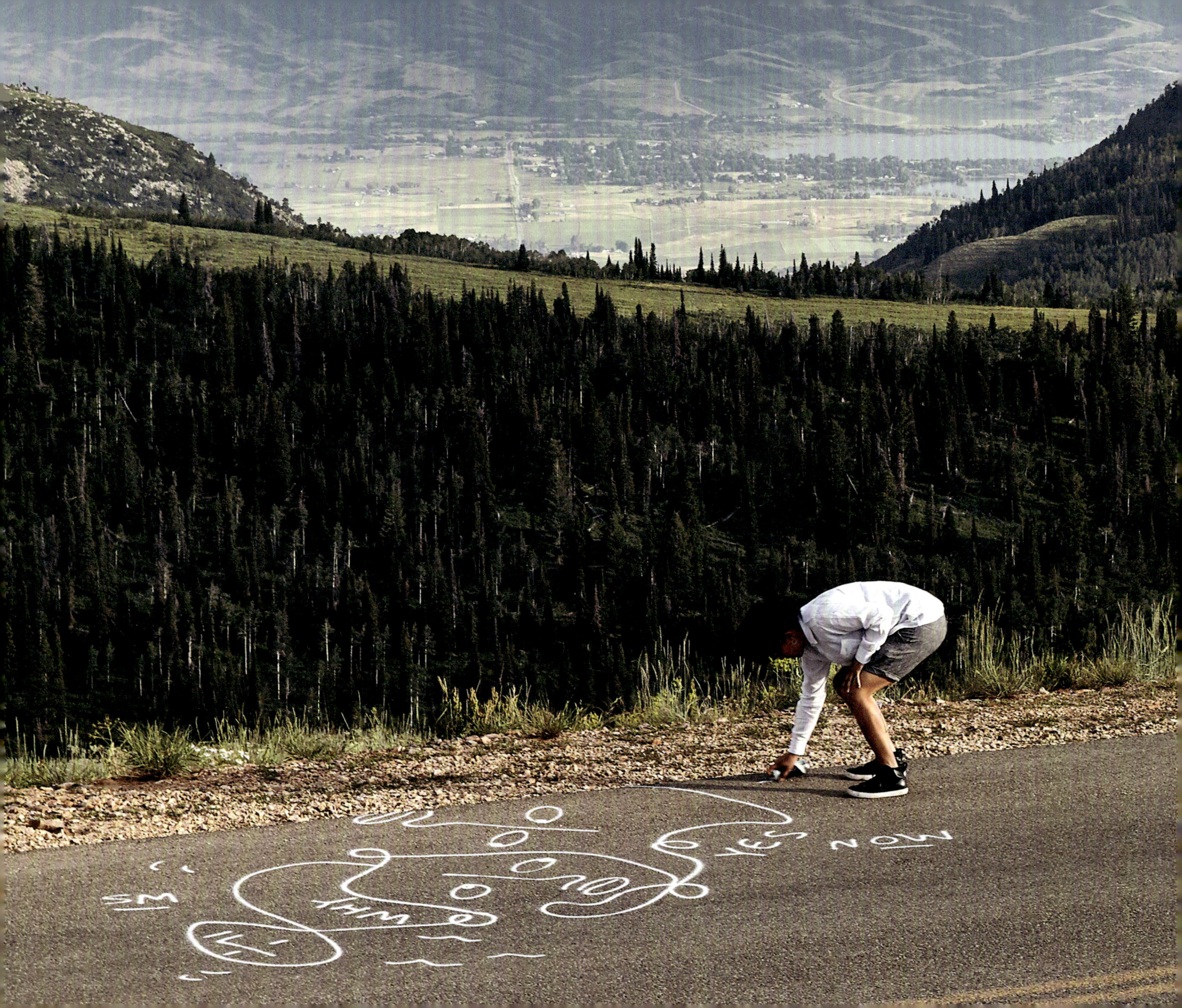

YES
NOW
WHY

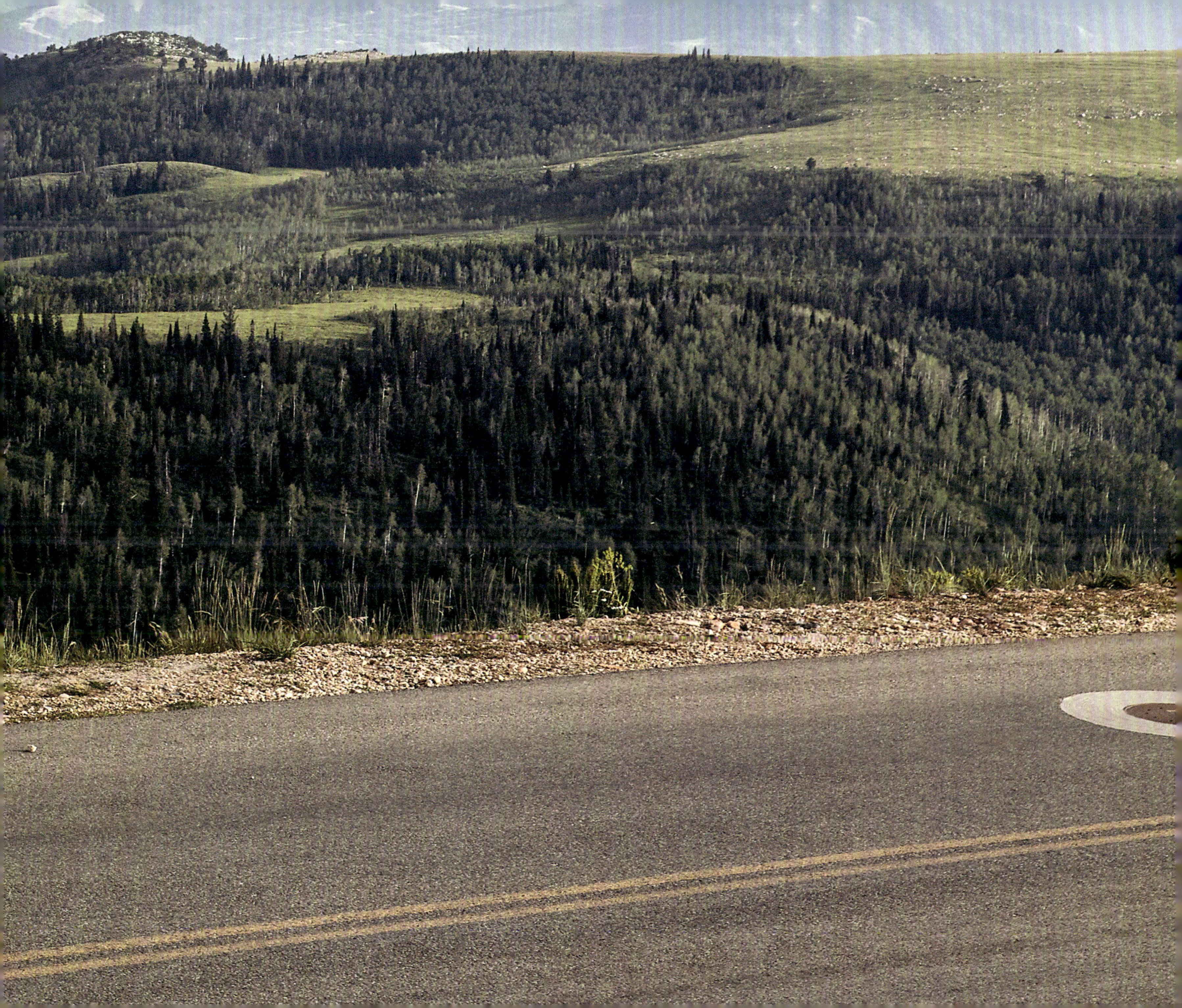

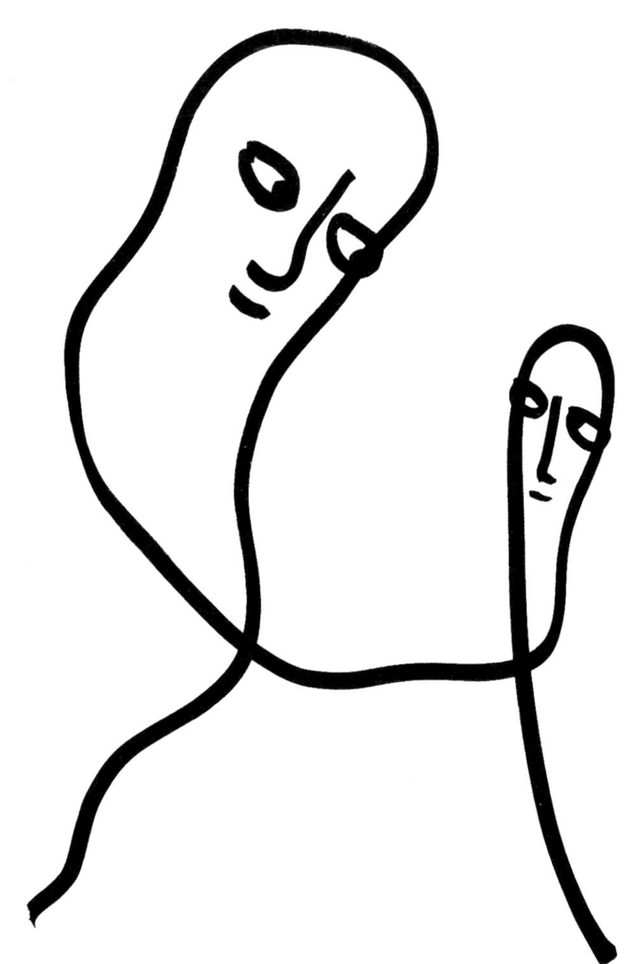

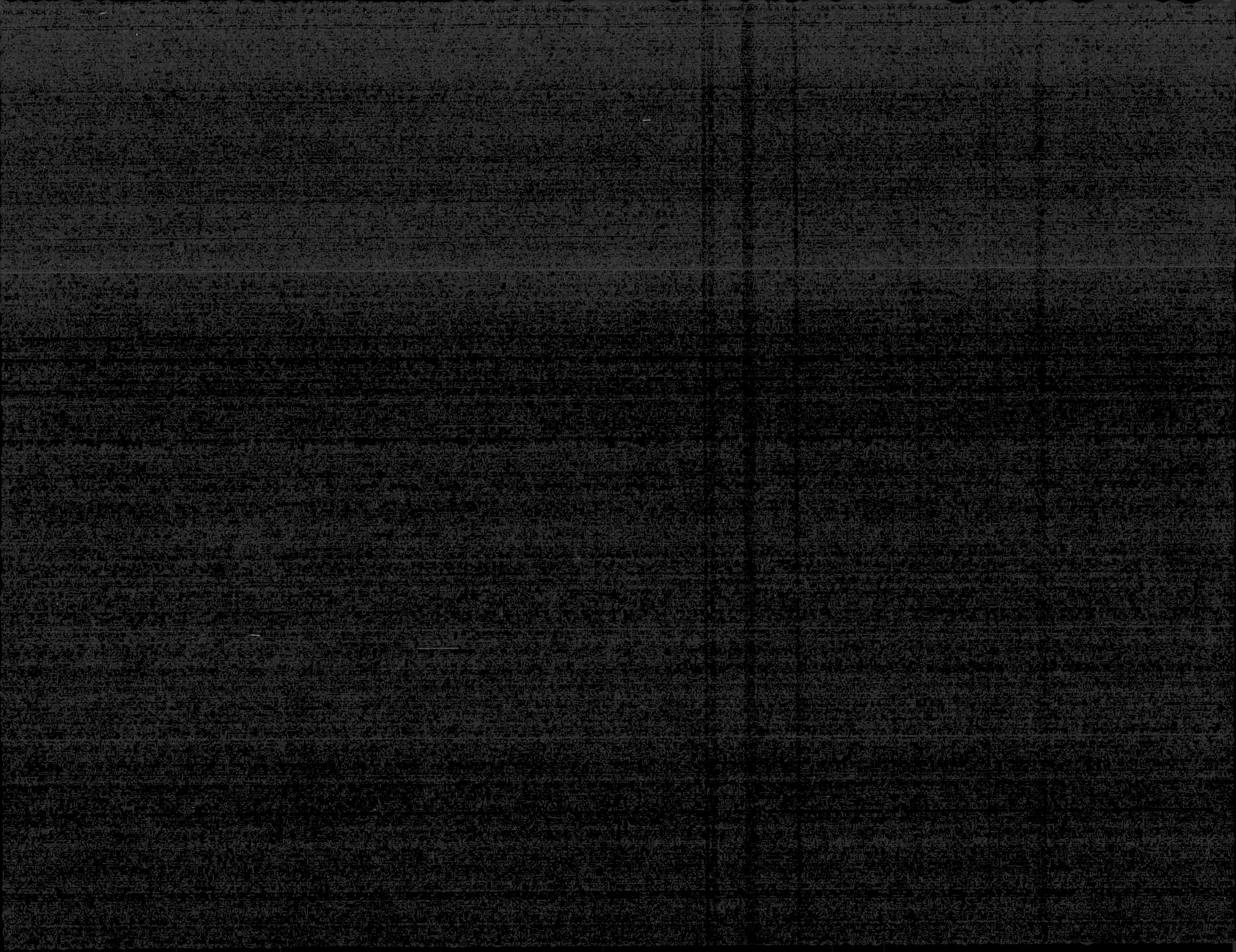